LIFE  LINES

# LIFE LINES

## Australian women's letters and diaries, 1788–1840

Patricia Clarke and Dale Spender

ALLEN & UNWIN

First published in 1992

Allen & Unwin Australia
8 Napier Street, North Sydney, NSW 2059

National Library of Australia
Cataloguing-in-publication entry:

Clarke, Patricia.
  Lifelines : Australian women's letters and diaries 1788–1840.

  Bibliography.
  ISBN 1 86373 124 5.

  1. Women—Australia—Correspondence.  2. Women—Australia—
  Diaries.  3. Women—Australia—Social conditions.  4. Australia—
  Social conditions—1788–1851.  I. Spender, Dale.  II. Title.

305.48894

Typeset in Times and Garamond
by Graphicraft Typesetters Ltd, Hong Kong
Printed in Singapore by Chong Moh Offset Printing Pte Ltd

# Contents

*Acknowledgments*                                                               *viii*

*Introduction*                                                                    *xi*

**1  Forced labour**                                                               **1**
Mary Talbot, Sarah Bird and other unnamed convicts
   *This desolate place of banishment*                                             1
Margaret Catchpole
   *I have been nursing lying-in women*                                           10
Lydia Esden
   *She is a most extraordinary clever woman*                                     17

**2  Farm managers**                                                             **20**
Elizabeth Macarthur
   *I have now a very good Dairy*                                                 20
Mary McDonald
   *As to fruit no country can equal it*                                          29
Eliza Walsh
   *A Lady can conduct a farm as well as a Gentleman*                             32
Anne Drysdale
   *We have got a good number of live stock*                                      35

**3  The work of the Lord**                                                      **39**
Eliza Marsden
   *Had we only a few pious friends*                                              39
Isabella Parry
   *Here is a moral wilderness of immorality and
   drunkenness*                                                                   43
Sarah Broughton
   *Mr C. Cowper, Mr Eyre & Mr Aspinall called*                                   46

4   **Shipboard travail**                                                    **49**
    Anna Josepha King
        *One of the poor women has drawn her last breath*          49
    Sarah Docker
        *A little after six Mary-Jane was born*                          54
    Sarah Brunskill
        *No pen can express the pain and agony of the heart*       59

5   **Charitable works**                                                    **61**
    Elizabeth Paterson
        *The Girls learn Housewifery and the use of the needle*   61
    Eliza Darling and Fanny Macleay
        *I am incessantly occupied with the School of Industry*    64

6   **Vice-regal duties**                                                   **70**
    Mary Putland
        *They are all treated with the same politeness*               70
    Elizabeth Macquarie
        *We spoke of the extraordinary events in New South
        Wales*                                                                  72
    Anne Bourke
        *There is a spirit of equality and independence here*       74
    Maria Gawler
        *We are still sleeping in tents and marquees*                 78

7   **Political observer**                                                  **80**
    Christiana Brooks
        *We want the rights of British subjects*                        80

8   **Working wives and mothers**                                     **94**
    Mary Wild
        *I never expect to have any more children*                    94
    Christiana Jane Blomfield
        *Most people add one to their family each year*             97
    Sophy Dumaresq
        *I wash & dress baby*                                              105

9   **Pathmakers**                                                         **110**
    Elizabeth Hawkins
        *The fatigue to mother and myself was very great*         110
    Elizabeth Fenton
        *Would to Heaven my confinement were well over*        121
    Jane Franklin
        *I write from an 'Encampment on the right bank of
        the Murray'*                                                        130

**10   Shopkeepers and needlewomen**      **137**
Sarah Thornton
    *I furnish my shop to the best advantage*      137
Ann Hordern
    *Checked shirts and satin slops fetch a great price*      138
Eliza Ward
    *Her lawful Commands every where gladly do*      141
Isabella Gibson
    *I had engaged to do apholsterary needlework*      144
Mary Carpenter
    *I shall sell the few stores I brought with me*      148

**11   Homemakers**      **149**
Janet Ranken
    *We are all come here to make money*      149
Octavia Dawson
    *I do not like it here at all*      154
Mary Thomas
    *Everything was in the roughest fashion imaginable*      156
Jane Synnot
    *Mama does not admire the Colonists at all*      162

**12   Work in isolation**      **166**
Ann Gore
    *Society we have none*      166
Margaret Menzies
    *We made ourselves comfortable in one room*      169
Sarah Burnell
    *I have not been out of the valley for two years*      175
Annabella Innes
    *I like my studies very much indeed*      177

**13   Health care**      **180**
Ellen Viveash
    *In sickness and in health*      180

**14   Sacrifice and science**      **188**
Georgiana Molloy
    *She could not be without flowers*      188

**15   Working with words**      **209**
Frances Louisa Bussell, Elizabeth Capel Bussell,
Frances Louisa Bussell (senior)
    *Family correspondents*      209

*Notes*      *237*
*Bibliography*      *246*
*Index*      *250*

# *Acknowledgments*

Debra Adelaide was one of the initiators of this project and we would like to thank her for all her brilliant detective work in discovering so many of the sources included in the volume; it was she who did some of the original scholarly and painstaking transcribing, and whose efforts helped to inspire us to undertake the task of compiling a narrative from women's letters and diaries.

We are also extremely grateful to the staff of the Mitchell Library for their willing help, their co-operation, and the benefit of their experience. Margaret Burn has been an invaluable resource and Di Rhodes has shared her time and skills with a generosity well beyond the call of duty; our regret is that space has not permitted the inclusion of Annie Baxter's diaries—which in their original form were so memorably 'deciphered' and 'deconstructed' by Di Rhodes. Many thanks too are owed to Elizabeth Imashev, the Pictures Librarian, who has used her impressive knowledge and ingenuity to help locate the relevant portraits of the women authors.

Members of the staff of the Battye Library have been superb in response to telephone requests, and the need for computer space, and have helped locate manuscripts, as well as provide information on the period. Thanks are due particularly to Candy Jane Henderson, who has forwarded details and photocopies by post. Again, we regret that it has not been possible to include all of the excellent examples that were uncovered and clarified—Louisa Clifton's diary among them.

We wish to thank the staffs of the National Library, particularly in the Petherick and Manuscripts Rooms, La Trobe Library and the Archives Office of Tasmania. Margaret O'Hagan of the Fryer Library of the University of Queensland helped to convince us that, regrettably, there were no available sources in that state. We thank the Mitchell

Library, State Library of New South Wales, for permission to publish material from the Macarthur papers, Piper papers, Marsden family letters, King family papers, Paterson papers, Bligh papers, Macquarie papers, Wild family papers, Henry Dumaresq letters, Hassall correspondence, and from the letters of Janet Ranken, Mary McDonald, Isabella Gibson (and to the Royston and District Local Historical Society, England which holds the original), Emily Curtis (and the owner of the original copy) and the owners of Anne Bourke's journal and Jane Synnot's letters, copies of which are held in the Mitchell Library; to the Archives Office of Tasmania for permission to publish material from the Dumaresq papers; P. L. Brown for permission to quote extracts from Anne Drysdale's diary from the *Clyde Company papers* and the La Trobe Collection, State Library of Victoria which holds the original; Mr S. Docker and the La Trobe Collection regarding Sarah Docker's diary; the National Library of Australia for permission to publish extracts from the diaries of Christiana Brooks and Sarah Broughton, the journal of Margaret Menzies, the letters of Elizabeth Hawkins, Jane Franklin, Octavia Dawson, Margaret Catchpole (and the Mitchell Library which holds the originals) and Ann Gore (and the Cambridgeshire Record Office, England, holder of the originals); and any copyright holders whom we may have failed to contact, inadvertently or through lack of information.

We would like to acknowledge our indebtedness to Lesley and Marsden Hordern for permission to use Ann Horden's story from Lesley Horden's *Children of One Family*; Helen Wilson, Lyons, ACT and Phyl Blomfield, Sydney, who kindly gave permission for the use of (and lent copies of) Christiana Blomfield's letters and Throsby Zouch, Swinger Hill, ACT for help in locating these letters; Pamela Statham for her permission to use *The Tanner Letters*; Professor Sandy Yarwood, Sydney, NSW for advice regarding the letters of Eliza Marsden.

Carmel O'Connor undertook some very valuable research in Sydney for which we are most grateful. Kirsten Lees, with her customary goodwill, energy and meticulousness checked references and photocopied material; and Sue Martin strained her eyes in helping to transcribe Annie Baxter's diary. Georgina Whallin diligently and undauntedly checked transcripts against originals, and many more friends helped to decode some of the barely discernible entries in journals and letters. We would like to thank Robyn Daniels for her wealth of information on the wonders of Western Australia—on Augusta, Busselton, the Swan River settlements and the flora and fauna of the area. The Busselton Historical Society also deserves praise for its achievements in its own right, as well as for the assistance it provided.

Lynne Spender has been an absolutely necessary 'in house' editor, giving support, encouragement, criticism and corrections, often in the form of letters. And Sue Jarvis has been a model of sensitivity and tact as she has undertaken the difficult task of 'cutting' the manuscript.

We would also like to acknowledge that we have enjoyed working with each other immensely; that it has been a stimulating and satisfying process 'combining' our interests, research findings and enthusiasms for women's personal chronicles of the past. This volume, then, is both a 'collection' and a record of our 'conversation'.

*Patricia Clarke and Dale Spender, July 1991*

# Introduction

*Lifelines* is a narrative which incorporates many of the known letters and diaries of women from the period 1788–1840. The writers come from the colonies of New South Wales, Van Diemen's Land (Tasmania), Victoria, South Australia and Swan River (Western Australia); regrettably no such material from Queensland seems to have survived. All of the writers are white.

Because we think that the hard labour of women during these years of colonisation has sometimes been overlooked, and because so many of the diaries and letters were necessarily concerned with the work that women were required to do, we have focused on women's work in the extracts we have chosen to use. We have also organised the chapters along these lines.

However, we did not just want to look at the 'messages' of these writers; we wanted to look at the 'medium' as well. This volume is not simply a story about the first fifty years of colonisation from the perspective of white women; nor is it just an account of their lives in the women's own words. It is a study of women's literary endeavours and achievements during this period, a study which helps to reveal the importance of letters and diaries as a literary form, and which suggests the central role that they played in women's daily lives. It is a collection which draws together the personal chronicles of colonial women and which begins to uncover the valuable historical and artistic legacy they bequeathed.

## Virtue and necessity

Of the women who sailed with the First Fleet, few—if any—had *chosen* their destination. One thousand and thirty men, women and children were aboard the ships which anchored in Botany Bay on 26 January 1788, after a voyage of almost nine months. While it is obvious that the 188 convict women had no say in the matter, a consideration which often goes unnoted is that most of the 'free' wives and female members of the accompanying familes were also fulfilling obligations, rather than *choosing* a new land.

For the free men—the officers and officials of the Crown—it was very different. The establishment of the colony of New South Wales afforded numerous advantageous possibilities: there were reputations to be won, fortunes to be made, advancements to be earned by acts of dedication and daring. The way might be hard, the risks great and the difficulties many, but personal prospects could be decidedly improved by a tour of duty in the colony and choices could be made accordingly. For the women, however, there were no such obvious promises of reward or fulfilment.

Because of the position of women in late eighteenth century Britain, it was possible for almost any woman—including 'free' women—to become a victim of compulsory migration; all that was needed was that she be dependent upon a man who elected to embark on such a venture. Any female member of a family, regardless of age or relationship, could be uprooted and transplanted if she did not have the social and financial means for self-maintenance. Very few women enjoyed such a privileged status.

Wives could find themselves en route to Australia against their will. In much the same circumstances were the adult unmarried women—daughters, aunts, sisters and widows—who had no place else to go. And then there were those who were co-opted because their energies were desperately needed; at a time when a woman could give birth to many children over an extended period, the services of elder daughters were frequently commandeered for the work of childrearing. And of course, there was always the possibility of a mother's death—in which case the duties of the household could fall to a daughter, aunt or other female relative.

As well, there were the mothers of mothers who may have had no other choice than to take the home that their daughter could provide for them. Indeed, what can be stated with some certainty is that in the absence of an independent means of support, almost any woman could be obliged to remain within the family circle, no matter where it was located and no matter what links had to be severed in the process. Duty and necessity, rather than choice, provided the framework of most women's lives during this period.

Louisa Clifton, for example, was an eldest daughter. When her family elected to move to Australind (Western Australia) in the 1840s, it was clear that her contribution to an increasing family (with an invalid mother) was absolutely essential. When she embarked from England, she left behind romance, as well as friends, and many of her diary entries reveal her resolve to resign herself to a life of serving the family interest (see the diary of Louisa Clifton).[1]

Being coerced or cajoled into crossing the ocean, however, was a practice by no means confined to the young. When Elizabeth Hawkins, the first white woman to cross the Blue Mountains, made the tortuous and terrifying journey, she not only had her many children with her, but also her elderly mother (see Chapter 9). As it is unlikely that anyone would wittingly and willingly subject themselves to such an ordeal, it is safe to assume that Elizabeth Hawkins' mother had financial as well as emotional reasons for travelling with her relatives.

This, of course, was the crux for women. Denied access to education and professional occupation, eighteenth century white women encountered extraordinary financial difficulties. That working women were often unable to provide for themselves is amply illustrated by the fact that so many of them were convicts, transported for the crimes of stealing food for themselves and their children. For women who were not engaged in paid work, the possibilities for self-sufficiency were often not much better. Apart from those who received an allowance, which afforded a measure of financial independence (an arrangement enjoyed by very few and one which could be terminated on marriage, when wives were not permitted to own property), the primary occupation that was open to women was that of finding a man to support them.

Theoretically it was a woman's *choice* to marry; in practice, many women were pressured into it, particularly if there were money problems. Marriage in the eighteenth century—and indeed, well into the twentieth —was a *trade*, argued the twentieth century suffragist and feminist Cicely Hamilton, with women obliged to exchange their intellectual, physical and sexual services in return for board and lodging.[2]

To be forced into this demeaning and often brutalising barter arrangement was the fate of many eighteenth century women, and understandably there were protests about the injustice, the injury and the indignity of the practice. Even in the seventeenth century there were women writers, such as the outstanding playwright Aphra Behn and the scholar Mary Astell, who denounced the way women were obliged to sell themselves in marriage, and then as wives were denied legal existence and the right to own property.[3] In the eighteenth century, Frances Sheridan was just one of the many women writers who took up her pen to point to the pain and the perils that were a consequence of women's lack of power.

In 1761 she published a remarkable novel, *The Memoirs of Miss Sidney*

*Bidulph*, which tackled the issue of women's duty, and degradation. In brief, Sidney is called upon by her impoverished and widowed mother to marry an undesirable but wealthy man in the interest of obtaining money to set up her son, Sidney's brother. According to the morality of the time, the dutiful Sidney owed complete obedience to her mother and was obliged to fulfil her wishes, despite realising that to trade herself in marriage would be against her moral standards—not to mention her personal preferences! The novel gave rise to much controversy and heated debate,[4] and although Frances Sheridan opened up many new possibilities when she challenged the bounds of duty and the debasement of marriage, she also acknowledged that she was dealing primarily with a philosophical issue: most women simply did not have the luxury of being able to please themselves—and the author was no exception. Less than thirty years later, little had changed, and most of the women who sailed with the First Fleet were in much the same predicament. Their actions were governed by necessity.

This was the period when men had passed a law which entitled them to take their wives sexually whenever and wherever they so desired. Women had no rights; they were legally obliged to comply. And with little or no reliable contraception available at the time, the enforcement of conjugal rights could also mean that women were compelled to undergo pregnancy and birth against their will, as many women in this volume testify. (See particularly Georgiana Molloy in Chapter 14.)

These, together with women's failing health, are pressing issues in achieving some understanding of the nature of women's reality, but few answers or insights are to be found in the literature of the period. There is an almost resounding silence on this issue.

One of the few women to break the taboo and to speak about women's repeated and unwanted impregnations was the great eighteenth century philosopher Mary Wollstonecraft. In her novel, *Maria, The Wrongs of Women* (published posthumously in 1798), she portrays the anguish of a wife who has been impregnated against her will by a brutish husband. Although violated by the pregnancy, and deeply resentful of the man (and the society) she sees as responsible, Maria nonetheless manages the almost impossible task of deploring the conception and cherishing the child. In the world of English literature, Maria stands almost alone as the woman who gives voice to her anger and bitterness at the way in which enforced pregnancy is legalised.

Not that Maria was able to do much to alter her situation. If an eighteenth century woman came to the conclusion that her marriage had been a dreadful mistake (and quite a few of them did) there were not many options open to her, as Mary Wollstonecraft makes clear. In her terms, marriage was nothing other than legal prostitution, with wives in the invidious position of having less control over their person and their price than the *illegal* prostitute. The worst feature of the whole appalling business was that, for the wives, the contract could not be ended. There was really no divorce available, and 'separation' was socially out of the question; for the virtuous woman there was no alternative to the husband, no matter how appalling his behaviour. (The not-so-virtuous often found other alternatives, as Babette Smith reveals in her excellent coverage of women convicts, *A Cargo of Women.*[5])

A woman could not make her husband leave, nor was there anywhere that she could go. She had no entitlement to her good name, her person, her property or her children. A wife 'cannot drive an unfaithful husband from his house, nor separate, or tear, his children from him, however culpable he may be' comments Mary Wollstonecraft in *Maria*. And it was not simply the loss of financial support which prevented a wife from leaving a disastrous marriage. For, even if her husband did not go so far as to force his disobedient wife to return (as he was legally entitled to do) it may have been impossible for her to find an accepted place in the community. Further, without any rights to her children, there was no way she could take them with her. Mary Wollstonecraft deplores, and denounces the double standard:

'The situation of a woman separated from her husband, is undoubtedly very different from a man who has left his wife. He, with lordly dignity, has shaken of a clog; and the allowing her food and raiment is thought sufficient to secure his reputation from taint. And, should she have been inconsiderate, he will be celebrated for his generosity and and forbearance. Such is the respect paid to the master-key of property! A woman, on the contrary, resigning what is termed her natural protector (though he never was so, but in name) is despised and shunned, for asserting the independence of mind distinctive of a rational being, and spurning at slavery.'[6]

Mary Wollstonecraft's *Vindication of the Rights of Woman*—the classic analysis of unfair treatment of the fair sex—was published in 1792, just four years after the women of the First Fleet went ashore in Australia. The book provided an awesome overview of the painful absence of choice and liberty in women's lives, and would have been no less relevant in some respects to the women in the colonies than it was to those who stayed in England. Yet, in any history of white occupation, this lack of choice, this absence of independence and autonomy and the implications it had for women's lives, has failed to be fully recognised.

For example, it is not uncommon to find that the women convicts who became pregnant on the voyage are referred to as 'prostitutes'. Mary Wollstonecraft would definitely have repudiated this particular terminology; she would have insisted that it was a gross misrepresentation of the women's situation. In her analysis, prostitutes would have been immeasurably better off, in that (unlike the convict women) they would have had some measure of control over their own conduct. This was a far cry from the conditions endured by the women prisoners. No one could be familiar with the state in which these women were transported and still believe that they had any choice about their sexual availability. They were virtually slaves, at the mercy of their gaolers, and they were completely powerless to pre-empt any of the sexual demands which were made of them.

But what Mary Wollstonecraft would have understood—and quickly challenged—was the way the convict women were condemned for their loss of moral virtue and lowering of moral standards. As if the women had any say in the matter! As if it were their fault that they had been sexually commandeered and impregnated!

How would the world have looked to these women when they set foot upon the soil of New South Wales? Taking into account the fact that many of them would not have chosen to make the voyage, and that those (both convict and free) who were pregnant had not necessarily chosen their condition, what would they have felt when they contemplated the strange land, when they were able to comprehend that they were so far from home, from all that was familiar and reassuring? That Octavia Dawson could write that 'letters are the only comfort' (see Octavia Dawson, Chapter 11) gives some idea of the bleakness of women's lives and the importance of correspondence with those back home.

Many of the women feared for their safety—for their very lives—and of course their terror was not only understandable, but entirely justified. As well as many of the same risks that the men faced, as women they had to contend with additional ones as well. Their health and well-being were jeopardised by pregnancy and 'confinement'; no doubt many of the women lived with the constant spectre of death hanging over them. Sadly, their worst fears were too often realised. The death of a mother in childbirth brings to an end the letters and journal entries of a number of the women included in this volume.

**Hard labour**

No woman stepped ashore in Australia in 1788 and lived a life of luxury or ease. Apart from the life-threatening women's work of pregnancy, labour, nursing and childrearing—not to mention the backbreaking and wearying labour of 'homemaking'—there was an urgent and insistent need to establish shelter and to provide food. Famine was a real risk in the early period.

For more than fifty years—the period covered by these letters and journal entries—all women were obliged to work in some form, as the fledgling colony did not have sufficient resources to support members of the community in a state of idleness. Even women of 'refinement', and those who took their place among the 'upper class' were required to play their part. From governors' ladies to indentured servants and convicts, women toiled at every known task.

Elizabeth Macarthur, for example, survived nine pregnancies. At the same time she was responsible for running a substantial and diverse enterprise (which came to include servants as well as convicts). For many years she managed the thriving and expanding business of Elizabeth Farm—growing crops, breeding sheep, developing a dairy—while she continued to supervise the education of those of her children who had not returned 'home', and while she corresponded on a regular basis with her family and friends in England. As every woman can well appreciate, it wasn't just the physical work that was so demanding; all the organisational detail involved could prove to be the most stressful, tiring and frustrating part. That Elizabeth Macarthur spent many a night worrying about how to manage all her many responsibilities is patently clear from her correspondence (see Elizabeth Macarthur, Chapter 2).

In 1798—ten years after the colony had been founded—Elizabeth Macarthur wrote to her friend Bridget Kingdon to give her some idea of the nature of colonial existence. The very inventory of tasks and trusts and duties is exhausting. And one reason that there were so many decisions to make and so much to do was—as she informs her dear friend living in 'civilised' England—that 'shops there are none', in New South Wales. Everything needed for the entire household had to be produced upon the premises—or ordered months or years in advance from the home country, which in contrast was earning itself a reputation as a nation of shopkeepers.

In the community that Elizabeth Macarthur describes, the general rule seems to be that if you can't supply it yourself, you can't have it. While this led to some innovative responses, it is also clear that the population endured many privations and shortages.

At the other end of the fifty-year time spectrum—and from the other side of the continent to Elizabeth Macarthur—Georgiana Molloy's letters from Augusta in the 1830s and 1840s contain numerous requests for goods—from books to rakes and cottons and dress materials—and probably even more cries of weariness and distress at being the sole nursemaid, educator and seamstress for her growing family. Even a woman such as Sophy Dumaresq, who was among the most privileged of the white community, was obliged to work in a way that would never have been countenanced in England. (See Sophy Dumaresq, Chapter 8.)

She too 'raised' her own child, although the absence of suitable servants was no doubt the overriding consideration in these circumstances.

It was not just the work itself which was such a problem for genteel eighteenth and early nineteenth century women. Work—and particularly paid, purposeful, professional work—was, for 'a lady', forbidden. At the very time that white women of all classes were engaged in unequivocal hard work in Australia, the cult of the 'kept' woman was becoming firmly entrenched in industralised Britain. 'Ladies' were expected to be ornamental, decorative, accomplished and amusing, but were criticised— even ostracised—if they engaged in intellectual pursuits or attempted to embark upon professional work or earn a decent living. This was another gross injustice that Mary Wollstonecraft railed against; to her it was a source of women's intellectual and financial impoverishment and a necessary condition of their dependence.

However, for the women whose work was absolutely essential in the Australian context, but who nonetheless aspired to the status of ladies, there was a genuine conflict of interests. When the definition of a lady was a woman who never dirtied her hands with trade or dulled her sensibilities with the crude business of living, how could they take on the most menial tasks and still preserve their distinction as desirable objects of refinement?

And this wasn't the sum total of their difficult predicament. Once work was thrust upon them—while ever it was not so great as to be mentally and physically tortuous—there were those who would have affirmed Mary Wollstonecraft's assertions that the work could be stimulating, satisfying, even exhilarating and enjoyable. More than a few women whose letters are included here became businesswomen, landholders and property owners—as well as becoming financially self-sufficient.

One of the topics that preoccupies the colonial letter writers through-out the decades is that of trying to conform to the desired standards of 'home' while breaking just about every genteel rule in their daily exist-ence. When a lady was not supposed to do her own washing, prepare her own meals, suckle her own child or sew her own clothes—let alone engage in buying and selling, or embark on breeding, grazing or dairying enterprises—and when in the colonies these activities could not be abandoned (and in many cases would not be abandoned even when the demands for women's labour were not so pressing), there were many colonial women who were confronted with real difficulties. They did not want to be disowned or dismissed by their familes and friends in England as rough and coarse creatures without manners or breeding, so their task was to convince their audience that they suffered no loss of refinement—despite the hard work and lack of civilising influences.

'The society has not degenerated in the least & instead of anyone or anything for the Swan, I should say selectness and refinement are more prevalent than in England. Yet no one scruples to assist in the duties of the menage,' Fanny Bussell wrote reassuringly from the Swan River settlement to her mother in England (26 January 1833). Along with her siblings (and later her mother), Fanny Bussell worked extraordinarily hard in establishing the family property (the area now known as Busselton). Well aware that she was risking her status as a lady, she became increasingly conscious of her form and image. Ridiculous as it may now seem, she (like many women of her position and period) went to even greater lengths than in England to preserve the right appearances. In her insistence on being more English than the English, in her persistence with dress and demeanour totally unsuitable for the primitive Australian conditions, it could be argued that Fanny Bussell was among the first subscribers to the phenomenon of 'cultural cringe'. (See Frances Louisa Bussell, Chapter 15.)

But if some of the ruses that women used to pass themselves off as ladies were successful, there were also some rationalisations that were highly transparent, and on occasion pathetic. They simply served to signal that there was a growing gulf between the lifestyles and values of the colonials and those of the custodians of standards and morality who had not ventured from their parlours in England.

While some women might have worried about hard work (and hard cash) undermining their status and eroding their sensibilities, there were others for whom such esoteric issues were irrelevant. Convict women had no status to lose, and for many of them the fundamental issue was whether they would survive the appalling conditions of their lives and work and the disparagement of their human worth. Some letters and diaries included in the volume help to give an idea of the savage and systematic way in which these women were abused, exploited and discriminated against (see Chapter 1).

But even when separated from young children while serving their sentences, even when ill-treated, overworked and reviled, there were still convict women and servant women who were able to take advantage of some of the opportunities that the colonies provided. Margaret Catchpole was not the only convict woman to become a property holder, and although there was no shortage of hard labour and no end to the suffering and disappointments she endured, she did not return to England even when she acquired the money to make the voyage. While she had often stated that her one wish in life was to go back to the country of her birth, she finally decided that it was Australia which had provided her with financial security and an esteemed position in the community.

Unfortunately, much of the work that women undertook in the early days of the colony has not always received the same attention and admiration as the work of the men. This cannot be because there was not enough of it to cause comment. On the contrary, it could readily be argued that women then did a double shift, often performing the work traditionally undertaken by men, as well as doing the work that only women can do. Nor can the neglect of women's work be because the labours of men were more dangerous, daring or daunting. From the accounts that the women give of their lives in their diaries and letters, it is clear that their contribution to the establishment of the colony was both enormous and essential, and that it calls for fuller acknowledgment and appreciation. It is also obvious that the women who set sail from England, who set foot on Australian soil and survived, were changed markedly by the challenges, the labours and the opportunities that their new life provided.

Individually and collectively, these women dealt with the fears, contended with the threats and generally comforted those around them, while still having enough resources to reassure and comfort those back home. Their letters and diaries were often expressly written for that purpose. If their records reveal lives of hardship and self-sacrifice, they also contain telling tales of personal growth and satisfaction, and stand as a testimonial to some of the rewards of colonial existence.

Women were tested by the difficult and often dreadful demands of colonial survival; their response was innovative, valuable, liberating and of course courageous. While only a few might have chosen their new home, there were many who found that their choices had multiplied upon arrival. Women's letters and diaries from 1788 to 1840 chronicle the hard labour that women performed, but they also point to the independent lifestyle that these women were beginning to forge, to like and to justify. It is easy to see some of the seeds of a sturdy self-reliance being sown during the period.

## The need for writing

Not all the women who landed in Australia during the first years of colonisation were able to write. However, it is surprising how many of them—convict women included—were literate. In fact, this high level of literacy across class barriers raises some interesting issues and emphasises some of the problems which women had in common. When *all* women were denied access to education and the study of reading and writing, it is a rather futile exercise trying to decide who has more or less education than others; there is no systematic way of determining which women were able to overcome the obstacles and acquire the skills of literacy, and which women were not. So much depended on personal circumstances and individual motivation.

But it is precisely because women were denied education, occupation and mobility that reading and writing became such important attributes in eighteenth and early nineteenth century women's lives. When as a sex you were not permitted to attend school or university, when you were not permitted a public role or allowed entry to any of the established professions, when the only work available to you was limited to the menial, the sexual or the domestic—and when there was little chance that you could go out and about because it was either improper or unaffordable—how were you to know anything about the world beyond the immediate confines of your own four walls? Death by intellectual starvation is how Florence Nightingale described this narrow, sterile life.[7]

So closely were the horizons of women circumscribed that today it is difficult to comprehend the conditions of their daily life. There were no mass media to bring information into the homes to which women were confined. The newspapers of the time were circulated mainly in places such as coffee-houses, where no decent woman would venture, and were not considered appropriate reading matter for women anyway. For this reason, Eliza Haywood had launched *The Female Spectator* in 1744 on the grounds that it would educate women in some of the dangers and dramas of the wide and wicked world. It was supposed to be morally instructive, and therefore would not be out of place in a respectable home. One of the forerunners of women's magazines, it helped to fill an enormous information gap in the eighteenth century.[8]

Women were cut off from just about every source of intellectual stimulation—with no professions, no political presence, and no great arts participation. And they were also effectively cut off from each other and the collective experience of women. They were isolated in paid work where the opportunities for social intercourse were very few and the workload often so heavy that there was little inclination for communication. And they were isolated from one another as small communities broke up and the drift to the cities accelerated. In these narrowed circumstances, it is no wonder that women were often desperate to know more about the world, about human nature, about ideas and the workings of society, even about the fears and aspirations of the woman next door. Kept in such ignorance, women had no way of getting beyond the 'here and now', no basis for organising and intepreting their experience, no context for evaluating, judging or operating in the world—unless, of course, they could learn to read and write.

The obvious solution, and the entrance to the world beyond their own private enclosure, was through books. Not surprisingly, women made extraordinary efforts to become readers. But there were no graded exercises or attractive reading schemes for their purposes. On the contrary, it is the absence of help which characterises their passion for both reading *and* writing. One of the most striking features of women's accounts of their own educational histories is the number who declare that they taught themselves to read at a very early age, and not infrequently from the Bible—the only reading matter that they could find. Mary Wollstonecraft even taught herself German from a dictionary so that she could be paid as a translator.

Women had to learn for themselves—and not just because they had no established schools or trained teachers. (As Antonia Fraser points out, the education of women deteriorated markedly after Henry VIII abolished the convents which prepared teachers and trained girls.[9]) They had to teach themselves in the face of active opposition, for it was widely believed that literacy 'unfitted' women for being dutiful and docile wives. There was probably an element of truth in this assertion, for the very good reason that reading enabled women to have access to opinions other than those of the men in their lives; once they could read—and get to the books—they were in a position to know other things, even to disagree, which is precisely why they were initially discouraged from taking up reading.

So 'contaminating' was literacy supposed to be that there were many women of birth and breeding who were dissuaded from ever acquiring the habit. And it was certainly considered unwise to allow working women to taste such dangerous fruits, although they too showed great ingenuity in acquiring the skills; there were even women who were known as the Milkwomen poets.[10] When literacy was finally extended to the working classes, it was granted in stages, with the first concession being that members should be allowed to learn to *read* only, so that they could study the Bible and learn the lessons of meekness and obedience. Only later was *writing*—which could be used to corrupt others—officially allowed; clearly there were working women who did not wait for permission to learn to write and read.

The medical profession also lent weight to the case against women's literacy. Evidence was frequently advanced to support the contention that writing and reading were bad for women's health, and could result in a range of reproductive diseases. It was not uncommon to find respected medical practitioners declaring that women's brains would burst and their uteruses atrophy if they were exposed to the risks of writing and reading.[11] And as it was widely believed that the uterus was the source of all women's moods and maladies, the insistence that the greatest single cause of uterine disease was novel reading was not without its adherents.

But if it was considered prudent to keep women from books, it was also considered appropriate for women to write letters. And when it comes to women's literary life, it was *letter writing* that was to be the loophole that allowed many writers and readers to slip through.

Letters were part of the private rather than the public realm and so fitted well with women's domain. They were a means of maintaining relationships, rather than of promoting dissension and inciting riots (real fears at the time, and grounds for transportation), so they were not viewed with the same suspicion as other literary activities. The task of letter writing did not call upon the writer to mix with men or know the ways of the world—or to earn a reputation—as public forms of author- ship required; rather, letter writing was a form of family communication which could be conducteed from within an intimate circle, and which could even be used to sustain relationships when families were scattered and divided. In short, it was expedient to classify letter writing as women's business, so women were permitted to write letters when they were not allowed to write anything else, as Virginia Woolf wryly observed. 'Letters did not count,' she contended in *A Room of One's Own*. 'A woman might write letters while she was sitting by her father's sick bed. She could write them by the fire whilst the men talked without disturbing them.'[12] And because letter writing was not seen as dangerous or a threat and was generally permitted, eighteenth century women took to letter writing with a vengeance.

They wrote out of a need to express their frustration at the aridity of their lives. They wrote to satisfy their curiosity, to find out what was happening to other people in other places. They wrote to relieve the boredom, to cultivate networks and to forge friendships. They wrote to develop their style, their sense of self, their ability to have *agency*; to some the very act of writing was proof of existence, an acknowledgment of an inner life, a psyche, an intellectual resource.

It is a mark of women's extraordinary literary achievement that they were able to transform into a profession the only activity as authors that was allowed them. For out of women's letter writing emerged the novel. It is no coincidence that the first novels were epistolary—fictions which were constructed from a series of letters. And it is no coincidence that most eighteenth century novels were written by women.

Women wrote novels to get in touch with other women; women read novels to find out how other women lived. In the absence of educational institutions to foster a spirit of inquiry and to provide information, the novel became the basis of women's knowledge, a common curriculum for women who were literate. (In many ways this is still the role played by books in the lives of contemporary women—hence the spectacular growth of women's presses, bookshops and literary activities.)

Women writers began to explore some of the problems of the day: they posed moral questions, addressed philosophical issues, presented a range of characters, choices and consequences, and extended women's horizons in an imaginative and stimulating manner. At the end of the eighteenth century and into the nineteenth there was a flowering of women's fictional talents where virtually every topic was taken up to become the substance of women's literature. This was when Fanny Burney published her superb novels (beginning in 1778 with *Evelina*, a novel in letters), and when the marvellous novels of Maria Edgeworth appeared. Mary Wollstonecraft's philosophy and fiction were printed at the end of the eighteenth century and the astonishing novels of her daughter, Mary Shelley, were best sellers in the early nineteenth century (with Fanny Bussell commenting on her reading of *The Last Man* (1826) from Augusta). There were Ann Radcliffe's Gothic novels challenging the boundaries of scientific explanation, Mary Brunton's writings questioning the boundaries of self-righteousness and Jane Austen's explorations of values and virtue—all of which qualified as a stimulating form of education.

Women seized the opportunity that had opened to them. They turned letter writing into a paying and prestigious profession which men could not initially control and from which they could not exclude women (as they did in the professions of medicine, law, religion, etc.). This pattern changed later, when novel writing became a pursuit for men. It is worth noting that during the eighteenth century, when women were the leading writers, men made use of women's pseudonyms in order to get their novels published; but by the middle of the nineteenth century, men had achieved such prominence that there were protests from them about the women who entered the profession under false pretences by the use of male pseudonyms, as in the case of the Bronte sisters.[13]

When it came to the novel, women developed a genre which was compatible with their own experiences and circumstances. Using letters as the lever to open the door to a literary life for women writers—and readers—was a remarkable accomplishment; this was the context in which colonial women were writing their copious letters and diaries.

Many of the letters (and diaries) included in this volume provide clear and creative examples of the connections between women's letter writing and the growth and development of fiction. This is partly because the conditions which applied in the colonies brought out some of the characteristics which were readily incorporated in the emerging form of the novel. For example, the colonial women had so many exciting stories to tell that it was almost impossible for them to write an account that was without intrigue, interest or drama of some sort. The letters and diaries in this volume have been chosen on the basis of their interest, and because they are representative of some aspect of early colonial life.

For obvious reasons, these letters also developed some of the features of suspense associated with the writing of serials. When there were such long periods between ships which could take the letters to their destination, it was not uncommon for women to write in weekly or monthly instalments, with each episode ending on a note of tension as the author was called away to deal with a crisis, a catastrophe or a cry for help. Understandably, then, the next page or the next entry was eagerly sought. What happened after the author had put the letter aside? And months— sometimes even a year—after the letter had been written, was the writer still there, or had tragedy intervened in the interim so that the English audience was reading a lively account from someone who had already 'passed on'? This was *real* drama, and given the colonial conditions it is not surprising that letters from the Antipodes were so popular. They could provide a narrative that would rival the escapades of Robinson Crusoe or Evelina, and a family saga which could do justice to the works of Charlotte Lennox[14] or Charles Dickens.

Writing was not always an indulgence or even a pleasant pastime in the colonial era. Letter writing was often another necessity. In order to stay in touch with loved ones back home—so that the family should not fade from the writer's memory, or (perhaps more importantly) so the writer should not fade from family memory—letters had to be written to keep communication and contact alive. And of course there was also the kind of writing that was required to obtain the goods that the colony could not provide. So writing was not time off; it was a form of work in its own right.

Because women had the *need* to write, whatever other pressures were on them, they had to make time for this additional chore. And once in the habit of writing, it was but a small step for many of them to become proficient in the art. Again it is interesting to note how the need to read prompted many women from all walks of life to acquire the skill—and the passion—to pursue the practice so avidly, and it seems that the need to write prompted colonial women from all walks of life to pick up their pens and create a body of literature that is a rich and inspirational heritage.

The letters in this volume reveal the intensity, the urgency, the necessity that was behind the efforts of so many of the writers; they also reveal the extent of the talent and the crafting that was responsible for this impressive literary work. When there were so few opportunities for the exercise of choice, assessment or judgement, and so few occasions which encouraged or allowed self-actualisation, the attraction of letter writing could be immense; it could stir and challenge the creativity of the woman writer and promote a sense of power and pleasure in the achievement of the writing.

For some of the women, writing became a central part of their existence over many years. For Elizabeth Macarthur, for example, letters became the vital thread that linked her with friends and family in England— including her sons, who left Australia to be educated 'at home'. Her letters also provided her with her own forum where she could communicate with her peers, where she could explore and explain some of the experiments she was carrying out on the farm, as well as being able to confide some of her hopes and fears, her successes and failures.

For the Bussells, letters became the very stuff of family life through periods of separation, as mother and daughters kept up the lively flow of information which united and nurtured the family members. When from this base, correspondence was conducted with friends and acquaintances, there can be no mistaking the message of family security, solidarity and intimacy that the letters intended. They were meant to mould the individuals into family unit, and they more than achieved their purpose.

Sometimes it was relatively easy for colonial women to present their lives in an extremely positive light to their English counterparts. There was certainly much about the excitement and the freedom, about the challenge, the change and the fulfilment, that English women—whose daily existence was governed by edicts on decency and decorum—could find very appealing. And there was much, too, in the style of writing that lent itself to the minimisation of the bad and the maximisation of the good news.

Because so many women did not want to give undue worry or concern to mothers, sisters, daughters and friends in the old country (and it is quite astonishing just how many of the letters are between women), they were often very careful about the way they referred to potentially sad or disturbing incidents. Why cause alarm over tragedies which might never occur? The tendency was to omit any predictions about difficulty or distress, but to proclaim the joys and delights that followed an ordeal or test of endurance.

So there were times when a life-threatening pregnancy was not revealed, but the celebration of the the birth of a child was thankfully announced. And this role as the giver of good news could be a splendid one for the letter writer. To give an account of the drama *after* the house had been burnt down—but when everyone was safe and well; to describe the trials and terrors of the journey *after* the Blue Mountains had been crossed—but when no injuries were sustained, was to be at the centre of an adventure story that had a happy ending. And this was the vantage point from which women reported the drought, the flood, the illness of a family member: *after* the danger had passed and the event had been distanced, transformed by the writer's art into a marvellously entertaining episode.

This is not to suggest that there are no heartfelt or pitiful cries in the letters; some of the most moving descriptions of loss, pain and anguish are contained within these pages. But it is to suggest that there were few women who ended their letters on a plaintive note or in a tone of unnerving despair. Although cries of wretchedness, weariness and loneliness pierce many of the entries, they are more often found in the diaries—the communication with self rather than with others.

When Georgiana Molloy writes about the death of her daughter three days after her birth, and the death of her son who drowned in a well, her letters are not a piteous plea for consolation or comfort. They are written after the initial and deadening grief has become more manageable, after she has come to terms with these awful events in her own mind and *she* is in a position to provide succour and reassurance to her correspondents. Yet she remains the heroine of the narrative—though it has more of the hallmarks of a tragedy than a romance or adventure story.

That these letters lend themselves to being read aloud is no accident. The writers knew how their letters could be 'staged' to provide the home entertainment and they shaped their words accordingly. While they may have been rushed, written under pressure, and never of the standard that their authors would have liked (a complaint made by many writers of serials with deadlines to meet, Charles Dickens being no exception) there can be no doubting their success as narratives; they have everything from comfort to suspense, from tragedy to romance, from philosophy to shopping lists, from the exotic to the familiar. They are an impressive achievement from some amazing women.

Letters, of course, were not the only forms of personal writing that women engaged in. Journals, too, could be a part of the colonial women's reality and they developed their own distinctive features in response to the Antipodean imperative. When women stepped ashore during those first fifty years of colonisation, it was not their only concern to keep in touch with those left behind; they also felt the need to keep in touch with themselves. For they had been thrown into a very different environment from anything they had known before and, in learning to cope with the new demands that confronted them, they were becoming very different people. To be cut off from all that was familiar—from the faces, the places, the circumstances which provided the feedback that shaped the nature of each individual, from the definitions as a mother's daughter, a child's nurturer, a member of a particular community or congregation—was in itself sufficient to cause an identity crisis. And when to this was added all the traumas and pressures of a strange and unknown land, and all the risks of death and disintegration which were a part of the daily landscape, it is understandable that women should have needed a space, a refuge to unburden their souls and sort out their thoughts. Today we would recognise their need for counselling.

But from 1788 to 1840 no such luxuries were available. So it was to a diary that many women turned. They made of their journals a companion, a comforter, a confidante. They found themselves in writing themselves, a reality which can still be constructed through the process of personal writing.

The journal entries included here are often difficult to distinguish from the serial letters. One reason for the overlap is that some of the women specifically wrote journals to send back home, so there is a notion of a public audience in their composition. Both Fanny and Bessie Bussell tried to keep daily records to send to their mother and, understandably, once a journal is for someone else's eyes other than one's own, it does have different qualities and assumes a different tone.

Of course the dividing line between a diary written solely for oneself and one written with other readers in mind can never be definitive. After all, how many journal writers have dreamt of their work being found, published and acclaimed after their death and have written with such an audience in mind? How many women included in these pages would have 'fantasised' about their words being preserved, printed and presented for study more than a century after their death? The very sense of an audience can lead to shifts in style . . . an interesting study in its own right.

No doubt some of the women in these pages would have thought that publication was no less than their due (Jane Franklin, perhaps, who had a positive sense of self, or the members of the Bussell family who had a strong belief in the importance of their own family records). But there are also women whose entries are included here who would have been deeply distressed to think of their most private hopes and hurts being paraded for public view. This is also an issue which needs to be taken into account in any appreciation of women's personal chronicles. To what extent do we invade another's privacy when we peruse their personal world without their permission? Is such behaviour ethical? And is this an inherent part of the attraction of diary/letter reading—being able to know the details of a life that the subject would have preferred to have kept secret?

What we do know about diary and letter writing is that it often provides a means for self-realisation—for consciously constructing an identity, for presenting a particular profile, for externalising the self and looking on one's own identity as an observer. This can be both exhilarating and enlightening. But in eighteenth and nineteenth century Australia, if there were rewards to be gained in terms of personal growth and human contact from this literary exercise, there were also difficulties to be overcome. One factor which should not be lost sight of is just how hard it was for women to write. Every letter sent, every journal record made, represents a triumph of determination.

First of all there was the problem of time; while women today legitimately complain about the double shifts, about the workload and the exhaustion that goes with the attempt to be superwoman, the contributions of women in this volume make it abundantly clear that the *burden* of women's work is not a new phenomenon. Indeed, it is salutary to note just what demands were made on women's time, not just in relation to hours, but in terms of the physical labour that homemaking required. Sleep was a luxury for many of our foremothers, and leisure was a concept that was often unknown. So women had to 'make time' for diary keeping and letter writing, and it was often at the expense of some other important—even essential—responsibility; for Georgiana Molloy, the conflict between letter writing and sewing the much-needed clothes for her children was a constant and harrowing one.

Even if the time could be made, there was the cost to be considered. Paper was precious, and very expensive, as it all had to be shipped from England and was often difficult to obtain (there were no stationers around to ensure a ready supply). Because it was so costly and so scarce, one measure of economy that was adopted was to write twice upon the page—first across the page and then again across it after it had been turned at right angles (see illustration on page 1 of the pictorial section in this volume). This was an exacting task in terms of writing and reading, and added to the difficulties.

Then, too, there was the cost of postage; not until 1840 did the 'penny postage' come in. Prior to that time, the cost of postage was determined by the distance and the letter size and was often paid by the *recipient*; with letters of more than one sheet being charged at twice the rate, it is no wonder that for many women in Australia the cost of getting extensive news from home was exorbitant.

Time, money and trepidation were the problems associated with 'letters home', for even when the paper was purchased and the letters penned, the difficulties were not necessarily all overcome. When would a ship sail? How safe would it be? How long would it take to reach its destination? Among the letters included in this volume are those which testify to the tyranny of distance. Letters which have been so long on the high seas that fortunes have changed dramatically; writers or receivers— or their loved ones—may have died in the interim, or births, deaths and marriages have altered the frames of reference.

Because there are so many common contexts, yet so many individual stories, represented in these diaries and letters, the possibilities for organisation were numerous and varied. For many reasons, however, we elected to arrange the entries around the theme of women's labour. One rationale for this was that women's work was so pervasive it united all the contributions; another was that women's work has often been devalued and neglected in historical coverage and interpretation. So we thought it fitting to take the opportunity to present women's accounts of their work, in their own words.

Not all the diaries and letters that were available have been included here. And of course, what is available is in itself a source for further study. Why have some sources been preserved and others not? Is the climate in Queensland a contributing factor to the paucity of appropriate material, or is there some other explanation associated with philosophy, state policy or educational institutions? Apart from confining the selection to approximately the first fifty years after white invasion, we were also concerned to cover a range of people, places and experiences. And while, unfortunately, there is no material from Queensland, the other states of Western Australia, South Australia, Tasmania (Van Diemen's Land), Victoria and New South Wales are all well represented, as are women of all ages and classes.

We have included the accounts of convict women, of farming women, of commercial women, of religious, philanthropic and vice-regal women. We have included the work of travel, from on board ship to crossing the mountains or pioneering in places where no Europeans had previously been. We have included the work of homemaking: of being wife, mother, daughter, cook, clothesmaker, gardener, correspondent, educator, nurse and midwife—as well as many other roles. And we have chosen entries which help to show how much time and energy women have put into women's work—into creating and maintaining family ties and relationships, into developing and managing the emotional realm which is integral to the quality of human life.

We have selected material which reveals women's achievements and failures, which testifies to their joys and their pain. We have included the letters of Georgiana Molloy, who, from the depths of despair and isolation, was able to respond to the intellectual challenge of her environment and to become one of the first white scientists to appreciate the richness and variety of Australian flora and fauna.

We have tried to let as many white women as possible speak for themselves, and to provide first-hand accounts of colonial life. And while many of them were conscious of the displacement of the Aboriginal people, we are conscious that their view is partial and prejudiced. There is another story yet to be told which will help to place the accounts of these white women in perspective.

## Note on spellings

Extracts from letters and diaries have been reproduced in this book as closely as possible to the originals. Spelling has not been altered and usually attention has not been drawn to incorrect or archaic spelling. An exception has been made with the letters of Margaret Catchpole which are difficult to read in their original phonetical spelling. In a few cases paragraphing has been added but generally unparagraphed letters and diary entries have remained unaltered. Similarly punctuation (sometimes indistinct or indecipherable in the original) has been added or altered only when essential for understanding. Underlining in letters and diaries is indicated in the book by italics, as are the names of ships. Raised letters have not been reproduced. In a number of cases, words were missing (for example, because of holes in the paper) or illegible. These have been indicated by using square brackets and a question mark where a word couldn't be deciphered, using square brackets around a word where that word was a likely one, or using square brackets, a word and a question mark where a guess was made as to the probable word.

# 1
# Forced labour

## Mary Talbot, Sarah Bird and other unnamed convicts

*This desolate place of banishment*

When the First Fleet arrived in Sydney in 1788 with its cargo of convicts, women made up just over one-quarter of the total. Like the male convicts, their role was to work under the direction of officials and guards in establishing a European settlement at Sydney Cove. In the first years of the colony, the main official role of women convicts was to work as servants for officers or for the few private settlers to whom they were assigned. Their work included the complete range of domestic duties from cooking, washing and gardening to nursing the sick. Later some were employed making clothes, an occupation that many had followed before being sentenced.

Many of the men, both officials and convicts, saw the unofficial role of the women convicts as prostitutes or concubines. The more fortunate got married, or entered steady relationships, some with fellow convicts and others with emancipists or men who had arrived free. Some women became joint workers in their husbands' businesses or farms. Some enterprising women began their own businesses, often as shopkeepers or innkeepers. Marriage, either legal or de facto, could give women convicts security and protection from unwanted attentions, a situation exacerbated by the disproportionate numbers of men and women.

The written words of women convicts, although very meagre, give a direct insight into their role in the convict era. Few letters—and no diaries as far as is known—have survived from the 23 000 women

1

convicts transported to New South Wales and Tasmania. For the many who were illiterate, their inability to contact their families and friends, and sometimes even their small children left behind in England, Ireland or Scotland, was an added punishment. For those who were literate, there were other obstacles. Paper was expensive, mails were infrequent and letters were often lost in transmission or in shipwrecks. Even when these obstacles were overcome, letters from convicts were generally sent to poorer families, who were often forced by the upheaval of the Industrial Revolution to move from place to place. Not surprisingly, few letters have survived.

Anyone looking for the intimate, written records of women convicts in the early years of settlement is forced to take second best. These are the letters written by women convicts which were published in newspapers in Britain. In some cases, these may have been written on behalf of the women; in other cases they appear to have been improved on or standardised in terms of style and grammar. Some may have been written with publication in mind, rather than as purely private communications.

Fortunately for our purposes, the first of these letters was written by one of the 188 women convicts transported on the First Fleet. Recent research reveals that far more of these convicts were literate than had been thought.[1] The women who were transported to Australia included many with a surprising range of talents. For example, Isabella Rosson, described as a laundress and mantua maker (dressmaker) who was sentenced to seven years for stealing, set up a school in Sydney with her husband, fellow convict William Richardson, after their marriage in 1789. Mary Johnson, described as a milliner and also sentenced to seven years for stealing, founded a school at Parramatta in 1791. Over a quarter of the women who arrived in the First Fleet and who married within the next two years were able to write their names in the marriage register.

The first letter by a woman convict appeared in a collection of British Museum Papers entitled 'Newspaper Extracts 1785–1797' which were reprinted in *Historical Records of New South Wales*.[2] Unaddressed, unsigned and headed 'Letter from a Female Convict', it tells of the desolation and privations suffered by the 188 women and 548 men convicts landed in a strange country after a voyage of between eight and nine months half way around the world. The writer of the letter probably arrived on the *Lady Penrhyn*, which carried more than half the female convicts.

The letter was written on 14 November 1788, between six and seven months after the landing. Although short, it is a remarkable piece of writing. Apart from conveying in striking words the desolation felt by this forlorn group, it touches on almost all aspects of life at the settlement, including the privations suffered by women prisoners, particularly those with young children or pregnant, because of a lack of clothes and food.

The letter also contains one of the first comments by a European woman on the Aborigines. It is not surprising that this comment echoes the ideas of the time, deeply ingrained in all classes of European society, that it was legitimate to take land from the original inhabitants and that any defence they made of their land was regarded as an unjustified attack. This unknown woman convict wrote:

'I take the first opportunity that has been given us to acquaint you with our disconsolate situation in this solitary waste of the creation. Our passage, you may have heard by the first ships, was tolerably favourable; but the inconveniences since suffered for want of shelter, bedding &c., are not to be imagined by any stranger. However, we have now two streets, if four rows of the most miserable huts you can possibly conceive of deserve that name. Windows they have none, as from the Governor's house, &c., now nearly finished, no glass could be spared; so that lattices of twigs are made by our people to supply their places. At the extremity of the lines, where since our arrival the dead are buried, there is a place called the church-yard; but we hear, as soon as a sufficient quantity of bricks can be made, a church is to be built, and named St. Philip, after the Governor.

'Notwithstanding all our presents, the savages still continue to do us all the injury they can, which makes the soldiers' duty very hard, and much dissatisfaction among the officers. I know not how many of our people have been killed.

'As for the distresses of the women, they are past description, as they are deprived of tea and other things they were indulged in in the voyage by the seamen, and as they are all totally unprovided with clothes, those who have young children are quite wretched. Besides this, though a number of marriages have taken place, several women, who became pregnant on the voyage, and are since left by their partners, who have returned to England, are not likely even here to form any fresh connections.

'We are comforted with the hopes of a supply of tea from China, and flattered with getting riches when the settlement is complete, and the hemp which the place produces is brought to perfection. Our kingaroo [sic] rats are like mutton, but much leaner; and there is a kind of chickweed so much in taste like our spinach that no difference can be discerned. Something like a ground ivy is used for tea; but a scarcity of salt and sugar makes our best meals insipid. The separation of several of us to an uninhabited island was like a second transportation. In short, every one is so taken up with their own misfortunes that they have no pity to bestow upon others. All our letters are examined by an officer, but a friend takes this for me privately. The ships sail tomorrow.'

Although ships with supplies of food and other necessities were expected from England, and their arrival was eagerly awaited, none arrived during the whole of 1789 or the first half of 1790. The next extant letter was written by a woman convict who sailed on the *Lady Juliana*, the first convict ship to leave England after the First Fleet. The ship sailed from England on 29 July 1789 with 226 women prisoners, but did not reach Sydney until 3 June 1790.

The letter, described as an extract, was printed in the *Morning Chronicle*[3] on 4 August 1791. The *Lady Juliana* gained a reputation for prostitution: a steward, John Nicol, in a gossipy account of the voyage, wrote 'every man on board took a wife from among the convicts'.[4] The writer of this letter may have been encouraged to write as she did in an effort to counter such reports. It seems obvious from the letter that she wrote under the influence of the agent, Lieutenant Thomas Edgar, an elderly sailor described by Nicol as a 'kind, humane man' who was 'very kind' to the convicts.

When children were born on board, a convict named Mrs Barnsley, who was later to practise in New South Wales, acted as midwife, Edgar is said to have distributed baby clothes donated by 'the ladies of England'.[5]

During the extremely long voyage of nearly a year, which included stops at Tenerife and St Jago and forty-five days at Rio de Janeiro, the captain of the *Lady Juliana* put about twenty women convicts to work making shirts from some linen he had brought aboard. Because of the shortage of clothing in Sydney, he was able to sell the shirts at a great profit after the ship landed.[6] One woman convict was assigned to look after the sheep on board the *Lady Juliana*. She did not lose a single sheep.[7]

The letter-writer gives some valuable information about the condition of the settlement, which had been reduced to semi-starvation because of the non-arrival of supplies from England. During this period of nearly two and a half years, during which shortages and the feeling of isolation escalated, it increasingly appeared to the inhabitants that the small closed community with its dwindling resources had been forgotten. Rations had been reduced in March and again in April 1790.

The letter also contains a first-hand account of the terrible plight of the convicts transported on the Second Fleet ships, the *Neptune*, *Surprize* and *Scarborough*. These ships, which arrived soon after the *Lady Juliana*, had the highest mortality rate in the history of transportation. During the voyage, the convicts were starved, heavily ironed and confined to the foetid holds. Apart from the 267 who died on the voyage, many others were carried ashore filthy and in the last stages of emaciation and disease, and died soon after.

In her letter, this *Lady Juliana* convict writes of the deplorable state of women prisoners in Sydney, deprived of essentials such as tea and clothes, living in windowless houses and dependent on unfamiliar animals, birds and vegetation as substitutes for the meat and bread to which they were accustomed.

The writer was one of the many women convicts employed in sewing. On the voyage she had probably been among the shirt-makers and soon after her arrival she was employed making badly needed clothes from material which arrived on the supply ship, the *Justinian*, on 20 June 1790. The letter was written on 24 July 1790, a month after the arrival of the Second Fleet, and she begins by contrasting the comparatively good treatment on the *Lady Juliana* with that on the Second Fleet ships.

'We arrived here safe after a long voyage, in very good health, thanks to our good agent [Lieutenant T. Edgar], on board, and the gentleman in England who sent us out, as we had everything that we could expect from them, and all our provisions were good. We landed here 223 women and twelve children; only three women died, and one child.[8] Five or six were born on board the ship; they had great care taken of them, and baby linen and every necessary for them were ready made to be put on.

'The greatest part of the women were immediately sent to Norfolk Island, a place about 100 miles from here, but very bad for shipping; there is no place to land but in fine weather. The *Sirius*, man-of-war, was lost at this place about six or seven months ago, when she carried some men and women from here. She landed them all safe, but lost almost all their provisions.

'This place was in a very starving condition before we arrived, and on allowance of only 2lb. of flour and 2lb. of pork for each man for a week, and these were almost starved, and could not work but three hours in the day; they had no heart, and the ground won't grow anything, only in spots here and there. There is a place called Rose Hill, about twenty miles from this, where, they say, there are four cornfields, but it does not grow much wheat; we are now much in want of almost everything; we have hardly any cloaths; but since the *Scarborough*, *Neptune*, and *Surprize* arrived we have had a blanket and a rug given us, and we hope to have some cloaths, as the *Justinian*, a ship that came from London with provisions, [is] bringing some cloth and linen, and we are to make the cloaths.

'Oh! if you had but seen the shocking sight of the poor creatures that came out in the three ships it would make your heart bleed; they were almost dead, very few could stand, and they were obliged to fling them as you would goods, and hoist them out of the ships, they were so feeble; and they died ten or twelve of a day when they first landed; but some of them are getting better. There died in their [this] way on board the *Neptune*, 183 men and 12 women, and in the *Scarborough*, 67 men, and in the *Surprize*, 85. They were not so long as we were in coming here, but they were confined, and had bad victuals and stinking water. The Governor was very angry, and scolded the captains a great deal, and, I heard, intended to write to London about it, for I heard him say it was murdering them. It, to be sure, was a melancholy sight. What a difference between us and them. God bless our good agent (I don't mean the captain). We had no reason to complain against him for anything; all our provisions and cloaths were good.

'I don't think I ever shall get away from this place to come again to see you without an order from England, for some of the men's times were out, and they went and spoke to the Governor of it, and told him that they would not work. He told them he could not send them home without orders from London, and if they would not work they should have nothing to eat, so they almost all went again to work, except ten, who were saucy, and the Governor ordered then a good flogging; but all that came from London in the First Fleet time will be out in less than two years' time. I hope that you will try to get an order for me, that I may once more see you all.'

An unfortunate Irishwoman, Mary Talbot, was the first woman convict letter-writer whose identity is known. Mary had begun her 'journey' when she migrated from Ireland to London to find work. There she had been forced into stealing when she was left without support for herself and her children after her husband, a stonemason, was injured at work and taken to hospital.

Tried for stealing linen from a London shop, Mary Talbot was sentenced to seven years' transportation. She escaped from a ship at Gravesend in an attempt to see her children, but was retaken and sentenced to death, her execution being delayed until after the birth of a child she was expecting. After about a year in Newgate prison, her sentence was commuted to transportation for life, but she protested that she preferred death as transportation would mean separation from her children. She was taken back to Newgate 'in strong convulsions, and her shrieks were re-echoed through the whole gaol' but her protests did not result in any change in her sentence. On 16 February 1791 she sailed on the *Mary Ann*, which arrived in Sydney on 9 July 1791.

Mary Talbot wrote her letter during the voyage, on 29 March 1791.

It was posted to Dublin from St Jago, the only port at which the *Mary Ann* stopped, and published in the *Dublin Chronicle* on 1 November 1791.[9]

The most poignant part of Mary Talbot's letter is her distress at being parted from her children, whose welfare dominated her life. For women convicts with children, separation was the most dreadful effect of a sentence of transportation. Terrible as the conditions were in English gaols, imprisonment there held out the hope that women might occasionally see their children and even eventually be reunited with them. Once they sailed for Australia, there was little hope of seeing their children again. This was to be true of Mary Talbot, a woman whose cry for her children echoes through the centuries.

Her letter was addressed to 'a gentleman' in England about whom nothing is known except that he had tried, without success, to keep Mary Talbot's family together by attempting to arrange their transportation as a family to America.[10] Addressed 'Most honoured Sir', the letter read:

'Your past kindness to me induces me to trouble you with some account of where I am, and what kind of voyage I have had; the latter, however, cannot be a very favourable one, for we have been surrounded by danger. We sailed from Portsmouth the 23rd of February, with the wind much against us, and were so much in danger that we feared we should have shared the fate of a ship which was lost within sight of us. Our good captain very kindly dropped anchor at the Nore, but did not stop more than one night, and sailed for the Downs, where we sent our pilot on shore. On the 25th and 26th, along the coast, we had a violent storm, which lasted twenty-four hours. During every moment of its continuance we expected to perish, and were washed out of our beds between decks, while the sea-sickness and the groans and shrieks of so many unhappy wretches made the situation we were in truly distressing, for there were 138 women and five children, two of the latter born after we sailed, and only one died on our passage hither, where we remain no longer than is necessary to repair the ship and take in water. Our captain hopes we shall arrive at Botany Bay in August, if it please God the weather should prove favourable . . . The 16th of March we crossed the Line, where we were dipped in a tub of salt-water by the sailors, and tarred all over, it being a rule amongst them to make every one pay so much money or undergo this, and we all shared the same fate. I have been greatly distressed for want of money, because I came away without being able to see my husband.

'If, sir, you have any success in your application for my pardon, you can send it me by any of the captains coming out to Botany Bay, which, I am sure, your goodness will endeavour to do for the sake of my motherless children; they are the only cause of my anxiety and unhappiness. I hope your generous exertions, aided by the goodness of God, will one day restore me to them; yet, whether you succeed or not, that God, I sincerely hope, will reward you—fully reward you—for your past unequalled kindness to me. Pray, sir, be good enough to let my husband know you have had a letter from me, and beg him to take care of my dear children. I think it hard I did not see him before I sailed, for we laid a week at Gravesend, and I should have left my country less sorrowfully had I given him my last charges and bade him farewell . . .

'We are much better off than we expected, and have as much liberty as our unhappy situation possibly allows. I am much better in my health than I have been for some time, and with God's assistance and yours I do not despair of yet living to be a comfort to my children. This, sir, is the only prayer for herself in the heart of one bound in duty and by gratitude to pray for you and your family as long as her life and heart have power to think of or utter a prayer to God, and who is your most humble and obedient servant, Mary Talbot.'

There was no happy ending to Mary Talbot's story. The burial of a Mary Talbot is recorded at Sydney on 28 August 1791, only seven weeks after her arrival.[11]

Towards the end of 1792, a woman convict whose name is not known wrote a short letter from Parramatta. Though settlement had spread from Sydney to the west, where there was better land, there were still severe shortages of food, as this woman's letter shows. Before crops were grown in any quantity in New South Wales, the colony was dependent on the uncertain arrival of supply ships. At times the rations were so low the people virtually starved.

The letter written by this unidentified woman, dated 23 November 1792, was published in the 14 June 1793 edition of the Dublin *Public Advertiser*.[12] Describing herself as 'an afflicted supplicant' she wrote that she 'most humbly takes the liberty to acquaint you of her sad distress in this desolate place of banishment, which is very severe; principally occasioned by hardships and shortness of provisions. We have during my short stay here lost near 1,500 souls from these causes.' The letter was addressed to a benefactor who had helped her previously. She concluded by asking for some money because of 'the dearness of food and my poverty'.

The only other letter which is known to exist written by a woman convict during the first decade of the convict colony is quite different in tone and content from the others. Signed 'S.B.', it appears to have been written by Sarah Bird, who was sentenced in July 1794 for stealing and arrived in Sydney on the female transport *Indispensible* on 30

April 1796. When it appeared in the London *True Briton* on 10 November 1798, it was described as being from 'a woman lately transported to Botany Bay to her father'.[13]

Sarah Bird's letter is full of news of her success. From her letter it seems that not only did she have financial resources, but she was, for a convict, remarkably free on the voyage to land at ports and buy goods. Once arrived in New South Wales she does not appear to have been constrained by her sentence. Although she denies this in her letter, the probable explanation is that she had a lover among the officers on board and that she operated under his protection. Once in New South Wales she was able to trade the goods she had bought at ports on the voyage to great financial advantage. Although she would have been assigned to work for an employer, her competence and financial resources apparently allowed her to take charge very quickly.

If her letter is to be believed, six months after her arrival Sarah Bird had worked the system so successfully she had a house, a range of livestock and poultry and was conducting an inn. Her story shows her to be woman of enterprise. It is a striking example of the diversity of convict experience. But it is possible that she exaggerated her successes to induce some of her family to follow her to New South Wales. Nevertheless, it is obvious that Sarah Bird was a very successful entrepreneur.

When she wrote her letter, ten years had passed since the arrival of the first convicts. Already there were many emancipated convicts who were doing well in business and farming. The settlement was no longer a small desperate group clinging to Sydney Cove. In good seasons the colony could grow its own food and trading flourished. Sarah Bird wrote to her father:

'I take the first opportunity of informing you of my safe arrival in this remote quarter of the world after a pretty good passage of six months. Since my arrival I have purchased a house, for which I gave £20, and the following articles, which are three turkies, at 15s. each; three sucking-pigs, at 10s.; a pair of pigeons at 8s.; a yard-dog, £2; two muscovy ducks, at 10s. each; three English ducks, at 5s., each; and a goat, five guineas; six geese at 15s. each. I have got a large garden to the house, and a licence. The sign is the "Three Jolly Settlers".

'I have met with tolerable good success in the public line. I did a little trade in the passage here in a number of small articles, such as sugar, tea, tobacco, thread, snuff, needles, and every thing that I could get anything by. The needles are a shilling a paper here, and fine thread is sixpence a skain. I have sold my petticoats at two guineas each, and my long black coat at ten guineas, which shews that black silk sells well here; the edging that I gave 1s. 8d. per yard for in England, I got 5s. for it here. I have sold all the worst of my cloaths, as wearing apparel brings a good price. I bought a roll of tobacco at Rio Janeiro, of 54 lb. weight, which cost me 20s., which I was cheated out of; I could have got 12s. a pound for it here. I likewise bought a cwt. of sugar there, and also many other articles. Rum sells for 1s. 6d. per gallon there, and here, at times, 32. Any person coming from England with a few hundred pounds laid out at any of the ports that shipping touch at coming here are liable to make a fortune. Shoes that cost 4s. or 5s., a pair in England will bring from 10s to 15s here.

'On our passage here we buried only two women and two children. The climate is very healthful and likewise very fertile, as there are two crops a year of almost everything; and I really believe, with the assistance of God, by the time that I have paid the forfeit, according to the laws of my country, I shall acquire a little money to return home with, which I have not the smallest doubt of, and to be a comfort to you at the latter end of your days.

'Any person that should have a mind to come out here as a settler, by applying at the Secretary of State's Office, may have a free passage, and likewise two men and a farm here, which is great encouragement. I should be very glad to hear from you the first opportunity. I live by myself, and did not do as the rest of the women did on the passage, which was, every one of them that could had a husband. I shall conclude with giving my kind love to my brothers and sisters, nieces and nephews, so am, dear father, your ever dutiful, loving and affectionate daughter till death.'

Sarah Bird's good fortune did not continue indefinitely. Apparently convicted of an offence in New South Wales, she was sent to the penal settlement on Norfolk Island, where on 8 January 1804, John Morris, the man she had lived with for some years, escaped from gaol and attacked Sarah in her house. He gashed her throat from ear to ear and cut her left arm as she attempted to ward off his blows, her shrieks bringing constables and neighbours to her assistance. Morris was put on trial for attempting to murder Sarah and a gaoler, Edward Garth.[14]

This later misfortune cannot detract from Sarah Bird's achievements as a trader, shopkeeper and innkeeper, one of the colony's first businesswomen.

## Margaret Catchpole

*I have been nursing lying-in women*

Margaret Catchpole is an enduring example of the ability of an upright, spirited woman to rise from the degradation of banishment as a convict to a position of independence and self-worth. She brought with her valuable skills in nursing, housekeeping and farming which, through her ability to cope with the challenges of a convict society, she was able to use to the full not only to her own advantage but to that of the people of New South Wales.

Margaret Catchpole was born in 1762 in the county of Suffolk, into the deprived and poor labouring class of eighteenth century rural England, a daughter of Elizabeth Catchpole and a farm labourer whose name is unknown. She grew up on the farms where her father worked as a labourer, becoming a skilled horse rider. When old enough, probably at the age of 10 or 12, she became a house servant and was later employed as a nurse and housekeeper for Mrs John Cobbold, wife of an Ipswich brewer. There she learned to read and write.

Her life was apparently uneventful until she left the Cobbolds in 1795. Two years later, at the age of 35, when she had been unemployed and ill for some time, she stole Cobbold's gelding and rode to London— a distance of about 120 kilometres—in ten hours. She was captured, tried for stealing the horse and sentenced to death, but the sentence was commuted to seven years' transportation. In 1800, while confined in Ipswich gaol waiting to be transported, she made a daring escape by using a clothesline to scale the 6.7 metre wall. When recaptured, she was again sentenced to death, the sentence being commuted to transportation for life.

Margaret Catchpole was transported on the *Nile*, arriving in Sydney on 14 December 1801. Nearly 40 when she arrived, she possessed skills in nursing and housekeeping that were desperately needed in the colony. Within two days she was assigned to work as a cook in the household of the Commissary, John Palmer, and his American wife Susan. Margaret's practical abilities and the maturity of her outlook, combined with a kindly employer, made the serving of her sentence more bearable than it was for many other women convicts, who were often viciously exploited by their employers. As her reputation as a competent nurse spread, her services were in demand. She nursed Mrs Elizabeth Rouse, wife of the superintendant of public works at Parramatta, through a difficult childbirth. She became a farm overseer for the Rouses, who had travelled as free settlers on the same ship, the *Nile*, and she worked for other well-known pioneering families including the Faithfulls and Dights. With her childhood experience of practical agriculture, she gradually built up herds of animals until she became a small farmer in her own right. During this time, she corresponded with her uncle and with her former employer, Mrs Cobbold.

As Margaret Catchpole's letters are written in phonetical English which is at times hard to decipher, they are reproduced here with conventional English spelling and divided into paragraphs. On 21 January 1802,[15] soon after her arrival, when she wrote to Mrs Cobbold, her life as a model convict had already begun. Although subject to few restrictions herself, she had great sympathy for those more unfortunate who were sent to Norfolk Island or to the Coal River (Newcastle), the punishment centres for convicts who offended against rules in New South Wales.

'With great pleasure I take up my pen to acquaint you, my good lady, of my safe arrival at Port Jackson, New South Wales, Sydney on the 20th day of December 1801, and as I was a going to be landed, on the left hand of me it put me in mind of the Cliff, both the houses and likewise the hills, so as it put me in very good spirits, seeing a place so much like my own native home, it is a great deal more like England than ever I could expect to have seen, for here is garden stuff of all kinds, except gooseberries and currants and apples . . .

'The wheat harvest was almost over just as I landed. Here wheat is 8 shillings per bushel. At this time here is 2 crops in the summer, one with wheat and one with Indian corn. The winter is but very short as they tell me . . .

' . . . I am [not] in such great trouble at present. But God only knows how it might be for here is many a one that has been here for many years and they have their poor head shaved and sent up to the Coal River and there carry coals from daylight in the morning, till dark at night, and half starved. But I hear that it is going to be put by and so it had need, for it is very cruel indeed. Norfolk Island is a bad place, enough to send any poor creature with a steel collar on their poor necks. But I will take good care of myself from that.

'I am pretty well off at present for I was taken off the stores 2 days after I landed so I have no government work to do nor they have nothing to do with me only when here be a general muster then I must appear to let them know I am here, and if I have a mind to go up to Parramatta or Toongabbie or Hawkesbury, I have to get a pass, or else I should be taken up and put into prison, for a very little will do that here . . . I cannot say that I like this country, no never shall.'

The following year, on 2 May 1803,[16] she wrote to her uncle, Richard House of Ipswich, and her aunt asking for news about friends and relatives and expressing the hope that:

' . . . they are all dutiful to you in your old days, for I never wish no one to come here into such a wicked country so God in heaven bless you and good night.

'I am well beloved by all that know me and that is a comfort for I always was going into better company than myself that is amongst free people where they make as much of me as if I was a lady because I am the Commissary's cook.'

In a postscript she added:

'I have at this time a man that keep me company and would marry me if like. But I am not for marrying he is a gardener he come out as a Botanist and be allowed one hundred pounds per year and this provision found him and a man fetch wood and water and one to go out with him to collect seeds and see skins and all sorts of curiosities.'

By the time she wrote another letter to her uncle and aunt Margaret had spent two years working for the Rouse family and had at one stage been left in charge of their farm at Richmond Hill. She had begun to build up her own herds by taking livestock in payment for her services as a midwife. It was as a small farmer that she became one of the victims of the devastating flood in March 1806 on the Hawkesbury River. Margaret herself was saved by the arrival of a rescue boat, but others were drowned, many thousands of cattle were lost and wheat crops were inundated and destroyed. Margaret Catchpole's letter of 8 October 1806[17] contains the only eyewitness account of this devastating event, the enormity of which overwhelmed the settlers and led to the colony suffering a severe food shortage with great rises in the cost of food.

In the first part of the letter she referred to the welcome arrival of a box from her uncle and aunt, then she continued:

'[I have] been for this 2 years past up the country at Richmond Hill. I went there to nurse one Mrs Rouse, a very respectful person. They came from England free, they respect me as one of their own family for Mrs Rouse with this last child she had told her husband that she must [have] died because [?if] I was not there. Mr Rouse did live up at Richmond at his farm. But the Governor gave him a place to be superintendant and master builder at the lumberyard Parramatta. Then I was left overseer at his farm. But it was so lonesome for me so I left.

'But I have got four ewes and nine breeding goats, 3 wethers and seven young ones that is all my stock at present. Mr Rouse keeps them and charges me nothing for them. I should had six pigs but this place has been so flooded that I thought once must all been lost that how I came so very ill being in the water up to my middle.

'As you well know I have a good spirit I was trying to save what I could and I and Mrs Dight and her 3 children went upon the loft for safety we had not been there [long] before the chimney went down and middle wall went, then I expected the next chimney to go and all the walls and then to be crushed to dead for the water was about five feet deep in the house at that time it was that depth in about 2 hours.

'Mr Dight and his 2 men were gone to knock down the pigsties and pig runs to drive the pigs away so we were left alone but great providence turned up a boat to save us from a watery grave, come and took us away I was more frightened then than all the way going over. This happened the 22 of last March, houses and barns and wheat stacks and the Indian corn that was not gathered it washed all away before the stream. Some poor creatures riding in their houses some on their barns crying out for God sake to be saved others firing their guns in the greatest distress for a boat. There was many thousands of head of all kind of cattle was lost and as many bushells of all sorts was lost of grain so now this place is in great distress for wheat. Last Saturday October the 5th it sold at the market for 3 pounds fifteen shillings per bushell and Indian corn at 3 pounds 10 per bushell, that is four pecks, beef 2 shillings, mutton the same, fresh pork not to be got, salt pork 1 and sixpence per pound, sugar 16 per pound, tea is not to be got. But when it was it was 3 pounds for a pound of tea and I have bought a pound of tea for 26 pound and a bushell of wheat for 5 shillings . . . everything is very dear, the wheat is coming in the ear, but the crops look very light.

'But my dear uncle and aunt I do not know any want bless God for I have been nursing lying-in women and I will take that care I will not want. It is a great word to say but I am well beloved amongst my betters. I never have known anything of punishment since I have been here only that I cannot get no tea that is all the same . . .

'I myself will not have no husband. But here is no women but must have some sort of a man, some women do very well indeed.

'Uncle I told you I was a going to a farm but I did not. I lived a little while in a little house of my own. I did not like that so I went to nurse one Mrs Skinner . . . then I went to nurse Mrs Rouse and stopped with her one year and then went to Mrs Dight's, there is where I was a year then I was left at Mr Rouse's farm and from there I went to Mrs Dight's to nurse her and from there I went to Mrs Wood and from there to nurse Mrs Rouse again. Now I am going to Mrs Faithfull, Mrs Wood's sister their names were Pitt when they came into the country they were some relation to Lord Nelson, a very good family, very well and much respected. Old Mrs Pitt is very fond of me but I shall I believe soon go to live by myself.'

In another letter, Margaret observes: 'It is a wonderful country for to have children, even very old women have them that never had none before.'[18]

Two more floods had devastated the Hawkesbury district some months before Margaret Catchpole wrote on 8 October 1809.[19] In this letter she again gives an invaluable first-hand account of these disasters. Living on her own farm she had incurred big losses in the floods. Again she expresses a longing to return to her home country.

'If I can but once more have my liberty restored to me to return to my own native land for I am almost brokenhearted, first with the floods & with fear with such surprising high winds that cleared acres of standing timber and trees that were of a very great size. We were afraid to stop indoors. My good lady, here has been a flood in the month of May which distressed us very much, then next flood on the last day of July and the first day of August, the biggest that was ever known by white men—it went over the tops of the houses, and the many poor creatures crying out for mercy, crying out for boats, firing of guns in distress, it was shocking to hear. This is the second time that one Thomas Lacey, wife and family was carried away in their barn, standing on the man made holes through the thatch and was taken out by men in boats and their lives happily saved some just expiring as they were picked up off their houses, barns, stacks and such as the poor creatures could get on . . .

'I rent a small farm about 20 acres but half of it cleared. I live in my little cottage all alone except a little child or two come to stop with me—my good Lady, you know I am very fond of children. I hired a man to work my ground I should have done very well had not this shocking flood come, it has made me very poor, my loss is about fifty pounds and within a very little of losing my own life.'

The last surviving letter written by Margaret Catchpole is to her uncle and aunt and dated 2 September 1811[20] from Richmond Hill. She was still a convict and still longing for her native land, but she maintained her fierce independence. After referring to the news of a cousin who had married, she continued:

'I am not and almost fifty years old, nor do I not intend. I hope to see home once more and to see dear cousin Charles weigh me a pound of tea for me and that fine strong young man, Samuel, to make me a pair of shoes, and poor Lucy to thread my needle for my eyes are not so good as they were. But thank God I can do so well as I do. I rent a little farm about fifteen acres, but half of it standing timber and the cleared ground, I hire men to put in my corn and I work a great deal myself. I have got 30 sheep and forty goats and 30 pigs and 2 dogs they take care of me for I live all alone, not one in the house. There is a house within twenty 2 rood of me. I have a good many friends that I go to see when I think proper such as I have nursed when they lay-in they cannot do without me. I am looked upon very well thank God. I hope to get a few pounds to come home . . .

' . . . I do not grow young myself I have lost all my front teeth, I can stir about as brisk as ever and in good spirits. Dear Uncle I hope when you write again you will send me word of all my friends and thank you for the newspapers, and I wish I could send you some, but there is not time, the ship is going to sail directly so I must conclude with my sincere love to you and all my cousins and pray to God to keep his Bless upon you all and not forgetting myself adieu.'

Margaret Catchpole was pardoned on 31 January 1814 but, although free to do so, she did not return to England. She may have considered that after paying her fare home she would not have had sufficient money left to keep herself in England. Or perhaps, faced with the opportunity to return to England, she may have realised how much she had become attached to her independent life and her prospects in New South Wales. She spent the rest of her life running a small store at Richmond and continuing with her work as a nurse. In 1819, while nursing a shepherd ill with influenza on the Pitts' property near Richmond, she caught the disease from him and died on 13 May, aged 58. She was buried in the churchyard of St Peter's Anglican Church, Richmond.

Margaret Catchpole's letters are the only known record of a woman convict's life in her own words over a considerable period during the early years of the settlement at Sydney. Because she was intelligent and observant, her letters are a rich direct source of information about many aspects of life in those days.

A sensible woman who behaved circumspectly, she was fortunate to have skills that were in short supply. Because of these, her life as a convict was relatively free from restrictions and punishments. Partly because of her own skills and partly because of her mature disposition, which enabled her to make the most of her life within the rules governing convicts, Margaret Catchpole triumphed over the experience of being transported for life to a penal colony on the other side of the world. Though she often expressed her longing to return to her home, she spent little time bemoaning her lot. Instead she used her skills as a nurse to help others and her knowledge of practical agriculture to become a small farmer. With her indomitable spirit, she survived the devastation of the Hawkesbury floods and continued to support herself into old age.

Her success in life was achieved without marrying. This was very unusual in a society where men vastly outnumbered women and where marriage or a continuing relationship was available to almost all women. Even those reluctant to form these relationships usually found that they were necessary as protection against indiscriminate sexual attacks or exploitation and against the lawlessness of society. Margaret Catchpole was different. She valued her independence too highly to attach herself to any man.

## Lydia Esden

*She is a most extraordinary clever woman*

Like many other women convicts, Lydia Esden was a victim of sexual exploitation. When she arrived in New South Wales in 1820 she was pregnant to a ship's officer, one of the many victims of officers and sailors on the convict transports, to whom women prisoners were fair game. With no power and no rights, they had little option but to submit. Some convict transports gained reputations as floating brothels, but even in ships where some efforts were made to protect the women, prostitution and rape were common. It is fortunate that Lydia Esden's story is available in her own words, as it represents the stories of many others.

As Lydia Astell (either Astell or Esden is an incorrect recording of her name), a 25-year-old mantua maker and shoe binder, she was sentenced to fourteen years' transportation at Middlesex on 24 March 1819 for having forged notes in her possession. She was transported on the *Janus*, which arrived in Sydney on 3 May 1820.[21]

Within a short time, Lydia Esden and Mary Long, another woman transported on the same ship, were assigned as servants to Nicholas Bayly, a prominent landowner at Bayly Park, Cabramatta. Both were pregnant, as were many other *Janus* women who, after arrival, had been assigned to settlers or sent to the Female Factory at Parramatta. Lydia Esden and Mary Long refused to work for Bayly and on 24 May left Bayly Park, explaining in a letter that they intended to go to Sydney. After they were brought back, Bayly agreed to ask the Governor for permission for them to go to Sydney if they would write stating why they wanted to go.

Lydia Esden, who could write, made her statement in the following letter. It is the letter of a woman prepared to fight vehemently for her rights, yet possessing a touching naivety in imagining, erroneously, that her lover, the ship's officer John Hedges, would adhere to promises to support her. The letter reveals the devastating position in which many women convicts found themselves, not only sentenced to a remote country but finding themselves pregnant on arrival after being prostituted either through rape or because of the position of mastery the officers enjoyed. Lydia Esden's letter was addressed to her employer, Nicholas Bayly of Bayly Park.

'Honoured Sir,

'My Fellings is Mutch Hurt At the Disponding News I Heard From you This morning, That of Being Put off with The Passes, As you have given me But Little Hopes After prommising me you Would. Sir! I hope to god, you Will Not be Worse than your word; For If so I Never Shall Be Happy; And In Respect To my Conduct Dureing my Absence Hope you have Not So Bad An Opinion Of me, As To Think me So Base As To Treat your Kindness and Ungratitude By Behaveing Ill, Or Not Comming Back To the Time you may Think proper To Allow me, Sir, I Promise you Faithfully I will Not Incrouth one Hour, Sir! I Do Not Wish to take Any Rash Stepts with Mr Hedges, As He Is Willing To make Acknowledgement, providing He As Interview with me. The Reason Things was Not Settled Before Wee parted was Wee Expected I Should have Being Able To have gone To See him with Out Any trouble, And being Wholely Out of his power To Come To me, makes me To Intreet So Hard For A pass. Sir! If Not Intrueding, Lett me Once more Beg For A pass to parramata, and If I Cannot goe Any Further, I will send For him to meet me there, Which Will Not Hesitate One moment In Executing the Command I Know. Wat makes me So Anchous Is the Ship Is going A Waleing, And I Am Shure He will Not Stay But very Little Longer. As He would Loose the Season For It. If He Did, I should mutch wish if you would send For Ann This Eveing, And I will pay the Expence, And happey so to do, For to Supply my place, wile I am gone. Sir! I hope you will Not Denigh me This Request, Or I am A Lost Woman. Sir! I have maney Thing To say to him, As he will goe To see My Famley, which will Be Of grate Concolation To me, And Satisfaction To them. For god sake, Sir, Take It Into Concideration, And grant me my Request, Though I Acknowledge It very Early To Ask Favours, Sir, there Seamed to Be a Dought Ariseing Concerning My Being with Child, But I am Not Desceved. It would Be well If I was; Nor Did I Entend To Name; But When you put the question To me, I Could Not Denigh the Truth.

'I hope, Sir, you will grant This Request To-morrow Or Tuesday, As then I should Be Able To Return By The Latter part Of the week, And Help with the work.'[22]

Nicholas Bayly referred the matter to the Governor, who decided the women were not to receive passes to travel. On 5 June 1820, Bayly wrote to the Governor:

'The two Women from the Janus would make most excellent Servants, if they chose; indeed Lydia Esden is a most extraordinary clever woman, and as a Servant is hardly to be excelled; but to counterbalance those qualities, she can make herself one of the greatest blackguards in the universe, but as yet that has only been amongst her fellow servants.'[23]

Governor Macquarie directed Judge Advocate Wylde and the Bench of Magistrates at Sydney to investigate the allegations. They took evidence from Captain Thomas J. Mowat, Ann Moore, wife of Corporal

Moore, 48th Regiment, who had travelled on the ship, Fathers Conolly and Therry, Lydia Esden and Mary Long. The inquiry found that 'Prostitution did prevail in a great degree on board the said Ship throughout the Voyage from England to this Territory; that due exertions were not made on the part of the Captain and officers to repress and prevent the same; and that the matter of Charge, as against the Captain and Officers of the said Ship individually in that respect, is true and well founded in fact'.[24]

The allegations of prostitution on the *Janus* were investigated rigorously, probably because of the presence on board of two Catholic priests— Father Philip Conolly and Father John Joseph Therry—who could be expected to make reports to the authorities in London. Similar events took place on other ships transporting women convicts without being investigated.

Lydia Esden had the strength of character to recover from the injustice of her treatment at the beginning of her sentence. She was to display in her life the cleverness Nicholas Bayly had noted and to rise above the circumstances of her conviction in England and abandonment by her lover in Sydney. After having a son, named John, soon after she arrived, the following year she married Thomas Barns, a police constable, at St John's, Parramatta. In 1825, in partnership with Charles Williams, she held a licence for the Macquarie Tavern in Pitt Street, Sydney. After her husband was promoted to Police Constable at Bathurst (he was later a gaoler at Bathurst Gaol), Lydia held the licences for several hotels in Bathurst.[25]

# 2
# Farm managers

**Elizabeth Macarthur**

*I have now a very good Dairy*

When Elizabeth Macarthur stepped ashore at Port Jackson in June 1790 she was one of the very few free women in the colony, the only 'lady' of any standing and the only woman with a claim to an education of any depth. It was fortunate that she also had an equable nature, a strong sense of duty, an aptitude for management, the vision to see beyond immediate problems and—perhaps most importantly—a background in a farming community. For two periods of her life, totalling twelve years, she was to be in charge of the largest farming enterprise in New South Wales.

Elizabeth Macarthur was born on 14 August 1766 at Bridgerule, a village in the farmlands of the border country of the English counties of Devon and Cornwall, the daughter of a yeoman farmer. After the death of her father, Richard Veale, and her mother's remarriage, she lived with her maternal grandfather and with the family of Rev. John Kingdon, vicar of Bridgerule. His daughter Bridget remained her great friend and correspondent.

At the age of 22 she married John Macarthur, an army officer recently promoted to lieutenant after volunteering for service in the New South Wales Corps. Elizabeth told her mother:

'You will be surprised that even I who appear so timid and irresolute should be a warm advocate of this scheme. So it is, and believe me I shall be greatly disappointed if anything happens to impede it. I forsee how terrific and gloomy this will appear to you. To me at first it had the same appearance, while I suffered myself to be blinded by common and vulgar prejudices. I have not now, nor I trust shall ever have one scruple or regret, but what relates to you.'[1]

Elizabeth and her husband sailed on the notorious Second Fleet. They travelled first on the *Neptune*, before transferring to the *Scarborough*. To the Macarthurs the voyage was extremely distressing. John Macarthur suffered a near fatal illness, their baby son Edward was so ill it was feared he would die, and Elizabeth was unable to leave her quarters for weeks at a time. Their situation on board these ships was infinitely superior to that of the convicts, yet even so the Macarthurs suffered considerably. Overwhelmed by her own problems, Elizabeth had no reserves of sympathy left for the starving, vermin-infested, brutally treated convicts. On the *Neptune* they had only part of a cabin, partitioned off from some female convicts, and the animosity of the captain made their movement on the ship almost impossible. Elizabeth wrote of this time:

'Without hope of relief, I was fain to content myself within the narrow limits of a wretched cabin, for to add to the horrors of the common passage to the deck, Captain Nepean ordered it to be made into a hospital for the sick, the consequence of which was that I never left my cabin till I finally quitted the ship. Thus precluded from the general advantages that even the convicts enjoyed—air and exercise—no language can express, no imagination conceive the misery I experienced. Approaching near the equator—the heat insupportable—we were assailed with noisome stenches, that even in the cold of an English winter, hourly effusions of oil of tar could not dispel, two sides of it surrounded with wretches whose dreadful imprecations and shocking discourses ever rang in my distracted ears, a sickly infant constantly claiming maternal cares, my spirits failing, my health forsaking me, nothing but the speedy change which took place,[2] could have prevented me from falling a helpless victim to the unheard of inhumanity of a set of monsters whose triumph and pleasure seemed to consist in aggravating my distresses.'[3]

Elizabeth Macarthur recovered quickly from the voyage. Although she regarded the posting to New South Wales as temporary, there was nothing of the parvenu in her approach to life in Sydney. With most of her household work done by convict servants, she saw her main roles as the setting of social standards and the nurturing of a society of responsible people. The extracts that follow from a letter to her friend Bridget Kingdon, written nine months after her arrival,[4] show her identification with the concerns of the small community, her acceptance of and interest in the strange world around her and her efforts to create a circle of friends whose standards were similar to her own. Even in this early letter, her keen interest in the possibilities of farming is apparent.

'On my first landing every thing was new to me, every Bird, every Insect, Flower, &c. in short all was novelty around me, and was noticed with a degree of eager curiosity, and perturbation, that after a while subsided into that calmness, I have already described.'

She wrote of her friendship with William Dawes, an officer in the marines interested in scientific subjects, Captain Watkin Tench, author of books describing the voyage of the First Fleet and the settlement at Sydney, and naval surgeon George Worgan who lent her his piano. After trying unsuccessfully to learn astronomy from William Dawes, she sought some other occupation.

'Still I wanted something, to fill up a certain vacancy, in my time which could neither be done by writing, reading, or conversation, to the two first I did not feel myself always inclined, and the latter was not in my power having no female friend to unbend my mind to, nor a single Woman with whom I could converse with any satisfaction to myself the Clergymans Wife[5] being a person in whose society I could reap neither profit or pleasure. These considerations made me still anxious to learn some easy Science to fill up the vacuum of many a Solitary day, and at length under the auspices of Mr Dawes: I have made a small progress in Botany, no Country can exhibit a more Copious field for Botanical knowledge, than this. I am arrived so far, as to be able to class and order, all common plants. I have found great pleasure in my Study; every Walk furnishd me with subjects to put in practice, that Theory I had before gaind by reading but Alas my botanical pursuits were most unwelcomely interrupted by Mr. McArthurs being attack'd by a severe illness . . . '

She observed that the soil had not proved suitable for the growing of crops, particularly without regular rain.

' . . . our Gardens produce nothing, all is burnt up, indeed, the Soil must be allow'd to be most wretched and totally unfit for growing any European productions, tho' you would scarcely believe this, as the face of the ground at this moment, where it is in its native State is flourishing even to luxuriance; producing fine Shrubs, Trees, and Flowers which by their lively tints, afford a most agreeable Landscape. Beauty I have heard from some of my unletterd Country Men is but skin deep, I am sure the remark holds good in N.S. Wales—where all the Beauty is literally on the Surface, but I believe I must allow it has Symetry [sic] of form also to recommend it, as the ground in all the parts that have been discoverd is charmingly turned and diversified by agreeable Vallies, and gently rising Hills but Still those beauties are all exterior. Many Gentlemen have penetrated far into the Country, but they find little difference in the appearance of the Soil . . . '

In the course of this very long letter, Elizabeth commented at great length on the role of women in Aboriginal society:

' . . . the Women appear to be under very great subjection, and are employ'd in the most Laborious part of their Work. They fish, and also make the Lines and Hooks and indeed seem very little otherways than slaves to their husbands. They weave their Lines from the Bark of a certain tree . . . Their hooks they grind into form from a shell, they perform this with great dexerity upon any rough stone . . . '

At the end of the letter, Elizabeth returns to the difficulties of maintaining a group of suitable friends in such a place. 'My spirits are at this time low very low,' she writes, 'tomorrow we lose some valuable members of our small Society, and some very good friends. In so small a Society we sensibly feel the loss of every Member more particularly those that are endear'd to us by acts of kindness and friendship from that circumstance . . . '

Shortly afterwards, on 18 March 1791, she wrote to her mother, Mrs Leach.[6] The themes in the letter were those that were to dominate her life for the next 60 years—her family, the maintenance of suitable friendships and the prospects for agriculture.

' . . . I hope you have received all my former letters . . . the second from this place giving an account of the voyage, of Mr. Macarthur's dangerous illness & surprising recovery, & of my being, in consequence of fatigue & anxiety, thrown into premature labour, & delivered of a little Girl who lived but for an hour.

' . . . In my last letter I mentioned there being a select number of Officers here, who had been very attentive to us & I am happy to say that we still experience the same attention from them; & however much I may want female society, Mr Macarthur can have no reason to complain. The Governor has been in the habit of sending us some little thing or other every day . . .

'We have not attempted any thing in the farming way. Our Neighbours succeed so badly, that we are not encouraged to follow their example. The Government Farm did not this year, in Grain, return three times the seed that had been sown. This great failure is attributable to a very dry season, but it is a general opinion that this Country is not well adapted for Corn.

'The Grape thrives remarkably well. The Governor sent me some bunches this Season as fine as any I ever tasted, & there is little doubt but in a very few years there will be plenty—we have also very fine Melons. They are raised with little or no trouble, the Sun being sufficient to ripen them, without any forcing whatever & bringing them to a great size & flavour. One day after the Cloth was removed, when I happened to dine at Government House a Melon was produced weighing 30 1bs. We have need of cooling fruit in the warm season—particularly when the hot scorching winds set in . . . '

In a letter written on 18 November 1791,[7] Elizabeth writes of the improved prospects for female friendships. She found Anna Josepha King, wife of Lieutenant Governor Philip Gidley King, congenial company:

' . . . our little Circle has been of late quite brilliant; we are constantly making little parties in boats up & down the various inlets of the Harbour, taking refreshments with us, & dining out under an awning upon some pleasant point of Land, or in some of the Creeks or Coves in which for Twenty miles together these waters abound. There are so many Ladies in the Regiment that I am not likely to feel the want of female society as I first did.'

Another letter, dated 21 December 1793,[8] contained news of the beginning of the Macarthurs' farm at Parramatta on land granted by Lieutenant Governor Francis Grose, who was in charge of the settlement for two years following the departure of Governor Phillip in December 1792. Within a few years their grant was to be the most important farming enterprise in New South Wales. Elizabeth was also pleased with another gift from Major Grose:

'I have one Gift more to speak of—it is a very fine Cow in Calf, of which I am very proud . . . to a Family in this Country in its present situation, it is a Gift beyond any value that can be placed upon it.'

When she wrote the following year, on 22 August 1794,[9] the family was living on its farm at Parramatta named Elizabeth Farm. From the Macarthurs' viewpoint there had been an amazing change in the colony following the departure of Governor Phillip. They had a grant of 250 acres and, with the use of convict labour, already had 20 acres under wheat, 80 acres prepared for Indian corn and potatoes and the remainder mostly cleared of timber. Their produce had already brought in £400 and their granaries were stocked with 1800 bushels of corn. They possessed a great number of livestock, including goats, hogs and poultry, and their table was constantly supplied with wild ducks and kangaroos. Their house was surrounded by a vineyard, fruit trees and a garden. Their four-roomed brick house built in the centre of the farm was comfortable and spacious.

When she wrote to her friend Bridget Kingdon in 1798,[10] Elizabeth reported the great success of the Macarthurs' thriving farming enterprises, with her own involvement in the running of the farm obvious. Her letter contains a valuable record of the economic system operating in New South Wales and the use of convict labour—not matters that women generally were thought to be interested in. But Elizabeth Macarthur was vitally interested, and she assumed her correspondent would be also. The only worry she expresses in the letter concerns the education of her children, by then numbering five.

'This Country possesses numerous advantages to persons holding appointments under Government; It seems the only part of the Globe where quiet is to be expected—We enjoy here one of the finest Climates in the world—The necessaries of life are abundant, & a fruitful soil affords us many luxuries. Nothing induces me to wish for a change but the difficulty of educating our children, & were it otherwise it would be unjust towards them to confine them to so narrow a society. My desire is that they may see a little more of the world, & better learn to appreciate this retirement . . .

' . . . Our Farm, which contains from four to five hundred acres, is bounded on three sides by Water. This is particularly convenient. We have at this time, about one hundred & twenty acres in wheat, all in a promising state. Our Gardens with fruit & vegetables are extensive & produce abundantly. It is now Spring, & the Eye is delighted with a most beautiful variegated landscape—Almonds—Apricots, Pear and Apple Trees are in full bloom. The native shrubs are also in flower, & the whole Country gives a graceful perfume. There is a very good Carriage road new made from hence to Sydney, which by land is distant about fourteen miles; & another from this to the river Hawkesbury, which is about twenty miles from hence in a direct line across the Country—Parramatta is a central position between both—I have once visited the Hawkesbury & made the journey on horse back . . .

'Our stock of cattle is large, we have now Fifty head, a dozen Horses, & about a thousand Sheep. You may conclude from this that we kill mutton, but hitherto we have not been so extravagant. Next year, Mr. Macarthur tells me, we may begin. I have now a very good Dairy, & in general make a sufficiency of Butter to supply the Family, but it is at present so great an object to rear the calves, that we are careful not to rob them of too much milk—We use our Horses for pleasure & profit—they alternatively run in the Chaise or Cart . . .

'. . . Mr. Macarthur has frequently in his Employment thirty or forty people whom we pay weekly for their labour. Eight are employed as Stock keepers, & in the Garden, Stables & House five more, besides women servants, these we both feed & clothe, or at least we furnish them with the means of providing clothes for themselves. We have but two men fed at the expense of the Crown, altho' there are persons who contrive to get twenty or more, which the Governor does not or will not notice.

'You will wonder how a return is made for the daily expense which it must appear to you we incur. In the first place some thousands of persons are fed from the public Stores—perhaps three & four thousand, all of whom were formerly supplied with flour from England to meet the demand for Bread. But since so many individuals have cleared Farms, & have thereby been enabled to raise a great quantity of grain in the Country, which at the present time is purchased by the Commissary at 10/- a bushel, & issued for what are termed rations—or the proportionate quantity due to each person instead of Flour. In payment for which the Commissary issues a receipt approved of by the Government. These receipts pass current here as Coin & are taken by Masters of Ships & other adventurers who come to these Ports with Merchandize for sale. When any number of these have been accumulated in the hands of individuals, they are returned to the Commissary who gives a Bill on the Treasury in England for them. These Bills amount to thirty or forty thousand Pounds annually. How long Govt may continue so expensive a plan it would be difficult to foresee . . .

'We fatten & kill a great number of Hogs in the year, which enables us to feed a large establishment of servants. These labourers are such as have been Convicts, & whose time of transportation has expired. They then cease to be fed at the expense of Government, & employ themselves as they please. Some endeavour to procure a passage home to England; some become Settlers, & others hire themselves out for labour. They demand an Enormous price, seldom less than 4/- or 5/- a day. For such as have many in their employment it becomes necessary to keep on hand large supplies of such articles as are most needed by these people for shops there are none—The Officers in the Colony with a few others possessed of money or credit in England unite together & purchase the Cargoes of such Vessels as repair to this Country from various Quarters. Two or more are chosen from the number to bargain for the Cargo offered for sale which is then divided amongst them, in proportion to the amount of their subscriptions. This arrangement prevents monopoly, & the imposition that would otherwise be practised by Masters of Ships. These details which may seem prolix are necessary to shew you the mode in which we are, in our infant condition, compelled to proceed.'

It was fortunate that Elizabeth Macarthur had taken an active interest in the Macarthurs' farming and business affairs. In 1801 John Macarthur was sent to England by Acting Governor Philip King under arrest, after duelling with his commanding officer, Colonel William Paterson. He was not to return for four years. Macarthur was by then the largest landowner in the colony and had the largest flock of sheep. During this time, Elizabeth was left in charge of the family's extensive farming and business affairs in New South Wales. She also had the care of three young children, including a baby, William, born in 1800. Two other children accompanied their father to England, where the eldest, Edward, was already at school.

None of the letters Elizabeth wrote to her husband during this time have survived, but there is an occasional glimpse of the magnitude of her problems from other letters. On 15 April 1804 she told Captain John Piper,[11] then serving on Norfolk Island:

'The management of our concerns gets bothersome to me in the extreme, and I am perpetually annoyed by some vexation or other ...

'By the return of the American I accidentally learnt that a large case of Bananna's were in the ship for me ... I was rather disappointed in not hearing from Broughton, because it really is of some consequence to me to know, whether there is a chance of my getting a supply of Pork for my stock-keeper upon better terms that I can purchase it here—get it salted. My Bargain with K's has been attended with much vexation and I have every reason to suppose that the most unfair advantage has been taken of me, without my having the means of redress—had I known the Man before, I should have taken closer precautions.

'I find myself getting into a detail of complaints, with which, I really beg your pardon for troubling you.'

This letter also contained news of the danger she and her children experienced during the Castle Hill rebellion by Irish convicts. While drinking tea at the home of Samuel Marsden, the Anglican clergyman at Parramatta, Elizabeth was told by a servant that the rebels had reached her Seven Hills farm and were approaching Parramatta. The flames from burning Castle Hill were visible from Parramatta. With Mrs Marsden and wives of two officials, Elizabeth Macarthur escaped with her children by boat down the river to Sydney.

During her husband's absence, Elizabeth managed the Macarthurs' land, producing and despatching the wool from ever-increasing flocks that supported not only her household and her numerous workforce but her husband and older children in England, with their diverse legal and educational expenses.

When her husband again went to England in 1809 after his involvement in the overthrow of Governor William Bligh by the officers of the New South Wales Corps, Elizabeth was again left in sole charge. Macarthur was not to return for nearly nine years. He took with him two more sons to join those already in England, leaving Elizabeth with her delicate eldest daughter Elizabeth, her partially paralysed daughter Mary, and her last child, Emmeline, whom she had borne at the age of 42.

Reassuming control of the now vastly expanded pastoral and agricultural estates and involved business ventures, she was the epitome of the capable pioneer woman, riding out to the farms at Seven Hills and Toongabbie and camping in the slab hut at the Cowpastures (later the site of Camden Park estate). She was not tempted to sell up and return to England as her husband suggested. She had come to love the land and to enjoy her responsibility and authority.

Though the letters she must have written to her husband during his absence no longer exist, it is possible to piece together a few of her problems. On 3 August 1810, Macarthur, in a letter to Elizabeth,[12] acknowledged the demands and difficulties she faced.

'I am perfectly aware, my beloved wife, of the difficulties you have to contend with, and fully convinced that not one woman in a thousand, (no one that I know) would have resolution and perseverance to contend with them at all, much more to surmount them in the manner that you have so happily done.'

Some of her responsibilities during these years are apparent in a letter she wrote to Eliza Kingdon in March 1816:[13]

'I am much oppressed with care on account of our stock establishments at our distant farms, at the Cowpastures, having been disturbed by the incursions of the natives. The savages have burnt and destroyed the shepherds' habitations, and I daily hear of some fresh calamity . . . Two years ago a faithful old servant who had lived with us since we first came to the Colony was barbarously murdered by them and a poor defenceless woman also. Three of my people are now reported to be missing, but I trust they will be found unhurt . . .

'My cares are many and anxious and I have so long been deprived of assistance from any Male Branch of the Family that I cannot say I am comfortable or happy.'

John Macarthur's long-delayed return to Australia occurred towards the end of 1817. Elizabeth wrote on 11 December 1817 to Eliza Kingdon:[14]

'I am yet scarcely sensible of the extent of my happiness, and indeed I can hardly persuade myself that so many of the dear members of our family are united again under the same roof.'

Her days of sole responsibility for a huge farming and business enterprise were over.

There were further calls on Elizabeth's reserves of strength when, towards the end of his life, her husband declined into insanity, accusing her of adultery and insisting that she move from her own home. John Macarthur died in 1834.

Elizabeth died in 1850 at the age of 83. She had arrived in New South Wales two years after the first settlement and lived to the eve of the gold rushes. The famine, isolation, and scarcity of women friends which marked her early years in the colony were far behind. Throughout her life, her family and its status, and her commitment to her value system concerning society, were important parts of her character. Her most remarkable achievement, however, was her management of the Macarthurs' complex agricultural and business empire over two periods totalling nearly thirteen years.

## Mary McDonald

*As to fruit no country can equal it*

In 1806, a former convict, Mary McDonald, wrote to her daughter in England telling her that Australia was a wonderful country and begging her to emigrate with her family. She wrote of the prolific wheat yields, abundant fruit crops and fine cattle on the land she farmed with her husband at the Field of Mars.

There is also in her letter a strikingly emotive phrase describing the heart-wrenching separation many women convicts endured when forcibly separated from their children. She longed for her daughter's safe arrival, 'that I may once embrace you in my longing arms to clasp you'.

Mother and daughter had been separated for at least sixteen, and perhaps nineteen, years. Mary McDonald, then Mary Oliver, was convicted and sentenced to transportation in Kent in 1787. Her crime and the length of her sentence are unknown and, owing to confusing records, it is not clear whether she was transported on the *Lady Juliana* which arrived in 1790 or the *Mary Ann* which arrived the following year.

Soon after her arrival she was assigned as housekeeper to Alexander McDonald, who had arrived as a Marine with the First Fleet and was then a settler on a grant at the Field of Mars in the Ryde district. They married in 1793, Mary being then about 45 and McDonald about 50.

Piecing together news items which appeared in the *Sydney Gazette* over the next two decades, it appears they were successful farmers. By 1810 McDonald was supplying wool shorn from his sheep to the Female Factory at Parramatta and was entitled to receive cloth from the Factory in return.

When Mary McDonald wrote to her daughter, Barbara, on 14 June 1806,[15] urging her to emigrate to New South Wales with her family, she painted an attractive picture of her life as the wife of a farmer. It is obvious from the letter that Mary herself was closely involved in the work of the farm and she wrote proudly of their magnificent crops and stock. 'My dear Barbara', she wrote:

'I Received boath your Letters, one wrote by yourself and the other by Mr Watson, which gave me such joy that my pen or word cannot express the sentiments of my heart as I never Received any account of you my dear Chield since I parted with you—but thank the almighty that is now removed by hearing my dear Barbara has an affectionate husband and three Children, you mention everything being at an enormous price in England and a Husbandman's wages being so low that you can hardly exist.'

After giving her daughter details of how to apply for a free passage, Mary continued:

'Here my Dear is the most healthful country in all the Globe for there is nothing that grows in a hot or Cold Country but comes to the Greatest perfection here, for Instance one acre of wheat will produce from Forty to Fifty Bushels of wheat—and as to fruit no country can equal it, and our Cattle is farr beyond in size and meat to your finest cattle in England. So my Dear do not loose a moments time when you receive this but use all your Interest and endeavours to come to the Garden of the World.

'My Husband came free to the Coloney along with Governor Phillips and gives me every encouragement to send for you he haveing great possesion of land here and haveing no children he had will'd everything that he posseses here to me, as he has an Estate in the Hilands of Scotland, our situation in this Coloney is the most plesent of any and I am very sure if please the almighty that you arive safe in this Coloney that you will think yourself a Blesd Family for your happy abode once more my prayer shall be for your spedey passage and safe arival that I may once embrace you in my longing arms to clasp you and to put you in possesion with what the almighty has bestowed upon us, my Husband joins me with his love to you and your family and hopes to have the pleasure of puting you in possesion of an Estate where he past many happy day.'

Mails took many months to reach England. By the time Mary McDonald wrote again on 3 November 1807,[16] her daughter had been imprisoned, but Mary still hoped that she would come to New South Wales. Again indicating her close involvement in running the farm, she gave detailed instructions to Barbara about what seeds were suitable for growing in Australia and how they should be carried on the voyage. 'My dear daughter', she wrote:

'This is to acquaint you that I Received your affectionate letter of 30th Augst by Mary Boyd a female convict from your Gaol, and it gives me the Greatest pleasure to here of your wealfare. Before you Receive this I expect that you have Received from a gentleman who went home from this place in his Majesty ship Buffulo Ten Pounds Stery, a Gold Ring & Necklace &c which my Husband sent you as a small token of his friendship, and should you come here he will make you a present of one Hundred Acres of land, if you can get to come to this place be sure to bring all kinds of fruit seeds such as all kinds of cherrystones Nectern stones, plum stones and the Different kinds of Curant Seed & Goosbury seeds with the Walnut chestnut filbert and the heasell nut which must be packed in Different Papers and put into a large bottle well corkd and Seald and then packed up in a small Box if you do not take care of the seed according to the order it will be of no use to bring or send them and if you do and the seeds will answer here you will make a fortune soon any Kinds of Market Peach in Garden Seeds will be very servisable & a few Kinds of Putoatoes that is most in voge with you at home, if you can bring a little hop seeds & a pound or two of Cloverseed—Should be very happy to here from you as soon as you can and acquaint me if you Received what I sent you and if you mean to come as me and my husband is geting on in years and will have no person to leave what we have if you do not come . . .

'P.S. If you can come bring some thread as it is one shilling a Skean here and Tobacco £3 a Pound and sugar 8 shillings a Pound and Spirits £1–10 a Bottle and all other things according—my Husband & I joins in our love to your Husband you and your family.'

The correspondence may have continued, as in October 1811 Mary McDonald's name was among those listed as having overseas letters waiting to be collected.[17] As her daughter's married name is unknown, it is not possible to check whether Barbara and her family ever migrated to New South Wales, although it seems probable that they did not.

Mary McDonald's life did not end happily. In December 1821 an inquest was held into the deaths of Mary, her husband and a neighbouring farmer, Thomas Styles. The three were travelling in McDonald's boat when they drowned, the verdict being 'Accidentally drowned, in consequence of the whole party being in a state of intoxication, and quarrelling.'[18]

Mary was then 73 and her husband 78. Quarter Master Sergeant George McDonald (apparently a relative) and Colour Sergeant James Smith of the 48th Regiment applied for probate of McDonald's will, but a legal battle followed with a creditor of the estate who applied to auction McDonald's farm and 'Dwelling-house and Premises' at the Field of Mars.[19] The McDonalds' property was later known as Rose Farm; the house still exists in the suburb of Ermington.[20]

## Eliza Walsh

*A Lady can conduct a farm as well as a Gentleman*

All the letters in this book, apart from these written by Eliza Walsh, are personal and intimate communications written to family or friends. Eliza's letters are exceptions—they are official letters written to several New South Wales governors and the Secretary of State for the Colonies, Earl Bathurst. They are included because of their great interest in showing the extraordinary difficulties put in the way of women who wanted to lead independent lives in New South Wales.

Eliza arrived on the *Globe* in January 1819 with her sister and her brother-in-law, Frederick Drennan, who had been appointed Deputy Commissary.[21] From the moment she landed, Eliza determined to become a farmer in her own right. By 17 January 1821, when she wrote to Governor Macquarie requesting a grant of land, she had already purchased a small farm.[22]

'I beg leave to state to Your Excellency that I have made up my mind to settle a Farm in this Country, and that I have already purchased one, about 3 miles from Mr Bell's at Richmond Hill, where I have horned Cattle and Stock, which amount to upwards of £1,000.

'I can also command £1,000 more, if Your Excellency will be so kind as to make me a Grant of Land with the usual indulgences to Settlers according to means, I can exhibit for cultivation and rearing of Cattle.'

A man in Eliza's position, and with her financial resources, would have been given a grant almost automatically, but Governor Macquarie's reply to her was short and definite: 'I cannot comply with your request, it being contrary to the Regulations to give Grants of land to Ladies,' he wrote.[23]

On the same day on which she received Governor Macquarie's reply, 19 January 1821, Eliza wrote to Commissioner J. T. Bigge, who had been sent from London to make a wide-ranging inquiry into the transportation of convicts and the administration of the colony. Bigge was critical of Macquarie's administration and the two men were mutually antagonistic. Eliza's letter, apart from furthering her own cause, was useful to Bigge because it contained ammunition against Macquarie.

Eliza told Bigge that, despite Macquarie's statement that it was against regulations to grant land to females, he had granted land to several women. She cited Mrs Susannah Matilda Ward, a widow with a large family, formerly Matron of the Female Orphan School, who had received a grant of 640 acres on the Paterson River in the Hunter River district, as well as Mrs Gore, wife of Provost-Marshal William Gore, and Mrs Allan, wife of the Deputy Commissary General, David Allan, both of whom had received grants. She claimed that because of Macquarie's 'habit' of granting land to females, she had been 'induced' to believe she would receive a grant. This would allow her to conduct her cattle farm on a larger scale and would be not only of benefit to her but to the colony. She concluded, 'it does not appear altogether a just measure to exclude Ladies from making use of their money for the benefit of the Colony in consequence of their Sex, nor can it be deemed a real objection that a Lady could not be able to conduct a Farm as well as a Gentleman'.[24]

Bigge sent her letter to Macquarie, asking what regulations precluded the granting of land to single ladies. Macquarie had to admit that he had received no instructions either for or against the granting of land to single women, but added, 'I consider it a bad practice (except in some extraordinary and pressing case of necessity) and very injurious to the Interest of the Colony to give grants of Land to single women'. He believed single women were incapable of cultivating land. 'Some large tracts of Land, granted by my Predecessors to Women and Children many years since, remain still unimproved and unprofitable,' he wrote. Macquarie referred the matter to the authorities in England for decision,[25] but his term as governor ended soon afterwards without any grant being made.

On 19 January 1822, less than two months after Sir Thomas Brisbane took over as Governor, Eliza Walsh wrote to him enclosing all her previous correspondence. She asked him 'to grant me the Land I have solicited under the stated Stipulations'.[26] When still nothing happened, Eliza, on 14 February 1823, confronted the Colonial Secretary, Frederick Goulburn, who advised her to put her case to the Secretary of State for Colonies, Earl Bathurst, in London. She did so in a memorial[27] in which she reiterated the details of her tenacious but unsuccessful attempts to obtain a grant of land. In support she said:

'1st. That the stated Ground of the late Governor's objection to granting Land to unmarried Females, is of itself no way valid, such Lands not being more subject to be neglected than those of other Individuals, where the circumstances of the Parties are similar, and

'2ndly. That Grants of Land to both married and single women as well as Children, have been and are by no means infrequent; that therefore Memorialist as precedent directs and analogies in her favour, and

'3rd. Waving [sic] all consideration of the abstract principles on which was founded the stated objection of the late Governor to such Grants, that no such Grounds of objection could be discovered in Memorialist's particular case, Memoralist is willing to give every required Security for the due fulfillment of the Stipulations, that might be attached to any Land that might be granted to her.

'Your Lordship's Memorialist here rests her case, and adverting to the difficulties and the exergencies [sic] connected with those more particularly of providing for an increasing Herd of Horned Cattle, amounting to upwards of One Thousand and eighty Head, with no ground on which to depasture them with the exception of the small allotment, before mentioned, purchased by herself, and which now, from the common that was contiguous to it having been lately divided in Grants to various Individuals, is unequal to their support, trusts that she will not appear obtrusive in thus addressing Your Lordship, and, under the hope that the mere circumstance of Sex will not be allowed to operate to her prejudice, ventures to solicit that Your Lordship will be pleased to allow to her a Grant of Land of such extent, as to Your Lordship may see fit. And Your Lordship's Memorialist as in duty bound will ever pray.'

This memorial was dated 17 February 1823. More than three years later, on 28 June 1826, Earl Bathurst wrote to Governor Darling, who had succeeded Sir Thomas Brisbane as Governor of New South Wales:

'I am not aware of any reason why females, who are unmarried, should be secluded [?precluded] from holding Lands in the Colony, provided they possess sufficient funds for the purpose, intend bona fide to reside on their Lands and to fulfill any other stipulations which may be required of them in common with all other Grantees. You will therefore consider yourself at liberty to comply with the Petitioner's request, unless upon enquiring you shall find that there existed other reasons for refusing it than those which appear from the Memorial or from the correspondence with which it is accompanied.'

Eventually Eliza Walsh received a grant of 1280 acres on the Paterson River in the Hunter Valley,[28] adjoining grants made to John Galt Smith whom she had married in 1823.[29] At the 1828 census, John Galt Smith and Eliza were recorded living at Woodville House, Woodville, on the Paterson River in the Hunter Valley, north of Maitland. She was then 39 and her husband 34. They had a 2610 acre farm, 1000 acres cleared and 30 acres under cultivation. The farm ran only 347 cattle, many less than Eliza had run at Cabramatta when she was farming independently.

## Anne Drysdale

*We have got a good number of live stock*

At the age of 47, Anne Drysdale, a daughter of the town clerk of Kirkcaldy, Fifeshire, Scotland, sailed on the *Indus* for Port Phillip, arriving on 16 March 1840. A single woman who had farmed on her own account in Scotland, she intended to take up farming in the Port Phillip district, founded only six years previously.

With a capital of only £1250 she had to search for land in the unsettled bush well beyond the established farms near Melbourne. After a few months, with the help of a friend, Dr Alexander Thomson from Aberdeen, who had land on the Barwon River near Geelong, she succeeded in securing the Boronggoop run of 10 000 acres in the same district. Also through Dr Thomson, she met Caroline Newcomb, who became her companion and partner in farming. Caroline had emigrated from London to Hobart in 1833, at the age of 21. In 1836 she moved to Melbourne as governess to the children of John Batman, the city's founder, and later to the Geelong district. The two women shared a deep religious conviction which guided their lives.

Anne Drysdale's quiet determination, equable temperament and cheerful tolerance is evident in the diary she kept, recording their farming enterprise. The following extracts describe a few episodes during her settling at Boronggoop with Caroline Newcomb.[30]

*'August 9th [1841],*
'On Monday, Miss Newcomb, Jane, & I took up our residence at Boronggoop. We found Armstrong & Owens digging the garden, which is fenced. This is Thursday night, & every thing is now nearly arranged in the house; we have also got a number of garden & flower seeds put in the ground.

'Miss Newcomb, who is my partner, I hope for life, is the best & most clever person I have ever met with; there seems to be magic in her touch, every thing she does is done so well & so quickly. Our arrangement for the day is as follows: rise at 7 O'clock, break fast at 8 (previously to which we have prayers, at which Miss N. presides, & prays extempore very beautifully), dinner at 2 (& excellent dinners we have, as Vere, Armstrong's wife, turns out to be a good cook), at $^1/_2$ past 6 tea, prayers at 8, & to bed at 10.

'*Saturday, 14th [August]* . . .

'We have got a good number of live stock to begin with. Miss Newcomb bought a mare some years since, which had 2 fillies—the eldest probably in foal, the youngest 7 months. I have 2 mares, Constance & Venus, both we hope in foal: the names of Miss N's, Diana, Silvia, & Bessy. She has fine cows, Patch & Logie, with heifer calves, & is to have a 3d in a few months. We have a pair of turkeys, the cock from Mrs Thomson, the hen from Mrs Fisher; a pair of geese from Mrs Thomson; a flock of pigs, which Miss N. brought up by hand: we have besides nearly 2 Dozn of fine fowls. the pigs here graze like horses, & do no mischief: the horses cost nothing for keeping, except tether ropes for those wanted to ride; the others roam at thier pleasure.

'The hut, or rather cottage, is now very comfortable & nice. It consists of a parlour, bed room, & dressing, & a small bed room for strangers; a kitchen & bed room behind, & a store room; also a little passage between the kitchen & parlour. We have got a tolerably good Piano, 9 American chairs, & the floors covered with Indian matting; the walls are all covered with bagging, white washed, & the wood painted. All this, with the zink cottage windows, looks very nice, & I think, with the blessing of God, we have every prospect of being very happy.

'*Saturday, Augt 27th* . . .

'Today the storm continued, but Dr Thomson came down to take Jane home—he brought a schedule for me to fill up, in which there must be an exact account given of the number of stock, people employed, stations & quantity of land, &c. The return given in would amuse the commissioners: 1,400 sheep—the majority of these have lambs by their side, but being not weaned are not mentioned; 10 head of cattle, 5 mares; for this small number of stock the names of labourers amounted to 12, including the six children of Armstrong; 10,000 acres occupied, & 1 acre in cultivation! Capt Pollock, a friend of Dr Thomson's, a settler about 40 miles up the country, called; he has brought me a pair of Emu's eggs, & a shell. Miss N. has been very unwell all this day.

'*Saturday, 18th Sept*

'At 2 O'clock yesterdy morng we were awoke by a loud coo-ey (the sound always employed here to be heard at a distance): on listening, we perceived the bleating of the lambs was no longer to be heard; they had knocked down the hurdles & got out. All the men ran, nearly without cloaths, & in about an hour they were all safe again . . .

*'Wednesday, 22d...*

'... on Monday about 4 O'clock the ploughing began. The place we fixed on is in the Marsh, close to the river. The potatoes are put into the ground every 3d turn of the plough. No previous working! no dung! we shall see the result. This day about 2 O'clock the ploughing was finished; it looks about 1¹/₂ Acres. The rest of this day, Mr Read's Blks & our own were employed drawing wood for a brush fence.

*'8th Octr, Friday:*

'Yesterday the wool shed was finished. It looks very well 30 feet in length, by 14 wide; a skilling or verandah along one side, under which some sheep are to be placed all night, that they may be ready to shear in the morning, otherwise they would be so wet with dew that men could not begin till 9 or 10. We yesterday hired 4 shearers; they are to have £1 Per Hund, & 5/- Per day to assist in washing & making a washing place; the men are drawing logs for this, & the shearers come on Monday.

'We yesterday transplanted 30 young almond trees. After dinner to-day, Miss N. rode to Corio. We are all well, & quite happy. We find the days two short for all we have to do, which is proof we do not weary.

*'Tuesday, 12th Octr*

'... All the shearers arrived in the morning, & were engaged the whole day making a washing place, which consists of long logs or spars put out in the river between 2 trees; the spars form 2 pens, into the first of which the sheep are flung & allowed to swim awhile; they are then pushed by a forked stick under the middle spar, & men with flat sticks rub off the dirt, after which they swim out by an approach, & go dripping & exhausted to join their companions...

*'Monday, Novr 1t*

'... all last week the shearing has been going on nicely ... the sheep are found to be quite clean & free from a single spot of scab, a rare occurrance in this colony ...

'... This is indeed a very happy, quiet life, & I have nothing left to wish for. How much cause have I to be grateful to God for having placed me in such a situation, & for having given me such an excellent, pious, & kind friend. Sir George Gipps, the Governor of New S. Wales, paid a visit to Geelong some days since, but as he only remained 3 and ¹/₂ hours, he could not see much of the place; but he was much pleased with what he saw.

*'Thursday, 18th [November]*

'... Yesterday, the 17th, at day break, Miss N. went to see Venus & brought me the intelligence that she had a foal. I went out & saw it, a colt; but a fine, large boned fellow, bay, with a star on the forehead. To day, while we were at dinner, Jamima [Jemima Scott Armstrong] announced that Di, Miss N.'s mare, had a foal; we all left our dinner & ran out—a beautiful bay filly. We expect Constance to follow in a few days . . .

*Thursday, Decm 2d*

'On Saturday night the wind blew so violently that we could not sleep: the sheep yards were blown down, & both the flocks which are at home got out; but all the men were got out, & soon put all right again. On Sunday it was so stormy, we did not attempt to go to church.

' . . . On Teusday we marked some of the bales of wool, & yesterday Armstrong took the first load, five, to Corio: he brought a box from Kirkcaldy, with Marmalade, all run out, leaving at the bottom of each jar only the orange skins; but there are some cases of preserved meat, & a little lambs' wool & worsted for knitting, which is a great pleasure.

' . . . We have had a good deal of rain last night & to day, which was much wanted, as the grass begins to look brown. We transplanted a number of lettuces, cabbages & cauliflowers. We have now plenty of peas & cabbages, &c.'

Anne Drysdale's farming venture went well. In 1843 the partners acquired the Coryule run on the Bellarine Peninsula and in 1848 obtained the freehold title they had always wanted. By the time the government subdivided and sold their Boronggoop station in 1852, they were established in a fine stone homestead at Coryule overlooking Port Phillip Bay. Anne Drysdale died at Coryule on 11 May 1853. Caroline Newcomb continued to farm the Coryule property and to take an active part in local affairs. On 27 November 1861 she married the Wesleyan minister, Rev. James Davy Dodgson, at Drysdale, the township named after her partner. She died in 1874.

# 3
# *The work of the Lord*

## Eliza Marsden

*Had we only a few pious friends*

Eliza Marsden[1] arrived in New South Wales in 1794 as the young wife of the Reverend Samuel Marsden, who had been appointed assistant Anglican chaplain in the colony. For the next 40 years she was to steadfastly fill the roles she saw as her destiny in life—as a helper in her husband's ministry and a homemaker and mother. During those years, Samuel Marsden became a dominant figure in New South Wales as a clergyman, magistrate and landowner. Known as the 'flogging parson', he has come down in history with a reputation for cruelty towards convicts and prejudice towards emancipists.

In letters to her friends, the Stokes family in Cheapside, London, Eliza made few comments on her husband's public activities. Instead, her writing portrays society through the eyes of a woman who yearned to carry out 'the Lord's grand design'. To Eliza Marsden, society in New South Wales consisted (apart from a few families) of the irreligious and the corrupt. She longed for the standards of English society and the friendship of people who valued religion. Apart from Elizabeth Macarthur and Mrs Johnson, wife of the Anglican chaplain, Rev. Richard Johnson, there were few women with whom Eliza Marsden wanted to associate. Like Elizabeth Macarthur, she excluded as beyond the pale those who had come to the colony as convicts. This exclusion extended to the great majority of officials who kept convict mistresses or de facto wives.

Eliza's first child, a daughter, Ann, was born on 2 March 1794 while the *William*, the ship on which the Marsdens travelled from England, was being buffeted by a storm off Van Diemen's Land. When she first wrote to the Stokes family, Eliza was happy that her daughter, by then nine months old, was thriving. She had made a friend at Parramatta in Elizabeth Macarthur, 'a very pleasant agreeable Lady' and to her surprise had found in Sydney several women she regarded as 'Ladies', although they spoke only of 'worldly' things. She wrote on 13 December 1794 from Parramatta:[2]

'I experience a great loss of Religious Society. Our general conversation in company is very different from what I have been accustomed to in England. It all turns upon worldly affairs. Religion is seldom a subject of conversation excepting to ridicule its doctrines or professions, never to edify one another. There appears humanly speaking little prospect of doing good—however I do not despair for the work is not man's but the Lord's. I trust we are not forgotten at a Throne of Grace by the faithful in England. The Lord had some grand design in sending his gospel to this dark benighted part of the world . . .'

In a letter written on 1 May 1796[3] Eliza again expressed her feeling of isolation in a community where religion was given little importance.

'I long for an opportunity of conversing with you face to face. This would enable me to open my mind more fully than I can now do with paper and ink but whether I shall ever be indulged with that privilege or no is still in the dark womb of Providence. We seem in our present situation to be almost totally cut off from all connexion with the world especially the virtuous part of it . . . Had we only a few pious friends to pass away an hour with it would render this colony more tolerable.

'The want of a place for public worship is still to be recognised. We have not one at Parramatta nor any likely to be. So little attention being paid to the ministers makes Religion appear contemptible. Sometimes Mr. Marsden preaches in a Convict hut, sometimes in a place appropriated for Corn and at times does not know where he is to perform it, which often makes him quite uneasy and puts him out of temper both with the place and people.

'With respect to myself I enjoy both my health and spirits pretty well equally as well as when in England. I thank you for kind attention to my daughter; the book you sent her I hope she will live to benefit by. She now can talk pretty well and is an entertaining companion to a fond mother whose feelings you will readily excuse.'

The continuing fragility of food supplies is apparent in a letter Eliza wrote on 6 September 1799.[4] Although New South Wales had been established for eleven years and the Macarthurs and a few other farmers

40

were harvesting good crops, the colony still depended for many essentials on supplies sent from England. It was a major crisis when a ship was lost or overdue. Referring to the loss of the *Lady Shore*,[5] Eliza wrote:

'If what Mr. Marsden had in her had come safe it would have made us very comfortable as at that time we was without any of the comforts of life such as Tea, Sugar, Wine Spirits &c. It was very laughable to see us sit down as formerly to Balm Tea or Wheat Coffee sometimes without Sugar.'

Though her love and attachment to her children is very evident, Eliza Marsden contemplated parting with her 5-year-old daughter because she believed it was impossible for her to be educated in the 'corrupt' society of New South Wales.

'I own it would have been a severe trial to part with her, but the manners of the people are so corrupt and we cannot get proper servants about us, and there being not one good school that I should have been very happy to have heard of her being safe with my mother. She is now 5$\frac{1}{2}$ years old, she reads a little and works very neat. Last Christmas we were near losing her by an intermitting fever but the Lord in answer to our prayers spared her I hope for his honor and our comfort.

'My Charles is seventeen months old and that is a very entertaining as well as mischievous age. Your goodness will excuse me for saying so much of my children. You must remember I am a young mother . . . '

Despite her misgivings, when Ann was six years old, Eliza sent her to England to be brought up by a relative, Mrs Betty Scott of Hull. In a letter written on 22 August 1801[6] to Mary Stokes, Eliza wrote that she could 'not express the pain' it cost her to part from her daughter.

When she wrote next, Eliza Marsden had the sad news of the death of one of her children to convey. Apprehension concerning the death of children was a subject never far from the surface in her letters, but she felt her son's death so deeply that she found it difficult to write about, although he had been dead more than a year. In her letter dated 13 November 1802,[7] she wrote first of comparatively mundane matters, only later broaching the details of her son's death.

'I daily regret the loss of Mrs. Johnson's society from this country so much so that I have not visited Sydney but once since she left it and that was to wean my little girl Elizabeth. Our society of married ladies increase, there are now twenty. There never were so many at a time since the Colony was established. I wished I could say we increased in divine things, but we still continue in the same depraved state as ever. You who have so many privileges can have no idea of our situation.

'You have no doubt heard what an affliction we have been visited with in the melancholy death of our dear little boy. We was going to the farm a servant was driving him and me in a single horse chaise. Mr Marsden was on horseback when a man twenty yards from our own home carelessly run a wheelbarrow directly under the wheel of the chaise and overturned it, and my dear child never stirred more. I received no hurt myself though I was but two months of my time. I am conscious that his was a happy translation yet dear Madam picture to yourself my feelings to have him in health and spirits and the next moment to behold him in the arms of Death. I was wonderfully supported and had one consolation which the world cannot give neither take away. He who is faithful has promised when thou passest through the waters I will be with thee and through the rivers they shall not overflow thee. God is a refuge & strength, a very present help in time of need. This is the first time I have taken up my pen to write to England since I lost him though it is now fifteen months. I am afraid I am very sinful. I often think could I know his little thoughts he would reprove me for wishing him back in this troublesome world, but his removal has stirred me up to be more earnest in Divine things, and though he cannot come to me I may meet him in that place, where sin & sorrow and sighing are fore ever done away. I have still one little girl & boy with me the youngest John is a little turned of a twelve month old.'

A year later her son John, born two months after the death of Charles, died as a result of being scalded in the kitchen.

In a letter written on 15 January 1805,[8] Eliza Marsden again faces the prospect of having to part with a daughter—on this occasion Elizabeth, who was nearing the age when it was considered necessary to send her to England to be educated. Apart from this topic, the main theme of the letter is the 'great wickedness' of New South Wales and the prospects for change through religion. She wrote to Mrs Stokes:

'You no doubt wonder how we are going on. Much in the old dull and uncomfortable way with respect to religion. Yet there is one thing which has a promising appearance. There is more attention payed [sic] to the Sabbath. Mr Marsden has both at Sydney and at Parramatta a very large congregation which is voluntary, so that by degrees they may be brought to fear his name and we do not know what the Lord may do for this Colony. He may yet raise up a faithful people to publish his name and though I may not live to see it yet it is a consoling hope that he will not entirely forsake this place, which at times I am almost tempted to think he will do for its great wickedness. You who live in the midst of Gospel blaze know not what it is to live among a people entirely ignorant of

God and his ways. At times I feel so dead and lifeless that I think I have never been a child of God and doubt whether I shall ever enjoy those seasons of grace which has afforded me such real comfort. Let me beg dear Madam an interest in your prayers, that I may be enabled so to run that I may receive the prize of everlasting life . . .

'My family is the same in number as when I wrote last—a girl & boy. Elizabeth grows a great girl and it is time she was in England, but I do not think I can muster courage to part with her. Charles[9] is also an engaging little fellow and I trust he will be spared to us.'

In 1807 the Marsdens visited England, taking their children, Elizabeth, Charles and the baby Mary (another child, Jane, was born in England). They did not return to Sydney until early in 1810. The following year, during the birth of her last child, Martha, Eliza suffered a stroke which left her paralysed in the right arm. She died in 1835, survived by five daughters and a son.

## Isabella Parry

*Here is a moral wilderness of immorality and drunkenness*

In 1830, when Isabella Parry went to live at Port Stephens on the edge of the settled areas north of Sydney, she took with her the pious values of the evangelical Christian faith she shared with her husband.

A daughter of Sir John Stanley, Isabella had married Arctic explorer and naval officer Captain (William) Edward Parry in 1826 in Cheshire, England. In 1829, the year he was knighted for his efforts to reach the North Pole, Sir Edward Parry was appointed Commissioner of the Australian Agricultural Company. The company had been set up in 1824 with a million-acre grant of land in the Port Stephens district to promote the growth of merino wool and other agricultural products. By the time Parry arrived, a combination of poor management and the use of large areas of land unsuitable for sheep had left the company with disaffected employees, dwindling flocks and a crisis of confidence among investors.

Sydney had few visitors as famous as Sir Edward Parry. As soon as Isabella and Edward's arrival on the *William* on 13 December 1829 became known, there was a stream of important callers, including Colonial Secretary Alexander Macleay, Governor Darling's private secretary Colonel Henry Dumaresq, the Surveyor General Sir Thomas Mitchell, Archdeacon William Broughton, John Macarthur and other members of the Macarthur family who were involved in the Australian Agricultural Company.

When Parry left for Port Stephens on 6 January, Isabella (who was expecting her first child) was not well enough to accompany him. The Governor's wife, Eliza Darling, insisted that she move to Government House, where eight days later she gave birth to twins, a boy and a girl. At first the lives of Isabella and her babies were despaired of, particularly the boy who was a small baby. His survival was attributed to Eliza Darling who, although in bad health herself, suckled the baby for two days and nights. Parry wrote to his family, 'Mrs Darling has been a guardian angel to our dear Isabella and her babes'.[10] Doubting that the twins could live, Mrs Darling had them christened Edward and Isabella after their parents.

A few months later, Parry returned to Sydney to take his wife and children to Port Stephens, north of Newcastle, where they made their home at Tahlee, the residence provided for the Australian Agricultural Commissioner. In addition to managing the huge run-down estate, Parry found himself magistrate and minister to some 500 people, half of them convicts. Both Isabella and Edward were shocked at the 'moral wilderness',[11] at the wickedness, immorality and drunkenness they found among the employees of the company, convicts and Aborigines. Schools were unknown and at the first divine service Parry held, only about twenty persons attended, and none of them women. Soon Isabella was deeply involved in providing for the spiritual and educational needs of the people.

Isabella Parry's letters have great interest for their description of life at this isolated outpost. There are descriptions of the Aborigines, of a devastating bushfire, of Christmas in a small community and many other aspects of life in the bush not previously described in a woman's words.

The Parrys established a school at Tahlee and Edward Parry took over the duties of clergyman in addition to his work in running the affairs of the Australian Agricultural Commission. Isabella Parry wrote to Edward's mother from Tahlee House on 7 July 1830:[12]

'God grant that his preaching may be blessed to some of these poor ignorant creatures! For four years they have never heard the word of God preached to them, and they really appeared to live "without God in the world". There is always now a full congregation, and, I must say, a most attentive one. Our school is also going on as well as we could wish, and we have forty-two scholars. No little heathen could have been more ignorant; but I hope that, in future, God's name and word will be more known and lived than hitherto. Earnestly do we pray that this may be the case. We must expect to meet with disappointments and trials; but when we consider whose work we are doing, no difficulties ought to discourage us. May God give us strength to persevere! You might, perhaps, suppose that our greatest difficulties arise from the convicts, but I must say that we have not found this to be the case. The free people are far the worst, and most difficult to manage, because they think they may do as they like; and, while they set such a bad example, we cannot wonder that the prisoners do not improve. For the latter we have set up an adult school. Some of them wished to learn to read, and we are anxious to encourage them, as a means of keeping them out of mischief, and amusing them in the evening.'

On 19 December 1831 Isabella Parry wrote a graphic account of a bushfire in a letter to her mother Lady Stanley.[13]

'We have lately experienced another disadvantage of a newly cultivated country, and have witnessed what I have only heard of before, and read in Cooper's novels.—I mean the burning of the woods, and it is, indeed, a fearful and extraordinary sight. For the last fortnight, the whole country around has been in a blaze, and between this place and the Gloucester, a distance of more than seventy miles, there is scarcely a blade of grass left: it is one continued black plain, and the stems of the trees are all scorched and blackened. We were in hopes we should have escaped, near the house, but, after two or three days, we saw there was but little prospect of our avoiding the general destruction. Just as we were coming home from church, last Sunday, a man came running to say that the fire had reached his house, and was rapidly approaching our garden. Immediately all hands were sent off to save the poor garden, and, I am happy to say, succeeded, though it was only by a few minutes. Edward made them set fire to a broad space all round, and this was only just completed when the fire reached the place we had burnt, and, finding no food to supply its flames, turned off in another direction.'

In another letter dated 17 March 1831,[14] Isabella describes a visit to Booral and Stroud, villages on the Karuah River inland from Tahlee. The Australian Agricultural Company had set up a school at Stroud but although schools were, (after religion,) her greatest interest, she wrote not of the school but of the beauty of the country. Her sense of duty is evident in the fact that she visited every home in the small settlement.

Isabella had a further two children before the family left Tahlee in the middle of 1834 to return to England. Isabella's years in the isolated settlement at Port Stephens, plus constant childbearing, undermined her health. She had another six children before her death in England in 1841.

## Sarah Broughton

*Mr C. Cowper, Mr Eyre & Mr Aspinall called*

Sarah Broughton was a conscientious and supportive wife and mother who undertook the social duties of her position as the wife of a prominent churchman without complaint. Married to William Grant Broughton, Bishop of Australia, she met and entertained the right people, returned social calls and carried out all the social obligations demanded by her position. She did not see her role as being a proselytising or evangelical one, although she had spent her entire life in Anglican rectories.

The daughter of the rector at St Mildred's, Canterbury, Kent, Sarah Francis married William Broughton in 1818, the year he was ordained a priest. For the first nine years of their married life, they lived at Hartley Wespall, Hampshire, where Broughton was a curate, then at Farnham, Surrey and then at the Tower of London, where Broughton became chaplain until he was offered the position of archdeacon in New South Wales.

Sarah and her two daughters, Mary Phoebe and Emily, sailed with Broughton on the convict ship *John*, reaching Sydney on 13 September 1829. He was created Bishop in 1836. The Broughtons' home in Sydney was Tusculum, a lovely stone house designed by John Verge, in Manning Street, Darlinghurst. Sarah was an inveterate diary-keeper—she kept a diary during a visit she made with her husband to England in 1834 and again in 1837–38, in which she recorded her life in Sydney. In writing that is now faint and difficult to read, she listed daily events, the people she and her daughters visited and the people who called on them, her husband's movements and the state of the weather. There is little about her personal feelings or opinions apart from her anxiety about her husband when he was away from Sydney on frequent visits to parishes in the bush. These extracts give an idea of the narrow scope of her diary.[15]

*Jany 1st [1837] Sunday*
'The girls with Mary Davies & myself went to St James Church in the morng. Phoebe walked to church in the aft & returned with Mrs Jones in the omnibus. A thunderstorm in the evening. My dear husband left home the 25th of last month for Bong Bong, Goulburn, Yass &c.

*Jany 3*
'A hot wind & very large fire in the bush on the North Shore. I heard from my dear husband, from Mr Throsby's. The heat was so overcoming that the girls & I laid down on our beds after dinner. Walked in the verandah after tea, & heard the Band playing at the Basoon.

*Jany 4th*
'Mrs James Busby called to take leave. Very hot. Thunder & rain nearly all day. Cleared up towards evening. Mrs Scott, Mrs J. Mitchell & Capt. Crozier called. Another thunderstorm between 9 and 10 o'clock. Old Green came.

*Jany 5th*
'Mrs Jones & Mrs Ferriter called. Also Capt. Hobson. After dinner I went with the 3 girls to call on Mrs Macquoid. Miss Macquoid, Louisa & Dickey went for a walk with us down to the point—the two latter drank tea with us. Very cool & pleasant all day.

*Jany 8th*
'We went to St. James Church in Mr Macquoid's carriage & walked home. My dear Brother's letters reached me with the melancholy, but not unexpected intelligence of my dearest Mother's death on the 23d Augt last. Very thankful am I to Almighty God that she was to the very last free from pain, & although I was not permitted to be with her I bow with submission to the will of God & with a grateful heart for all his mercies humbly trusting to meet him my dear Father & all we love on earth in a better world.

*Jany 9th*
'Mary Davies went to Sydney with Mr Macquoid who kindly offered to assist me getting our mourning for us. Several friends called but I could not see them.

*Jany 11th*
'I wrote to my dear husband to inform him of my dear Mother's death. John Davies dined with his sister & went to Parramatta after dinner. Mr. Cowper kindly called on me after dinner, & I had a long chat with him about my dear Mother. I also saw Mrs & Miss Macquoid. Dear Julia's birthday, 12 years old.

*Jany 13th*
'Mr & Mrs Mackey called. Hot wind all day which lasted till 8 o'clock when we had a Brickfielder [the wind which came from the area of the brickfields]. Got another letter from my dear husband, from Capt. Ross's, he having been detained there by illness, & was prevented going on to Yass.

*Jany 15th*
'Harry got our mourning we went for the service to St James's Church in Jones's carriage Boyd went home to see his wife, was taken ill & was not able to return to us. Young also very poorly.

*Jany 18th*
'I received a most comforting and kind letter from my husband in answer to the one I wrote to announce my dear Mother's death, assuring me he was quite recovered. It rained very hard all day.

*Jany 20th*
'I wrote to my dear husband at Liverpool not expecting to see him till tomorrow, when to my great joy he arrived home safe & well, thank God, though wet through, just as we had finished tea, having come all the way from Mr. C. Cowper's in pouring rain.

*Jany 22nd*
'We all went to St James Church in the morng in Mr Jones's carriage. The Bishop preached. Did not go in the afternoon, it was so wet, but it held up for a short time after dinner when we all walked on the Verandah for some time. A little thunder in the evening & rained again very hard.

*Jany 24*
'Fine day. Mr Riddell called before breakfast. The Bishop went to a meeting at St James's Church when he returned brought the news of the Governor's resignation.

*Jany 25th*
'Mr Macquoid, Mr Biscoe, Mr Bell, Mr C. Cowper, Mr Eyre & Mr Aspinall called.

*Jany 26th*
'The 49th Anniversary of the Foundation of the Colony. The Bishop went to see the Governor. Mr Cowper, Mr M. Cowper, Mr Campbell & Sarah, Col. & Mrs Shadforth, Mr Riddell & Mr & Mrs Macleay called.

Sarah Broughton's diary continues in a similar fashion through the rest of 1837 and 1838. Interestingly, her daughter, Mary Phoebe Broughton, kept a diary during this period which was a virtual imitation of her mother's, detailing the same events and visits, and the details of daily life in an almost identical fashion.

Sarah Broughton died in Sydney in 1848. In 1844 Mary Phoebe Broughton married William Barker Boydell and went to live at Caergwrle on the Allyn River in the Hunter Valley. She had four daughters and six sons before her death on 30 July 1867 at the age of 47, a few months after the birth of her last child.[16]

# 4

# *Shipboard travail*

## Anna Josepha King

*One of the poor women has drawn her last breath*

The long voyage by sailing ship was the experience that united all people who travelled to Australia in the early days of settlement, whether they were officials, convicts, wealthy settlers, poor emigrants or middle-class professionals. To almost all, it was an experience they never forgot. The name of the ship on which they travelled remained engraved on their memories and it forever afterwards was used as a distinguishing mark in official records—for instance, censuses. The friendships made and the enmities remembered, along with first sight of the new land, remained in their memories forevermore.

The journey was a testing time also. The courage, stamina and spirit with which emigrants faced the dangers of the sea were often a trial run for the qualities they would need in their new country. For women the voyage had traumatic aspects over and above those shared with men. Many women did not emigrate of their own choice. Apart from the conscripted convicts, the decision to emigrate was made for many women by officialdom if they were the wives of officials, or by their husbands if they were free settlers. Women convicts, of course, had no control over their sentence of transportation, which often meant a heart-rending separation from their children. For women, the stress of unwillingly facing the prospect of life in a strange and unknown country added to their apprehensions of a dangerous sea voyage.

During the voyage, the family responsibilities of many women were of heightened importance. Many were responsible for young children and many gave birth on board ship. Mothers of young children had the concern of safeguarding their children against infectious diseases and injury.

These sometimes dangerous and usually prolonged voyages were unique and many women kept diaries of their experiences, even women who did not regularly write in journals at other times in their lives.

Anna Josepha King kept a diary of her voyage to Australia on the *Speedy* in 1799 when she travelled as the wife of the man appointed to succeed Governor Hunter as the third governor of New South Wales. It was not her first voyage to the Pacific. In 1791, a few days after her marriage to her cousin Philip Gidley King, she sailed for Norfolk Island where King resumed his position as commandant and lieutenant governor. There she faced, with equanimity and kindness, her position as stepmother to King's illegitimate sons, Sydney and Norfolk, the children of his liaison with convict Ann Inett. Six weeks after her arrival at Norfolk Island, Anna Josepha gave birth to her first child, Phillip Parker King. In the next four years on Norfolk Island, she had two daughters, one of whom died young. Another daughter was born on the voyage back to England in 1796.

The whaling vessel *Speedy*, on which the Kings embarked in November 1799, also carried fifty women convicts and stores for the settlement at New South Wales. Anna Josepha's diary gives a graphic picture of the hazards of voyages such as these, the illnesses, accidents and deaths that occurred and the devastating effects of these tragedies.

Anna Josepha brought only her youngest child, Elizabeth, with her, leaving the two older children in England to be educated. In her diary, her anguish at parting with Phillip and Maria is apparent, as is her concern for the other passengers on board ship. Though Anna Josepha did not endure the same hardships and restrictions as the convict women, she had an understanding nature and reserves of sympathy for their plight. Even for her the voyage was not easy—her husband was often ill, the sea was so rough that her housemaid, Jane Dundas, was badly hurt when she tumbled down the companionway, and her baby, Elizabeth, suffered such a fall that everyone thought she had been killed. Generally in her diary Anna Josepha King shows pity for the convict women, whose position in the heat and rough weather was far more uncomfortable than her own. In rough weather the battens in the convict quarters were fastened, '& for all this precaution they are all wet as drowned rats—it is bad management to have their beds so near to deck,' she wrote.

Some of the fears and incidents she recorded give an idea of the risks of such a voyage. At first there were fears that the ship would be captured by the French Fleet. When that danger had passed, King became very ill and Anna Josepha faced the prospect that he might not survive the voyage. Among the convicts, one woman lost her reason and died, an event that had such an effect on the other convicts that several nights later they believed they saw the dead woman's spirit among them. Several other convict women also died, including one woman who left an orphan baby. After they left Cape Town, the ship's doctor became insane, a boy who fell during rough weather nearly bit off his tongue, a convict woman splintered her leg badly in a fall down the hatchway and another scalded her foot. When a man called Wise, a master weaver travelling to New South Wales to take charge of the government manufacture of linen and wool, was lost overboard, his young wife and two children had to continue the voyage to an unknown future without a breadwinner.

Though Anna Josepha King was constantly worried about her husband's health, the following extracts from her diary[1] show that she also had time to take an interest in the convict passengers. Sometimes she was critical of them, but her sympathy and concern for their welfare was easily aroused.

*'Dec. 25th*
'This being Christmas Day all the Officers dined with us—our dinner consisted of a boiled leg of mutton, three roast fowls & a very fine ham, with a good mince pie as could be made on board ship—The ladies seem to be very happy & by way of a treat they had a little dance for about 2 hours, it was much amusement for us to look at them. Some attempted Irish, other Scotch steps & in truth I could scarcely make out any sort of step, but a country jump. At tea King was taken with a violent pain in his knee, which lasted all the evening—the weather very sultry. This sudden change of weather is the cause of much sickness.—The man that I before mentioned as being sick is at this time very weak & low, two women not expected to recover, a child very ill.

*'Dec. 26th*
'King very ill, gout flying about him. A fine breeze & dreadfully hot . . . A woman dangerously ill—two children the same.

*'Dec. 28th*
'King dangerously ill with a bad complaint in his stomach—Gout in knees, elbow hips & 1 foot—in the course of a day the obstruction was removed. Gout very bad—but I thank God the worst part of his complaint is mending.—One of the poor women that was so ill has just drawn her last breath after a long illness. She has left a very young child about 7 months—of course we shall not let it want whilst on board—

51

Capt. Questead has appointed a very good sort of elderly woman to take care of it—& should it live to reach our destined port, I shall be happy to protect a poor little orphan . . .

### *Jan. 19th*
'. . . this being Sunday our ladies dressed out very neat & clean—excepting *one* that calls herself Lady Underhill—she complains very much that she can't wear the things Government provided for her & unfortunately she has very few others. I never saw such a proud creature in my life . . .

### *Jan 23rd*
'. . . I find myself very poorly with a bad cold. King I am happy to say is in good health he finds his warm bath of greatest use to him—it is a large tin shoe painted green big enough to put his whole body when he bathes—it is placed outside the cabin door under the companion—where it is filled with warm water a sail is thrown over the companion which covers him from everything—others take a dip after him. Capt. Questead still very poorly the Dr. taken very unwell—orphan better—child very ill . . . '

When they arrived at the Cape of Good Hope, Anna King had an important social role as the wife of the man appointed Governor of New South Wales. They were entertained at many events.

### *Feb 4th*
'. . . Our mornings were very much taken by receiving & paying morning visits. Invitations pouring in hourly for dinner parties which filled up the whole of the time of our stay. . . . I dined 2 public days at General Dundas'—where we sat down the first time 16 & the second 35—I cannot help observing how extremely pleasant & agreeable Mrs. Dundas conducts herself—she is very much beloved. I had the honour to know her when she was Miss Cumming of the Isle of Wight—she is not in the least altered—now being the 1st Lady in Rank in the Cape of Good Hope. Mrs. Blake, Sir George Young's niece is being much liked among the Dutch ladies. Her politeness to me I cannot forget always—Having now passed the time allotted for the ship's stay at the Cape we were preparing to embark—the Governor & other friends very anxious for us to stay a day longer to go to the Assembly—& with much reluctance I must say King consented that we should stay—he being anxious to make our destination—however we staid—expecting an amusement of this kind I had provided myself with a dress so that I was not only ready in mind & wish—but dress also . . . '

After the social interlude at the Cape, shipboard life resumed. A few weeks later, Anna wrote about a threatened fire on board, a very much dreaded event.

*'Feb. 22 & 23rd*
'The morning very unpleasant—heavy rain thunder & lightning. All on board tolerably well—A great smoke & smell alarmed the Capt & us in our cabin. I had wondered whence it came—the Capt's servant had been down in the gun room under our Cabin to get a box for King, he had left the candle burning in this place & it burned down to its end—it caught the bag he had fastened it to by sticking the grease to the bag, which was rice belonging to us—this was smouldering—then got to a bag of twine when the smell more distinct of fire & smoke alarmed us. God only knows what our lots would have been—for the gun room is as packed of everything that would have burnt at a great rate—& a cask or 2 of spirits would have helped to blow us up—I ran upon Deck & it was raining hard—in fact I did not know where to go for I thought all was over—we must be lost—it was very soon put out as the boy remembered the candle. It cannot be surprised these little frights make me something of a *coward*—for this is my name now & I cannot help it, as I trust please God I live, my next voyage will be the last, the thoughts that I will keep up my spirits & with the wind fair—the faster we go the sooner I shall be blessed with the sight of my dearest children—pray God grant we may all live to return.'

When they arrived safely at Port Jackson on 15 April 1800, Anna finished her shipboard diary:

'I was very happy to put my foot once more on dry land—& I hope never to take another voyage after arriving again in England for I am quite sick of the *Seas*.'

Anna Josepha King was the first governor's wife to live in New South Wales; Governor Arthur Phillip had left his wife in England and Governor Hunter was unmarried. During the six years when King was governor, she shared his labours and difficulties, her influence being so marked that she was known as 'Queen Josepha'. Her most important work was the establishment, with her friend from Norfolk Island days, Elizabeth Paterson, wife of the Lieutenant Governor, of the Orphan Institution (see Chapter 5), the first public social welfare activity undertaken by women in New South Wales.

When King's term ended in 1806, she sailed with him on the *Buffalo* on a nightmare journey around Cape Horn which lasted nine months. King, who had been ill on several occasions during their married life, died in 1811, leaving Anna Josepha a widow at 43, with a son and three

53

daughters. After more than 20 years in England, she returned for the third time to Australia in 1832 to live with her daughter Maria, married to Hannibal Hawkins Macarthur, at their property The Vineyard at Parramatta. She died there in 1844 at the age of 79.

## Sarah Docker

*A little after six Mary-Jane was born*

Sarah Docker had her first living child while travelling to Australia on a sailing ship in 1828. Already, at 25, she had the qualities of maturity and independence that were to make her a successful pioneer in north-eastern Victoria.

As Sarah Bristow of Liverpool, she had married Joseph Docker, the assistant curate at the Anglican Church at Southport, Lancashire. She gave birth to a stillborn child before sailing in June 1828 on the *Adams* for Australia, where Rev. Joseph Docker had an appointment as a Colonial Chaplain[2]. During the voyage, Sarah Docker kept a diary which describes the problems and the boredom of a long sea voyage. Through it shines a picture of an assured young woman with definite opinions, already possessed of great strength of character. The following extracts are taken from the diary she kept from 16 June to 11 November 1828.[3]

*'Wednesday 18th*
'In the Morning we were surprised to find that a Storm was prevailing. I was the first who felt its effects, feeling very sick about 5 oclock and continuing to vomit during the whole of the day most of the Passengers felt the effects of the motion in a slighter degree. Without any particular incident we approached Margate and as the wind being directly contrary we anchored a short distance from the shore and I have since much regretted that I was too unwell to take even a slight view of the Place.

*'Thursday 19th*
'We left Margate about six oclock in the morning and anchored off deal [Deal] at eleven when we were obliged to remain from contrary winds. About five in the evening the Doctor and Wm Docker went on shore with the Pilot who was leaving us. The Captain, although unwilling for them to leave the vessel granted them permission to stay on shore until nine, at the same time telling them that he would not wait longer for them if the wind rose. About nine the wind became favourable, and the Captain and passengers were anxious to sail. The Captain stated, that if as he expected, the wind should rise, it would be extremely

dangerous remaining so near to shore. I was so displeased with the thoughtlessness that I would have consented to leave them, but Mr Do, thought it would be imprudent, while we were hesitating the wind suddenly changed and obliged us to remain.

*'Saturday 21st*
' . . . Mrs D., Jane and myself continued very sick. The young men amused themselves with cockfighting and Cards.

*'Friday 27th June*
'Nothing particular occurred during the week. I still continued very sick and became so weak that I could scarcely sit up. About 6 oclock this morning I felt very unwell and had the Doctor and Mrs Davies called up, and a little after six *Mary-Jane* was born. She was so very small that I was inclined to think she was born a month too soon, but the Doctor thought it was owing to my have been so very sick.

'At 9 oclock Mr D. baptized our little girl and gave her the name of Mary Jane. After my confinement I never was the least sick, and should have been up in a day or two but that the weather was exceedingly stormy, and the Ship was very much tossed. Mr. D. was so very unwell that he almost thought he should not survive the passage.

*'Sunday 6th*
'July I went into the Cabin for the first time after my confinement, and looked so well that the Captain said he should scarcely have known me for the same person. We were this day about 90 miles from Cape [F]inistere.

*'Saturday 12 July*
'Mrs. Davies took Mary on Deck for the first time.

*'Monday 21st July*
'We had a fine view of St Antonio one of the Cape De Verts Islands. I paid Mrs Davies £1–10 for dressing Mary for the first month. Mary is much improved. Mrs is related to the Davies's of Neston and knew my Aunt and Miss Wilson and most persons in that neighbourhood.

*'Saturday 26th July*
'About one oclock we met with the *Ganges* a ship sailing from Calcutta to London, we were sufficiently near to speak to them with a trumpet, and could plainly see the Passengers on Deck; one of them, a little boy, clapped his hands, seemed quite delighted with seeing us. I believe I was the only person on board who did not heartily enjoy the sight, but I felt so disappointed at not being able to put a letter which I had previously written on board the *Ganges* that I could scarcely bear to look at it.

*'Monday 11th Aug.*
'Having passed the Line yesterday all the passengers, myself and Mary excepted went through the ceremony of ducking. I sat on Deck and was much entertained with seeing them all one by one brought up blindfolded and well drenched in water, out of respect to Mr. D. the sailors only threw a tub of water on him, but most of the others had their faces pitched and were thrown backwards into a sail full of water. When all was over Mr. D. gave the men £1.10. The other passengers gave some 10/- and some 20/-.

*'Saturday Aug 30th*
'This morning Jane fell from the top of the Cabin stairs to the bottom, and hurt herself very much, we thought it very fortunate that she had not Mary in her arms, as she had *previous* to this time frequently carried her up and down.

*'Wednesday September 17th*
'Jane is now perfectly recovered from the effects of her fall. The weather is now very cold; and the thick Fogs which come over the sea almost every quarter of hour remind us forcibly of a November day.

*'Friday 26th Sept.*
'Very early in the morning several Whales were seen at a distance, and one in particular, lifted his head above the water a considerable way, and remained in that position a considerable time to the great delight and astonishment of all on deck. In the evening the first Mate took a Porpoise, there was great rejoicing on the occasion, as we were all anxious to have a near view of this singular Fish it was soon killed and bled more than any Pig our butcher then cut it up; the flesh had exactly the appearance of Pork, particularly about the face. The Sailors were very glad of it to eat, and we all tasted the liver which you would not have known from that of a Pig. Numbers of Sea Birds were Shot. Last Sunday I put Mary into short petticoats, she is grown very fat, and has Aunt Elizabeth's double chin, but it is impossible to say who she will be like. The Captain and all the passengers seem very fond of her, she is so very quiet and goodhumoured.

*'Sunday 28th Sept.*
'We sailed all day with a fine breeze, about four in the afternoon the wind became much higher, and the sea washed over the Deck so that we were obliged to go into the Cabin. About twelve oclock I was awaked by a quantity of water pouring upon my bed; we called for a light, and were informed that the Companion door had been left open and the sea had rushed down the stairs. It is difficult to describe the scene of noise and confusion which we witnessed, the rattling of Boxes, Chairs, and

decanters, as they rolled about the Cabin; the creeking of the Ship, together with the frequent rushing in of water. There was an almost continual glare of lightening. It may appear strange, but I was more inclined to laugh at the noise and confusion than to feel the slightest apprehension of danger.

'Saturday 4th Oct
' . . . About this time we lost many of our comforts, our white Biscuits, Cheese, Porter, and desert were all finished, and the Coals were getting very low that we could have nothing but boiled Meat. Some of the passengers appeared very much discontented, but as Mr. D. was well, and Mary very fat I did not mind.

'Monday 13 Oct 1828
'This morning we met with a Dutch ship, and sent out a boat to enquire if they could let us have some coals. The Captain *gave* us 3 baskets but would not *sell* any.

'Wednesday 5th Nov
' . . . About 4 oclock A.M. we had the first sight of New Holland, and at 11 we came in sight of King's Island; the day was delightful, and we had a moderate breeze.

'Thursday 6th Nov.
'About 4 this morning the Mate informed us the land was very near. The morning was very fine, and we were all soon on deck. Nothing could exceed the beauty of the scenery, we passed on the left, Wilson's promontory, and the Coast of New Holland, about 4 miles distant, to the right we saw Rotondo, Sir Roger Curtis's groop, and the Monceer Islands.

'Sunday 9th Nov.
'We had this morning got to the north of Jervis's Bay. We could plainly see the smoke from numbers of fires along the Coast. You can form but little idea of the joy which we felt at being so only a few hours sail distant from Sydney. Yesterday we expected to be at Sydney today and even talked of going to Church. But today the wind being quite contrary we were obliged to tack about, and made very little progress.

'Tuesday 11th Nov.
'We were this morning wakened by a violent storm of Thunder and Lightening. The Thunder broke just over our heads, and the heavens appeared to be in one continual blaze. The Captain who had been frequently to the East Indies said he had never before witnessed any-thing to equal it. About 4 the rain fell in torrents, and the thunder and Lightning gradually ceased. An hour after we had a violent Hail storm, which however lasted only a few minutes, but the hailstones were some

of them the size of large marbles. We now slept for a couple of hours, and upon waking found ourselves close to the Harbour of Port Jackson, before which we were detained some time during this time Jane and I were very busy packing up our bedding &c &c and dressing ourselves and Mary for our first appearance in Sydney. We had just completed our preparations when we entered the Harbour. The scenery became every moment more and more beautiful reminding us forcibly of the Lake scenery in Cumberland. Hill above Hill rose on each side of us; the three Islands named Shark, Garden and Pinchgut now presented themselves. Pinchgut took its name from having been in former times the prison for the worst of the Convicts. We anchored between the entrance of the Cove and Pinchgut Island, when a Customhouse officer came on board and politely congratulated us on our safe arrival. After taking charge of Letters of which the Captain had, he civilly offered to convey any of us on shore in his boat. Mr. D., myself, Jane, Mary, and Tom accepted his offer and were soon landed at Sydney. Mr. D. proceeded immediately to the Colonial office, and we walked up to the Rose Inn, where we thought we might possibly lodge, as the woman came from Birmingham and we brought a letter from her father. It was a hot summers day, so that we soon felt much tired with walking, we arrived at last at a wooden Cottage which we were told was the Rose, after waiting a considerable time at the door we were shown into a little room and told that Mrs Still would be with us in a moment, in about half an hour Mrs St. made her appearance after asking a few questions about Birmingham &c she begged to be excused a few *moments* longer that she might change her dress which indeed I thought highly requisite. I will now give you an idea of her appearance, she had on a dirty thin Muslin gown, confined at the waist by a string, and a still dirtier chemise peeping below it, and as she was immensely fat you may imagine what an appearance she would make, without stays, and without stockings. Mr D. then joined us, and informed me that finding the Governor and Archdeacon were both absent from Sydney he called upon Mr Cowper one of the Senior Chaplains who went with him and engaged rooms for us at the principal Hotel. Mr Cowper is a plain, quiet, puritanical sort of character, and Mrs C. rather formal they have four Sons, and one Daughter who is lately married, and was presented by the Governor with a grant of land on the occasion; the Sons are most of them settled in the Colony. They politely invited us to dinner at four. In the evening the Rev. R. Hill called upon us and invited us to dine with them the following day.'

Some months after their arrival, Joseph Docker became rector of St Matthew's Church, Windsor. However, seeing the opportunities in farming, he resigned in 1833 and he and Sarah settled on a farm named

Clifton near Windsor, where they remained for four years. Then, encouraged by the accounts of Major Thomas Mitchell's explorations, they decided to move to the Port Phillip district and take up a run. By the time the family set out for the journey south, Sarah had six children. They travelled with servants, a flock of sheep, cattle and a boat in which to cross the Murray at Crossing-Place (later Albury).

After an adventurous and difficult journey lasting seven months they arrived in September 1838 at a station on the Ovens River called Bontharambo, previously held by George Faithfull who had abandoned it after his shepherds had been murdered by Aborigines. The story of Sarah and Joseph Docker and their family at Bontharambo is an epic of pioneering settlement. Their journey south and their first years at Bontharambo are described in a retrospective journal by Mary Jane Docker, the child born during the voyage on the *Adams*.[4]

In the diary kept by Sarah Docker on the *Adams*, it is possible to see the qualities that later made her such a successful pioneer. She died on 17 May 1864, survived by seven of her eleven children. By that time Bontharambo was graced by a stone mansion, and the Docker family were known as outstanding pioneers of the Wangaratta district.

## Sarah Brunskill

*No pen can express the pain and agony of the heart*

Sarah Brunskill's tragic experience in losing her two children on the voyage to South Australia was only too common. The majority of deaths on emigrant ships occurred when epidemic diseases swept through crowded and unhealthy cabins. Sarah wrote to her parents in Ely on 27 November 1838:[5]

'I every day defer writing, but the day must come when it must be done, but oh! no pen can express with truth the pain and agony of the heart that dictates. We sailed from Plymouth with a fair wind on Tuesday, 13th November. My throat after applying leeches was better, and so I thought our dear children were, but hopes were vain; in a day or so they gradually began to decline, and on Wednesday, 21st, at ten minutes past seven in the morning, our dear boy breathed his last on my lap. Oh, how can I proceed! My heart is almost ready to burst. Soon after four o'clock his body was consigned to the deep about 90 miles from Oporto. Our dear girl still was left us; for her we prayed that she might be saved. But no, God in his good time thought fit to take her also to Himself. About half-past twelve her dear spirit flew to that mansion from which no traveller returns, so you see in less than 24 hours our darlings were both in the bosom of their God. Poor Mrs. Richman's third child is going to be buried this afternoon, but they still have three left. Eight children have died since we left London. Mrs. Richman's first suffered the same as our dear boy, the other two from sore throats, with which almost everyone has been attacked, and had it not been for the leeches I should have gone also. My tongue began to swell, and I could scarcely speak or breathe, but now both George and myself are well, with the exception of weakness . . .

'The warm weather here brings out swarms of small flies, cockroaches and bugs, the last mentioned on comparison are trifling inconveniences . . .

'There is another child dead to-day, making in all 17, and I believe all could have been saved with care and proper medical attention.

'We have had three children born on board. One was dead and the others with their mothers are doing well. The ship is like a little town, so much scandal and ill-nature, and prying into each other's affairs, you would hardly believe. We have found the preserved meat the last eleven weeks so bad that we cannot eat it, and that is served to us three times a week. What a treat a little fresh meat will be to us, but this voyage will reconcile us to many things on shore we should have thought very hardly of had we gone from England to Australia without it.'

Sarah Brunskill reached Adelaide on the *D'Auvergne* on 21 March 1839. Despite her tragic voyage, she was able to tell her parents soon after she arrived, 'If you were all here I should not wish to return'.

# 5
# Charitable works

**Elizabeth Paterson**

*The Girls learn Housewifery and the use of the needle*

Elizabeth Paterson and Anna Josepha King (see Chapter 4) were the first women in Australian history to undertake charitable work in an organised way. In 1800, just twelve years after the establishment of the colony of New South Wales, the two women were involved in starting a home for orphans and they remained active members of the committee which ran the home. As wives of the two most senior office-holders in the land— Anna Josepha's husband was Governor King and Elizabeth's husband was Lieutenant Governor Paterson—their involvement could have been a token gesture; but in fact both were extremely conscientious, paying daily visits to the orphanage.[1]

Philip Gidley and Anna Josepha King had became interested in looking after orphaned and abandoned children while he was in charge of the settlement at Norfolk Island. They set up an Orphan School there and when they reached Sydney in July 1800 were dismayed when they found so many children abandoned 'to every kind of wretchedness and vice'. King decided that a home was needed not only for orphans, but for neglected children who should be taken away 'from the vicious example of their abandoned parents'.[2]

The Orphan Institution was established soon afterwards in a house opposite the Military Barracks on what is now the corner of Bridge and George Streets. The committee appointed to supervise the Institution consisted of Anna Josepha King, Elizabeth Paterson, Rev. Richard

Johnson, Rev. Samuel Marsden and surgeons William Balmain and John Harris.

Elizabeth Paterson had first arrived in Sydney with her husband, New South Wales Corps officer Captain William Paterson, in October 1791. They left almost immediately for Norfolk Island, where Paterson served until March 1793 when he returned to Sydney to act as administrator for nine months. In 1796 Elizabeth accompanied her sick husband back to England, but he was ordered back to Sydney in 1799.

It is fortunate that in a letter written to her uncle, Lieutenant Johnson of Liverpool, soon after she became involved in the establishment of the Orphan Institution, Elizabeth included a first-hand account of its aims.[3] At the beginning of her letter she expressed her fears about a possible uprising by Irish convicts—'my terror is private assassination, breaking into our houses in the dead of night,' she wrote. Then she continued:

'Governor King who has now the command, will make many regulations for the security, as far as in his power, of the Colony—and likewise some attention to the rising generation, to which hitherto none has been paid, for certainly if we ever hope for worth or honesty in this settlement, we must look to them for it, and not the present degenerate mortals. A school is now establishing on a very extensive plan, for the reception of all orphans, and other children whose parents are not proper for such a charge, under the management of the Govr and a Committee—these children are to be entirely secluded from the other people— and brought up in habits of religion and industry—some branches of manufactories will be by means of this seminary put on foot particularly making linnen and woollen cloths the latter to be procured from the Fleece of a remarkable fine breed of Spanish Sheep already in the Country—and the former from the Flax which grows spontaneous in the Woods. This with their education and the Boys learning different Trades, and the Girls Housewifery and the use of the needle, will be full employment.—This arrangement gives me great satisfaction—as there are now above a thousand children in the place. I cannot help looking forward to the time when the young Men will become useful members of Society and the Women faithful and industrious wives. Everyone must hope for our success in so laudable an undertaking—and if no material interruption takes place—we shall soon have it on a permanent establishment.—I hope when an opportunity offers to hear from you— it is now fifteen months since we left England, and I have not heard from any Friend I have.—Col. Patersons whole time is totally taken up with his two capacities, particularly under the present circumstances, either hearing evidences, or in the Field with the Men, and I am often lonely enough, and sometimes perhaps fancy things worse than they are—but however with respect to My Dear Sister I am always easy, under your protection I can have no fear.—I have now only to add Col. P. best respects. [I]f any thing more happens before the sailing of the ship I will mention it to my sister.'

Elizabeth Paterson continued to be involved in the running of the Orphan Institution. During the next few years there are many reports of committee meetings signed by A. J. (Anna Josepha) King and E. (Elizabeth) Paterson. On 23 February 1802 the committee reported that the 54 children in the Institution had 'made Considerable Improvements both in their Morals and Education, considering the Situations from whence they have been taken'. The report also stated that, following recent extensions, the committee expected to be able to take double the number of children.[4]

The French explorer, Nicholas Baudin, was so impressed with the Institution—and perhaps also mindful of the eminent standing of the committee members—when he visited Sydney in 1802 that he sent a donation of fifty pounds sterling.[5]

The premises in Captain William Kent's old house in George Street, although extended and augmented by additional buildings, were regarded as temporary. Plans were made to transfer the school to a new building at Parramatta, but this idea was abandoned during Governor Bligh's term.

In 1810 there were plans for the school to pay for itself by taking in plain needlework to be done by the girls under the supervision of the matron.[6] The same year, Governor Macquarie, who had succeeded Governor Bligh, directed that a Female Orphan School be built on 60 acres at Parramatta. The foundation stone was laid on 23 September 1813 and the Governor's wife, Elizabeth Macquarie, continued the practice of vice-regal involvement by not only becoming patroness but by making the school her principal public activity (see Chapter 6).

By then Elizabeth Paterson had departed from New South Wales. In 1804 her husband was sent to Van Diemen's Land to found a settlement at Port Dalrymple, but eventually had to return to Sydney to take charge following the arrest of Governor Bligh by members of the New South Wales Corps. After the arrival of Governor Lachlan Macquarie, Paterson sailed for England, but he died at sea off Cape Horn on 21 June 1810.

In 1814, in Bath, Elizabeth Paterson married Francis Grose, after whom her first husband had named the Grose River in 1793 for his efforts in attempting to find a route over the Blue Mountains. Grose died only two months after the marriage. Elizabeth died at Bath in 1825, aged about 65 years. She was childless.

## Eliza Darling and Fanny Macleay

*I am incessantly occupied with the School of Industry*

The Female School of Industry, begun in Sydney in 1826, was the first colonial charity to be founded and managed entirely by women. The aim of the school was described in an advertisement calling for subscribers, published in the *Sydney Gazette* on 18 March 1826 as being 'the education of female servants'. The school planned to take twenty girls aged 7 to 14, who would be supported entirely by the institution, plus others who would be admitted if their parents or friends undertook to pay £10 a year for their upkeep. All would be educated in every branch of housework, plain needlework, knitting, spinning, reading, writing, the first four rules of arithmetic and the catechism of the Church of England. (Catholics were specifically excluded.) Girls were to be the responsibility of the school until the age of 18, but were eligible for employment as servants at 14. The school was to be run by a Ladies' Committee which would meet once a month, with two members making weekly visits.

The patroness was the Governor's wife, Eliza Darling, who was the dominant force in the establishment of the school and who was to be associated closely with its running until she left the colony in 1831. The Macleay family—daughters of Colonial Secretary Alexander Macleay—provided many of the officeholders on the School of Industry committee. The Macleays were tied to the Governor's family not only by official links through Alexander Macleay holding the chief public service office, but by developing personal ties. In 1830 one of the Macleay daughters, Christiana, married Eliza Darling's brother, William John Dumaresq. Christiana was treasurer of the committee which ran the School of Industry, Fanny Macleay was secretary and other Macleay sisters, Kennethina and Rosa Roberta, were committee members. One or other of the Macleay sisters was to hold the positions of secretary and treasurer for the school's first ten years.

The school began in temporary accommodation in a cottage in Castlereagh Street under a matron, Mrs Kingsmill, and in September 1826 moved to the former cavalry barracks in Macquarie Street, made available by Governor Darling who arranged renovations. The matron was responsible for the day-to-day running of the school, but a sub-committee of Eliza Darling and the Macleay sisters took responsibility for management, staff and finances, including enrolments, dismissals and expulsions, physical welfare, clothing, education, religious instruction and discipline. The sub-committee met every Wednesday at the school and in effect ran the institution.

The school gained support from affluent subscribers who, as well as approving its high-principled purpose in rescuing children from poverty and moral danger, also appreciated having first call on the services of the graduates.[7]

At times Eliza Darling was an almost daily visitor. The rationale for the school accorded very well with her evangelical Christianity, and the institution was modelled on the School of Industry in Cheltenham, England, where Eliza grew up. Like the Schools of Industry in England, it aimed to rescue poor, unemployed or orphaned girls from the immorality of the streets and the influence of their parents, if any, and to educate and train them, providing a moral as well as a practical education.

Eliza was born at West Bromwich in 1798, the fourth child of Lieutenant Colonel John Dumaresq and his wife, formerly Ann Jones. Her father died when she was six, leaving her mother to bring up her six children in straitened circumstances. From her mother, Eliza received a deeply religious upbringing. Through her brothers Henry and William, who became army officers, Eliza met Ralph Darling, then a 45-year-old major general. Although 26 years younger, Eliza married him at Cheltenham on 13 October 1817. The result was a new life for Eliza and opportunities for advancement for her brothers.

Darling was appointed governor of New South Wales in 1825 and sailed with his wife, four children and her brothers, William and Edward, on the *Catherine Stewart Forbes* on 29 July 1825, another brother Henry having preceded them. The party arrived in Sydney on 17 December 1825 and remained in Sydney for nearly six years. During that time Eliza had three more children, followed by a miscarriage in 1830; she was often ill and sometimes confined to her bed for lengthy periods.

This did not prevent her from undertaking philanthropic activities. She attended meetings of the Benevolent Society, reorganising the lying-in branch to separate it from the other work of the society, helped the Sydney Dispensary provide the poor with medical advice, actively supported the Sunday School movement and took part in the work of the government-run Female Orphan School (see earlier in this Chapter), in addition to her major public activity in establishing the Female School of Industry.[8]

Her close personal interest in the School of Industry is indicated in letters she wrote to her brother, Edward, who had settled in Van Diemen's Land. On 18 April 1826,[9] in a letter in which she also described other activities which competed for her time with the School of Industry, she wrote:

'We are, that is myself—Mrs Powell, Wells & the Misses Macleay all as busy as possible making *grand* preparations for the very *grand Ball*, to be given here on the King's Birth-night—Mr Fraser & Mr Reid are both also very active, and Mr Condamine is to have one side of the Room as *his* Charge—to fit up with *Bayonets*, Flags, Gun Barrels—&c—one window to be taken out; & a wooden platform & shed to be built outside for the Band.—Mr Fraser is to bring in Four large *Gum* Trees— and make Garlands &c—Mr Reid is painting silk Lamps—and we Ladies are making Roses & Lilies, and Golden Crowns. &c &c—

'Then I assure you the School of Industry gives me a good deal of employment—Plans for the *interior* arrangement of the Building—Plans for the management—Rules to draw up—Notes to write.—Clothes *bought; cut out; made*, and all done under my own eye—not to say a word, of the yet uncomfortable & unfinished state of our *own* domestic arrangements—Clothing for Convict Servants—Rewards to Dr—Presses to make—Closets to fit up—Rooms to furnish &c—. This is to give you an Idea of *my* Business—that of a Public Nature seems endless, & I much fear the Governor will be ill, without we can *make* him take more exercise . . . '

On 24 May 1826,[10] in another letter to Edward Dumaresq, she wrote:

'I assure you I do not look upon myself as possessing by any means a *Sinecure*—We too have a Ladies Committee's and our *Minutes* & our *Resolutions* &c—and consider ourselves as People of some Importance . . . The Governor keeps quite well in spite of writing thirteen & sometimes fourteen Hours a day, and taking no exercise—the Children have recovered their English Roses—and look "in my Eyes"—quite beautiful—as for myself, tho' I am now *five Months* in the way to produce a young Australian I have never been so well since I married—I have not mentioned *my situation* to Mama or Marianne as it would only render them for some months anxious and uneasy . . . I am incessantly occupied with the School of Industry & have myself turned *overseer*, in transforming the orderlies Stables into the School House and by dint of Bribery, giving the men a Supper of Bread & Cheese & a Glass of Grog, we shall soon I hope get into the House.'

When she wrote to her brother on 27 November 1826,[11] she had given birth to a son, Augustus, who, after being very ill following his birth, was thriving. The School of Industry remained of great concern:

'I myself *should* be I think (indeed I must say I *am*) wonderly well if I had but rest, but I have much more to occupy both mind & Body than I have strength for, nothing is done I find, without *personal* exertion & superintendance & now my School is begun, I must not let it be neglected—But it is needly to attempt giving you an account of all I have or fancy I *ought* to have to do . . . '

Fanny Macleay also mentioned the School of Industry when she wrote to her brother, William Sharp Macleay, in England. She was a reluctant, although long-serving, office bearer, who appears to have been dragooned into helping under the influence of Eliza Darling's position. Fanny complained of her involvement in the school to her brother on 21 April 1826:[12]

'Mrs Darling has instituted a School of Industry for young Girls and sorely against my good will has appointed me Treasurer & Secretary. I am very angry—Papa well pleased.'

When the school had been running in its permanent premises for about a month she wrote on 8 October 1826:[13]

'... my time is very fully occupied with our School already I begin to sicken at the thoughts of it—One has such wretches to deal with and the trouble seems endless—I wish they had a better Secretary with all my heart, then I might amuse myself a little.'

The next year Fanny had another unpleasant chore—preparing the committee's annual report. She wrote to her brother on 25 March 1827:[14]

'I have a job on hand which worries me—I, as Secretary of the School of Industry, have to draw up a report of our proceedings—I wish I could have your assistance Oh! how I wish I was clever in any way.'

Fund raising was a constant task for the committee running the school. On 28 April 1829 Fanny told her brother:[15]

'We are all quite well here and have been enjoying all kinds of gaities—Birth-night Balls, Races and *what nots* as for me I am half dead with fatigue for in a short space of a fortnight we had ball dresses to make up (and fancy or contrive, which was not the least annoying part of the business), a long report to draw up of the proceedings of the School of Industry, a thing I quite detest, and also pretty bagatelles to make for a Sale in aid of the School funds. That we were industrious, or rather that the Gentlemen were generous you will easily believe when I tell you that the Sale of Ladies work brought the Treasurer between 80 & 90 pounds! *Our* stall took the most money about 25 pds.'

With the Darlings soon to leave the colony, Fanny was still active on the school's behalf in 1831. She wrote on 27 April 1831:[16]

'I have been busy with my School Children who last week underwent a long examination by the Archdeacon and were much commended. I have been busy penning my *Report* and also in making little fancy works for our Annual Sale. This took place yesterday and how much do you suppose the Ladies obtained for their little, foolish trumpery—no less than 90 pounds—Is not this a charitable place?'

Frances Leonora (Fanny) Macleay, born in 1793, had arrived in Sydney in January 1826 just after Governor Darling's arrival, her father having been appointed Colonial Secretary. She was one of six unmarried daughters of Alexander and Eliza Macleay. The family immediately joined the small elite circle of people attached to Government House, Ralph and Eliza Darling and the Governor's brothers-in-law, William and Henry Dumaresq. The Darlings, at least in their early years in New South Wales (in contrast to the former governor, Sir Thomas Brisbane), enjoyed entertaining, and there was a round of dinners, suppers, dances, balls, races, regattas and family celebrations.

Fanny's mother, Eliza Macleay, saw New South Wales, with its numbers of eligible bachelors, as a promising society in which to launch her daughters. This suited some of the daughters, but not Fanny. She resented her mother's efforts to marry her to Sir John Jamison, often referred to as the 'wealthy knight of Regentville', and Eliza Darling's efforts to marry her to her brother, Henry Dumaresq. At the start she was an acute and caustic observer of Sydney society, critical of the obsession with making money, then she joined several evangelical and philanthropic societies, including the Female School of Industry. As her letters show, she was a somewhat reluctant helper in this activity.

Fanny's real interest was the environment. In London, unusually for a woman, she had taken an interest in natural history which was an absorbing passion of the male members of the Macleay family. She maintained her father's scientific collection and in New South Wales became the main assistant to him and to her brother William Sharp Macleay in collecting botanical and entomological specimens and in making drawings and paintings of them to send to England.[17]

At the age of 43, Fanny Macleay married Thomas Cudbert Harington, assistant to her father as Colonial Secretary. She died six weeks later.

The Female School of Industry was regarded as very successful and drew compliments from visitors. With a strong demand for places, Eliza Darling endeavoured to find additional accommodation in Sydney. In November 1828 she and her husband bought at their own expense a cottage at Parramatta which in July 1829 opened with four children; however, the Parramatta branch survived only until 1835. The Female School of Industry proved to be one of New South Wales's longest surviving charities. After existing for just over a century, it was absorbed by the Church of England Committee for Homes and Hostels for Children in 1927.

After her husband was recalled to England, Eliza Darling sailed from

Sydney with her family in October 1831 on the *Hoogly*. During the voyage she had another child, Charlotte Amelia, and her last child, Agnes, was born in England two years later. There she devoted her energies to the education of her children and later the careers of her sons and the marriages of her daughters. Eliza Darling died at Hartfield, East Sussex, on 3 September 1868 aged 66, leaving four daughters and three sons.

# 6
# Vice-regal duties

## Mary Putland

*They are all treated with the same politeness*

When William Bligh sailed for Sydney to take over the position of governor from Philip Gidley King, his eldest daughter, Mary, the wife of his aide Lieutenant John Putland, accompanied him. His wife and his other five daughters stayed in England, so Mary assumed the role of governor's lady. She and her father arrived in Sydney on 6 August 1806 to find the colony in great distress, partly due to disastrous floods in the Hawkesbury and partly because of the falling off in the arrival of convicts and stores. Bligh attempted some reforms, but his irascible temper soon made him extremely unpopular.

Mary, passionately and single-mindedly devoted to her father's interests, was well aware of the hostility towards him and the plotting behind his back. But her sense of duty demanded that she maintain the correct procedures in entertaining prominent citizens (including her father's enemies) to social occasions at Government House. Although she acted in a coldly correct manner, Mary Putland could be an implacable enemy.

In appearance, style and force of character she was one of the most striking women to live in colonial New South Wales, often dressing unconventionally in trousers rather than petticoats. To Ellis Bent, deputy judge advocate, she was 'conceited and affected' to a greater degree than any other woman he had ever seen, 'everything is studied about her—her walk—her talking—every thing'. According to Bent she had inherited her father's violent temper. She was 'extremely violent and

70

passionate', he wrote, repeating gossip that she had often flung plates or candlesticks at her father's head. Perhaps her main fault in Bent's eyes was that she was a woman who was 'very clever, & accomplished'.[1] An opponent of Governor Bligh's cause, Bent was a prejudiced observer.

The most interesting part of a letter Mary wrote to her mother on 10 October 1807,[2] fourteen months after her arrival in New South Wales, concerns her public role as her father's confidante and hostess. It also contains many expressions of her deep attachment to and interest in her family, and her worry about her husband's health. She wrote:

'Papa is quite well, but dreadfully harrassed by business & the trouble-some set of people he has to deal with, in general he gives great satis-faction but there are a few that we suspect wish to oppose him; as yet they have done nothing openly, tho' it is known their *Tools* have been at work some time; that is they are trying to find something in Papas conduct to write home upon, but which I am sure, from his great cir-cumspection they will not be able to do with honor to themselves. Mr. [John] McArthur is one of the party; the others are the Military Officers, but they are all invited to the house & treated with the same politeness as usual.

'I wish I could tell you that Putland is as well as my Father; since you last heard from us he has been continually ailing, & has had every symptom of a Consumption, for these two months past he has been confined to his room, but is now I trust in God gradually recovering: you may suppose he has required my whole attention & that except a dinner party now & then of eight or ten persons, we have not had any— In May Papa sent him to Norfolk Island as a sea passage was much recommended but it was not of any service to him his Surgeon is a clever man & tells me I need not make myself at all uneasy, therefore I beg my dear Mama you will not do either; before my next I trust he will be much recovered . . .

'I cannot express how much we were delighted with Betsey's Picture; we think it the strongest likeness that can possibly be taken & the Drawing beautifully done: we can never repay & convey the pleasure it has given us. It is a long time since we have had any arrival from England or India, the Colony is in great distress for articles from the latter country; but nothing would do my spirits as much good just now as letters from you my dear Mama & another Picture—Putland joins with me in affec. love to you, my dear sisters, & Henry, a letter from Papa will accompany this, so I need not say more for him than that it is astonish-ing to me how he gets through the multiplicity of business he does without impairing his health—That this may find you all in health & happiness.'

Mary's husband, John Putland, died on 4 January 1808. In the same month, Bligh was arrested by rebel officers of the New South Wales Corps and remained in confinement in Sydney, apart from a period spent in Van Diemen's Land, until he eventually sailed for England on 12 May 1810. Mary, who remained devoted to her father and his cause, intended to accompany him, but a few days before his ship sailed, she married the Lieutenant Governor, Lieutenant Colonel Maurice O'Connell, who had arrived with Governor Macquarie in December 1809.

Mary left New South Wales in 1814 when O'Connell's regiment was sent to Ceylon. They returned to Sydney in 1838 after O'Connell, by then major-general and a knight, had been appointed to the command of the forces. O'Connell was administrator of New South Wales for a short period in 1846 between the departure of Governor Gipps and the arrival of Governor Fitzroy. He died in Sydney in 1848 just as he was about to sail for England. Mary, the mother of two sons and a daughter, lived in Paris for some years and then in London, where she died in 1864.

## Elizabeth Macquarie

*We spoke of the extraordinary events in New South Wales*

Two years after 29-year-old Elizabeth Henrietta Campbell of Airds, Scotland, married her distant kinsman, Lachlan Macquarie, in 1807 as his second wife, her husband was appointed to take over the governorship of New South Wales from the deposed Governor William Bligh.

During the voyage to New South Wales on the *Dromedary*, Elizabeth Macquarie kept a journal, as did so many other travellers including other vice-regal ladies. Extracts from her journal indicate her observant nature and her interest in events, particularly her concern about the situation her husband would find in New South Wales following the rebellion against Bligh. She was to remain interested and took an active role throughout his governorship.

During the voyage of over six months, the Macquaries were anxious for any news of the situation they would find in New South Wales. When they reached Rio de Janeiro, they were relieved to find that Lieutenant Colonel George Johnston, who had led the rebellion against Governor Bligh, had passed through the port only four days previously on his way to England to answer charges. Two of Johnston's party, Surgeon General Dr Thomas Jamison and Dr John Harris, stayed on at Rio; from them the Macquaries heard news of events in New South Wales. Elizabeth recorded their meeting in her journal:[3]

'It may naturally be supposed that the causes for our being sent on this unexpected service, & the probable state we should find the Colony in, was very frequently the subject of conversation; we had the smallest expectation of obtaining any information regarding the state of things till our arrival at the Cape, & even then it was very doubtful that we should; but to our surprise found that Col. Johnson [Johnston] Mr Macarthur Drs Jamison and Harris, had arrived at Rio shortly before us . . .

'We had a good deal of conversation with Dr Jamison regarding the extraordinary events which had taken place in New South Wales, and it appeared to us that *even by their own account* the conduct of those persons who had acted against the Government was not to be justified or even excused; we felt sorry that a man such as Col. Johnson was described to us, should have committed himself as he has done, by an act of the most open and daring rebellion, by which in as far as it appears to us, he will probably forfeit a life, which has till this unfortunate period, been spent in the service of his King and Country.

'Colonel Macquarie has felt it quite a relief to him, his having quitted the Colony before his arrival, and by that means having spared him the pain of taking measures which the service required, but which no officer could feel easy at being obliged to have recourse to, particularly on this occasion; Col. Johnson being a man of amiable character, and in their early years an intimate companion of his own . . . '

When the Macquaries arrived in New South Wales at the end of 1809, they found the colony torn by factions. Some of the policies Macquarie adopted, especially that favouring emancipists, were controversial. Throughout, Elizabeth supported him and took a great interest in many aspects of colonial society, including the welfare of women convicts and Aborigines and the planning and building of Sydney. She had brought with her from England a collection of books on architecture which her husband and his architect Francis Greenway used in the design of buildings in Sydney. Elizabeth herself planned the road running around the inside of the Government Domain to the point which, like the road, was named after her.

Elizabeth accompanied her husband on several arduous journeys. In 1811 they went to Van Diemen's Land and in 1815 they travelled over the newly crossed Blue Mountains. In 1818 she accompanied her husband to the Hunter in a brig named after her, the *Elizabeth Henrietta.*

It is unfortunate that the few letters of Elizabeth Macquarie that have survived are family letters concerned with family matters and tell little of her life in New South Wales. The most intense emotion expressed in them concerns her love for and pride in her young son. Her first child, a daughter named Jane, had died a few months after her birth in 1808.

In 1814, to the great joy of both parents, a son, Lachlan, was born in Sydney. In one letter Elizabeth expresses a mother's pride that her son, then only just a few days past his third birthday, knew his 'letters'. She wrote to her niece, Mary Maclaine of Lochbuy, on 7 April 1817 from Sydney:[4]

'. . . as you do me the favour to ask for a lock of Lachlan's hair I have great pleasure in sending it and also a little sketch of his face which though by no means well done serves to give an idea of him . . .

'I hope you employ the spare time which you must now have in the improvement of your music there is not a day I have in which I do not envy the idle time I passed at your time of life nothing can be more true than that youth is the season of improvement for at an after period of life we are generally as much engaged in the necessary occupations of life as to render it impossible to devote much time to any other subject . . .

'Little Lachlan has this moment come from school and delighted me more than you can think by pointing out a great many of his letters . . .'

The Macquaries left New South Wales early in 1822 to make their home at Macquarie's estate on the Scottish island of Mull. When Macquarie took ill during a visit to London in 1824 Elizabeth hastened there and was with him when he died. Elizabeth Macquarie died at Jarvisfield, Mull, on 11 March 1835.

## Anne Bourke

*There is a spirit of equality and independence here*

Anne Maria Bourke, a daughter of the newly appointed governor Sir Richard Bourke, arrived in Sydney on the *Margaret* on 3 December 1831. During the voyage, Anne's mother, Elizabeth Bourke, became ill and nearly died; there were also many other problems common to sea voyages. Like some other vice-regal ladies, including Anna Josepha King and Elizabeth Macquarie, Anne Bourke kept a diary of this uncomfortable and distressing voyage; fortunately she continued her diary for a short time after the vice-regal family landed in Sydney.

Although imperviously upper class, with a superior attitude, Anne's diary has freshness and charm. Some of her views are naive, but in things that mattered—for instance, in judging the temper and outlook of the inhabitants of Sydney—she was a wise observer.

Anne Bourke was born in the mid-1800s into a family that had been part of the Irish Protestant ascendancy for some generations. She grew up at the Bourke family estate, Thornhill, in County Limerick, and accompanied her parents to the Cape of Good Hope where her father was Governor from 1825 to 1828. With her mother's health uncertain and her eldest sister, Mary Jane, married and settled in England, she again accompanied her parents when her father was appointed Governor of New South Wales, expecting that she would substitute on occasions for her mother as hostess at Government House.

Her diary contains lengthy descriptions of Sydney, particularly Government House and its immediate surroundings, and there are also long accounts of the climate. These first impressions are very interesting, but these extracts have been chosen with an emphasis on her comments on people and society rather than the more descriptive sections. The diary is in the form of a diary/letter written to her younger sister, addressed as 'dearest Fanny'.[5]

'*6th December*
'Government House . . . Papa landed at twelve, with the usual ceremonies of guns and cheering and bands playing and soldiers marching, the commission was read in the veranda and then a levy. Last night the town was very handsomely illuminated with every manner of rockets, squibs, guns from the batteries and ships, the *Margaret's* were really quite fine, and an immense bonfire was lighted . . . which gave a beautiful effect to the shipping, the cheering was tremendous. The staff (wives and all) had a holiday and stayed at their hotel, only Mr. Innis and Dr. Stevenson dined with us, however after dinner as we were standing in the veranda, they all walked up together and we drank tea out of doors, the effect was very good, the evening was so sultry, and to add to the scene the lightning was beyond any thing I ever saw . . . We sat up till eleven the fireworks were kept up the greater part of the night. Today is hotter than I ever felt it at the Cape, it is like a fiery furnace out of doors. We went to church last Sunday, Mrs McLeay sent her carriage for me, it is a very large church and our pew is very large and comfortable, it held the whole staff, including Mr. Innis who is at present Papa's chaplain, he comes every morning to read prayers and breakfasts with us. Archdeacon Broughton preached us a tolerably good sermon—St. James' is the church, it has a good organ and very good singers.

'*8th [December]*
'I have been very busy unpacking these two days, tho' we have not got half the things from the ship yet. We experienced the day before yesterday the only disagreeable part of this climate which is the hot northwest wind, it blew with great force for about 5 hours, during which time the heat was insufferable, I never felt any thing like it at the Cape nor has Capt. W. at the Mauritius . . . My piano forte is very well thank you, the master of the 17th Band is now tuning it, I shall have all the

evening to tune myself up, as Papa and staff including Mr. Innis and Dr. Stevenson, dine at the mess of the 39th Regt. commanded by Col. Lindsey. Dick was gazetted today to be private secretary by command of his Excellency. A great number of ladies have left their cards, more than I thought were in the colony, I have not seen any of them. Mama does not yet come down stairs, she is I hope getting stronger but very slowly . . . Every place Mr. Innis goes to they ask him so many questions about me, whether I am fond of gaiety, and whether I dance, and all manner of questions, which he together with his answers tells me every morning . . .

' *10th [December]*

'I am today established in my room and have unpacked most of the things, fancy the wet getting thro' the tin cases to our dresses, however we have escaped tolerably well, my satin slip is quite dished and one of my gowns a little, we are fortunate it is no worse, we reckoned the *Margaret* a dry ship but we find that there is hardly a box that is not more or less touched by salt water, the only thing really injured is the chariot, the linen what with water and cockroaches is completely in tatters, there being no lining silk in the colony it is relined with cloth, which will be very hot . . . The town is, I hear, very bad, but only saw George Street which is wide and has some very good shops. Our two nearest neighbours are Mr. McLeay, the colonial secretary, and Mr. Chief Justice Forbes, they have houses just outside the entrance gate which formerly belonged to the Government. They are both very civil and send to know how Mama is every day, we have not seen the ladies of the family yet. The Westmacotts have got a cottage in the grounds which belonged to Col. Dumaresq and family . . . [The newspapers] give [Governor Bourke] a great number of hints in the papers, indeed I should say instructions as to his behaviour, pointing out the faults of Genl. Darling all good points of Governors Macquarie and Brisbane. They beg he will spend his income in the colony like a Prince and show himself about the town, and not shut himself up as his predecessor did and save money (as they elegantly express it) "to the tune of 20,000£" whilst he was here. I very much doubt any body's saving that sum in six years, out of five thousand a year—everything is very dear except just the bare necessaries of meat and bread and I believe they are cheap. You know how I hate the liberty of the press and it is most terribly free here.

' *14th [December]*

'A ship came in this morning, the *Bussorah merchant* from Dublin, she brings out our solicitor general, and a great many convicts, amongst others that horrible Mr. Luke Dillon, what a creature to have in the same colony as one . . .

*'19th [December]*
'We had a little petit dinner party yesterday consisting of Colonel Lindsey and a Mr. Therry, who is Commissioner of the court of Enquiry, Watty of course and his wife. The two strangers are both agreeable people, Colonel Lindsey is very like old Hal in manner and face, he is an old bachelor, and the commandant here. Mrs. W. begins to *stick out* very much, but she behaved very well, I believe she is afraid of Dick and me, she sees we laugh at people so much. Of course I sung, and of course they said such singing was never heard in the colony before, there are very few if any singers here, but a good many ladies play the harp and pianoforte very well . . . I get up at six o'clock every morning they are so heavenly, at first I tried going out, but I found it had the usual effect of knocking me up for the remainder of the day, besides giving me such a weakness in my back as almost to prevent my walking across the room. I applied to Dr. Stevenson and he made me leave off walking and told me to drink a double allowance of port wine, which has restored me entirely to my usual vulgar health, and I have appropriated the hours to practising as I am not then interrupted till breakfast, after that you are as well to be in the streets as in the drawing room, the veranda is a complete thoroughfare to Papa's room, and they generally stray into the drawing room.

*'23rd [December]*
'We cannot drive out today, as it is blowing what they call here a *brick fielder*, a strong wind which blowing over some very large brick fields to the back of the town, brings such a terrible deal of brick dust with it as to darken every object in the town, it generally blows after a hot northwest wind, which we experienced a little last night. Much worse than a southeaster. That I have seen of the place I like very much, the people I cannot speak about not having seen any of them.

*'27th [December]*
'Yesterday some of the Sydney gentlemen came to present an address to the Governor to congratulate him on having assumed the government, in this address they had the bad taste to mix up a little abuse of Mr. McLeay the colonial secretary, who having been the adviser and friend of Genl. Darling is very unpopular. Papa plainly shewed them in his answer that he did not like it, and hoped there would be no party spirit shewn for the future. These people will certainly be very much harder to manage than the Dutch, they are not half so tractable, and there is a spirit of equality and independence amongst them which I should think will require a great deal of delicacy to manage. We had yesterday Chief Justice Forbes and Mr. McLeay, two or three more men to dinner, the former is a tremendous talker but very agreeable, Mr.

McLeay is only famous for the immense size of his legs, which Capt. Hunter and I nearly died of yesterday, we laughed so much at them.'

Within six months of their arrival in Sydney, Anne's mother had died and Anne assumed the role of the governor's hostess. During his term as governor, Bourke made journeys far and wide and Anne accompanied him on some of these. Late in 1832 she went west with him over the Blue Mountains to Bathurst, one day riding 15 miles before breakfast.

On 18 September 1833 Anne married Scottish-born Edward Deas Thomson who had been in Sydney since 1829 when he took up the appointment of clerk to the Executive and Legislative Councils.

Edward Deas Thomson succeeded Alexander Macleay as colonial secretary in 1837. For the next forty years, at first in this role and later as a parliamentarian and a leading supporter of many public institutions including the University of Sydney, he was a prominent figure in New South Wales public life. Anne, who had approached Sydney with some wariness in 1831, accepted the colony as her home after her marriage. When Edward Deas Thomson died in 1879 she was still alive, the mother of five daughters and three sons, several of whom had married into old colonial families, including the Campbells and Lawsons.

## Maria Gawler

*We are still sleeping in tents and marquees*

Even a governor's wife shared with more lowly immigrants the discomforts of a new settlement in the early years in South Australia. When Maria Gawler landed in the Colony on 12 October 1838, as the wife of the newly appointed Governor, she, her husband and their five children moved not into an official Government House, but into tents.

Maria, born in Derby, England, had married George Gawler, an Army officer, with whom she shared a devotion to evangelical Christianity, in 1820. Only five of their twelve children survived childhood.

A few months after arriving in Adelaide on 12 October 1838 on the *Pestonjee Bomanjee*, Maria Gawler wrote to her sister, addressed as 'My beloved Mary Anne', on 7 December 1838:[6]

'I shall most anxiously look for letters from Britain bearing glad tidings of your welfare. The distance between us is indeed depressingly great and to reflect on the probabilities and possibilities of the non-arrival of our letters is discouraging I allow—but that must not deter us from writing to each other; on the contrary, let us take every opportunity. Our general opportunities of sending letters are via Van Diemen's Land, for it is not once in six months that a vessel leaves this for England direct.

'If we could get you here without having to undergo the discomforts of a voyage I feel sure you would all be delighted with the country—a migration of capitalists is exceedingly wanted. Provisions are exceptionally dear and money as scarce . . .

'We are still sleeping in tents and marquees. Our new house will be very commodious—we are having our domain walled in and a well dug. Our present thatched mud cottage is very pleasantly situated fronting the River Torrens. I shall try and send a plan of our intended future residence and a sketch of our present . . .

'The land here is very dry and the grass parched, but in the Mount Lofty Range all agree that it is magnificent. My husband and Mr. Hall rode to the top of Mount Lofty the other day and returned quite delighted. They say we can judge nothing of the beauty either of country and scenery here—that about us is just like a nobleman's park nicely wooded and there is nothing in the scene to remind one that we are so far from our native land—we shall have some cows as our ground is railed in—at present we pay 8d. per quart for milk.

'The Captain of the *Lloyds* made me a present of a couple of ducks and a couple of fowls—valuable here—the former £1 a piece and the latter 11/-, eggs 4d. each. Tell dear Mrs. Henry with my love that I hope she will send me a dress and bonnet and cap each year such as she thinks suitable for a Governor's wife—the sun is very powerful, and she must consider that in her choice of colours and let either Miss Cox or Mrs. Beeland be employed to make them . . .

'I have not any brown sewing silk to mend my brown silk dress. I wish, therefore, my friends would recollect one in the way of different coloured sewing silks and beg our friends to muster some old clothing for the Aborigines. The most common print here is 1/- per yard. Send also some gauze cap ribbons. Only think that we are scorched with heat while perhaps you are freezing with cold. This climate is not one which pleases me. The air is mild and balmy, and we are told most healthy. It is not to be depended on—hot and cold—hot winds and dust smother oneself, furniture and victuals in an instant. The hot winds are as though putting your face to the mouth of a baker's oven . . . '

In South Australia, Maria and George Gawler interested themselves, as they had done in England, in establishing Sunday and infant schools and in charitable work, particularly among the migrants in the immigration depot, which Maria visited regularly. She returned to England with her family when her husband was recalled in 1841.

# 7
# *Political observer*

**Christiana Brooks**

*We want the rights of British subjects*

The diary Christiana Brooks kept from 1825 to 1829 is quite unlike most other diaries kept by women in early Australia. It records the events of government, the state of the colonial economy, her opinions of the governor and of various public servants, the advent of newspapers, her opinions about the Aborigines and many other subjects generally assumed to have been the province of men in the early nineteenth century. All her comments are recorded in an authoritative style.

Christiana Brooks was a close observer of events of government and a woman with definite opinions. Unlike many of her female contemporaries, who deferred to the opinions of their husbands, she was confident in her own views about how the governor, administrators and public servants should act. Family and social events are recorded sparingly in her diary. When they are mentioned, it is in the same detached style. Her daughter's wedding is recorded as it would be in a newspaper announcement, without emotion or embellishment.

Her comments, while opinionated, are usually judicious. For instance, when reporting measures taken to suppress attacks by Aborigines, she blames not these 'poor simple creatures' but the stockmen who assault the Aboriginal women, and the advance of European occupation. They had been 'deprived by the invasion of strangers, of both food and raiment', she wrote.

Christiana Brooks may have kept a diary from the time she arrived in

New South Wales in 1814, but if so the early volumes have not survived. What has been preserved is a diary she kept from 29 June 1825 to 31 December 1829. She was by then a mature woman, probably aged in her middle forties, the wife of Captain Richard Brooks and the mother of six daughters and a son.

She was born Christiana Passmore, the daughter of an East India Company sea captain. Her husband was also a sea captain, who had made several voyages to Australia, both as a captain of convict ships and as a trader, before deciding to settle in New South Wales. Christiana and six children accompanied him on the *Spring*, which arrived in Sydney on 8 March 1814. He exchanged the brig for a house at the corner of Pitt and Hunter Streets and, with the cargo, set up in business as a merchant. There Christiana had her seventh and last child.

In 1823 they moved to Denham Court, a property near Liverpool, where they built a beautiful house that became famous for its hospitality. Their six daughters made 'good marriages', most into prominent colonial families. At the time Christiana's diary began, her eldest daughter, Christiana Jane, was married to Lieutenant Thomas Valentine Blomfield and living at Dagworth on the Hunter. In 1827, during the course of the diary, her third daughter, Jane Maria, married Edward Cox of Mulgoa, a son of pioneer landowner William Cox. Later Mary Honoria married Lieutenant William Wilson, Honoria Rose married William Edward Riley of Raby, Maria married Lieutenant Henry Zouch and Charlotte Sophia married Nathaniel Stephen Powell of Turalla, Bungendore.

Although only extracts, the following entries show something of the richness of Christiana Brooks's diary.[1] She had comments on all subjects from bushrangers, social conditions, banking, concerts in Sydney, the Female School of Industry and epidemics to the price of leghorn bonnets and the state of agriculture. The opening section of these extracts begins with the arrival of General Ralph Darling on 17 December 1825 to take over as Governor of New South Wales. She held great expectations for the rule of General Darling and only gradually accepted that some of his actions were not popular and reluctantly expressed criticism.

*'Dec. 1825*
'On the 14 inst. I visited Sydney and did not return till the 21—as this was in itself a great event so great events might be expected, and General Darling's arrival on the 17th may be recorded as an era of some importance to the Colony of N. S. Wales. His Excellency was sworn in on 19, and on the 20th he landed publicly, and was attended with all due honours.—We *hope* great things from the administration of General D who is represented as being firm and impartial, just and determined; a character which if he merits is just what we need in a Governor.

'There are many changes about to take place in this Colony, and in our sister settlement of Van Diemens' Land. This is very encouraging to us as it shews we are increasing in importance as "a promising append-age to the British Territory's in the East".

'There is some change in the Members of Council and some additions under the denomination of an *Executive* Council. This is *all* we need at present. I would have the Governor *Supreme*, assisted and advised by his Council, but having a will of his own, I would also have *three* members . . . A Council chosen annually, by which change every party would be likely to have friends in the administration nothing can be better chosen than the present members—the head of the Law, of the Church, of the State and of the Mercantile and Landed interests—we ought to be con-tented, and I trust we shall have reason to be so.

*'Dec. 25*
'Christmas is always a time much to be dreaded in this country by the sober and well inclined. Drunken husbands distress their peacably dis-posed wives: and well disposed men have to lament the riotous dis-positions of their mates who cannot resist temptation which these holidays hold forth to jollity and intoxication.

*'Dec. 26*
'The Lieut. Governor had a short reign,[2] he seems inclined to be *the* Governor and has distinguished his brief administration by the establish-ment of a Post Office, and a regular Post throughout the territory, for which a General Order has been issued under his direction, and with the advice of senior members of Council.

*'January 7th 1826*
'The festivities of the season commenced at Denham Court on the second inst. (the first being on Sunday) and were kept up with great spirit by a party of sixteen from Sydney who were met here by all our country neighbours.—On Monday we set down at dinner forty in number—sixteen of whom were accommodated with beds in the house, besides fifteen servants in the kitchen and out houses . . .

*'Jany 10*
'The new Colonial Secretary[3] has arrived, and Major Goulburn has given up to him the cares and duties of an office of great responsibility during the later administration.—

'Nothing can promise more favourably than the energy with which General Darling has commenced his Government—that he is a man of *business* we have every reason to believe, and that he will cause "everyman to do his duty" we may be allowed to anticipate from the prompt government orders for the reorganization of the several Public Departments.

*Jany 26*

'I don't know how some of our great men will relish the late General Orders, but I imagine many of them will be quite unprepared to comply with them . . .

'During the Administration of Sir T B everything was left to the *Heads* of *Department*, but when the murmur of discontent rose at the inefficient measures adopted, these *petty sovereigns* would willingly have shifted the burden from their own shoulders.—General D if I mistake not will be *Governor* in *Chief*, and the Heads of Departments will no longer be allowed to consider themselves as so many Heads of the Colony, whether they be the *Accreditted Agents of the British Government* "or the trusty and well beloved of George the Fourth", or our own Kings' own *"Visitors"* all will find themselves subjected to the power of Major General *Ralph* Darling etc. etc. I confess for my part I would prefer one Tyrant if needs must, to half a score petty usurpers.—

*Feby 20th*

'The Governor has begun by giving dinner parties to about 20 persons, and seems inclined to be sociable with the better part of the inhabitants: It is said Mrs D is rather gay and is fond of dancing—the young folks *will have reason* to rejoice should anything like the old times in Governor Macquarie's day be revived.

*March 5*

'This is the anniversary of our landing in this Colony, and 12 years has made such an alteration in everything here that a comparison would be very amusing, say, "Sydney in the year 1816", and "Sydney in the year 1826", or we will take a less period and say 1817—the year which the Bank of N. S. Wales[4] was established: by the end of this year it is believed there will be *three* Banks, *three* newspapers and *three* steam engines—Bob Howe[5] says ADVANCE AUSTRALIA but this is advancing with rapid strides.

*March*

'The Governor's Orders appear to be issued without respect to persons, the highest in office, or the meanest subordinate appear to be equally called upon, equally required to do their duty. I for my part admire the prompt measures of General Darling, he requires of every man to do his duty as it is pointed out to him: *he* does not *need* any person to tell him what is necessary but appears to be a man of business equally for arranging and carrying into execution.—

*'March 15*

'The inhabitants of the country are once more restored to a state of security by the Execution of some, and the capture of almost all that desperate hords of bushrangers which have for many months been the scourge of the country—the efficient and prompt measures adopted by General D on this occasion will lend much to keep alive that respect and veneration for his character which already begin to manifest themselves toward him as Governor.

*'March*

'The School of Industry patronised by Mrs D seems better adapted in its plans as a system for the Orphan Institution, and could be carried with effect without any additional subscription—a plan of so much utility in a new Colony like this as "A School for the Education of Female Servants" will however not want support, I feel convinced, while the Ladies are only called upon for their *one pound one*, and a little of their time, and attention, and whence their names are associated in the same list with those of the polished, the feeling, the benevolent, and the conscientious Mrs A Mrs B Mrs C Mrs D and altho I entertain little hope that in the *present generation* it will be of much service while the population continues as about [?] male to one female, yet as the girls will be *taught* to do something useful, they may transmit their knowledge to their offspring and in time become a superior race to those who lounge over the shop doors in Sydney: A *half* dressed or *over* dressed generation—who seem born for no other purpose but to gossip with their male acquaintances.—

*'April 6th*

'We are beginning to have the *Australian* newspaper now regularly twice a week,[6] and it is expected the newspaper called the *Monitor*[7] will shortly make its appearance. I hope it will be a weekly paper—while we had but one "*Howes Weekly Gazette*" we looked for it with great avidity, when two of each weekly papers appeared we read them with great interest, but now we have four each week they frequently lay on the table for days without being perused. I indeed have lost all feeling of interests in the *Australian* since W has withdrawn his name as Editor.[8]

*'April 20*

'We have had almost incessant rain for ten days past, and the roads are nearly impassable, this is a great disappointment to us country folk who have invitations to Government House on 26th inst. and had the weather been favourable it would without doubt have been one of the most crowded partys ever witnessed in this Country—every person of respectability is asked, and all would be anxious to show their loyalty by taking their bow at Government House, not only in honour of His Majesty's Birthday, but to make Courtesys to His Excellency, who is known to be a great stickler for all the forms of Etiquette, of which he is a perfect pattern in his own conduct, never sparing himself where any *duty* demands his *time*, his *ear* or his *eye*.

*'May 12*
'The Aborigines Natives having assembled in unusual numbers in the County of Argyle in the neighbourhood of Lake George, and having evinced some hostility to the stock keepers of particular stations, the Govr. in his usual prompt manner has despatched a Detachment of the 40th and 57th Regts., with instructions to the Officers in Command to put themselves in communication with the Magistrates of that district. This hostility on the part of the Natives will I have no doubt be found, as it ever has been, to originate in outrages committed on them by the stock keepers, an ignorant and brutal race, who by their interference with the females of the aborigines provoke them to revenge—The Governor's Order upon this occasion is humane and liberal, promising equal justice to all. I doubt not the sight of *soldiers* will strike a panic in these poor simple creatures, and the Officer in Command is a man of experience, who will fully investigate the cause of their present hostility, and should he find that the stockmen and shepherds have committed any violence, or ill treated any of these inoffensive creatures, he will I earnestly hope, bring them forward that they may receive the punishment due to their cruelty.

*'May 19th*
'There are ARCH FIENDS in this place who seek to ruin all in which they are not themselves concerned—the Bank of N. S. Wales has been placed in rather a tottering state by the machinations of those enemys to mankind, but the *Champion* of *Australia* has been a match for them, and the impartiality of Government in rendering the Bank prompt assistance has averted for the present the evil apprehended. The *Directors* will, or ought, to learn prudence. They MUST limit their discounts, or we shall not have a Dollar left in the Country.

*'May 24*
'The new Journal the *MONITOR* made its appearance on the 19th, it appears moderate in its policies but from my own knowledge of the Editor, I know which side he is likely to enlist upon, and it is worthy of remark that the Aristocratic party have no advocates in our journalists— a symptom that this party is not very popular—There was a rumour some months ago of a newspaper to be Edited by a *certain great man*,

and supported by his partisans, nor do I believe the idea is altogether abandoned.

*'May 30th*
'The Council, it would seem, by a General Order in this weeks Gazette, are quite tired of the applications for *female servants* being addressed to them, and it is now simply specified that families who are in want of female servants may be supplied from the prisoners lately arrived in the Ship *Lady Rowena* describing what sort of servants are wanted, and which application is to be addressed in writing to the Principal Superintendant of Convicts.

*June 9th*
'The first Amateur Concert on the 7th was as well attended as could reasonably be expected considering it was not *set on foot* by the quality of Sydney; but as this is an amusement in which taste and science are combined, there is every hope it will be patronised *by those who give the tone* to fashion. The Subscription list has been augmented by one or two names of great respectability whose families, it is said, intend honouring the next Concert which is fixed for the 21st.

*June 21*
'. . . I had promised to visit the Infant School to see the Gas Light introduced into the Colony by a man named Wilson, and which altho on a small scale at present, is capable of being extended, if he meets with encouragement. I also wished to see the inside of the Scotch Church, which I am told is a very neat and commodious place of Worship, and is to be opened for Public Service very soon, it is a pretty plain but substantial building, and has a most beautiful and commanding situation.

*July 29*
'Much as our present Governor is to be admired for his energy and decision of character, yet there has arisen some discontent lately among the newly arrived emigrants for hitherto General D has not given a single Grant of Land, and consequently those settlers who arrived in the beginning of the year are seeing their finances daily diminish without an immediate prospect of getting on a Farm of their own—It is an old saying "While the grass grows the stead starves". Thus while *Commissioners* are *preparing* to start in order to *locate* and value the lands— while the members of the *Land Board* are suggesting the best method to apportion grants etc. etc. a poor man with a family, or a young man with little property, is hanging on in expectations of what, when he gets it, he will have no means left to stock, or cultivate. (a farm)
'This very serious grievance should be represented to the Governor,

for he is possibly ignorant how much this delay costs those who suffer by it.

'The Chamber of Commerce (a new institution) will be likely to benefit the Colony very materially, the members being respectable, wealthy and effective, and for the most part free of that *party spirit* which rages, and has always raged, in this community.

'Sept. 10th

'I do not quite agree with the *Monitor* this week in thinking a person with a capital of 750£ can do better for his family by "Renting a farm in England or Scotland" than by getting the Grant of one here because, tho' in the present time the poor settler may have some difficulty to contend with, it is next to impossible they can endure, besides with all the disabilities, the industrious cultivator has many advantages in emigrating here he would look in vain for in almost every other part of the world—The climate and the soil are good—fuel and provisions are cheap and plentiful: and a habitation however simple in construction, is sufficient to shelter him from the effects of heat and cold, and above all, his family will learn from their neighbours to do without any of those things which are *at home* reckoned necessarys, but which, in fact, are not essential to his happiness.

'I know some families who are now, and have been for the last 18 months, living on their grant of land in tents: They are indeed poor, but they are healthy, contented and cheerful: they have HOPE for their prospects, and INDEPENDENCE for their COMFORT, and when they die, what they have lived upon themselves, will descend to their children, and the same HOPES and the same INDEPENDENCE will be a legacy that pays no DUTY.

'Sept. 18th

'The Aborigines Natives both at Hunters River and in the New Country (Argyle) are still very hostile: several murders have been of late committed by them in the former District, and altho the Mounted Police have been actively engaged in pursuit of them, and have in those affrays shot two or three, yet they seem so far from being intimidated that they become daily more and more daring . . . things indeed now have gone so far that something decisive must be done to stop the progress of this evil, or the Stockmen and shepherds will not readily be persuaded to remain at the distant settlements while exposed to the animosity of a set of untutored savages. As these Natives have never before been known to proceed to such extremeties, there is reason to think some MOTIVE must exist for their present warfare, which if possible should be ascertained, and if six or eight of them could be brought in as prisoners, it is likely we should become acquainted with the cause of their animosity, and probably find it easy of remedy: perhaps our people have been the first aggressors, or possibly want of food may drive them to desperate measures, for it is a fact well known that wherever our stockmen abide, the Kangaroos and Opossums disappear, our dogs destroying them; and thus being driven from the coast, and this usual sustenance destroyed, it is no small evil to these poor simple creatures to be deprived by the invasion of strangers, of both food and rainment.

'*Sept. 29th*
'Bushranging in all its atrocity seems still to prevail instead of being subdued by the numerous executions that have taken place during the last six or eight months, and Housebreaking and Street Robbery was never so frequent in Sydney as during the winter—many reasons are assigned for this, but none of them satisfactorily account for it, as upon all hands it is agreed our Police was never better.

'General Darling with all the energy of a powerful mind constantly engaged for the welfare and good government of this people, has not on all occasions shown himself infallible—One error which he has committed which is likely to be an abiding evil: Whoever could persuade His Excellency to bring two hundred of such abandoned bad characters from Port Macquarie might be a friend to humanity but could have *thought* little about the effect likely to be produced: These men for the most part are notoriously of the worst description, and therefore, if indeed the Prison population were not sufficient to supply the demand for labour, the best that could have been done for the security of the Colonists would have been to work them in Ironed Gangs, till they had given some warranty of their good behaviour.

'*Nov. 20*
'The delightful rain of yesterday has made everything in the country look refreshed and beautiful: hope may now be entertained that the Epidemic Catarrh which has prevailed in the Colony for the last three weeks or a month will abate—this disorder which is indeed an influenza prevailed to a similar degree about six years ago, it then, as it has now, carried off some of the old inhabitants of the Colony: the population being now much larger, a greater number of Deaths have taken place. I think I have observed that it has been felt most severely by the native born youth of both sex, but there has been few, if any, deaths from this cause among them—those who have died (about 30) have been old persons with worn out constitutions.'

In the next extract, Christiana Brooks comments on the actions of Governor Darling towards Joseph Sudds and Patrick Thompson, privates in the 57th Regiment who deliberately committed theft, hoping to be discharged in New South Wales. Determined to deter others from this course, Darling made an example of them by changing their sentence of transportation for seven years to seven years' hard labour in the chain gangs. At a parade on 22 November 1826 the two privates, dressed in felons' clothes with iron collars attached by chains to leg irons, were drummed out of the regiment. Sudds died five days later. Darling's action in varying the sentence of the court was found to be illegal and he was ordered from London to release Thompson. Christiana Brooks remained an apologist for the Governor.

'Dec. 26

'For my own part I have never had but one opinion, which is that the Govr. will be able to justify his motives to the satisfaction of the British Government, just as I do not believe G D acted upon his own ideas only in a matter in which the military men were competent judges: secondly I believe he wished to strike terror into the soldiers comprising the Regiment, in Garrison, and that the irons put on the Prisoner were intended only to be used until he was fairly out of sight of his brother soldiers. If indeed G D had refused to attend to the representations made by the surgeon or surgeons "that Sudds was not in a state of health to bear the irons or undergo the whole punishment" then indeed he would merit the stigma thrown on his character, but we do not hear that any such representations was made, neither do we hear that the Judges or Attorney General made any remonstrance as to the illegality of the sentence, it is said Sudds was in a dropsy before any part of his sentence was carried into execution. What were the Surgeons about that they did not interfere—I do not deny however that the man died of a *broken heart* but whether such death can be attributed to the harshness of the sentence or to the man's own acute feelings I leave the *hair splitting* Dr W to convince the public.

'That G D is unpopular as a Governor is very true, but it is equally true that all the Governors who have gone before were as unpopular, and with less reason, for altho' G D has neither the [faith?] of Governor Mc or of Sir T B, he is as obstinate as the former, and not so easy and mild as the latter, and moreover he *makes every man do his duty* and I should not hestitate to take a wager that G D will remain as Governor for the next *Eleven Years*.

'Dec. 27

'A most daring robbery was committed almost at our very gate on Saturday evening, a Gentleman going on a visit to a near neighbour of ours, was stopped by two bushrangers who seized the bridle of his horse, but having extricated himself from their grasp, was fired at, the bullet of a Musquit entered the back of his neck behind one of the ears, and came out above the cheek below the eye—believing him to be dead they dragged him into a ditch, and relieved him of his watch and money—he was found in the morning quite insensible, and is now lying dangerously ill at the house of his friend, the great loss of blood he has suffered, and the coolness of the weather, are however favourable. Two suspicious persons have been brought into Liverpool this morning and it is greatly to be hoped if these are not actually the men who committed the atrocious deed, that their detention may lead to that of the gang to which they belong. The Governor with great promptitude came in person to Liverpool to enquire into all the circumstances, and has ordered an additional party of Mounted Patrols on duty in this neighbourhood.

*'Jany First 1827*
'The first daily newspaper has made its appearance this day.[9]

*'Jan 28th*
'On the 39th anniversary of the foundation of the Colony (Jany. 26th) a Public Meeting of all the free inhabitants of N.S. Wales was convened by the Sheriff for the purpose of petitioning the King and both Houses of Parliament, that Trial by Jury, and a House of Assembly be allowed in this Colony; the meeting was numerously and respectably attended, "The Hero of Australia" (one of her sons)[10] spoke at great length, and as a test that this speech was the voice of the popular feeling, "The loud cheers and great applause" which it excited bears ample testimony, as well as that those who are opposed to an application for these indulgences, were inexcusably absentees: fully aware, I imagine, that all they could advance would not gain one proselyte in that Assembly—I believe that nothing is more likely to promote Emigration to this Colony than being in possession of all the *rights* of *British subjects*. "Trial by Jury" first and foremost for which we are every year becoming more competent, and secondly "Taxation by Representation" which we may now with some face hope for, when it is known that our Colonial Revenue amounts to £65,000 annually which by a late calculation appears to be a Tax of £3 per head for every free adult in the Colony.

*'March 3*
' . . . This place [Sydney] which 10 or 12 years ago was a quiet country looking, thoroughly English looking Town, is now a crowded Bustling *Business like* City—the shops are well supplied generally speaking, and the price of Leghorn Bonnets are very high nothing wearable at less than *six guineas*! The price of Tea is very low—good black Tea being only about *one shilling* per pound by the chest.

*'April 12*
'It might be thought that Governor Darling is trying how unpopular he can make himself—his late measure is a rash one to say nothing

more of it, and he has placed a man of narrow mind, repulsive manners, and a selfish disposition, in the situation lately filled by a Gentleman every way the reverse of this character, a situation too, where conciliatory manners, and an obliging disposition is so necessary—*everybody* will feel the reverse, and the change is terrible loss to the Colony.[11]

*'April 18*
'Married this day at Campbell Town by the Revd. Mr Hassall Edward Cox Esq. of Mulgoa, son of Mr Cox Esq. of Claredon, to Jane Maria third daughter of Richd. Brooks Esq. of Denham Court.

*'May 4*
'An Act in Council passed on 3rd inst. entitled "an act for imposing a Duty upon all Newspaper and Papers of a like nature" has caused a great sensation in Sydney—this will indeed act as "a restriction on the Press". I wish I could say such a restriction was uncalled for, and unnecessary, but WE are too young a Country to be allowed *all* the privileges of a British people—Sir Thomas Brisbane allowed to this Colony the full liberty of the Press. General Darling has passed more than one act for the restriction of this liberty, and has thus rendered himself if possible more unpopular than heretofore. It is a pity his measures and his manners are not more conciliatory, for I believe *him* to be a well intentioned Governor, and I have no doubt the experience of seven years will render him far more agreeable to the inhabitants of N.S.W. during the last years of his Administration: for "be it Recorded" I think the administration will extend to *twelve years.*'

This entry refers to the *Newspaper Regulating Act* submitted by Governor Darling to the Legislative Council in April 1827 to curb newspapers, particularly the *Australian* and the *Monitor*, which had been extremely critical of his actions, particularly over the death of Sudds.

*'Oct. [1829]*
' . . . It is with real satisfaction that I make mention of the Schools of the Colony being in a promising state of progressive improvement—it is true the funds are still small, but the Government has done all that can be expected—the private subscriptions of the ladies of the Colony to clothe those whose parents are not able to provide decent habiliments, does much, and nothing is now wanted but that the parents themselves keep their children clean and decent and to show a willing mind to forward the views of those engaged in this benevolent purpose—it is much to be lamented that the idle dissolute characters of the parents defeat in a great measure the instruction offered gratis to all the poor inhabitants of this Colony—the hope of success must not however desert us, and as example does much, we must endeavour to stimulate those

who are well disposed and assiduous "our one pound one" and our "five pounds five" must not be wanting to complete the purpose of schools, more beneficial to the Colony than any other institutions that can be devised for rooting out gross ignorance and habitual fraility—

### *June 10 [1828]*

'"If people must be busy" it is as well that they should be busy in a good cause and that man deserves well of the country who is alive to its interests. Sir [John Jamison] "representations to the Authorities" of the distress generally of the country and the low state of Agriculture among the small settlers should from his rank and influence have a salutary effect in raising the wealthy Landed proprietors to active measures in rendering timely assistance. This can be done by a little stretch of liberallity on their part: let the gentlemen of the Agricultural Society meet and subscribe a sum for the purpose of purchasing the *first* Cargo of Wheat from Valpairaso, (and several are expected,) let them issue them at 10d. per bushell to the poor of the Colony and let each landed proprietor employ as many free men as they can find work for, nay let them *make work* if they can afford it and pay them in wheat, meat, tea, sugar, &c at a reasonable rate.

'Government also purchasing wheat as it comes in must endeavour to make the Prisoners useful at some great piece of work, building Wharfs, and Jettys, working the Coal Mines, building the Bridges, and making roads, the expense will no doubt be great, but when it is considered that in good seasons the settlers liberally employ all the Vagabond population which the Mother Country sends among us, it is but fair that the British Government should assist us in our distress, distress not brought upon ourselves by our own folly, but the dispensation of Providence—

### *July 10th*

'In my late journey to Sydney I have seen a great improvement in the buildings shops and general appearance, Sydney is becoming a large town, and from the well supplied shops, and the numberless well dressed people you meet in the street you are inclined to fancy yourself in the Capital of a flourishing Country, and so perfectly is everything English you could almost feel yourself within a hundred mile of London itself.'

At the time she was writing this diary, recording and commenting on public events with only an occasional reference to family matters, Christiana Brooks wrote in a much more intimate way, but with her usual sound sense, in her letters. This extract refers to the death of her baby grandson, the child of her son Henry and his wife, formerly Margaret Mackenzie. On 2 October 1826[12] she wrote to 'My dear Ms M'

'We were most concerned this morning to hear of the death of our poor little grandson. We are quite ignorant of the cause and of the duration of his illness but if he has, as I suppose, died in convulsions, I shall be satisfied that God has in his mercy removed the dear infant to save his parents and friends much anxiety and sorrow. I, you know, have always been fearful that the dreadful illness dear M [Margaret] experienced in the early stage of her pregnancy would fall upon the infant, and that it might be subject to fits, & wanting in some of its faculty's. I trust his poor Mother will bear this affliction with fortitude and that her health may not be affected. I hope she will now very soon be able to bear a journey better. Change of air and scene will have the tendency to strengthen both body and mind.'

Christiana Brooks died on 12 April 1835. She was buried in a vault at Denham Court with her husband, who had died two years earlier after being gored by a bull. The church of St Mary the Virgin, Denham Court, was built to enclose their remains.

Denham Court was left to the Brooks' eldest daughter Christiana Blomfield, the other children having been provided for in other ways. Christiana Blomfield's story is told in Chapter 8.

# 8
# Working wives and mothers

**Mary Wild**

*I never expect to have any more children*

By the time Mary Wild arrived in Sydney as an army wife, the colony had been established for nearly thirty years. Convicts were still arriving and power still rested with the Governor who reported to London, but there was a growing diversity in society. Mary Wild is an example of one class of women arriving at this time. Neither a convict nor a member of the ruling class, her interests were typical of a range of women in the middle sections of society.

Mary Wild arrived in Sydney on 8 August 1817 on the *Matilda*, which brought the 48th (Northamptonshire) Regiment of Foot under Lieutenant Colonel J. Erskine to New South Wales to take over from the 46th Regiment.[1] She travelled with her husband, the Adjutant of the 48th Regiment, and two children, Margaret Edwards, a child of a previous marriage, and a son John from her marriage to Adjutant Wild. She had lost two children. In contrast to some other women who, whether they really thought so or not, conventionally expressed pleasure at the arrival of further babies, Mary Wild was happy that she was unlikely to have more children.

Like army wives through the centuries, her role was to establish her family in a new environment in what she imagined would be a temporary posting. She had several successes to report in a letter she wrote to her sister in England in 1819. She had seen her daughter married—to

Lieutenant Charles J. Vandermeulen of the 48th Regiment—although admittedly the marriage settlement had been a considerable drain on the Wilds' finances. Her son was doing well at 'the best school' in Sydney. Socially, the family had gained considerable status by the move to New South Wales. Although holding only the relatively lowly rank of adjutant and hoping to be a lieutenant, her husband (and through him Mary Wild) was invited regularly to Government House.

The development of Sydney is apparent from her letter. The untidy rows of windowless houses had long since gone: 'the town of Sydney is very large,' Mary Wild wrote in a letter to her sister, Bess Cox, on 1 April 1819:[2]

'I . . . recd. 2 [letters] from my dear mother . . . I hope in the course of one year I shall be able to send her what will keep her comfortable while she lives, all that grieves me is that I did not bring her with me for my life is miserable about her, particularly as I have not had it in my power to send her money which I promised to do, but unforeseen circumstances prevented me, in the first place we drew 12 months pay leaving England, and our voyage here was made in five months, the money was all spent, and we had to live the other seven as well as we could, we bought a horse and paid an enormous sum for him, he died, and we were obliged to give £50 for another, we also had to purchase furniture as there is nothing allowd. in Barracks but the empty walls, after all this I could have sent something but for Margts. Marriage which took place on the 18th. of last May you may recollect Lieut. Vander Meulen, he is a very fine young man and I gladly embraced his offer, his Father is rich and as a younger Brother he has 3 thousand pounds one of which has been lodged in the Agents these 2 years for a company when they were married he was under orders to go on detachment to Van Diemens Land one thousand miles from here, and I was at great expense in providing everything for them, they saild. the week after and I have not seen her since, I hear from her almost every month he has got a Colonial situation of Naval Officer and Inspector of Government works, which is worth about 3 hundred a year besides his pay. I do not expect they will join the Regt. before we leave this which will be about 2 years— I have a deal of comfort in my dear John, he is almost a young man and very much like myself, he promises to be a good scholar he is at the best school here I pay £1–12 a month for him he is almost as tall as his Father—I never expect to have any more children and do not regret it if god spares me those two, my poor Harry and Mary, are well provided for in heaven, as it was god's will to take them I must be satisfied . . . do not forget to write often . . . if you knew the anxiety of my mind, and the pleasure it gives me to hear from you, you would write oftener . . . I am happy to inform you that poor Wild is in good health and still retains the Adjutancy, we are in hopes that he will very shortly get his Lieutenancy which if god spares him will be a good thing for us . . .

'This is a very fine country, the town of Sydney is very large & the Barracks beautiful, fruit and vegetables are plentiful they feed the pigs with peaches, potatoes are 1s. a hundred, beef and mutton 10d. a lb, eggs 2d. each, butter 3s.6d a lb, milk 8d a quart, and wearing apparel very dear, the best Mysore tea is 7s.6d and good black 3.6d a pound, sugar 10d, Indian goods are sometimes very cheap, but every thing from Europe dear, a common wine glass is 1s. and a plate 9d, every thing else in proportion, we had good rations when we arrived first but they have been taken from us, only 6 married privates to each company receive them, our present allowance is 12 lbs of good beef, 12 lbs of bread, and 2 quarts of rum per week and 2s.6d. a day for a horse, some of the Convicts have made their fortunes here, but if they rode in a Coach and six we dare not associate with them, they are all thieves and robbers, there are 8 to be hanged this week, they have regular events here and people of bad character are transported to New Castle to hard labour. The prisoners are obliged to work for Government from 6 in the morning until 3 in the afternoon. They are then at liberty to earn what they can for themselves, their allowance is 7 lbs of meat and the same of bread or flour each week, no spirits, there are many respectable settlers and good families which makes it very pleasant to us, we are often invited to Govrnt. House, and in short the military are much respected.'

Mary Wild's son John fulfilled his early promise at school. Following the half-yearly examinations at 'Doctor Halloran's establishment for liberal education' (later Sydney Grammar School) in June 1820, the two top students, John Wild and Henry Robinson, were presented with silver medals for their achievements.[3] It is interesting that Mary Wild, who had such a bad opinion of convicts, should choose this school for her son, as Halloran, a gifted teacher, had arrived in Sydney as a convict only one year previously, after being found guilty on a counterfeiting charge. He was granted a ticket of leave immediately and began his school in June 1819.

Mary Wild's expectation that they would return to England with the regiment was not realised. Officers of the Regiment (her husband had been promoted to lieutenant) were encouraged to sell their commissions and settle in New South Wales. Both Lieutenant Wild and his son received grants of land in the Camden district in 1826 and the family settled in this district. John Wild later held several important government appointments[4] and became a substantial landholder.

## Christiana Jane Blomfield

*Most people add one to their family each year*

Christiana Blomfield's letters to relatives in England are a wonderful source of information on family life and the role of a woman on a country property in New South Wales during the 1820s and 1830s. In her letters she describes all the vicissitudes of country life, from droughts, fluctuations in commodity prices, and the problems of educating children to the quiet joys of good seasons, a happy family and the improvement in the amenities of the district.

In the background is Christiana's constant childbearing, which she accepts with remarkable equanimity. Her family is always her first concern. She often expresses her happiness in her marriage, her intense interest in her children, her concerns for their education and the closeness of the relationship with her parents (Richard and Christiana Brooks), and her sisters. Her absorption in her family to the exclusion of wider events affecting the colony is in striking contrast to the concerns her mother expresses in her diary (see Chapter 7). It is only in her last surviving letter that Christiana Blomfield expresses more than passing views on wider issues such as the merits of convict and free labour.

Christiana Jane Brooks, born in Surrey, England on 13 January 1802 spent her childhood in Greenmile, Kent, and arrived in Sydney with her parents at the age of 12. On 3 August 1820, at the age of 18, she married Lieutenant Thomas Valentine Blomfield, who had arrived in Sydney in 1817 with the 48th (Northamptonshire) Regiment of Foot. Blomfield, born in 1793 at Dagworth, Old Newton, Suffolk, joined the army as an ensign in 1809 and served in the Peninsular War, being awarded the Military Service Medal with eight clasps. While her husband remained in the army, Christiana lived at her parents' home, Denham Court. In 1824 Christiana and Thomas Blomfield moved to a grant of 2000 acres on the Hunter River and, with money raised from the sale of Thomas's commission, they bought sheep and agricultural implements to add to the cattle herd they had established on Christiana's father's property.[5]

By the time they moved to the Hunter, Christiana had two sons, both born at Denham Court, Thomas Edwin in 1821 and Richard Henry in 1823. When she wrote to her sister-in-law Louisa Edwards on 2 June 1825,[6] she told her of their move to the Hunter and the birth of her third son, John Roe, on 27 October 1824 in Maitland.

'You will, I dare say, like to hear something of our farm, which is called Dagworth. It is a very pretty place. Our house stands on a hill from which we have a very extensive view. On one side we see through the trees part of Lake Lachland, and on all sides we see the mountains, which have a very wild and beautiful appearance. I must now give you a description of the way in which our house is built. The foundations are large trees of a very hard wood, called ironbark, and the walls are of the same wood. The logs are cut into lengths of ten feet and are then split into slabs, which are forged into grooves in the foundation, as also into the wall plates at the top. Over this is nailed weatherboards, and the roof is shingled, which has the appearance of a slated roof. The doors and window frames are made of cedar, and to the windows are fastened Venetian blinds, painted green, as are the doors. The house is painted white. The length of the house is sixty feet, with a verandah all round eight feet wide, which is a very necessary part of a house in this warm climate. It is also a good walk in rainy weather, and a nice place for the children to play in out of the sun. Our rooms are all on the ground floor. We shall have a parlour 14 feet wide and 20 feet long, a bedroom the same size, another bedroom 12 feet wide and 20 feet long, a storeroom for provisions and farming tools, etc., the same size, a small store room joining our bedroom 10 feet square, and a bedroom for Thomas and Richard the same size opening out of our room on the opposite side of the verandah, which we shall make a dairy of at present. I do not know if, after all my description, you will be able to make out what sort of a place it will be, and I think I can fancy my little niece exclaim, "Well, that will be a queer house of Uncle Tom's," but it is the style of most country houses here. "But there is no kitchen!" Louisa will say. The kitchens, on account of the heat, are generally detached buildings, very different to the comfortable ones in England. Indeed, all the houses in this country must strike a stranger as being very meanly furnished. The walls are generally painted, sometimes only bare whitewashed, with very little other furniture than a table and chairs, a fireplace with no grate, but wood fires burning on the stone hearth or placed on iron dogs. Window curtains are seldom seen; indeed everything that adds to the heat is taken away in summer time, which is eight months of the year. Indian matting is used instead of carpet. It is made of bamboo, and is very white and cool looking, but I must say I like to see a carpet in the middle of the room in winter time, for although not much colder than your summer we feel very chilly and enjoy sitting round a cheerful wood fire of an evening.

'Now I've told you what sort of a house we shall have when finished, I will tell you how we employ our time. In the summer time we rise early, but at this time of the year we get up about 7 o'clock. The children are awake at daylight and are soon dressed and running about. After we are dressed we have family prayers. Thomas reads them to myself, the children, and one or two female servants, and both Thomas and Richard kneel by their father and are quiet all the time. After prayers we get our breakfast. Richard and Thomas sit up with us, Richard by me and Thomas by his papa, and when they have drank their tea and eaten their bread and butter they are in a hurry to get down, so after "Thank God for my good breakfast," away they skip to play with their wheelbarrows, which is their chief amusement. After breakfast Thomas's mare is saddled and he goes to the farm, where he remains until 4 o'clock. In the meantime I sleep my baby, see the house put to rights, give out what is wanted for dinner, teach little Tom to read, and Richard comes to say his lesson, which is generally P for papa and M for mama, and C for cow or Onginge, as he calls orange. Tom is much amused and says "Poor little thing, he don't know better; when he is as big as me he will say it right, won't he, ma?" We do not dine till five, as Thomas cannot leave the farm sooner, or there would be little work done. After dinner the children are washed, have their tea and go to bed, after which Thomas and I walk in the verandah until it is dark, and he tells me what he has been doing at the farm. We get our tea comfortably together and enjoy an hour or two in quiet. I generally work and he reads to me, or we talk of the improvements we intend making when we get to "Dagworth". At nine or ten o'clock we have evening prayers and go to bed, and, if the children will let us, sleep very soundly. As we are 20 miles from any church we read the church service on Sunday to our servants twice a day and Bland's sermons or some other religious book. I dare say it will not be very long before we have a church and clergyman in the neighbourhood, as it is becoming a very populous district, and as I have always been used to attend public worship regularly, I shall be very glad when I can do so again, and take my children. Poor little Tom is always asking questions. The other day I had been telling him that if he was good and said his prayers that God would love him and give him everything. He said directly, "What, lots of pancakes and sugar?" Poor little innocent fellow, that is his idea of everything that is good, but he will, I hope, soon know better . . . '

By the time she wrote to her niece, Louisa Edwards, on 5 January 1828[7] Christiana had her fourth child and was expecting another.

'You ask me in one of your letters if you have any more cousins. I believe I have not written to you since the birth of our little girl, which event took place on the 30th of June, 1826. She is now eighteen months old; such a very fine child and beginning to be very interesting. Her name is Christiana Eliza Passmore, after my mother's maiden name. What will you say when I tell you perhaps ere you receive this letter you may have another little cousin. If a girl she shall be named Louisa Matilda; if a boy, Barrington. I think your Aunt Matilda will say we stock our house too fast now, but in this colony we are only considered very moderate folks. Most people add one to their family every year, and as there are so few disorders fatal to children in this colony there will in a few years be larger grown-up families in this part of the world than any other . . .

'Our three boys are all well and growing up fast, but they are as wild as young kangaroos and as mischievous as monkeys, but not unlike other children at their age. Thomas is still small of his age, but very sensible, manly, and quick at his lessons; very passionate but very affectionate, so that I do not despair of making him anything I please. Richard is a stout fellow, in my opinion a fine handsome boy, an excellent temper, but more mischievous than any of them. Johnny is a little innocent child, very fond of being made a pet of, rather odd looking, with very light blue eyes and light curly hair. He is quick like Thomas. It is a sad thing not having a school to send them to. I regret it more on account of keeping them away from our farm servants than from what they would learn. I take them myself to school for two hours every day, and Thomas is beginning to read very nicely. He can say the church and their other catechisms, besides several of Watt's hymns very nicely. Richard is rather dull, but I dare say he will improve by and by. I hope in another year to be able to send Thomas to the clergyman of our district to school, as he proposes taking a few pupils above eight years old. We will endeavour to bring Thomas forward as fast as we can and persuade Mr Wilkinson to take him before he is eight years old. He is a very nice man, and we should know he was taken care of in every sense and improved in moral as well as learning.'

During the previous year Christiana had visited her parents at Denham Court to attend the wedding of her sister, Jane, to Edward Cox, described in Christiana Brooks's diary (see Chapter 7).

*January 20th*
' . . . It was a happy meeting after an absence of nearly three years, and, could you have seen us all, I am sure you would have thought so. I went up rather sooner than I expected, to be present at the marriage of my second sister Jane, which took place on the 18th of April. She was twenty years old, and her husband one year more, so you will say they are a young couple; but he is a very steady, prudent young man and has a good farm and a pretty cottage, with everything a young couple could wish for to take his wife to. He is the youngest son of a Mr Cox who was paymaster to the first regiment that came to this country, and afterwards settled here. He is now a very rich man and has provided for all his family handsomely. My brother-in-law Edward is the fifth son that the old gentleman has seen married, and all are living with in a day's

journey of their father. Most of them have now large families, and I suppose Edward and my sister Jane will add to the 36 already bearing the name of Cox before many months pass.'

When she wrote to her sister-in-law, Louisa Edwards, in November 1828[8] Christiana had another child, Louisa Matilda, born on 18 April 1828, making it necessary to extend their house.

'When my father came to see us he brought us his carpenter to complete our house, and by his means we are enabled to make many additions which have added considerably to our comfort. Thomas has also been making great improvements on the farm by clearing land and making many enclosures. You who live in England can have no idea the labor it takes to bring land into a state of cultivation here, as also the great expense, but I must leave Thomas to tell you all these sort of things; he can explain better than I can.'

On 4 October 1829,[9] Christiana wrote to her husband's family thanking them for presents including a cigar which she 'had a great mind' to smoke herself 'as Thomas is not a smoker'.

'The books for the children were the best present you could have sent us, as there is a difficulty in obtaining such things here, and I assure you they afforded great amusement. Those to myself I value much, and I hope to benefit by the many useful lessons in them . . .

'Our two eldest boys have gone to school; they went to Newcastle, where the clergyman resides whom they are placed with, with their papa. The clergyman is a particular friend of ours, and I feel confident they will be taken every care of. Mr Wilkinson takes but six pupils, and our boys make two of that number. Poor Richard was delighted at the idea of going, as they are both very fond of Mr Wilkinson; but when night came he could not contain his feelings any longer; his little heart was full and he wanted his papa to bring him home again. He was quite reconciled when his papa wrote to him the next day, and Thomas equally happy. He has more spirit than Richard, and will fight his way in the world better.'

She wrote of her husband's visit to Sydney to finalise an additional grant of 560 acres and how drought was affecting their income.

'He has no money to spend this year, and it requires great economy to keep our head above water, as the three last years of drought have involved the colony in great difficulty. The almost total failure of the grain crops has taken all the money out of the colony to pay for the wheat imported from India, The Cape, and other places, consequently there has been a great fall in the prices of cattle, sheep and horses, neither of them being worth more than a third what they were two years ago. There is no more money left in the country, and several farmers and settlers have been ruined, particularly those who came here about three years ago, and who paid great prices for their cattle, etc . . .'

But she concluded optimistically:

'I must not leave off without telling you I am as happy as the first day of my marriage. I have more reason to be thankful every day with my lot in life, though we have not riches we have contentment, and are happy in the affections of each other, and our good, healthy little children.'

The education of her children was the major subject of Christiana's letter dated 2 April 1830[10] to her sister-in-law.

'I think I told you in my last that our two eldest boys were at school at the clergyman's of our district. They were at home at Xmas, and thought them much improved. They are good, affectionate little fellows, and so exactly of a size that they are always taken for twins. They are very fond of each other and are excellent companions. Johnnie is still at home, as we think him too young to send to school; besides we could not afford it just yet. We pay £40 a year for each of the boys; that is to say, we supply Mr. Wilkinson with the produce of our farm to that amount, for money is not to be had in these days. We send him beef, mutton, butter, cheese, bacon, etc., which answers his purpose as well as ours; otherwise we could not afford to send the boys. The seasons here have been so very bad for the last three years that it has been very ruinous to the settlers, and we have had no grain to sell, but, thank God, we have now had plenty of rain and the face of the country has quite changed, and we must hope for better times.

'I have another little nephew to introduce to you—Barrington Wingfield—who was born on the 28th January. I think he is the largest baby I ever saw, and very good. He's like the others, quite a Blomfield. We have made no alterations and improvements since I last wrote to you. We go on just in the same quiet way, never happier than when we are together. Thomas goes out but seldom, and I the same, for I never see any place I like so well as my own peaceful home, good husband, and affectionate children. I know we shall never be rich, but as long as we can make both ends meet and give our children a good plain education, without all the fine accomplishments, I shall be perfectly content.'

In the nine years between this and Christiana's last surviving letter, there were major changes in the life of the Blomfield family. Following

the death of her father in 1833 and her mother in 1835, Christiana
inherited Denham Court and the family moved there from the Hunter
district. By the time of her letter written on 10 November 1839[11] from
Denham Court, Christiana was expecting her eleventh child and was
also caring for the three orphan children of her sister Honoria, whose
death had followed closely that of her husband, William Riley, her
'dying request' being that the Blomfields should care for her children.

'They are so young as not to feel her loss, and they are in every respect
treated like our own. We have, in consequence to this addition to our
family, been obliged to add to our house. We have built a back wing,
containing a large nursery and sleeping room, with an enclosed verandah all around. They have just got into it, and it looks so comfortable
and nice. I do not know how many children we had when we last wrote
to you. We have now nine of our own,[12] and it is God's will in January
I shall add another to our already numerous party. Our four youngest
are boys, nice little fellows, some fair, some dark, some quiet, other
pickles, but all good dispositions. We have only two girls out of all our
number. The eldest, 13 last June, is a pretty, fair little girl, genteel and
gentle in manner. Louisa, as I have always described her, is a merry little
romp, and her brothers think her very pretty. They both go to school at
the Hunter, but now we are settled here we find it inconvenient their
being so far away, and as there is now a very excellent school in Sydney, kept by two young ladies lately come out, and who have been
accustomed to the education of young ladies, we are thinking of sending them there, at any rate Christiana, as their terms are high, £42 each
a year, and we cannot at present afford both. Our eldest boy, Tom, is
at present studying with a Mr. Clarke,[13] lately come out as headmaster
of the King's School. He is a clever man, and we wish Tom to have the
advantage of his instruction for some months. He is unsettled in his
disposition, having a strong inclination to a military life. His papa always
tells him it is of no use thinking of such things in these times, as he has
no interest to get him a commission. He sometimes asks me if his uncle
Edwin has none, and declares if war breaks out he will volunteer. We
wish him to turn his attention to a settler's life and assist his father in
managing his flock and herds. He is not ill-disposed, but giddy and
thoughtless, much liked by his companions, of a generous and courageous disposition, and a great lover of horses, while he is a famous
rider.

'Richard and John are both steady boys and will, we hope, soon take
an active part in the management of our up-country establishments. Our
sheep and cattle stations are nearly 300 miles from here. We have an
overseer and convicts and free men. There is great expense attending

these distant stations, in clothing and feeding the men, the shearing, and forming stockyards, men's huts, and in the payment of free labor, which takes away considerably from our profits. Our income arises principally from the sale of our wool, which we send to England, the sale of sheep for the butchers, and cattle also. We ought also to receive £200 a year from the rent of Dagworth farm at the Hunter, but we have not been fortunate in our servants, and our rent is considerably in arrears at present. The colony has been visited by a severe drought the last year. The crops were a total failure. Out of 70 acres we only reaped about 40 bushels, and we were not singular, so that we have been obliged to purchase flour for the establishment, as well as our up country stations . . . The shearing time has commenced in most parts of the country; some places they have finished but at Maneroo, where our stations are, it is colder, and we do not commence so soon. Tom will go up to superintend the shearing; as I do not like your brother to leave me during my confinement, which happens at rather an inconvenient time, when all our young folks will be at home for the holidays, but he will go up after I am about again, to muster our cattle, and as our herd is now about 1500 in number he will select some for sale, as it is difficult to get pasture for so many. We are obliged to rent land from the Government both for our sheep, cattle and horses; that is to say, we pay for a squatting license.

'They now tax our sheep, cattle and horses at so much a head; it is but a small sum on each annually, but I think we pay about £50 a year; and they talk of other taxes, so that we may expect in a year or two that the English Government will make the colony pay its own expenses. There is at present a great debate in our little council about these matters, and the colonials are becoming dissatisfied at the whole expenses of the police and gaol establishments being thrown upon the colony, which, composed as the colony is of the outcasts of England, must of necessity be very expensive, and we think all the expense ought not to be put upon us, particularly as convict labor has ceased. They will not now assign any more, and the emigrants do not come out in sufficient numbers to supply their place. Those that do come are a lazy, useless set, expecting very high wages, a large ration of meat, flour, tea, sugar, tobacco, and many of them having large families of young children, which they expect also to be fed. We prefer hiring the convicts who have become free or have obtained ticket of leave for good conduct. They are used to the ways of the colony and, rogues as they are, are more useful than the lazy set sent out. There are some exceptions certainly, but we suppose they are generally the sweepings from the parishes at home. They should send us unmarried men and women from the agricultural counties. They would easily obtain work and we should be glad to employ them. We give our farming men ten shillings a week and a ration of 10lbs. flour, 10lb. meat, 1½lb. sugar, 3oz. tea; and our female servants from £12 to £15 a year; £12, I should say, was the average wage for females.

'Sydney is becoming a large mercantile town. It is well supplied with English goods of every description. The shops are numerous and full of goods, and the people in Sydney—that is, the merchants, Government officers—all live in good style. Everyone keeps a carriage, as do many of the shopkeepers, and some of the handsomest equipages belong to persons who have once been convicts, but who have become rich men in a few years, not being overscrupulous in their dealings . . .

'We have not much confidence in our new Governor.[14] He is a Whig, and he is considered a time-server and has not the interest of the colony at heart . . .'

Christiana Blomfield's eleventh child, a boy, Frank Allman, was born on 7 January 1840 and her last child, Alfred, two years later, both at Denham Court. Christiana Blomfield died on 31 October 1852 at Denham Court, aged 50 and her husband, Thomas, died on 19 May 1857.

## Sophy Dumaresq

*I wash & dress baby*

Aristocratic and charming, Sophy Dumaresq was a member of the intimate circle of family and friends surrounding Governor Ralph Darling and his wife, formerly Eliza Dumaresq. When Darling sailed to Sydney on the *Catherine Stewart Forbes* in 1824 to take up his appointment as governor, his party included two of Eliza's brothers, William Dumaresq, who became inspector of roads and bridges, and Edward, who settled in Van Diemen's Land. Her eldest brother, Lieutenant Colonel Henry Dumaresq, Darling's private secretary, preceded the party to Sydney.

After he had been in New South Wales for three years, Henry Dumaresq, then aged 35, visited England on official business and on 19 August 1828, at St George's, Hanover Square, married Elizabeth Sophia (Sophy), elder daughter of Augustus Butler-Danvers, Earl of Lanesborough and his second wife, Eliza Bizarre (Bizzy) Sturt.

Sophy accompanied her husband when he returned to Sydney on 10 July 1829. While still in England she had had a miscarriage, but a few months after her arrival in Sydney she gave birth to a son, baptised Arthur Fitzroy Charles Dumaresq on 27 September 1829 at St James's Church, and known as Fitzroy.

A letter Sophy Dumaresq wrote from Sydney the following year gives an interesting insight into the development of her outlook—from a demure young bride, unable to 'talk abt. water closets' to her husband, to a mature young wife who wrote about toilet training her baby son and found that she now enjoyed her husband's risqué stories, which had once made her blush. She emerges from the letter as delightful, open and charming. She was never to enjoy living in New South Wales, but she approached her situation with inherent good nature. Perhaps she had little reason for complaint—she led a privileged life in a circle that included her sisters-in-law Eliza Darling and Christiana, daughter of the colonial secretary Alexander Macleay, who married William Dumaresq in 1830.

When she wrote this letter on 20 February 1830, her role is clearly defined as that of a young mother. Unlike Eliza Darling and some of the Macleay women, she was never to take a prominent part in charity work or in their particular interest, the establishment of the Female School of Industry. In this letter Sophy shows herself to be ecstatically happy with her baby son and her husband, despite finding nothing that she likes about living in New South Wales. Though the country is 'odious', she is personally 'very very happy'. A combination of bad convict servants and her own joy in her baby son makes her decide to care for him herself; the servant she had brought from England, Martha Petty, having left as she saw great opportunities for setting up in business as a milliner and dressmaker.

It is interesting to note Colonel Dumaresq's role as a father. Far from being a stereotype of a detached Victorian male uninterested in the 'nursery' aspects of his children's upbringing, he takes an active part. 'Where would you find another Papa to do as much?' Sophy asks.

Sophy wrote[15] to Mrs Winn, wife of Charles Winn, later second Baron Headley and Baronet of Nostell.

'I begin the day by rising abt. five o'clock, not from *choice*, but downright *compunction*, being dragged *neck & heels* out of bed if I show the slightest resistance, of course I need not name the perpetrator of so *tyrannical* an act, none but a *man & husband* cd. be guilty of such *cruelty*. My next act is to prepare to accompany Cornelia Darling in His [?Her] little Garden Chair to the bathing House abt. a miles distance, Col Dumaresq drives, & our party is increased by the addition of *my little Son* (How do you think it sounds? *I* fancy very oddly indeed) two Newfoundland dogs & a Spaniel. The three latter personages accompany me into the sea, where we all seem very much to enjoy ourselves. We return to breakfast at $^1/_2$ past eight, immediately after which Col Dumaresq leaves me to my own concerns, & attends the duties of his office (*alias Treadmill,*) for the remainder of the day my time is almost entirely engrossed by my baby, in this *odious* country (for I must call it so) it is impossible to trust the most trivial thing out of ones sight & since the departure of the Servants we brought with us from England, I am never comfortable in leaving home for a minute without him. My maid immediately commenced by following the terrible fashion of this part of the world of producing *olive branches,* & in consequence has set up for herself as *Milliner & dress Maker,* & I have no doubt will soon realize a fortune. She made a bonnet out of a piece of Gauze I gave her (wh. was literally the fag end of one of the famous *East Riding Turbans*) wh. she sold for 30s. On her departure poor baby & I were left to the mercy of a Convict Woman who had been with us four months previously & had as far as I cd. judge behaved perfectly well. I was prejudiced in her favor the more because she was Yorkshire, & spoke the dialect *charmingly.* When she was more immediately placed under my observation however, I began to suspect she was fonder of the Brandy bottle than I quite approved of & this idea was only too well confirmed soon after, by her coming upstairs to me so intoxicated that she scarcely knew what I said to her, & on attempting to undress the baby exposed herself so much that I took him from her & ever since have dressed & undressed him myself. Her *conduct* was altogether so abominable that Col Dumaresq sent her off to the Watch House from whence she was committed to the Penitentiary for 6 months.

'It is one of the most serious objections to the Country & certainly a great evil, I mean the difficulty almost amounting to an impossibility of procuring servants with the requisites generally applied for, namely *Honesty, Sobriety, & obliging disposition.* If one qualification is met with, there is sure to be an absence of the others. In my own individual case however I probably *care* less, at least *feel* the inconvenience less than others who are more addicted to straying where "two or three are gathered together". I really never leave my own quiet home to go any where in search of Society, not one of the Gowns belonging to my Wedding paraphernalia have been *put-together* since their arrival in this Kangaroo Land; & till the parties at Govern' House are resumed I think they are likely to remain a long time in their packing cases—I have rather digressed from the account I was giving you of *the order* of the day, the rest is soon told however; after breakfast I wash & dress baby, *order dinner* (wh by the bye I absolutely detest, all the other cares of housekeeping included,) & to play with & amuse him till 4 or 5 o'clock when I trot over to invade Col Dumaresq's office & bring him back with me to an early dinner after which we ride out till 8 or 9, & by ten I am in bed, with my baby boy lying on the outside *at my feet,* where he now sleeps, being very hot weather, in general however he has his own little

Cot wh. is placed by his *papas* side, who is *the very best nurse* you can imagine.—I will give you an instance of this assertion. Whenever his boy wakes during the night wh. he usually does two or three times for me to nurse him, Col Dumaresq takes him up & *holds him out*, wh the *young man* quite understands & immediately performs what is required of him. Where wd. you find another Papa to do as much? By the bye it is quite extraordinary how *used* I am become to *these sort of things*: I am really *now* downright impudent, *almost improper, wh. you know was not the case once*. I was obliged to get you & Louise to talk abt. Water closets for me to Col Dumaresq. Do you remember? At present however I cd. save you the trouble but it is all my husbands fault; Stories he used to tell & make me blush at, I now enjoy extremely & think very good fun. In short I realize the old Proverb "Evil Communication, &c." You know the rest—I am thinking if I have written to you since my confinement, & cannot recollect having done so, I must therefore now assure you, that Little Fitzroy is a very nice little fellow, (in his Nurses—ma & papas opinion at least) & is becoming more engaging & intelligent Every day. His eyes & complexion are the most clear & brilliant possible, but unluckily he has got my mouth instead of his papas wh. is a dire mistake, & a nose wh. makes one rather uncomfortable not knowing how it is to *turn out*, at present *however, it turns up*.—I think I have employed more of the paper in writing abt. *self* than I ought to have done, but will not apologize because I am vain enough to imagine that the subject is not uninteresting to you my dearest Mrs Winn . . . What is there I wd. not give to see you all, & show you my little mannikin, but alas I see no prospect of such happiness being in store for me. This is not the Country for making fortunes; it is only calculated for living *in*, not *out* of it & unless Col Dumaresq gets some Govt. appointment wh. wd. *pay tolerably*, (wh. I now see no chance of, being disappointed of the *Treasuryship*,) I fear there is no reason against our passing the remainder of our lives here. Even if this place was the Paradise the Prejudiced & Enthusiastic represent in point of Climate, Scenery &c, such advantages wd. not compensate to me for the complete separation wh. exists between myself & those dearly loved friends I have left; I had rather be doomed to live in a perpetual yellow London fog & be within *their* reach, than in the *finest situation & climate* at 1600 miles [?] distance. *I am* however greatly disappointed in New South Wales in every instance that I have heard it given credit for. The climate *to me* is *detestable*, The Lower orders of people more depraved than I cd. have conceived possible, & the Country is dull & heavy & gloomy in the extreme. Every succeeding day however only proves to me more forcibly that *place* has very little to do with happiness, for I decidedly do not like the climate or admire the Character of the Country in general,

Sydney being excepted as beautiful yet I am *very very* happy. If we were not forbidden to praise ones own, I shd. launch out in Col Dumaresqs, nothing can exceed his care, tenderness, cheerfulness & unremitting solicitude towards me in Every way . . . By the bye I must particularly mention that he wants a few yards of Silk to cover his stocks with, he says that Mr Winn will know what sort it shd. be, *I imagined*, it shd. resemble the lining of a certain old coat of his, in fact of the *tatters* of wh. my first born *sweet* baby was wrapped in the night of my unexpected accouchement in the Salon at Nostel, however Col Dumaresq says he thinks it shd. be a kind of ribbed silk, whereas what I allude to, (& have now,) is a *twill*—I have a great deal more I might say, but so many letters are on my mind to write, that I can indulge myself no longer in lengthening this.'

Soon after she wrote this letter, Sophy and her husband moved to his land grant at St Heliers near Muswellbrook. In 1833, when Henry was appointed Commissioner of the Australian Agricultural Company, succeeding Sir Edward Parry, they moved to Port Stephens. Henry died at Tahlee House, Port Stephens on 5 March 1838 at the age of 46. By then Sophy had seven children. In addition to her first-born, Fitzroy, Louisa was born in 1830, Harriet in 1832, Algernon in 1833, Henry in 1835, Cornelia in 1837 and Priscilla in 1838. A few years later Sophy returned to England with her children.

# 9
## *Pathmakers*

**Elizabeth Hawkins**

*The fatigue to mother and myself was very great*

Travelling did not end for some women when they landed at an Australian port. As European settlement spread from Sydney and Hobart, and later from the other capitals, women found themselves travelling overland, often on horrendous journeys into virtually unknown country to settle on farms at the edge of settlement. When Elizabeth Hawkins set off with her family to cross the Blue Mountains in 1822, they were the first family of free settlers to cross the formidable mountain barrier which had barred the way westwards for a quarter of a century. Only nine years before Elizabeth Hawkins made her epic journey, explorers Lawson, Wentworth and Blaxland had succeeded in crossing the Mountains and had glimpsed from Mount York the fertile plains beyond. Elizabeth Hawkins, her husband, her eight children aged from less than twelve months to twelve years and her 70-year-old mother, Mrs Lilly, set off in 1822 for Bathurst, the centre of these plains.

The Hawkins family arrived in Sydney on 11 January 1822 on the *Mistral*, hoping that by migrating their prospects of supporting and providing for their large family would be better than they had been in England. Elizabeth's husband, naval officer Thomas Fitzherbert Hawkins, had fought in the Napoleonic Wars but soon after the war ended he was one of the many naval officers compulsorily retired. He went into business in London but lost money.

His wife, formerly Elizabeth Lilly, was born in Kent on 15 July 1783 and they married at Deal on 15 June 1802. At the time they emigrated to New South Wales they had eight children, several of whom are mentioned in Elizabeth's account of the family's journey across the Blue Mountains. They included Tom, aged 12$^1$/$_2$ who was regarded as a man rather than a boy, riding his own horse; four girls, Eliza, Helen, Louisa and Ann; the delicate George and the baby Edward.

In April, a few months after their arrival in Sydney, Thomas Hawkins was appointed Commissariat Storekeeper at Bathurst. The family set out with all their family possessions, clothes and food in a wagon, three drays and a tilted cart on the 220 kilometre journey which was to take eighteen days. They chose a female servant from the Female Factory at Parramatta and they were accompanied by eight male convicts.

Elizabeth wrote an account of the journey over the Blue Mountains in a long letter to her sister, Mrs Ann Bowling of Hammersmith.[1] The hardships and dangers of this journey are so vividly described that the letter speaks for itself. It is a gripping story of an adventure undertaken with great determination and spirit by a family group thrown into a world entirely without the comforts, and most of all without the security, to which they were accustomed. Yet they were buoyed by the prospects ahead for themselves and their children. One night, sitting outside their tent, Elizabeth Hawkins wrote that she was experiencing for the first time no 'dread for the future'.

At one stage in their journey they passed a clergyman returning to Sydney from Bathurst, whom Elizabeth Hawkins identified later as Rev. Samuel Marsden. He remarked to the party:'I congratulate you. You are going to the land of Goshen'.[2]

The family left Sydney on 5 April 1822 and by evening had reached Rooty Hill. After resting the next day, Sunday, they travelled to the banks of the Nepean River, but could get only part of their goods across before nightfall. During the next few days they were delayed further by rain and then by having to dry out their belongings. Sir John Jamison, living nearby, invited them to dine. On Tuesday 12 April they began their journey over the mountains:

'I had now before me this most tremendous journey. I was told I de-served to be immortalised for the attempt and that Govt. could not do too much for us for taking such a family to a settlement where none had ever gone before. I mean no family of free settlers and very few others. Every thing that could be done for us was done by officers to make it as comfortable as possible.

'In addition to our luggage, we had to take corn for the cattle as in the mountains there is not sufficient grass for them, and we also had provisions for ourselves and 9 men that accompanied us. In consequence of this we were obliged to leave many things behind. We now commenced with two drays with 5 bullocks each, 1 dray with 4 horses, and our own cart with 2; they had no more carts to give us. Amidst the good wishes of all, not excepting a party of natives who had come to bid us welcome we commenced. We had not proceeded more than a quarter of a mile before we came to a small stream of water with a sandy bottom and banks. Here the second dray with the bullocks sank: the storekeeper, superintendent and overseer from Emu witnessing our stoppage, came to our assistance. The two latter did not quit us until night. It employed us an hour to extricate the dray, it was accomplished without the horses of the other being added to it. We now slowly proceeded about a quarter of a mile further and now, my dear, imagine me at the foot of a tremendous mountain, the difficulty of passing which is I suppose as great or greater than any known road in the world, not from the road being bad, as it has been made and is hard all the way but the difficulty lies in the extreme steepness of the ascent & descent, the hollow places and the large ragged pieces of rock. You will perhaps imagine, as I had done, that the mountains are perfectly barren. For 40 miles they are barren of herbage for cattle but as far as the eye can reach even from the summit of the highest every hill and dale is covered with wood, lofty trees and small shrubs many of them blooming with the most delicate flowers, the colours so beautiful that the highest circles in England would prize them. These mountains appear solid rocks, hardly any earth on the surface. This land seems as if it was never intended for human beings to inhabit. There are no roots or substitutes for bread no fruits or vegetables on which men could subsist, but almost everything will grow which is brought to it.

'We now began our ascent up the first Lapstone Hill, so called from all the stones being like a cobbler's lap stone, the horses got on very well, but the bullocks could not, so we were obliged to unload, have a cart from Emu, and send back some of our luggage, even then the horses were obliged when they reached the top to return and assist them. We only performed the distance of one mile and a half that day. Our tent was for the first time pitched, the fatigue to mother and myself was very great every night after the journey in preparing beds and giving the children their food & the little ones were generally tired and cross little Edward in particular.

'It was a very moonlight night and all was novelty and delight to the elder children, immense fires were made in all directions we gave them their supper and after putting the younger to bed I came from the tent in which was a large fire, our drays and carts close in view. The men nine in number were busily employed in cooking in one place, our own man roasting a couple of fowls for our next days journey, at another the

men (convicts), not the most prepossessing in their appearance with the
glare of the fires and the reflection of the moon shining on them in
the midst of a forest formed altogether such a scene as I cannot describe
it resembled more a party of Banditti, such as I have read of than any
thing else. I turned from the view took the arm of Hawkins who was
seated at the table with the storekeeper and went to the back of the tent.
Here we saw Tom and the three elder girls trying who could make the
best fire as happy as it was possible for young hearts to be then I
seemed to pause it was a moment I shall never forget. For the first time
for many a long month I seemed capable of enjoying and feeling the
present moment without a dread for the future 'tis true we had in a
manner bade adieu to the world to our country and our friends, but in
our country we could no longer provide for our children and the world
from that cause had lost all its charms. You, Bowling and all my friends
and acquaintances, I thought of with regret but the dawn of independence was opening on us. Hawkins was again an officer under Government, a home to receive us, and the certainty under any circumstances
of never wanting the common necessaries of Life, you, my dear Ann,
must have suffered in mind what we had long suffered, to form an idea
of what we then felt. After a little while we returned to the table, there
were moments of such inward rest that Hawkins took up a flute belonging to one of the party and calling Eliza to us she danced in a place
where perhaps no one of her age had ever trod before . . . '

The next day they travelled to Springwood, where they were accommodated in a government stockkeeper's hut, occupied by a corporal and
two soldiers. Elizabeth thought, 'A good barn in England would have
been a palace to this place'.

'The corporal's wife an old woman who had been transported above
twenty years with fawning manners came forward to show us in. We
entered the kitchen which contained a long table and form and some
stumps of trees to answer the purpose of chairs of which there was not
one in the house. Several people were there to rest for the nights journey from Bathurst to Sydney. We were shown into the small back room
which had nothing in it but a sofa with slips of bark laid on it for the
seat, here I felt desolate and lonely it was nearly dark still Hawkins did
not arrive we got quite miserable. At length the storekeeper . . . arrived
and said to us that he could not get on without some horses being sent
to his assistance. It was nearly nine o'clock before he arrived. I went out
but such a scene of confusion as there appeared from the glare of the
fires the carts and drays the men tired with their days work, swearing
as they extricated the bullocks and horses, it was long before I could
distinguish Hawkins. I felt comparatively safe when I did. The old woman

a most depraved character and well-known thief with a candle held high above her head screamed out "Welcome to Springwood, sir." He said when he looked round he felt sure his welcome would be the loss of whatever she could steal from us, he was much fatigued not having had any refreshment all day. It was my intention when I first arrived to have pitched the tent on the green but it unfortunately was on top of the dray left with Hawkins but having my mattresses, I spread them in the storeroom, the earth was dirty, damp and cold we could not think of undressing the children and when in bed all looked most miserable, I lay down with my baby, a very few minutes convinced me I should get no rest, the bugs were crawling by hundreds the children were restless with them and the confinement of their clothes, the old woman had contrived to steal some spirits from our provision basket which with what had been given to her made her and the soldiers tipsy all was noise and confusement in doors, without swearing and wrangling with the men. Never did I pass a night equal to it. Hawkins remained all night on the green or in the cart watching, in addition to the other noises a flock of sheep had been driven into the yard and they to avoid the men came close to the house and kept up a continual pat with their feet. Could any of our romance writers have been in my situation they might have planned an interesting scene to add to the horrors of their volumes you may be certain we were happy when the morning came we got our breakfast and packing up our beds bade adieu to the house at Springwood.

'Mother, myself and three girls as the morning was fair walked on before, it was such a relief to get away from that place that I never enjoyed a walk more. We gathered most delicate nosegays from the flowering shrubs that grew amongst the trees you must understand that the whole of the road from the beginning to the end of the Mountains is cut entirely through a Forest, nor can you go in a direct line to Bathurst from one mountain to another but you are obliged often to wind round the edges of them and at times to look down such precipices as would make you shudder. We ascended our cart had now three bullocks as we had so much trouble to get on with two but we were worse off than ever as the ascent became worse they refused to drag and every few minutes first one and then another would lie down the dogs were summoned to bark at them and bite their noses to make them get up, the barking of the dogs, the bellowing of the bullocks and the swearing of the men made our heads ache and kept us in continual terror that was exactly the case every day of the journey. Frequently it was necessary we should all get out and more frequently our fears made us scream out: "Oh do let us get out I am sure there is danger." At length we came to a hill so steep it seemed as if we could never get up it, we alighted, and seating ourselves on a fallen tree waiting for the event we were on the side of it in front it was almost perpendicular behind was a valley so deep the eye could hardly distinguish the trees at the bottom, to gain the top of this mountain the road wound along the side, the first dray with the horses got up they were then brought back to assist the rest with the bullocks but they could not succeed in raising these from one rock to another with great noise a sudden effort was made and one shaft was broken this had to be repaired as well as we could some of the luggage taken off and with the assistance of the other horses, it was got up, the other was got up in like manner. When at the top the men who were much fatigued sought for a spring of water and with the addition of a bottle of rum were refreshed, we again set off, and for the last two miles it was perfectly dark attended by heavy rain you can suppose the danger and misery we rode in, not being able to see where we went we were obliged to go on until we came to water, there our tent was pitched in the road, and was dark damp and dirty we were obliged to remain in the cart until the bedding was put into the tent, of course we again lay down in our clothes, this very fatiguing day's journey we had only accomplished eight miles. For fear I should tire you with a repetition of the same scenes I will now tell you that every day on the journey from Emu to Bathurst we were subject to the same thing such as our bullocks lying down constantly the others not able to drag their load compelled to have the assistance of the horses, which caused great delay.

'Our provisions consisted of half a pig which was salted for us at Emu and some beef we had flour to make bread, tea, sugar, butter and when we stopped at night we made our tea and had some cold meat, it was our man's business every night to boil a piece of meat for the next day, and bake a cake under the iron pot, breakfast and supper were the only meals we had. I used to take a small basket in the cart with me, a little just to keep us from starving and some drink for baby and during the 11 nights we rested in the woods Hawkins never laid down until about three in the morning when the Overseer would get up and watch and never but twice did he take his clothes off as we occupied the tent, his only resting place was the cart. It rained the next morning, and every thing was very uncomfortable, the men went in search of the cattle they were obliged to be turned loose at night to get water and food, could not find them at all, after waiting some time we thought it better to proceed excepting one dray which the overseer was to watch while his men sought the bullocks. As the road this day was something better we got nine miles to two bark huts which had been erected by the men employed in mending the roads, but were now empty, we were very glad to take possession of one and our men of the other as it rained all day. In England you never saw anything like these huts and I fear from my description you will not understand them. Some stakes of trees are stuck in the ground the outside bark from the trees is tied together and to these with narrow strips of what is called stringy bark being tough it answers the purpose of cord, and the roof is done in the same manner. There was a kind of chimney, but neither window nor door but a space left to enter as many men had been obliged to sleep here all around were placed small stakes and across and on the top were laid pieces of bark so as to form a kind of broad shelf all round here we spread our beds. Mother and I soon found it was impossible to get any rest from the bugs and fleas Helen and Louisa were laid head to foot finding them restless we looked and found poor things that from some of the pieces of bark not being close to the outside, they had tumbled through and being suspended by their arms we had some difficulty to drag them up.'

During the night their bullocks strayed, delaying the party for a day. Then:

'The next morning was fine and we again ascended the cart this day we accomplished nine miles much in the same way as before. The following morning the 18th a morning never to be forgotten for to all my complaints about the road I was continually silenced by "Say nothing about it until you get to the big Noll." We were now within eleven miles of it but the roads being tolerably good and the morning fine in expectation of something very wonderful our spirits were by no means bad for after this day our greatest difficulties were over. Hawkins shot some birds the boys hunted a kangaroo rat we laughed and talked and went cheerfully on until we were within a mile of Mount York or more commonly called the Big Hill. I desired Tom to ride on and give us some account of it he soon came galloping back. "Oh Ma you will never get up I am sure you won't I can't see much of the road but I can see the valley you are to reach it is dreadful" our courage began to fail by the time we reached the top . . .

'The men began to cut down the trees necessary to chain behind the drays this appeared a terrible precaution to take we thought it better to commence our walk down first Tom led his pony, Hawkins his horse, we had proceeded but a short distance when it appeared so impossible for any cart to descend the place we were at that Hawkins refused to go any further with me, Ann was forced to be carried and Mother and myself had to carry Edward, how we got down I cannot tell but I believe the fear lest any accident should happen to him gave us strength and resolution to keep our own footing we were often obliged to sit down on a fallen tree but when we did the pains in our legs and the violent trembling all over us made it difficult to get up again we at last reached the bottom in safety. To give an account of the road is not in my power but you have read Miss Porter's "Scottish Chiefs" where the rocks and glens are so well described but even that can convey but a faint idea of this mountain. The descent is about a mile it is 4000 feet above the level of the sea all rocks and beauties awfully grand to behold but from it being impossible to make some parts of the road safe from the projecting pieces of rock we were rendered very uneasy about our luggage. It was about three o'clock when we seated ourselves on some trees it was extremely hot I had given a piece of sugar candy to one of the children in a small tin we had brought down and as Tom and Eliza found a spring of water the can became useful to us to drink from and the sugar served to quiet the little ones. We waited a considerable time and could hear nothing of the rest and then desired Tom to go and meet them and when he found them all safe to call out and an hour passed, and still we heard nothing. Mother and I then thought to walk a little way and listen some times we could just hear the sound of voices and all again was still we returned to our children. It was nearly sun set and in this country it is dark almost immediately. I asked Eliza if she would venture up with the female servant to enquire what we were to do, as I was convinced some accident had happened it was nearly dark when they returned with two cloaks, lantern and tinder box on account of the first dray having upset at what is called the 49 mile pinch and that the cart would be sent down to us. I soon after heard Tom's voice high above my head I blamed him for keeping me so long in suspense but he said I had desired him to call if they were safe which he did as soon as the dray was unloaded and reloaded tired as we were, all were employed in breaking wood and making fires it was quite dark before the cart came, in it were two great coats and a shawl a piece of bread and a little arrowroot. I gave it to the poor children to little Neddy I gave the arrowroot and we hushed him to sleep. Mother sat down with him in her lap before a fire Ann and George were wrapped up and laid on the ground beside her the four girls I laid in the cart with a great coat over them I began to feel very weary and chilly about 9 two drays arrived but to stand and listen as I had previously done to the noise of the men endeavouring to cheer the cattle and the dreadful rumbling with which they descended was enough to create a sensation of terror in a very stout heart to see them was impossible until they got close to us. Hawkins was still at the top of the hill remaining with the last drays which from the darkness and fatigue of the horses and men it was found could not be got down that night. They had now to get water and put the tea kettle on and some were obliged to walk up the hill and bring down our provisions and many things which we could not do without and two men to remain and watch the dray. Hawkins came down with the others very much fatigued we now had our supper and the tent pitched. It was 11 o'clock when ready for us we got the children from the ground and cart into it and laid ourselves down.

'The next morning we all felt the effects of being exposed so long in the night air and the great fatigue we had after breakfast we walked up to a small rock and sitting down viewed the scene around and felt thankful that the little property we possess was safe for the injury caused by the dray upsetting was trifling. Here as we sat we observed three persons winding among the trees in the valley on horseback they proved to be a clergyman from Parramatta [Samuel Marsden], another gentle-man, and a servant they spoke in rapture of the country from which they were returning. I now felt myself so ill from fatigue that I was forced to go into the tent and lie down I fell asleep and did not wake until the last dray came rumbling heavily by me. Before commencing the journey again which we did about one o'clock I cannot help re-marking on the extreme fatigue the men endured the preceding day without any refreshment from breakfast until their supper at 11 o'clock, one man in particular who was the head driver of our cart a Folkestone man a countryman of our own, behaved uncommonly well when the dray overturned nothing saved the lives of the horses and our property but the stump of a tree by the road side it was suspended over an immense precipice this man was the first who got to the top and hanging by the ropes laboured hard to lighten the dray he likewise was one who went at night to bring down our provisions. Hawkins told him his conduct had been such that he should strongly recommend him to the Com-manding Officer which he has done and in all probability he will either be made an overseer of a party or have a ticket of leave given so that he may work for himself which is reward given to them when their behaviour has been very good . . .

'I should say there never before was such a party of females without any protection for so many hours at the foot of the mountains had any snakes attacked us we should have lost our lives for none of us would have had the courage to kill them.'

After crossing Cox's River and finding pasture for their horses and bullocks, they stopped for a day. For Elizabeth it was a day of 'great fatigue' as she spent it 'giving the children all a good washing and change of clothes'. Then they resumed their journey.

'We again ascended our cart on the 21st we had been sitting for some time on the banks of the river seeing the whole cavalcade cross and when it came to our turn it was with many fears we did the water nearly up to the horses belly and the bottom covered with large pieces of rock and stone enough to overturn the cart and jolt us to death. A man offered to carry little Neddy over in his arms with anxious eyes I watched him through fear his feet might slip and our darling boy have his head dashed against a stone with talking swearing beating our poor bullocks we got safe on the bank on the opposite side. We had now a very long and steep hill before us and as usual they refused to go it was decided that we must have two good horses as it was impossible we could ever get on again Noby Redmond and Lion Lowe (names I can never forget) were placed in a dray with a horse behind and another before them but from its being a constant succession of steep hills we were only able that day to perform 8 miles and rested at 8 in a valley here we were joined by 5 more bullocks from Bathurst.

'We set off early the next morning after going 8 miles reached the Fish river after crossing which we had to ascend our last hill which was very long and very steep. I thought I could never have walked to the top the drays were a considerable time in getting up and were obliged to assist each other we now descended into a most beautiful country to Sidmouth Valley we had to go through a very bad swamp before we got to our resting place . . . We had now my dear Ann accomplished our journey over the mountains the last ten miles we had hardly a spot of level ground all was steep hills. We were now 18 miles from Bathurst the country extremely beautiful gently rising hills covered with wood. We passed Macquarie Plains crossed the Fish River and entered on the plains of Bathurst the road was good being determined to reach home that night we almost trotted which jolted us so dreadfully that I thought every bone would be disjointed it was as much as we could do to keep ourselves on the seats and hold the children as if to the very last our journey was to be made uncomfortable a fine rain began which beat in our faces and made us very cold. At length our house was pointed out to us what a welcome sight the rain was now fearful and before we could reach the home we had to cross the Macquarie River the most dangerous of all. You descend the steep bank and suddenly plunge into the water which was as high as the bottom of the cart the first dray got over but the rest being lower we were obliged to seek another ford for them. We remained alone the driver of the first brought one of his horses over, put it to ours and in we plunged we felt more alarmed for our personal safety at that moment than we had done during the whole journey we reached the opposite side, and all at one moment exclaimed we are over and a few minutes brought us to our house where there was a blazing wood fire to warm and cheer us.

'I have now my dear Bowling and Ann brought you to the end of my journey but I cannot close this long letter without adding a little more I tell Hawkins that had it been possible to have gone any further (as he was always famous for moving us about) we should have done it, but beyond here there is no road. Mother bore the fatigue uncommonly well a journey of such as I have described of 18 days was at her age a very great undertaking but she has recovered from it and is better than I am for I am very thin and not very strong. Our children are all well and happy.'

At Bathurst the Hawkins family lived at first in a three-roomed house made available to them while a two-storey house suitable for their large family was being built. 'Altogether,' Elizabeth told her sister, 'we have no reason to complain of our present situation . . .'

'I think there can be no doubt but we shall do well in a few years prosper but I would never persuade anyone with as large a family as mine and slender means as we possess to leave England for not one in a thousand could expect to be as fortunate as we have been for without the appointment we have and the assistance of the Govt. to bring us here we never could have come on without it we must have been subject to many hard-ships and privations that we have never felt . . .

'Tom and the children are all well George is the most delicate little Edward the plaything of our leisure moments and the darling of all he has ever been a treasured babe from an idea that he was deprived of those little comforts attached to infants he is a most healthy and lovely child and it will be worthy of remark that born in England his first birthday was spent at Bathurst the day on which his father took on himself the duties of commissariat no child so young I should think ever travelled so far.'

Thomas Hawkins remained in charge of the government stores at Bathurst for only about a year. Soon after arriving in the district, he selected 2000 acres on the Macquarie River and by 1828 held 2400 acres and was running substantial flocks of sheep and herds of cattle. He built a fine brick house, cleared and fenced the land, formed a garden and planted crops. In 1831 he sent wine made from his grapes to Sydney, the first wine made west of the Blue Mountains.

Gradually the number of women living near Bathurst increased, to some extent ending Elizabeth Hawkins's 'seclusion from the world'. Janet Ranken arrived the next year (see Chapter 11) and among other later arrivals were the Innes family and Captain and Mrs John Piper. As they became older, the Hawkins children were sent to school in Sydney.[3]

In the midst of his success as a farmer, Thomas Hawkins died aged 56 on 27 May 1837 while on a visit to Sydney. The property was let and Elizabeth Hawkins moved to Sydney, where she lived until her death on 6 April 1875 at the age of 91. She had thirteen children, two of whom had died in infancy in England. Three were born after the family settled at Bathurst.

## Elizabeth Fenton

*Would to Heaven my confinement were well over*

How Elizabeth Fenton differed from the archetypal sturdy pioneer! In 1829, on her first walk in Hobart, her black satin shoes filled with mud and water, yet she clung to these symbols of refined living. She was still wearing this most inappropriate footwear over a year later when she travelled over a rough track above the Derwent to her new home in the bush. Elizabeth came to Hobart from India, where she had been used to many servants and enjoyed a life requiring little exertion.

She was born Elizabeth Knox, probably in 1804, a daughter of Rev. John Russel Knox, rector of Lifford and afterwards of Innismagrath, Co. Leitrim, Ireland. In the middle of 1826 she married Captain Neil Campbell of the 13th Light Infantry and went with him to India where Campbell died about a year later. On 20 May 1828 in Calcutta Elizabeth married Campbell's fellow officer, Captain Michael Fenton, a 39-year-old Irishman from Castle Town, Co. Sligo. Soon after their marriage, Fenton resigned his commission and decided to emigrate to Australia. They chose Van Diemen's Land when Fenton was offered a position running the property of lawyer Charles Prinsep under an arrangement that he would receive a half-share of the increase in stock.

Fenton preceded his wife, who detoured to the Isle of France (Mauritius) to give birth to her first child, Flora, born in March 1829. Elizabeth sailed for Van Diemen's Land on the *Denmark Hill* in June that year. Her account of her arrival and the first year or so of her life in Tasmania is reproduced in extracts from her diary.[4]

Her style of writing is very interesting. It differs both from diaries in which the writer confides thoughts not intended for other eyes and from those containing a superficial, shorthand account of events. Elizabeth Fenton's diary is a dramatic account written for and intended to be read by others. It was probably posted in instalments to relatives and passed on from one to the other. Although basically a day-to-day diary kept at the time, there may have been some later rewriting and dramatisation. What these alterations were we will never know unless her original diary is discovered, but there is obviously enough of her contemporary writing to make it a valuable record of the arrival in Van Diemen's Land of a lady initially unsuited to colonial life and her gradual adaptation to it. Nightmares haunted her as she coped with convict servants she believed were malevolent, as well as hazardous travelling, the desperate illness of her baby and a further pregnancy. Alarming problems beset her arrival in Hobart.

*'11th August [1829].— On the River Derwent, in sight of Mount Wellington, and Hobarton.*

'Though there is but one thought absorbing my mind, I must not anticipate, but tell you that after seven weeks of most awful weather we got sight of land. You may judge my thankfulness, as three weeks we had been under water on deck, nor had the daylight entered my cabin. 'Tis vain now to waste time dwelling on all the suffering of such a period with a baby at my breast, but I may express how much valuable aid I had from my humble friend Mrs. Hughes, and kind attention from Mr. Betts, who nightly stopped to speak and cheer me, sometimes, if it was tempestuous, nursing Flora or assisting to bathe her and beguile our mutual discomfort.'

Immediately Elizabeth sought information about her husband, eventually discovering that he had sailed for Mauritius believing that his wife was still there. She reflected:

'I had taken this miserable voyage in vain, and was *alone* in Van Diemen's Land, while Fenton was retracing the perilous sea I had just crossed.

'Surely I am doomed in everything, and for me there is no haven of peace on this side of time.'

Elizabeth Fenton gained assistance from the port officer, Lieutenant Hill, Government Surveyor George Frankland and his wife, Ann, and Lieutenant Governor George Arthur in having a boat sent off to try to catch the *Orelia* which her husband had chartered to sail to Mauritius, intending, in addition to collecting his wife, to invest in a cargo of sugar to bring back to Van Diemen's Land. While anxiously waiting for news of the result, Mrs Fenton left her ship for a hotel in the company of the Franklands, George Frankland having been a close friend of her husband.

*'14th August Macquarie Hotel, Hobarton*

' . . . Then we took our way up Macquarie Street. About half-way I could not resist the temptation of stopping to lean upon a fence almost breathless, this being the longest walk I had taken for some years; and further being equipped in black satin shoes, they were penetrated by wet and fringed with mud. Mrs Frankland's recollections of the habits of India soon explained my distress, and the party kindly accommodated themselves to my feebleness and unequal strength until we reached the hotel, when, after inspecting the rooms ordered, Mr Frankland with equal kindness and tact proposed they should all leave me to rest for an hour, when he would return and take me to his house, which proposal I readily agreed to . . .

'On my return to the Macquarie Hotel, I felt so nervous, to sleep was impossible, and I stepped out on a little balcony to look on the waters with which my future destinies and that of my babe were mixed up, and on the strange stars above me . . .

'I have in the midst of other disjointed thoughts to-night half inclined to the idea of returning to India, if Fenton's return is hopeless. I must in this case have seven solitary months to spend here, how I know not . . .

'[*15th August*]
' . . . This is the third day since the departure of the whale-boat, one or two more must decide my measures.'

The whale boat succeeded in overtaking the ship in which Fenton was travelling and brought him back to Hobart, where Elizabeth was overjoyed to see him.

'[*August 17th*]
'I do not think any comparison can be fairly made between the love of a father and a mother for an *infant*. But he was evidently delighted with Flora. She could not be passed unnoticed by a stranger, and the dullest parent must have regarded with delight the lovely creature, just able to sit up and know it to be a *stranger* who embraced her. Visitors came in rapid succession. At length with Flora enveloped under the nurse's cloak, we proceeded to Mrs F.'s drawing room and spent a delightful evening; Fenton and Frankland were in such high spirits, and even the children seemed delighted to see him.'

After being reunited, the Fentons lived in Hobart for nearly a year. Fenton was often away in the bush looking after property for his partner Prinsep; Elizabeth was occupied with domestic arrangements and difficulties with servants.

'*3rd October*—
' . . . The perpetual encroachment of the servants on my time is indescribable. After our breakfast at eight o'clock, I order dinner and go with the cook to the store room, for anything requisite, for I need hardly remind you of the direful necessity of having to lock every-thing up yourself. Here my daily admonition is, "Take all you want *now*, for I will not come here again." Then perhaps the cook departs to the market for any small articles wanted; in an hour after, when perhaps I am nursing the baby or writing a letter, or arranging my clothes, a knock comes to

the door: "Please, mam, will you give me some rice, or some sugar or spice, or something else out of the storeroom?" It is in vain to remind the offender that I said I would not go there again. His or her "Very well, mam" will not supply the deficient article when dinner comes, and the only redress left me of "sending him in" will only give me another to pursue the self-same plan of annoyance, which is repeated in every family in the Colony . . .

'I may tell you here what my establishment consists of: a nurse, a cook, a laundress, a housemaid, a man who cuts wood and is groom; the boy I brought from India I have kept with the idea of training him for an inside servant; I cannot yet reconcile myself to the attendance of a convict, though I see them at every house in town, and admirable servants too. All *these* ideas I am told I shall lay aside and do as others do after a little experience. So this is my household at present. I asked the housemaid yesterday while I was giving her some work what she had been sent out to this Colony for : "Please mam, for *housebreaking*"; a very pretty, neat, dark-eyed girl.'

Early in 1830, Elizabeth Fenton's baby daughter became seriously ill.

'*7th February [1830].*—
'My dear friend, never did any of your dear letters reach me at a more critical moment than the last—of 29th of August—yet it lay three days *unread*. I opened it and looked at the signature, but read it I could not;—you will wonder when I tell you that my baby, the very light of my eyes, was then quite despaired of and given up by all but myself— even when there was no hope to any other, still I said She will not die. She is now out of danger and renews her wonted smiles and endearments. But oh! what have I suffered! Sleep has altogether forsaken me, my strength too is wasted; though I force myself to eat and drink for her sake, it oppresses, not revives me . . .'

'*5th May*
'And is this an anniversary of marriage? Eheu! What a bewildering dream, of a few nights since, this day recalls. I fancied myself yet unmarried and living in Ireland...I raised myself with an indescribable terror of *what*, of who, was *that child*. Nor was it till after I sat up in bed, and, by the lamp, looked steadily at her and at Fenton, both sound asleep, that I regained a conviction of my identity; but with renewed consciousness came also a faint and giddy sickness, which actually forced me to lie down and close my eyes. Floods of repressed tears at length enabled me to breathe, and I lay in sad and troubled rumination till daylight. *These* dreams are truly terrible, they seem to let loose all the long pent up waters of affliction on the soul. Indeed, for two days after,

I could not regain the composure of my mind. Strange voices seemed about me, and visionary shapes passing before my eyes . . . '

By July 1830 the Fentons were preparing to leave Hobart to live on Fenton's grant near New Norfolk. Writing retrospectively from Fenton Forest on 12 August 1830, Elizabeth Fenton described the journey. She was in the early stages of her next pregnancy and her husband had only partly recovered from a serious illness.

*'12th August [1830] Fenton Forest—*
' . . . On the 12th [of July] the weather had cleared; a very bright morning, too bright to last decided Fenton, and though he was extremely weak we set off in our buggy with Flora on my knee, her nurse and a girl from the Orphan Asylum having gone the evening before to wait our arrival at New Norfolk. I need not detail all promises to write and parting regrets. The thing was to be done one way or other, and though I felt both ill and very nervous, from knowing my illness was only the commencement of a period of indefinite suffering, I knew too, that the effort must be made, and the sooner the better for all parties . . .

'The [following] day seeming tolerably clear, we sent off the women in their bullock cart, calculating they would have good light to get home before us. To the nurse I gave the baby's night things, etc. etc. When *they* were gone and *we were going*, Mrs. Bridger [the innkeeper] came up to me with an important face to caution me with respect to my nurse, whom she believed to be one of the worst women in the Colony— everything that was bad and depraved—she had gone away nearly drunk, and was quite drunk on her arrival the day before. This was pleasant intelligence to one with my anticipations, but I thanked her warmly for her caution.

'We proceeded as far as a terrific ledge of rocks overhanging the river round which the road wound, midway between the river and a perpendicular cliff, along whose edge and at whose summit huge masses of rock jutted out and seemed as if they must inevitably crush us at every onward step; even the motion of the carriage below seemed sufficient to impel them forward, and through their angles you saw the sky above at intervals: these threatening on the left and the abyss of the river many fathoms below constituted together a fearful position. On entering this pass Fenton pulled up the hood of the buggy and drove our spirited horse on at full speed, expecting I might not observe our situation. I *did* see it, but forbore to speak until fairly past. I could not then resist remonstrating on such a mode of driving over such awful roads. We had no more precipices, but the road, if road it might be called, was a succession of gulfs and mire, through which it required the utmost effort of our fine horse to drag us. Every step I believed an upset inevitable.

I grasped the poor infant to save *her* from the bruises I received on every side. My comb was broken and my head cut by one sudden jolt, and I perceived too late the personal danger that such a journey exposed me to.

'If I might bear up until we reached the shelter of a house, was the extent of my wishes and expectations; as we stood to breathe the poor horse after toiling up a steep and slippery hill, a storm of blinding hail and snow swept down from the mountains in our faces, and Fenton had to get out and turn the carriage off the road where a clump of mimosas formed a shelter from the storm. He was drenched with rain and snow, and if my fears for myself were strong, you may judge what I dreaded at seeing him, who had just arisen from a bed of illness, in such a condition.

'The baby too, cold and hungry, was fretting on my knee, and I shed bitter tears over her as the gloom of the evening approached. After the storm was passed we again proceeded, but very slowly, the horse seeming quite spent. After toiling up another weary hill the snow again came on, and again we stopped. I then in despair inquired if there was no human habitation within reach where we might pass the night. He told me he thought we must be near the residence of Frederick Bell whom I had met at the Hamiltons; if we could find the entrance, as each side of the road was fenced with fallen trees piled on each other. After some difficulty we reached a gate and entered a waste of wood without trace of either man or animal, and drove onward at hazard, for now it was so dark we could barely distinguish one object from another.

'Judge of my distress at this juncture, with a sick infant on my knee and almost powerless with fear and cold myself. The distant bark of a dog was to me a sound whose blessedness I never shall forget, and then the report of a gun directed us where to drive, and we approached a dwelling. In the darkness the light of fires within was a joyful revelation.

'Without inquiry as to who were within, Fenton assisted me out and gave the child into the arms of a man, who informed him that Mr. Bell was just come back from Hobarton, and showed us into a small apartment where Mr. Bell sat drying himself before an immense fire. You may well imagine his amazement when I staggered in, faint and blind with the sudden glare of light—a lady and an infant, at such an hour!

'Most kind and cordial was our welcome—every effort of master and man to revive and refresh us was bestowed; a cup of nice soup brought for the baby, who seemed quite joyful at the sudden change from the darkness and storm without, to the cheerful scene; so after the refreshment of warm water and dry clothes for Fenton we joined Mr. Bell at his excellent dinner, though a late one. When it was concluded and we heard and told the "on dits" of the day, I had leisure to notice that Flora seemed flushed and her pulse rapid and unsteady. Mr Bell summoned his man "John" to procure me some water for a bath and told me he had a medicine chest, out of which I at once prepared the prescribed dose.

'It was then I recollected with dismay that I had not a single article to put on her, and she had always slept in flannel. *Here* was a difficulty beyond Mr. Bell's hospitality to remedy. The only linen article he could afford me was a *shirt* or a *sheet*, so selecting the former I divested myself of my only warm garment—my under petticoat—into which I put my *poor* Flora and gathered it round her throat somewhat in the fashion of a mantle. Over this was a muslin shirt confined round her waist with the band of my gown. Her papa's silk hankerchief bound her head, and in this guise she dropped asleep.

'Where to lay her down was my next perplexity, for Mr. Bell's accommodation was strictly that of a bachelor. He had slept in his sea cot swung in the only bedchamber, which he most kindly offered to us, and a couch was prepared on the floor, which no doubt might have been very comfortable for one person but for three was scanty quarters. Such as it was, I was very glad to see Fenton and Flora asleep thereon.

'It was extremely cold and how to manage the night without a fire or a lamp I could not divine. For myself, I was faint and shivering with cold, and nothing to put on but Mr. Bell's shirt, to which I added a sheet folded something as a shawl, and thus I laid me down on the hard edge of the cot fearing to disturb those who each needed sleep so much. I did not care to cover myself with the blankets lest the baby should be disturbed, and for her to sleep after taking calomel was of vital importance. My anxiety was too great for sleep and I lay watching her as long as the candle burned. But long and dreary was that vigil. Towards morning she awoke very sick, but as it was utterly dark my only mode of keeping her quiet was walking to and fro through the apartment with her in my arms, until Fenton woke.

'It was then the cold pale twilight of a winter morning, and I did not scruple to send him to rouse our friend "John" to get a fire made and some tea, of which we most thankfully partook. I was, in addition to loss of sleep and fatigue, struggling against the most overpowering sickness. The only thing I had to keep me up was, that after Flora was bathed and had got a sufficiency of warm nourishment, she appeared evidently relieved by the calomel, which I rejoiced I had so timely administered.

'It was one of those bright days which generally follow a snowstorm, warm and invigorating; but Mr. Bell strongly advised us to give up the idea of pursuing our journey on this side of the Derwent, as our buggy would never get through it. Fenton then took a survey of Mr. Bell's boat and said he would attempt the Indian mode of crossing, with the body of the vehicle in the boat, the wheels over the side. All who listened said it was impossible, but the thing was done, and the horse swam the river gallantly.

'I ought to tell you the object of this excursion was to gain a certain point where a boat would pass from the farm of a Mr. Barker to that of a Mr. Ballatine. Once at Mr. Ballatine's we were nearly on our own property, and could drive over the plains in an hour;—furthermore, I must tell you the said Mr Barker was introduced to me while getting into the buggy at the inn at New Norfolk as a "neighbour", and I "guess" my acknowledgment of him was not very alluring—for, truth to tell, he looked mean and dirty, and I should have forgotten him only for the present arrangement.

'On inquiring of Fenton who and what he was, he told me he was now a man of very large property, one of our squires! had been a shopkeeper, partner with another illustrious, Kemp, who still kept the concern in town, only *calling himself* an agent or merchant. They were among the very early settlers and had both feathered their nest in the "good old times" when they sold a pound of tea for £1,2p.6d.

'I had hoped when the river was safely passed my troubles were well over, but a new and very embarrassing dilemma presented itself; neither soothing nor force would induce our horse to go into the buggy (I mean into the shafts). They said it was fright at the uproar of crossing the water, but it was evident his resolution was taken, and whenever backed to the carriage he reared and plunged in a way that would have intimidated a more daring person than myself. It was then suggested that if once on the road, and out of sight of the water, he would get quiet and proceed; so Mr Bell kindly sent two men to drag the buggy into the road about a mile, *at least*, and bade us farewell, business requiring his return. He promised an early visit to Fenton Forest.

'The day was delightful, and with renewed hope and energy I took Flora in my arms and followed the procession, Fenton leading the horse while I took a path through the trees that seemed drier.

'I wish, my dear, I could honestly keep back one *fact*, which was that that I had been so very *absurd* as to set out on this expedition in black satin boots; but the truth must be told, otherwise you could not understand why it was that ever and anon I sat down to ease the pain of my bruised feet, for the boots were in fragments with the rough ground I had to walk through. Then finding the *mile* lengthened fearfully out, my strength quite failed. I put Flora, as the Indian women do, on my hips, on my back, tried to induce her to walk, all in vain. The thought of "Hagar in the desert" came to me as I lay down under a mimosa which spread bower-like over the footpath, and some few tears of weariness and pain were shed in spite of all my striving against them: and then again I pursued my way, with the double toil of trying to amuse the child as well as carry.

'The road attained, with some little difficulty the horse reluctantly was harnessed, but when he once got the rein he flew *on, on,* while I was breathless with horror, supposing some greater evil yet to come. We were on Macquarie plains and the way had hitherto been level, but steep hills were in view, which tenfold aggravated my horror. Fenton pointed out the site of Mr Barker's house, but my sight was dim with fear and weariness. My expedition seemed like that of Leonora and the Spectre Horseman.

'The road wound up a hill, whose inequalities and side motion were so dreadful that I implored Fenton to let me out, and not kill the infant, if he would himself. I vowed in my terror never again to let him drive me and at last succeeded in getting out with the baby. It was so close to Mr. Barker's house, and heedless of mire I got as far from the buggy as I could. Mr B. was at that moment engaged in the pastoral duty of ploughing, but he approached and offered me his arm, and so we neared his house, which was a new and capacious stone building of handsome appearance. To enter was *not* so easy for every species of filth you can imagine had been quietly deposited about the doors, and it was floating with mud. Hesitating how to emerge into this Augean pool, and dreading being overthrown by contact with large pigs if I invaded their "pleasure ground", I decided the point by letting Fenton carry me into the hall. A handsome hall it might have been, but just then seemed doing double duty of barn and scullery. I was introduced into the parlour, and after being told the lady of the mansion would instantly wait on me, the gentlemen went off to investigate the prospect of the boat and river . . . '

After further travel, Mrs Fenton glimpsed her new home.

'It was a long, shapeless, naked, brick cottage outside, but oh! within, there was confusion worse confounded. Every article of baggage that had been sent up, furniture, packing cases, had all been piled up, promiscuously, as they presented themselves. The vile servants we had sent out had profited by the opportunity to pillage everything they could abstract. All the farm servants had collected in the house and the nurse— my right-hand woman, as I took her to be—had opened a keg of rum for their refreshment; rum, tobacco, noise and dirt assailed every sense with horror and dismay.

'My choice of accommodation was not difficult, for there was only one apartment with a *door.* Turn where I would, comfort found I none. Oh! how I wished myself back in India after a comfortless dinner; by the time I got out some things for the child, weary of everything I undressed and went to bed, and I must fairly confess cried myself to sleep.'

During the second half of 1830, Elizabeth Fenton created order out of chaos in her new home. She ended the year, however, exceedingly worried about her husband's poor health and wishing 'to Heaven my confinement were well over and my capability to exert myself renewed'. At this point, according to a note by Sir Henry Lawrence who wrote the preface to her published journal, Elizabeth Fenton's journal ceased 'abruptly, and was never resumed in the same form'.

Elizabeth Fenton survived her early years in Tasmania to become a long-lived pioneer of the New Norfolk district and a mother of six. She died in her seventies in 1876, two years after the death of her husband who had recovered from his poor health to become a prominent Tasmanian politician and successful farmer.

## Jane Franklin

*I write from an Encampment on the right bank of the Murray*

During the time her husband was governor of Van Diemen's Land, Jane Franklin made Hobart a centre for intellectual activities. In 1839 she founded the first Royal Society for the advancement of science outside Britain and she bought land for a botanical garden where she had a museum of natural history built. She also initiated moves to aid the reformation of women prisoners and to promote the establishment of a state college.

Lady Franklin was also an indefatigable traveller. She was the first European woman to climb Mount Wellington and the first to travel overland from Melbourne to Sydney and from Hobart to Macquarie Harbour.

Born Jane Griffin in London on 4 December 1791, she was the daughter of a wealthy silk weaver of Huguenot descent. Until her marriage she spent much of her life travelling in Europe. In 1828, at the age of 37, she became the second wife of John Franklin, a noted Arctic explorer, who was knighted soon after. Early in 1837 they arrived in Van Diemen's Land on the *Fairlie*, following Sir John's appointment as Lieutenant Governor.

In 1839, deciding to travel overland from Melbourne to Sydney, Jane Franklin and her entourage left Hobart on the brig *Tamar*. They arrived in Melbourne on 3 April 1839 and left two days later for Sydney. In Lady Franklin's party were Sir John Franklin's niece and Lady Franklin's companion, Sophy Cracroft, military escort Captain William Moriarty, aide-de-camp Henry Elliot, physician and amateur naturalist Dr Edmund Hobson, police magistrate Frederick Powlett, a maid and a servant, two cart drivers and various military escorts.

Supported by such a party, Lady Franklin's journey did not equal in danger or rigour those of Elizabeth Hawkins over the Blue Mountains or even Elizabeth Fenton's short journey along the Derwent to New Norfolk in Tasmania. Nevertheless, it was the first overland journey between Melbourne and Sydney made by women and it gains interest from comments Lady Franklin made in her diary and in letters. Often regarded as the power behind her husband, her letters show that she had opinions on government and political matters and that she regarded her journey as an information-gathering exercise.

The journey was expected to take 28 days. Stations were established along part of the route and it was expected the party would have to sleep in the bush on only about five or six nights. Jane wrote to her husband on 5 April 1839 about her arrival and reception in Melbourne:[5]

'We landed in a mud bank on our left, (ascending the river) and found ready to receive us the same gentleman we thought we had left behind but who had taken a shorter cut to land; and many others collected there. Amongst these were Mr. Robinson (whose family had arrived a day or two before in the *Vansitart*) and Mr. Hawkey (of the *Fairlie*) dressed like a wild German youth, with flowing locks, moustachios &c. A smart little carriage having three seats for six people placed one behind the other, with a pair of horses was in waiting. The carriage bore on its pannels "From Melbourne to Geelong" with a Fox's head for a crest, and the motto "Tally Ho". It is the property of Mr Tulip Wright and is to start shortly as a regular stage coach also carrying the Mail, for Geelong, a distance now of 50 miles, but which will shortly when the punt is ready to cross an intervening salt water creek be only 40. Capt. Lonsdale informed me he had one room in his house at my service; but having learnt in my way that there was an Hotel with respectable accommodation I begged to prefer the latter as we could then be all together, a proposition which met with no opposition, and we accordingly drove to Mr. Fawkners Hotel where we were expected. Mr. F formerly kept the Cornwall Hotel at Launceston, and is the son of a man who came out in the first Convict ship to Port Phillip 36 years ago. They are not people of the first respectability but are doing well in this money making place. He is the Editor of a Newspaper, the *Patriot* and his printing press is in the room adjoining my bed room.

'Our first enquiries were of course as to the practibility of the road, and the fitness of the season, and as usual all difficulties vanished on a near approach. We could not possibly have chosen a fitter season of the year, nor have hit upon a more lucky moment, for rain had fallen and forage and water were said to be in sufficient quantity, and "the rains" were not likely to come on for a month to come. We have not heard a single dissenting voice upon these points. Two mounted policemen, one being a sergeant, were in readiness, and an additional one was intended but something prevented.—I thought *one* quite enough, but we were not to be excused from having two.

'On arriving at the Inn, Capt. Lonsdale asked me when I would like to receive visitors, and I told him at three, expecting thus to have an hour of quietness. Mrs Lonsdale however immediately arrived and sat with me above an hour before any one else came in. Then they came in, one after another for an hour and half, when finding myself and poor Sophy too, quite ill and absolutely unable to go through any more of it, I procured first some luncheon and then the same Mr Tulip Wright's carriage to be brought to the door in which we escaped from the rest. We were driven round about and through the Town and outskirts and ended with Capt. Lonsdale's residence w[h]ere we left the and returned home as it was getting dark. No one had ordered dinner and it was a long time before we could get some mutton chops.

'About eight or nine oclock we went out to see a Coroberry of the natives who are encamped in the outskirts and who, consisting of the tribes usually frequenting this port and of several more distant ones, are supposed to amount just now to about four or five hundred.

'The Coroberry of one of the stranger tribes was over before we arrived on the ground. After a long delay during which the men were painting themselves the home tribes began their dances. For this purpose they had thrown aside their skins or blankets and were perfectly naked (except bundles of heavy fringes hanging round their loins like aprons) their breasts, arms, and thighs and legs were marked with broad white belts of pipe clay and borders of the same were traced round their eyes. Round their ancles they wore large ruffs of the gum tree branches and in each hand they held a piece of hard wood which they were constantly employed in striking against each other. The leader of the band was an elderly man, dressed in a blanket who stood with his face towards a group of women squatted on the grass, and who beat time with their hands on some folded opossum skins, thus producing a dull, hollow accompaniment. They sang also the whole time, in the style of the Flinders Island people, led by the old man.

'With the exception of these songs there was little else which reminded us of the exhibition at Flinders. The principal feat performed by these savages was quite indescribable, it was performed by stretching out their legs as wide as possible, and making them quiver with great rapidity, and as if they didn't touch the ground, a deception aided by the boughs round their ancles. One would have thought the trunk of the body a prop on which to rest, while the lower limbs were thus shaking, apparently without touching the ground. They did not all commence simultaneously, but rapidly advanced one before the other, never clashing and constantly coming forward, and reminded me in this and in the manner in which they addressed themselves in face to the spectators of the kickers and jumpers and spinners on the Opera Boards. At last they formed a line close to our faces, changed their posture and measures, kicked up the dust with tremendous vehemence, in the way of a salute turned half round and with bent bodies and with extreme rapidity slank away. Mr. Robinson[6] and his family have not called on me, and he seems a little shy when I meet him, tho' always respectful.

'Dr. Hobson left the *Tamar* before we disembarked in order to visit his brother who is feeding his sheep somewhere near "Arthur's Seat" towards Western Port, and to our surprise he is not yet returned, tho' we have staid here a day longer than we intended, that is two days. I am now writing on Saturday the 6th. It was thought desirable that either now or at the next station the horses should have two days rest, not being after their voyage in their ordinary state of freshness. I thought it best therefore to stop an additional day here and was the more disposed to do this as we are entirely independent and put no one to inconvenience. Mr. Wright's carriage was again put in requisition yesterday, and we drove a few miles out of town towards mount Macedon on fine open grassy grounds of beautiful verdure in many places, and very scantily wooded. These grounds fell down towards the S.W. in low shelving banks, towards a dried lagoon whitened with salt and which is skirted on the farther side by what they call the South Yarra, the embouchure of which we had passed in our passage up to Melbourne. The scenery upon the whole is somewhat novel to our eyes, long accustomed to our own mountainous country, dense woods, and bush-encumbered ground-surfaces. It is however less picturesque and much tamer.

'The weather yesterday was extremely hot, and Mr. Wright's horses stopped short at every hillock.

'The horse bought at Launceston for the spring cart is found to be not fit for the journey, and another has been purchased at a higher price of Mr. Wright.

'Capt Lonsdale asked us yesterday (the 2d day) to dinner, but we were sure he was not displeased at our declining. I asked them to tea with Mr Simpson and a Lady who is staying at this hotel of the name of Wills, whose husband a magistrate of New South Wales has just set off overland for Sydney. Mr Simpson says you have congratulated him on an office he is not yet appointed to. He is an agreeable man, and we had much conversation about the people of Van Diemens Land.

*Lifelines*

'Capt Lonsdale received only yesterday a letter from Sir George Gipps begging him to do every thing for me. It seemed to give him increased zeal in my cause, but he said it was impossible for him to obey his instructions since I wanted nothing. He had received the first intimation of our intended arrival from Mr Forster a very short time ago. Mr Simpson said if he had known of it a week ago he would have gone with us to Sydney . . .

'We have had the greatest difficulty to make Mr Fawkner agree to take any payment for the accommodation, &c he has afforded us. "The honor was everything". This would not do, and at last Capt Moriarty has made him promise to make out his bill, but this is only on condition that I will honor his "library" with a visit. I suppose I must subscribe to the good man's paper in return, but as the other one is said to be the best of the two, this is a pity, and perhaps should lead to a double subscription or not at all. It is not probable that both will last. We hope to get today as far as Mr Thorloe's station 20 miles off, he is expecting us,—but the Deputation, does not arrive . . .'

By 20 April, Jane Franklin and her party had reached the River Murray. She wrote from an 'Encampment on the right bank of the Murray':

'We have arrived safely at this important point of our journey and I must commemmorate the event by dating a fresh sheet to you from it. Our last stage of 14 or 15 miles from Joe Slack's station was performed in about 5 hours, our progress having been somewhat interrupted by numerous creeks, and the descent from steep and awkward banks, into the reedy and occasionally inundated flats.

'The first few miles run along the lower declivities of some lightly wooded banks projecting from a range of hills which obtained a higher elevation on our right as we proceeded, but were only partially seen through the foliage of the intervening plain . . .

'The river here makes a deep bow, the bight of which is towards the E. and a little below it is the crossing-place or ford. The banks were not lofty, but were rather steep. They descended however in the present state of the river not into the water but upon a flat beach of shingles, which was a great advantage to me in crossing. The water in the deepest part did not come above the horses girths, and the current was not sufficiently strong to render it a matter of any difficulty to stem it. The water here may be 80 yards across, and the stream tho' thus easy of passage, was much more rapid than any we had hitherto seen. In times of flood it is dangerous on account of this rapidity as well as on account of the steepness of its banks. We were told that parson Docker's drays [see the article on Sarah Docker in chapter 4] had been overturned in it, and one bullock drowned on the occasion. Accidents to human life

134

have also occurred at this passage since it has become the high way between the old colony and the El dorado of Port Phillip. On the right bank of the Murray are two inhabited dwellings, and a smaller unfinished one, the latter belongs to a Mr Lewis whose cattle station we had passed 2 miles on the other side of the river. Of the former, one is the spacious hut of a Mr Brown erected for a store, and standing on the forest plain near the water, and the other is the station of the mounted Police perched upon the steep declivity (which a few hundred yards below Mr Brown's rises from the edge of the water) of the lofty and undulating bank. On a flat enclosed paddock between these two dwellings and meant as a reserve pasture for the horses of the mounted police we pitched our encampment rejoicing to have passed that formidable river which had hitherto been represented to us as the greatest obstacle we had to fear and at the same time to have accomplished half of our journey to Yass or 200 miles exactly in a fortnight . . .'

When she reached Yass on 2 May, Lady Franklin wrote not about her journey but about government affairs in Van Diemen's Land. The contents of the letter show quite clearly how closely she was involved in the affairs of government. Referring to a letter she had received from Mr Forster[7] she wrote:

'Pray tell him I am much pleased and obliged by it. He answers almost every point on which I wrote, and particularly as regards the Regatta extension meeting (upon which he greatly regrets my absence) the Horticultural Society, the Colonial Infant School, schoolmasters, in which he says he has encouragement from you that something will be done on an extended scale. He promises to use his influence at the Colonial office for Dr Hobson, whenever you have found a situation as Naturalist or in any other department for him, saying it is of no use to ask for general assistance. It seems by this that Mr F. does not understand that what is wanted at the Colonial Office is the making of the office of Naturalist, or does Mr F. mean that if you and the Legislative council created such an office, then would be the time to apply for the salary? Some public expression in the Council, perhaps, of the desirableness of such an appointment would be useful. The more I see of Dr Hobson the more anxious I am that the Colony should not lose the benefit of his services. He does not wish to live in any other part of the Colony but Hobarton, he could not carry on his researches to advantage elsewhere, nor would he care to practice elsewhere. Private practice in Hobarton, joined to the Naturalist situation is that which he prefers to all work. He has already pared a considerable number of things for the embryo Museum, and told me he had expended £200 of his own in skeletons and other things, which he has given to a Museum in England. He wishes the Museum at Hobarton to be in a miniature way, on the plan of the Universal Hunterian Museum at the College of Surgeons, the comparative anatomy being of the first importance.

'There seems from what Mr F. tells me every probability of your relation with the Attorney General coming to an end. I do hope it may be so, for it is impossible the credit of your Government can be supported without such a step . . . '

After diverging to travel through the Illawarra district, Jane and her party rejoined the road to Sydney at Campbelltown and were met at Liverpool by a carriage sent by the New South Wales Governor Sir George Gipps. During a lengthy stay at Government House, Lady Franklin continued writing letters telling her husband the latest Sydney political news, stating her opinions on the important people she met and advising him of her views on developments in the government at Hobart. Before sailing for Hobart on the *Medway* early in July, she travelled by ship to Newcastle, visited Port Stephens and toured the Hunter district.

The Franklins left Van Diemen's Land in 1843. Four years later Sir John Franklin, at the age of 59, led another naval expedition seeking a north-west passage through the Arctic. The expedition did not return and Lady Franklin spent the following years organising search parties for the lost expedition. In 1859 searchers in her ship, the *Fox*, brought back news that relics of the expedition had been found on the north-west coast of King William's Land. Franklin had died on 11 June 1847 within sight of the North-West Passage. Lady Franklin died in England on 18 July 1875.

Margaret Catchpole (*left*) (ink and grey wash, by an unknown artist, courtesy Dixson Library, State Library of New South Wales) and (*below*) a sample of handwriting, showing the economical measure of writing twice upon the page (courtesy Mitchell Library, State Library of New South Wales)

Elizabeth Macarthur (oil
portrait, n.d., courtesy Dixson
Galleries, State Library of New
South Wales)

Portrait of Mrs Samuel
Marsden (courtesy National
Library of Australia, Philip
Geeves collection)

Portrait of Anna Josepha King,
ca 1805. Oil on canvas, 61 ×
50.5 cm. (on loan from Mr
R. W. L. King, courtesy
National Library of Australia)

The Docker family (photograph, 1898, courtesy Mitchell Library, State Library
of New South Wales)

Mrs William Paterson (oil portrait by William Owen, n.d. courtesy Dixson Galleries, State Library of New South Wales)

Portrait of Eliza, wife of Governor Darling 1825, by John Linnell, 1792–1882. Oil on wood panel 30.3 × 24.5 cm (courtesy National Library of Australia)

Mary Putland (Lady Mary O'Connell. Watercolour on ivory miniature, c. 1790. Courtesy Dixson Galleries, State Library of New South Wales)

The Female School of Industry (courtesy National Library of Australia, ref. F1735 Australian Almanack & Sydney Directory)

Elizabeth Macquarie (miniature
on ivory, n.d., courtesy
Mitchell Library, State Library
of New South Wales)

Anne Bourke's mother,
Elizabeth Bourke (part of set
of 5 miniatures of Richard
Bourke and family, 1800.
Courtesy Mitchell Library,
State Library of New South
Wales)

Elizabeth Hawkins (courtesy
National Library of Australia,
ref. N/994.006/ROY, R.A.H.S.
Journal, Vol. IX, 1923, Part
IV, p. 179)

Ann Hordern (photograph,
n.d., courtesy Mitchell Library,
State Library of New South
Wales)

Mary Thomas (courtesy National
Library of Australia, ref. 994.2/
THO, The diaries and letters of
Mary Thomas, frontispiece)

Georgiana Molloy (courtesy
Busseltown Historical Association)

# 10
## Shopkeepers and needlewomen

### Sarah Thornton

*I furnish my shop to the best advantage*

Sarah Thornton's story is the inspiring tale of a woman sentenced to transportation for life who, through hard work and determination, became a successful businesswoman. In December 1813, Sarah, a needlewoman, was sentenced for stealing lace from a shop in London's Oxford Street. She arrived in Sydney in July 1814 on the *Broxbornebury* and her loyal husband Samuel, a tailor, followed later the same year as a free emigrant to join her. Together they set about making their living in the colony, as Sarah told her relatives in a letter, dated August 1820.[1] Despite her relative success, it is apparent from Sarah's letter that she felt her exile from her homeland very deeply and longed to return. It also emerges that she was one of many convicts about whom there was official confusion concerning the length of sentence caused when records were lost or temporarily mislaid. In Sarah's case the confusion was resolved. She wrote:

'Myself and my husband have had many hard struggles to gain the means of an honest livelihood. To accomplish it we have worked night & day. I thank God that he has crowned our endeavours with success. I rose early in the morning & went to market bringing home my articles on my head, *to furnish my shop* to the best advantage. With the greatest care of our little profits, & the greatest frugality in housekeeping, we collected together a small sum sufficient to buy a little house. I then applied to the Gentlemen of the Colony, for a Licence; which they not only granted, but said they would assist me & my husband in any way in their power, as they had noticed our industry and that we associated with none but persons of good character. This was very gratifying to me and I thank Heaven our efforts have answered our expectations.

'I often wish my dear friend, you could see my little family & they playing round me, while I am milking my cows, or making my bread. O that my voice could be heard by the young people in England, to deter them from evil ways & incline them to keep the path of virtue & honesty that they might not come to this wretched country where so much evil abounds. For though I have by a regular line of good conduct, & great privations arrived at a state of comfort, not one in twenty who is sent here, obtains even the necessaries of life, by their own industry, independent of support from the government. I now intreat your application at the Office of the Secretary of State, to enquire whether I am to remain here for life. I am told by a friend that came from England, that my sentence was only for seven years, & that I could once more return to my Native Country. O! do not neglect to make the inquiry. Think what it is to be an exile for ever from our friends or relations, who are dear to our hearts—Often with overflowing heart & tearful eye, do I think of you and the many endearing hours we have passed together with those other friends of our infancy & childhood. Yet I still feel happy in the thought that I have friends at the immeasurable distance, by whom I am still held in esteem though deprived of the blessing of their society—O my dear friend once more I conjure you by all that is dear to you & myself to make the inquiry, that if possible I may enjoy the hope of seeing you & my other relatives once more.'

Sarah was granted a conditional pardon in 1820 and a free pardon in November 1825. She was then free to return to England, but she died at Parramatta in November 1827 leaving at least five young children. One of her sons, George, who had been born at Macquarie Street on 23 December 1819, was Mayor of Sydney in 1853 and 1857, was twice elected to the Legislative Assembly and was a member of the Legislative Council for over 20 years.[2]

## Ann Hordern

*Checked shirts and satin slops fetch a great price*

It took only one day for Ann Hordern to size up the business opportunities after she arrived in colonial Sydney in 1825. She ended a letter to her parents with a request that they send out ginghams, prints, muslins, lace, ribbons, bonnet shapes and stays so that she could take advantage of the demand for these items among the well dressed women in Sydney. She specified that the stays should be big sizes, as the women 'run large'.

This was the small beginning of what her descendants were to develop into the famous Anthony Hordern department store.

Ann and Anthony Hordern arrived in Sydney in March 1825 on the *Phoenix*. Ann was the daughter of John Woodhead, a London stay- and bonnet-maker, originally from Retford, Nottinghamshire. Anthony, a native of Staffordshire, was working in the East End of London as a wheelwright and coachmaker when he married Ann. They are believed to have migrated because of antagonism by the Hordern family to their marriage; whatever the reason, they both seized the opportunities offered in the town of Sydney as soon as they stepped off the ship.

In a letter to her parents written just after their arrival, Ann gave an account of their voyage.[3] Travelling steerage with their three small sons, Ann was shocked at their first experience of Australia when their ship stopped at Hobart. There were 'dreadful murders and robberies continually'; judges sat six days a week to try the accused. 'I will leave you to judge the awful state of Van Diemen's Land,' she wrote. The town gave her 'a kind of disgust'. She had critical comments for the single-storey weatherboard houses, high rents, the prevailing drought and high prices for food and the 'rubbishy money', among other aspects of life in Hobart. The Horderns had considered settling in Van Diemen's Land, but then decided on Sydney.

'We landed most of the passengers at Van Diemen's Land but they would most of them have been glad to have gone back again to London if they had enough to have gone back with. The flies here are large and flyblow the meat before it is half cold; it is enough to turn one against it. There are a great many fleas and bugs; and many mosquitoes that bite worse than bugs. They sting one and leave a large bump and it is very tormenting in the hot weather.'

Despite forming these views of Hobart, Ann arrived in Sydney some days later with an open mind. Perhaps having seen Hobart she had made up her mind that she would have to like New South Wales as, in common with the emigrants who landed at Hobart, the Horderns almost certainly did not have the means to return to England. Her first impressions, when she glimpsed Sydney on 5 March 1825, were good, and once ashore her business brain worked overtime.

'We had a most beautiful view of Sydney. It looked very handsome as we lay in the harbor. The next day we went ashore and took a view of the town. It looked a very strange place. The houses are large and strong, in general built of brick or stone and here and there is one that looks like shops. A great many public houses and chandler shops. Trade is middling in general, but if people will strive they can get a living middling comfortably. Bread is 10d for a quartern, cheese 2s 4d a pound, butter 2s 6d, sugar 6d, tea 1s a pound, meat 7d, potatoes 1d, eggs 2½ each . . . I have one great comfort; Mr Hordern is very kind to me and the children and he does all in his power to comfort us and make us happy.'

After she had absorbed the prospects in Sydney, Ann added a post-script to her letter to her parents.

'I wish we had about £10 in your goods that I might begin in a little way. We shall endeavour to sell some of our things and save a little if we can and buy some wool to send you to sell for us, send the return in stays . . . Cotton ginghams, prints, muslins, and lace are very dear, checked shirts and satin slops and waistcoats fetch a great price . . . Bonnet shapes, ribbons and sewing silks as well. I wish you could be so kind as to trust us £10 or £20 worth of such as I have mentioned at cost price. We will endeavour to send you over as much wool as in our power for you to sell and pay for the goods with. The stays must be from 24 to 30 inches, no childrens and more 27 and upwards as women run large and slops thin as it is a warm climate.'

The Horderns set up house at 2 Upper Pitt Street, Sydney, on the southern extremity of the town on what is now the north-eastern corner of Pitt and Campbell Streets. Their trading began when on 21 April 1825 Anthony advertised in the *Sydney Gazette* offering to sell or exchange some of their own possessions—a gun and some English cured tongues—for the blue gum timber or fine wool materials he needed to begin his coachbuilding business.

On 14 July 1825[4] Ann advertised that she had begun business as a staymaker:

'Mrs Hordern, Long Stay and Corset Maker, Whalebone Manufacturer, from London, begs Leave to acquaint the Ladies, that she has commenced Business at No. 2 Upper Pitt-street, Sydney. Stays, made to Order, on the shortest notice, and in the most fashionable way, on reasonable terms; an assortment of Stays ready made. Staymakers supplied with Whalebone, ready dressed.'

When the goods she had ordered from her parents arrived, Ann was able to expand her business from staymaking to a general drapery warehouse. On 23 March 1827[5] she advertised again:

'MORE BARGAINS are now on sale at Mrs HORDERNS, No. 2 Upper Pitt-street, consisting of a Variety of good large size twilled Shawls, only 4s 6d. to 5s 6d. Sterling each, figured silk scarfs, from 9s. Sterling and upwards, prints, muslins, and a numerous assortment of other Articles, are now on Sale at the above Place.

'Two or Three respectable Young GIRLS, from the Age of 11 to 13 Years, are wanted to learn the Staymaking Business.'

Ann's business appears to have closed during 1828, when boom times gave way to recession, causing financial problems for many merchants. During the next few years she may have helped her husband run a tavern, the Coachmaker's Arms, which he had begun in 1827; she is also said to have run a stall at the markets opposite the tavern.

Ann was back in her own business by July 1831 when she opened a shop at No. 17 East King Street near Castlereagh Street, specialising in the sale of bonnets. In 1834[6] she advertised her 'SPLENDID STOCK of LADIES' and CHILDREN'S TUSCAN BONNETS', as well as leghorn and beaver hats, stays, chintz, prints and muslins, cloth cloaks, umbrellas, kid gloves, hankerchiefs and boots and shoes. The advertisement, headed 'BARGAINS IN BONNETS', carried a line drawing of a bonnet, the first such illustration published in Australia. During the following years, advertisements for her shop appeared regularly and her stock expanded to include sable, chinchilla and squirrel furs.

Ann's business was so successful that her husband abandoned the coachmaking business to which he had returned and joined his wife at her drapery store which became the first retail store to trade as 'Anthony Hordern'.

Ann's role as a mother continued during these years. In the thirteen years following her arrival, she had a further six children, several of whom died as babies. When she died on 18 January 1871, two daughters and four sons survived her.

Ann Hordern showed remarkable farsightedness and initiative in her determination to combine a commercial career with the bearing and raising of children. She was the driving force behind the establishment of her family's commercial ventures, which were to be developed by her descendants.

## Eliza Ward

*Her lawful Commands every where gladly do*

From the early years of settlement young people were apprenticed to trades. An original contract for such an indenture which has been

**NEW SOUTH WALES.** # THIS INDENTURE WITNESSETH, THAT

_[handwritten]_

doth put h__ self Apprentice to

to learn his or their Art, and with him or them, after the Manner of an Apprentice, to serve from _[handwritten]_
_[handwritten]_ unto the full End and Term of _[handwritten]_ Years from thence next following, to be complete
and ended; during which Term, the said Apprentice his said M__ faithfully shall serve, h__ Secrets keep;
h__ lawful Commands every where gladly do; he shall do no Damage to h__ said M__ nor see it done by
others, but to h__ Power shall let or forthwith give Notice to h__ said M__ of the same: The Goods of h__
said M__ __ he shall not waste, nor give or lend them unlawfully to any: __ he shall neither buy nor sell without
h__ M__ __ Leave: Taverns, Inns, or Alehouses __ he shall not haunt; at Cards, Dice, Tables, or any other
unlawful Games __ he shall not play; Matrimony __ he shall not contract; nor from the Service of h__ said __
Day or Night absent h__ self; but in all Things, as a faithful Apprentice, __ he shall behave h__ self towards h__ said
M__ and all h__ Family, during the said Term. And the said
for and in Consideration of the Sum of _[handwritten]_
to h__ in Hand well and truly paid by the said _[handwritten]_ the Receipt whereof
is hereby acknowledged, the said Apprentice in the Art of _[handwritten]_ which he now useth,
shall and will teach and instruct, or cause to be taught and instructed, in the best Way and Manner that __ he can; and shall
find unto the said Apprentice sufficient Meat, Drink, and Lodging, and all other Necessaries during
the said Term _[handwritten]_

AND for the true Performance of all and every the said Covenants and Agreements, each of the said Parties bindeth
h__ self the one to the other, firmly by these Presents. IN WITNESS whereof the Parties above-said to these Indentures
have interchangeably set their Hands and Seals, at _[handwritten]_ in this His Majesty's Territory of NEW
SOUTH WALES, the _[handwritten]_ Day of _[handwritten]_ in the _[handwritten]_
Year of the Reign of Our Sovereign Lord _[handwritten]_ of the United Kingdom of
Great Britain, King, Defender of the Faith, and so-forth, and in the Year of Our Lord One thousand eight hundred and _[handwritten]_

_Signed, Sealed, and delivered (no Stamps_
_being used in the Territory) in the_
_Presence of_

_[signatures]_

Eliza Ward Ewen

Indenture of Eliza Ward (courtesy National Library, manuscripts NLA MS 3334) preserved[7] documents the indenture of Eliza Ward in 1827 to Hannah Jones, a Sydney dressmaker. The form of indenture she and her employer signed was apparently modelled on the form used for many years in England. In archaic language she was bound to 'her said Mistress faithfully shall, her Secrets keep, her lawful Commands every where gladly do'. She agreed to 'do no Damage to her said Mistress nor see it done by others', not to waste her Mistress's goods and 'Taverns, Inns, or Alehouses she shall not haunt; at Cards, Dice, Tables, or any other unlawful Games she shall not play; Matrimony she shall not contract.'

Hannah Jones, probably the Hannah Jones described in the 1828 census[8] as householder of George Street, aged 45, who had come free to the colony on the *Broxbornebury* in 1814, agreed to teach Eliza dressmaking and supply her with meat, drink, washing and lodging on payment of £10. She was to pay Eliza 40 Spanish dollars in the first year of her apprenticeship and 48 in her second.

There is some confusion on the certificate of indenture, where Eliza's name is given as both Eliza Ward and Eliza Ward Euren. The 1828 census does not list any Eurens. It is likely the Eliza who is the subject of the certificate was Eliza Ward, aged 15, who with her mother, Amelia Ward, a housekeeper aged 40, and brother Joseph, aged 10, came free to New South Wales on the *Friendship* in 1818.[9]

In 1834 the New South Wales Legislative Council passed an Act putting the apprenticeship of juveniles on a legal basis. Called *An Act for Apprenticing the Children of the Male and Female Orphan Schools, and other Poor Children in the Colony of New South Wales*, it was passed on 4 July 1834.[10]

The Act provided for apprenticeship until the age of 21 or, for females, until marriage. It required the Master or Mistress to provide sufficient food, clothing and bedding and to ensure that their apprentices attended Divine Service on Sundays. They were required to pay into the Savings Bank a sum of £2 for males and 30/- for females for each of the last three years of a seven-year apprenticeship.

Apprentices could be transferred with the consent of a Justice from one Master to another. Masters or Mistresses could be fined up to £10 if complaints of misusage, refusal to provide food, cruelty or illtreatment, were upheld by Justices, but there were harsher punishments for apprentices found guilty of misdemenour or misbehaviour. They were to be put in gaol in solitary confinement on a diet of bread and water for up to fourteen days, then forwarded to the Male or Female Orphan Schools 'to be further disposed'.

## Isabella Gibson

*I had engaged to do apholsterary needlework*

A single letter written by Isabella Gibson gives a very valuable and rare insight into the life and thoughts of one of the thousands of single women who migrated to New South Wales under government-assisted schemes in the 1830s. Isabella arrived on 16 December 1833 on the *Layton*, which brought 284 single women to New South Wales as assisted migrants.[11] The women were chosen by the Emigration Commissioners in London under regulations adopted in 1831 to assist female migration. An advertisement published in England described the scheme:

'Single women and widows of good health and character, from 15 to 30 years of age, desirous of bettering their condition by emigrating to that healthy and highly prosperous colony, where the number of females compared with the entire population is about one in three, and where, consequently, from the great demand for servants and other female employments, the wages are comparatively high, may obtain a passage by this ship on payment of £5 only, as they will have the advantage of a free grant of £12 each from the Government, which grant, during the present year, will be confined to those females sent out by this Committee, and will cease after this ship is despatched.'[12]

As soon as the *Layton* arrived in Sydney, there were complaints similar to those made when the *Red Rover* and *Princess Royal* arrived the previous year and which were to continue to greet ships bringing female assisted migrants in future years. Typical of the comments was the allegation in the *Hobart Town Courier* that the *Layton* was loaded with prostitutes taken from the streets of London.[13] Whether they had worked as prostitutes or not, the great majority of the women came from London workhouses, to which they had been forced by poverty. Despite the advertisement inviting general applications, the Emigration Commissioners found it easier to gather groups of women from workhouses and charitable institutions rather than investigate applicants singly. In 1832 the *Red Rover* contained women from charitable institutions in Dublin and Cork, and those on the *Princess Royal* were taken from the Female Penitentiary, the Guardian Asylum and workhouses in various London parishes. The *Layton* and the other female migrant ship to sail in 1833, the *Bussorah Merchant*, contained many women from workhouses who were entirely destitute.[14]

As soon as the *Layton* arrived, the Colonial Secretary's Office advertised that the women were available for employment by 'respectable Married Housekeepers'. The shipping reporter on the *Sydney Gazette* belied the criticism of the women when he reported that several were 'very respectable-looking women' who would be a benefit to the colony.[15]

The shipping list for the *Layton*, unlike those for most ships on which assisted migrants sailed, does not contain individual details on the places the women came from, their occupation or religion. It records only where each migrant was employed after arrival in Sydney and her agreed weekly wage. Isabella Gibson's employer in George Street, Sydney engaged to pay her £8 a year.[16]

On 19 June the following year, Isabella wrote to her sister, Helen Gibson, from Jamieson Street, Sydney.[17] Apparently she had left her first employer and found work more in keeping with her skills. There is a disturbing desperation in her letter. She had not heard from her sister, although daily expecting a letter, during the seven months she had been in New South Wales, and her brother Richard (who was apparently to follow her) had not arrived. Although employed, she had to work very hard not only at sewing upholstery for which she was engaged, but also in doing housework. With the shortage of women in New South Wales, it was easy to marry, but unlike other single women who had travelled on the *Layton*, Isabella could not bring herself to accept an arranged marriage with a farmer up country whom she did not know.

Part of the motivation for bringing groups of single women to New South Wales was an attempt to overcome the great preponderance of males in the population, often stated to be a cause of immorality. Although officially Isabella Gibson arrived in New South Wales as part of this policy, her admirable personal reaction—that she was not going to be manipulated into marrying—indicates the range of reactions to government efforts to enter a complex area. At the same time as she was resisting marriage, Isabella Gibson—at least at the time she wrote this letter—was so desperate that she was seeking to return to England.

Her plea for letters is just one of many indications in women's correspondence of the overwhelming importance most attached to keeping in touch with their relatives at home. It also indicates the depth of deprivation that must have been felt by the very many who could not write. In giving a personal face to one of these generally anonymous women, her letter contradicts some of assumptions about their character. Isabella Gibson was neither a prostitute nor an unskilled pauper; neither was she intent on marrying at the first opportunity.

'I wrote home on the 17th of Febry last which letter I hope will reach London about this time informing you that we arrvd at Sydney on the 16 Decr and that I had engaged here with a Mr Hunt to do his apholsterary needle work, salary to be 8£ a year. For several months after landing I was afflicted with the scurvy and other complaints from which I am now got quite better of and at present in good health. I am much surprised and disappointed at receiving no letter from you considering how strictly I charged you to write soon and how faithfully you promised to do so. It is now ten months since I left home yet no letter from any of you. I regularly enquire at the post office every Packet that comes from England and as often return home disappointed. I can get no intelligence of the Mail Brigg the ship which Richard was to come by. It is conjectured here that the owners of it must have failed and in consiquence of that the ship will not come here at all at this time but if so it is strange he has not come out by any other ship whither he has changed his mind and is not coming at all or what has become of him I cannot ascertain. I form numberless conjectures but all in vain every day adds to my anxiety—I still remain at Mr Hunts and at the end of the first quarter had my wages raised from 2£ per quarter to 3 10£ which is 14£ a year this is the most they will give they are well satisfied with me or they would not have advanced it so much but in addition to my needlework I have now to make 8 beds and sweep out 6 rooms every morning. If I were assured that Richard would never come I would endeavour to return home as soon as possible if I could find it at all practicable but I doubt whither it will ever be in my power. Today I requisted the editor of a newspaper to advertise me to engage with any family that was going to England and wanted a female servant he said that he might do so but that I would find it a difficult matter to succeed there were such numerous applications of the same kind by people that were disappointed in their expectation of endeavouring to return home. He said that by advertising he thought I might procure a larger sallery if I could undertake to be a governess but in no other capacity accordingly I am going to advertise for a nursery governess (that is to begin young children and take the charge of them) free emigrants are sometimes allowed the priviledge of inserting an advertisement gratis in this newspaper so mine is at this time to be put in free of expense, but I do not well know what is best to do there are so very few places that is any way tolerable here that I am afraid to risk leaving Hunts they are such quiet people and have never once found fault with me since I came to their house. But I trust that providence will direct me for the best for I have none either to care for or assist me. Shop work of any kind is rarely to be had here what is sold in the shops is most all brought from London ready made Millinery and dressmaking are I understand better paid for than what the dressmakers made me to believe when I was trying amongst them for employment they charge from three shillings to 12 for making gowns and from 4 to 7 or 8 shillings for covering a silk or Velvet bonnet willow for bonnet shapes 1/6 per sheet and 2/6 or 3 sh when made into a shape it is mostly gause ribbon that they are trimmed with here and that is about 2 sh per yd. I lay out as little as possible on clothing but the family I am in require that their servants well dressed so I am obliged to do so. I had my straw bonnet cleaned & pressed lately for which I paid 2/6d. I regret that I have no person to live with me that I could trust or I would take a room and make bonnets and frocks and sell a few toys, penny dolls sell here for 6d each or take in apolstering needlework. Miss Vetch the Scotch woman is the only person I could put my confidence in and I understand she is expecting to be married soon to a farmer 150 miles up the country—A farmer and his family that came out with us in the ship went to live at that place and a few of his neighbour farmers employed him to return to Sidney and bespeak wives for them among the free women that he could recommend he fixed on Miss V. for one and she has had two letters from the man saying that he intends to come to Sidney soon when if they approve of each other at sight they will be directly married. If I was to give the least hint of such a thing being agreeable to me I might have the same opportunity but I could not bring my mind however destitute I may be to think of marrying any person I had no regard for on this account I declined accepting one offer I have had already from a man who has lived a while in this family as cook and butler an Englishman about 45 years of age he has been most of his life time a soldier & has now a pension of 15£ a year and a house and 20 acres of land from government about 70 miles from Sidney he has now left his service here and gone to live at his little property. A number of women that came out with me have married prisoners—Dear H I hope you will not on any account delay writing to me immediately on receiving this. On my own account I would like to see you here but for my fathers sake and your own I could not advise you to come because I am conscious by doing so you would run the risk of suffering more hardships than I would like to see any of you subjected to. I hope Christina is continuing better that my father is keeping his health and that all of you are well let me know if the cholera has been in London this summer. Being so close confined here I have almost no opportunity of hearing any news or seeing any of my ship acquaintances . . . I dread the coming of the warm weather again if I could get home I would not wish to remain here longer than the month of Feby next. If so I might have time to have an answer to this letter from you before I left here at all events if you are alive and well do not be so long in writing to me again.'

Isabella Gibson's letter was addressed to her sister, care of Mr Gibson, cowkeeper, 1 Ashlins Place, Drury Lane, London. There is no record of Isabella marrying in New South Wales; perhaps she returned to England.

## Mary Carpenter

*I shall sell the few stores I brought with me*

Mary Carpenter's happiness at the opportunities she saw ahead of her in Adelaide shines through a letter she wrote to her former employers in London. Other women recently arrived in Adelaide found the difficulties of living in a new settlement in tents or half-built houses extremely trying (see Mary Thomas, Chapter 11), but to Mary Carpenter, who had been a servant in London, everything about Adelaide and the country-side around it was exciting. She saw beauty and progress where others, expecting a different standard, did not. Soon after her arrival she prepared to set herself up in business by selling the goods she had brought with her and by taking in washing. Mary wrote on 9 May 1838 to 'My dear Mistress and Master':[18]

'I take this opportunity of writing to you, as Mr. __ tells me there will shortly be an opportunity of sending by post. I have written by the *Lord Goderich* but you will not have the letter for some time. By that vessel I have sent you a parrot, which I hope will arrive safe. This is a most beautiful country. I am sure no one would live in England if they could but know half of the beauties here. I hope many persons will come before long,—I am sure they will not regret it. I would not live in London again. This place is quite civilised—there is nothing rough or outlandish. We shall have the fine streets of London, but not all the vices. We have good buildings here, and plenty of everything. You may go for miles up the country any way—across the plains, park land, mountains, valleys, and sea coast—enjoying the most beautiful scenes, and either in winter or summer. If you don't like to walk or ride, you will be equally pleased with views from your parlour . . . We have here brickmaking, limeburning, and soon, I daresay, shall manufacture many other things. We have a great many cattle, a storehouse that covers an acre of land, and some fine buildings.

'I am much obliged for the mangle you sent me. I think I shall make it answer very well. Tomorrow I shall begin to sell the few stores I brought out with me. Mr Arthur G. says he thinks I shall do very well, and so I think . . . It is astonishing to see how much business is done here, and what a many houses there are—also carts and drays. An omnibus started last week, and we soon shall be quite English. I never was before so well as I am now. I must conclude with wishing you every blessing this life can give; and, if you will believe me, this colony is just the place for it.'

# 11
# Homemakers

## Janet Ranken

*We are all come here to make money*

Janet Ranken was a young Scotswoman, mature beyond her years, when she arrived in Australia in 1821. A woman of bold, forthright opinions on people and places, she had a clear view of why she and her husband and the other Scottish families who travelled on the same ship had come to Australia. Their aim was to be successful by acquiring land and making money.

As Janet Hutchinson of Kelloside, Dumfriesshire, she had faced family opposition when she decided to marry her first cousin, George Ranken, as Ranken had made up his mind to emigrate to Van Diemen's Land, a place Janet's mother thought was 'nothing but a desert'.[1] Janet eventually won over her family by getting Mrs Annabella Campbell, wife of Colonel John Campbell of Argyleshire, who was also emigrating, to write to her mother. Janet and George were married in May 1821 at Kelloside and sailed soon after on the *Lusitania*, which had been chartered by Colonel Campbell to convey his wife, thirteen children, his eldest daughter's husband, Mr Macleod and her three children and a retinue of servants to Australia. Janet Ranken became very friendly with the second eldest Campbell daughter, Lorn.

George Ranken travelled with letters of introduction to the Lieutenant Governor of Van Diemen's Land and the Governor of New South Wales, Sir Thomas Brisbane, who was a relative of Colonel Campbell. After arriving in Hobart on 28 October 1821, he decided to look at prospects in New South Wales and went on to Sydney, leaving his pregnant wife in Hobart.

While she waited alone in Hobart, Janet wrote to her sister, Margaret Hutchinson. Her letter contains one of the first descriptions of Hobart from the viewpoint of a woman who believed she would be making her home there. She maintains a healthy scepticism towards others, including Mrs Campbell, her senior in years, experience and standing. For instance, she takes Mrs Campbell's tale of miscarrying her twentieth child with a grain of salt and decides that, while she likes to visit her, she does not want Mrs Campbell for a 'door neighbour'.

Her scorn for money-grubbing settlers posing as friends, her disdain for those who believe their wealth to be a means of transcending class barriers and her refusal to acknowledge the existence of Mrs Lord because she was a 'convict woman' are balanced by contempt for the pretensions and pretences of her own class; 'in short,' she wrote, 'we are all come here to make money and money we will make by hook or by crook so to talk of friendship would be a sad prostitution of the word'. With a canny understanding of the tactics necessary for survival, she advises (herself as much as others) 'trust no one but for your own interest appear to trust every one'.

The undated letter to her sister Margaret, written just after Christmas 1821 (to which punctuation has been added to clarify the meaning), begins with an account of the voyage during which the ship was fired on at St Jago after the captain omitted to pay port dues, an event which disturbed most of the passengers.[2] Janet wrote:

'Mrs Campbell was very much frightened and ill for three weeks afterwords but fortunately for me I had not the sense to be frightened. Indeed Mrs Campbell was so much frightened that she told me she had miscarried her *twintyeth* child but gude forgie me I think she hardly sticks to the truth in family concerns she makes them all very young and for Mrs McLeod who has three children and is just about to have the fourth she is only twenty one or two and the young ladies three straping queens are from eighteen to fifteen but the youngest may pass for eighteen and the oldest for twinty six. Well we lost sight of St Jago and then we were becalmed for weeks together and but for harpooning sharks and shooting whales I dont know what the gentlemen would have done with themselves and the ladies generally were disputing which of their lords or brothers or lords to be (for there were some matches made up on the way) that had the merit of sending the poor shooten fishes to their long homes—

'And then, but this is rather a serious story, a young man of the name of Nicholson, a servant of Mrs Campbell, went to sleep in the jolly boat and was struck by the sun. He died on the ninth day afterwards and was buried on the day after his death. I never never will forget the sound of the deep and hollow plunge when the body was consined to its fathomless bed of rest. It was a calm day and every wave was as still as death till the mornin after his funeral when all at once there was a breeze got up and in twelve hours we were a hundred miles from poor Nicholson.

"No home no kiss no niver never
Sound shall his sleep be forever and ever"

'After leaving sight of St Jago and that was on the 17 of July we never saw land again till the 16th October when we arrived at King George's Sound the coast of New Holland . . . I never in my life suffered as much cold as I did for a fortnight before we reached the Cape till within a few days sail of Van Diemens. There we arrived all in good health upon the 28th Octr I did not get a house till the 31st but I got a very good one then and very far superior to any I expected. I see the hills out of my windows and I see beautiful little cottages with there fruteful gardens and hedges of roses and I see a very neat church and stipple and I can see a signal post where they hoist a large flag when ever they see a ship coming in at the foot of the river and this is just what I have been looking at. Brauchild[3] has been away at Sydney and I am expecting him home every day. I have never heard from him since he left this but by chance their was a vessel driven in here that was bound from Sydney to the Cape and brought word of the Grace—the ship George went in—being arrived at Sydney and that all passengers were well—

'Now I shall discribe this country but I cannot do I have never been farther out of the town than seven miles but what I have seen is most beautiful. However it is a very different still [style] of beauty from Jeffrey's Van Diemens Land—all that I have seen is more grand than beautiful. The river Derwent is a broad and deep river abounding with fish of many kinds, thickly wooded on both sides excepting here and there a patch of cultivated land with fine thriving crops. The sail up the river from this to Restdown [Risdon] a distance of five miles is very fine quite like the scenery in our highlands of Scotland. Mrs Campbell has taken Restdown for a few months. George thought of taking part of the house but I did not like that. Mrs Campbell does best to *visit* she will give you a highland welcome when you go to see her but I should not like to be *door neighbours*. I have been there spending my christmass . . . Every thing is *dear* beyond all calculation excepting mutton bread and tea . . . meat is the same as in England, the bread is as good and rather cheeper, good black teas from 4/ to 5/ a pound, green from 5/ to 6/6, butter from 5/ to 7/6 per lb—Oh a kingdom per a dozen eggs from 2/ to 3/ a Dozn. I bought a pair of young ducks the other day the coast

151

6/ and I paid for eight little chickens that had not left there Mother 12/ the potatoes were for a long time 4d a lb but I can buy them now for three halfpennys. Every kind of kitchen goods are modarite in prise if you buy a quantity together. There is an Indian ship here at present and I have bought a bag at 7d per lb theirs a nice pickle . . . O I wish I had brought a great many things here that I have not. I have written a list of things which I really would require if Willie could find it convenient to send them—

'The society here is abominable. Mr Lord[4] a man worth half a million money is married to a convict woman. The Leut Governor Mr Sorell is married but he left his own wife in England and brought another mans wife[5] with him in her stead. Mrs Lord sent her daughter Miss Lord and her sister Mrs Simpson to call upon me when I came here but I have never returned the call yet nor shall I although wile Governor McWharie [Macquarie] and his lady were here paying there last visit Mrs Lord was Mrs McWharies most intimate friend and I have been advised to visit her but they say "evil communication corrupts good manners" so I shall rather be without the kindnesses that Mrs Lord has in her power to show me than visit her. The Colonel surgeon and his lady[6] are a very pleasant pair she was the only daughter of Coln Davies[7] late Leut Governor of this place and Dr Scot [Scott] is a Scotch man. I find myself at home when I go to see them and Dr Scot is always ready to give his advice when it is asked.

'There are a great many settlers come out here this season all of them the grandest people ever I saw they are surely come to spend and not to make money as for their wives and daughters they are so much of fine things that they cannot put on there own clothes they must all have maids to do that for them and there papas are all Majors Colonels and for Captains they are like to knock one another down that is never *hard* if you may find them *clarks* to some of the great store keepers here. Major Bell the commander in chief and his wife called upon me. Mrs Bell is a good sort of person but I hate the Major. In short we are all come here to make money and money we will have by hook or by crook so to talk of friendship would be a sad prostitution of the word *trust no one* but for your own *interest* appear to trust every one. I shall sertainly here from Scotlan by some of these ship arrived here yesterday morning *on one* day since I came here there were four large ships anchored here from London. The horses here are dreadfully expensive, any thing good will coast £80 or £100 a dollar here is thought no more of than a penny in Scotland this to me is incomprehensible but even so it is . . .

'I believe we shall have very few settlers from England after this I heard the other day that nobody would get more than 200 acres let their property be ever so great. This may not be true but we shall soon hear from Sydney &c &c I meant to have written to Bettie and Jane Mitchell but I find I shant have time you must let them try to read this. My dear Margaret be assured that I am very happy and do not regrate coming here . . . '

This one letter, with its robust, outspoken views, was to be the last letter Janet Ranken wrote from Hobart. Her husband, George, had in the meantime arrived in Sydney on the same day that Sir Thomas Brisbane assumed command of the colony. George Ranken met Brisbane briefly, and determined to settle in New South Wales. He told his wife he regretted stopping at Van Diemen's Land. She would be delighted with Sydney, he wrote; in New South Wales 'sheep and all kinds of stock' were 'far superior' and 'the society is excellent'.[8]

George returned to Hobart to collect Janet and they sailed to Sydney on the *Venus* on 10 February 1822. They were kindly received by Captain John Piper, Naval Officer at Sydney and soon leased Piper's property, Petersham, of 2000 acres. Janet Ranken's first child, a son, George Somerville, was born at Petersham on 31 March 1822.

In 1822, when the first land grants were made available over the Blue Mountains in the Bathurst district, Ranken selected a 2000-acre grant and named it Kelloshiel. Having found Petersham too close to Sydney, 'a stage for travellers, and a drive for the town people,'[9] Janet Ranken complained, they moved to Kelloshiel in 1823. Like Elizabeth Hawkins the previous year (see Chapter 9) Janet Ranken faced the formidable journey over the Blue Mountains to reach Bathurst. She and her husband rode, while their child and his nurse travelled in a tilted cart and their possessions were carried in two bullock drays. Janet Ranken found only two women she considered gentlewomen west of the mountains, one being Elizabeth Hawkins. Although comfortable herself, she was sorry for the plight of many settlers. 'Oh!' she wrote to her sister-in-law, 'if you saw the misery that many people bring themselves to in this country, who have been in opulence at home. How sad to see accomplished, delicate women, living in the back parts, eating pork and damper.'[10]

The Rankens flourished at Kelloshiel and in the 1830s enlarged their estate by acquiring Sir Thomas Iceley's nearby Saltram estate.

In 1837 George Ranken leased his properties for four years and in January 1838 sailed with Janet and their nine children for Scotland, where they rented an estate, sending their four sons to be educated in Germany. However, a disastrous drought cut short their stay and they returned to Bathurst in 1841.

The family suffered great sorrow in losing all their four daughters and two sons, some in Scotland and some in Australia, within the space of six years. George Ranken died in London in 1861 during a visit to England. Janet Ranken died at a family property on 20 October 1883, aged 87.

The next generation of Rankens produced writings of lasting interest. Mrs W. B. Ranken, the wife of Janet and George Ranken's second son, published *The Rankens of Bathurst* (1916), a grandson, George, wrote a novel *Wyndabyne* (1895) and a nephew, William Hugh Ranken, wrote *The Dominion of Australia* (1874).

## Octavia Dawson

*I do not like it here at all*

Octavia Dawson, like many other women who migrated to Australia in the early years of settlement, had difficulty in adapting to a life she found so different, and so challenging to her cherished ideas of a stratified class system. There were not only material problems such as the scarcity of goods and commodities; more importantly, there was the major problem of social dislocation. How did one fit into this new society where rich people were once convicts and where a relative might choose a drunkard for a wife?

Octavia solved this problem by being very selective in extending friendship. The only friends she made in Hobart were a merchant and a banker and his wife who was 'very clever'. In the latter at least, she chose well. These friends were Stephen Adey, managing agent for the Van Diemen's Land Company, and his wife formerly Lucy Leman Rede. Lucy Adey had herself written poetry and came from a family of writers, actors and dramatists well known in literary London. Her sister, Mary Leman Grimstone, who lived with the Adeys in Tasmania from 1826 to 1829, had had several volumes of poems published and had written one novel. In Van Diemen's Land she was to write another, *Woman's Love*, an early feminist novel.[11]

Octavia Dawson wrote to her cousin in Belfast on 11 August 1829, soon after she and her husband, Samuel Robinson Dawson, arrived to settle in Van Diemen's Land. She was still to make the necessary adjustment, but she was eventually to find her own niche in society and in the process, like many other women, to introduce many of her own values into Australian society. Her initial difficulties in fitting in were accentuated because she found the people in Van Diemen's Land 'either very high or very low', either upper class and military or naval, or the convict and ex-convict lower class. The only way she found of preserving her integrity in these early days was to shun the company of those below and aspire to those above and not once question the values and ideals which were so hard to graft on to this society. She was shocked that 'George', who appears to be her brother, should so easily succumb to the mores of this new society by marrying a woman who was a drunkard and who apparently had been a prostitute.

In the major aspect of their new life, their choice of occupation, the Dawsons illustrate that the benefits of migration usually outweighed the problems of adjustment. City dwellers at home, they found no difficulty in becoming farmers in Tasmania.

In these early days, however, writing a letter back home, where the old values for which she was so nostalgic reigned, was one way of preserving the illusion that nothing need change. She wrote on 11 August 1829[12] from Claremont, Van Diemen's Land, to Robert J. Tennant who was keeping an eye on her young son left in school in Belfast. While Octavia was prepared to risk her daughters, Jane and Martha, to the mercy of a colonial education, she apparently believed a son needed an education 'at home'.

'According to promise but not as to time I write to you but I have so little to say that is so much that I cannot find words to express it so it will amount to the same thing in the end and you will have a short letter about nothing. In the first place I was to tell you how I like the place, I do not like it at all the country I must say is beautiful no person can find fault with it but then it is a new colony and there is a great deal for a settler to encounter particularly a female, next the people, they are either very *high* or very *low* the upper class are all military or naval men such as Cols Majors and Capns. that you have no chance with them and the lower class are convicts. There is such a party spirit amongst them that if you are at all noticed you must be either one side or other so that it makes you quite uncomfortable, as for us we know very few. We know the gentleman who transacts business for Sam his Son and Daughter and a Mr & Mrs Aidey[13] he is a banker and she is a very clever woman— but these are all that I am on visiting terms with so you see our circle is not very extensive and now that we have left Hobart Town for the bush I dont expect to see them often either oh! how often do I wish for some of my friends to be nigh me but it is all in vain. I suppose you have heard of Georges marriage poor fellow he has done for himself forever I have only seen him at a distance since our arrival if she had been any kind of woman that I could have been on terms with how comfortable it wd have been for me but it seems as if I was to be disappointed in everything—it seems she was well known on the Commercial Road as Betty Duff god knows how true it is but this I know that she is one of the greatest drinkers and one of the worst tempered women

I have ever met with. What think you of Sams turning farmer and me making Butter and Cheese but alas! I am sorry to say that we have not a cow or hen yet on our farm—so much for my beginning we are about five miles from town across the river the greatest want of these farms is the want of water we have to draw every drop we use from what they call a Lagoon a mile off and every thing we want we have to send to town for Eggs are 2/3 per dozn and fowls 5/ and all these kind of things in proportion as for milk we seldom see it now—firing is the only thing we have cheap and that we have for the cutting. I wish you would take a trip over here and see us . . . T[here] are a great many respectable families here from Ireland . . . and now dear Robert how is my own boy I trust you have an eye as you promised and that you make him go over his lessons often. I hope he will be all I could wish Jane and Martha often talk of you they are all quite well but not gone to school yet. They send you a kiss I hope my dear Father is in good health I am sure this is a country he would like if he saw it your father I know would—Dear Robert may I depend on your writing to me soon you know that letters are the only comfort I have now and I trust you will add to it if you should happen to be in London when the ship arrives that this goes by I wish you would see the Captain he will be able to tell you all about us as he is the Capn we came out with and he could give you all the information about George as they wd be anxious at home to know of him his name is Elder of the ship *Pyramus*—Sam joins with me in affectionate remembrances and believe me to remain dr Robert your ever affectionate Cousin and Friend.'

Samuel Robinson became a substantial farmer at Claremont, Kangaroo Point, later called Bellerive, on the east bank of the Derwent, and when the Municipality of Clarence Plains was formed in 1860, he was elected a councillor.[14]

Octavia and Samuel's son, also named Samuel Robinson Dawson, took up land at Rosedale in Gippsland, Victoria, where he also called his property Claremont. Octavia may have considered they were well established in the upper circles of society when her granddaughter, Octavia Charlotte Dawson, married Phillip Gidley King, a grandson of Admiral Phillip Parker King, at Rosedale in 1877.[15]

**Mary Thomas**

*Everything was in the roughest fashion imaginable*

Mary Thomas arrived in Adelaide in 1836 on the first ship to bring settlers to South Australia. The journal she kept and the letters she wrote[16] of the family's voyage on the *Africaine* and their first years of pioneering in a new colony are very valuable in adding a woman's view to the official records of those early years.

Mary was a well educated woman who had published a volume of verse, *Serious Poems*, in London in 1831. Born Mary Harris at Southampton, England, on 30 August 1787, she married Robert Thomas, a printer, bookseller and stationer, at Southampton on 18 January 1818. Her husband was attracted by E. G. Wakefield's ideas for the colonisation of South Australia and in 1836 bought 134 acres of land in the proposed province. He was a valuable addition to the group of first settlers. Before sailing, he produced in London the first number of the *South Australian Gazette and Colonial Register* and after arriving in South Australia he printed Governor Hindmarsh's proclamation of the province on 28 December 1836. In June the following year he produced the first colonial edition of his newspaper, which became a weekly in 1838.

Mary Thomas's journal and letters provide a vivid picture of the difficulties and achievements of the first settlers. As she struggled to maintain some semblance of family life and the values of her upbringing in the tent which was her first home, she balanced her lingering love for her native land with the economic necessity for the family's move to a new unknown land.

The Thomas party including, in addition to three daughters and a son, two printers, two agricultural labourers and a servant, sailed on the *Africaine*, which left England towards the end of June 1836. The last sight of the Isle of Wight hills, Mary wrote, 'and the reflection that in all probability it would be the last cost me some tears'. When several of the children suffered severe illnesses during the voyage, Mary Thomas nursed them day and night, at one stage spending 'five nights without taking my clothes off'.

When the *Africaine* reached Holdfast Bay, at Glenelg, south of Adelaide, on 10 November 1836, Mary Thomas recorded their first days in South Australia:[17]

*'November 11.*
'This day Mr. Thomas and our two agricultural labourers went on shore with our tents, and the weather being rough they did not return. The next day they were occupied in receiving the luggage, as it was landed on the beach, and conveying what was necessary for present use to a site some distance away, where our tents were to be pitched. As everything had to be carried by hand, there being no other mode of conveyance, it was no trifling labour, especially through untrodden paths often full of holes, and with grass three or four feet high.

'November 13. This day the girls and I packed up our bedding and such things as remained in the cabin, and went on shore to the place of our present destination . . . We had two tents, the smaller of which the men had erected, and of which we, with part of our family, that is, our three daughters and the young woman who came out with us as assistant, took possession, gladly enough, though everything was in the roughest fashion imaginable. The two men located themselves on the sandhills, making a circle with packages and furniture and sleeping in the middle.

'As for my two sons (for Robert had now joined us for the present)[18] I made up a bed with a thick mattress on the ground in the open air, and as near as I could with safety to a large fire, and saw them asleep before I ventured to retire myself. My anxiety, however, would not suffer me to sleep much for that and many succeeding nights. Towards morning, however, I fell into a slumber out of which I was suddenly startled at about 5 o'clock by the loud crowing of a cock, which, with some hens we brought from the Cape of Good Hope, had roosted in a bush close at the back of our tent. I got up at the summons and hastily dressing myself went to see after my boys, both of whom I found fast asleep. The quilt that covered them was so saturated with dew that I could have wrung the water out of it.'

In a letter written on 14 October 1838 to her brother, George Harris of Southampton, in which she described the family's move from Glenelg to the site chosen for the city of Adelaide, Mary was frank in disclosing the family's reasons for leaving England.[19]

'I will now tell you some of the reasons which induced us to leave England. In the first place the lease of our house had nearly expired. It was greatly out of repair, partly owing to the next house above having been pulled down and rebuilt a short time before. This caused ours to give way, though I could not make Mr Thomas believe it was in so bad a state as it really was. I knew if we stayed to the end of the lease we should have heavy delapidations to pay for. I also knew this would put him in a terrible rage, as I estimated them to be at least £200, and to prove that I was right in my conjecture Mr Baugh has since informed us that the repairs took £300. Added to this, Robert wished to go abroad, and William was not likely to be placed at any business. Mr Baugh wished very much to have him as an apprentice, and I did not like to see him idle away his time at home. The scheme of this new colony happened to be starting just at the time. We first heard of it from Dr. Inman, of Portsmouth, who came up to London to purchase some land in it for one of his sons, who is now here. It was thought to be an excellent opportunity for young men of talent to try their fortunes, especially as the plan on which this colony is founded is considered to be superior to all others; and as neither of my boys is deficient in genius or education I flattered myself that, with attention and industry, they might become at some time or other possessed of considerable property. Besides this Frances's health, which was never good in London, I hoped might be improved by a sea voyage and change of climate. These were the principal reasons which made me encourage rather than otherwise Mr. Thomas's inclination to become a landholder in this new Province. Accordingly he purchased 134 acres, each at twelve shillings per acre, which also entitled him to two in the principal town, and these were purchased several months before we left England. In my latter object I have not succeeded so well as I could have wished for Frances is the same here as in London, never well long together, but with regard to the boys they are both likely to do well.

'By his drawings and some maps which were exhibited at the committee rooms Robert obtained a situation under the principal surveyor and came over in the *Cygnet* three months before we did, on the 21st March, and is now in partnership with Colonel Light and three others as land agents and surveyors under the name of "Light, Finnis, & Co." They are likely to realize a very good income, being the principal firm in town. Robert is acknowledged to be equal to any draughtsman in the colony, though we have some very clever men, here, and in mapping and ornamental writing superior. Perhaps you may have seen engravings from some of his maps, with his name attached to them. Several went to England for that purpose, but I do not know if they are yet published. William is overseer of the printing office, and is very useful and industrious . . .

'When we left England my mind was so filled with anxiety on account of the children, and I was so harassed with fatigue and the bustle of packing up that I scarcely gave it a thought that I was quitting my native land in all probability for ever, but I had not been long on board before I wept bitterly at the reflection, as I often do even now. Nor should I ever have made up my mind to leave it but for the sake of the boys, and I trust that it will all turn out for the best, though we have suffered a great deal and endured many hardships which in England you would think it almost impossible to go through.

'I forgot to mention that when we were at Chalton Mr. Thomas engaged two of Mr. Martin's men as agriculturists—Jacobs and Windebank—and I also engaged Mary Lillywhite, of the same place, as servant and companion, for she lived with us the same as my own family. Unfortunately, however, she was too much of the fine lady to give me much assistance. They all came up to London the day before we sailed. We also engaged two printers—one a journeyman, the other a turnover apprentice—and two other young men, we being entitled by the money we paid for the land to take out ten labourers or servants, free of expense, who were bound to remain for one year, but we have not one of them now. Jacobs and Windebank left us after some months, as the land could not be taken possession of so soon as we expected, and we had no employment for them suitable to their inclinations. About twelve months ago Mary Lillywhite married our printer, whose name is Fisher, and they both left us but still reside in Adelaide. Since then I have been without a servant, having no accommodation for one in my present habitation unless I allowed her to sit at my table and sleep with the girls, which I will never submit to, especially here, where the servants are becoming as saucy and independent as they are in America. Both servants and labourers being scarce they get too much wages by half.'

After describing their landing at Glenelg and their stay there in tents for several months, while the site for the capital was chosen, Mary Thomas recounted her husband's purchase of town lots in Adelaide in March 1837. She continued:

'We came here [Adelaide] on the 1st of June, 1837. Mr. Thomas and the boys came up some time before, as the printing press was obliged to be set up here, and resided in the tents until September, while this building was finishing. Since then we have been within these walls, which are built of mud, and the roof is of boards. We have a stone house in progress, and when we remove into it I hope it will be the last remove we shall make till we return to dear old England!

'Mr. Thomas, who is perfectly infatuated with this country, does not seem to anticipate such an event, but I do, and so do the girls, and I feel confident, please God, at some time or other such will be the case.

'This is certainly a very fine country, and capable of the highest improvements. Doubtless those who are born and brought up here will think of it as we do of our native country, that there is no other like it in the world; but to those who know what England is, and recollect the comfort there enjoyed, it never can bear a comparison, notwithstanding its luxuriant plains, its magnificent trees, its ranges of lofty hills, and scenery often sublime. The soil, too, can doubtless be made to reproduce nearly all the fruits and vegetables of the known world. We have a garden in which we have abundance of the latter and some of the former in cultivation, but the vegetables have not the sweetness of those in England and generally run to seed before they have attained half their size. This may perhaps be remedied by proper management, the plants being, like ourselves, not yet acclimatized.

'And now, having spoken of the climate, I cannot say that it is by any means as agreeable as I expected, according to the accounts which were given of it, and in this respect I am much disappointed. The heat, which was said to be seldom greater than it is in England, is sometimes so intense as to be scarcely endurable. I have seen the thermometer at 105 degrees four days following in this room where I am writing. The mud houses are by far the coolest. One day I placed the thermometer out in the sun to see the effect. In a few minutes it rose to 155 degrees. Sometimes the weather is very cold; the wind is often extremely boisterous, carrying up whirlwinds of dust, and the rains are so heavy that they literally come down in torrents. Moreover, the atmosphere is subject to great and sudden changes from heat to cold, cold to heat, much more than is the case with the climate of England, so long proverbial for its changeableness. The mornings and evenings here are often cold enough for a good fire, while in the middle of the day the heat is almost insupportable . . .

'This, as I said before, is a very beautiful country, and for those who wish to better their condition they cannot do amiss in coming here, provided they be sober and industrious and can make up their minds to endure many things which in England would be considered unreasonable, and yet nothing in comparison to what we underwent when there was not a house to be seen or a thing that could be done except by manual labour. All our goods had to be brought from the beach by hand, as no such animal as a horse or a bullock was then in the colony. Now there are thousands of both, with carts and every convenience for carrying baggage and passengers, and lodgings either at inns or private houses; and yet those who have been accustomed to English comforts will find themselves very deficient of them in many respects, unless they reckon among them hundreds of rats and mice, thousands of fleas and flies, millions of ants and mosquitoes, and many other such annoyances. Therefore I would advise all those who are doing well in England to remain there, but I would by no means discourage any man, who wishes to try his fortune in South Australia, especially if he has a family, as there is plenty of scope for industry, ingenuity, and talent of every kind . . .

'I forgot to tell you that our population exceeds four thousand, and several more ships are expected. Streets are rapidly forming in all directions in regular lines, for the city is laid out on a particular plan, which cannot be deviated from, and in a few years this will be a magnificent place. We have already a church built of stone and of considerable dimensions, and a clock has lately been fixed in it. This we find of great use as all our watches are stopped, influenced, I suppose, by the climate. This is a general complaint. Mr. Thomas is making bricks on his country sections. These are in great demand, and are now used in preference to mud. When we built our house stone was the only thing to be had. Of course our fuel is wood, which I fear will soon become scarce. It is already very dear, owing to the great consumption, and although we have plenty on our lands the carriage is expensive. No doubt this country contains much coal, which will be very profitable to anyone who may discover it. We have abundance of goods of all kinds, almost as cheap as in England, but provisions are dear. Fresh meat 1/- per pound; fresh butter 3/6; salt butter 2/6; and bread 1/8 per loaf, all of which have been much more. We sometimes get fish. The water is not so good or so plentiful as in England. Neither is the air so bracing or refreshing. Frequently there is a hot and scorching wind, which, while it lasts, is almost past endurance. With all the advantages of this fine country it will never bear comparison with dear old England, where I hope to end my days in peace and comfort. This is all I desire for I have no ambition to be rich, and though we may wish, with the blessing of God, to obtain a competence here we must go to England to enjoy it.

'In my next I will give you some account of the natives, who are an inoffensive people, but extremely ignorant. About 500 of them went yesterday to the Bay [Glenelg] to meet our new Governor and ran by the side of his horse to Adelaide. Our children went to hear the proclamation read in front of Government House.'

Mary Thomas continued her journal and her letter-writing as she faced the difficulties of adjusting to a new country that did not always live up to her expectations. Her husband continued to bring out the *South Australian Register* and in 1839 bought the rival *Adelaide Chronicle and South Australian Advertiser*. The *Register*, always critical of Governor Gawler, criticised him strongly in September 1840 for ordering the execution of two Aborigines suspected of murdering some settlers. In retaliation, the Government withdrew all its advertising, worth £1650 a year, from Thomas's paper. Thomas visited England to protest, but was unsuccessful in getting the decision reversed. In 1842 he returned to Adelaide insolvent and sold the *Register*. From 1845 to 1852 he was a government inspector of weights and measures. He died in 1860, survived by Mary, three sons and two daughters.

Mary Thomas did not return to her native country. She died in Adelaide in 1875. The Thomas family's association with the *Register* was later re-established when a grandson, Robert Kyffin, a parliamentary reporter, became general manager of the *South Australian Register*.

## Jane Synnot

*Mama does not admire the Colonists at all*

When Jane Synnot wrote to her aunt in Ireland from Invermay, Launceston, in March 1838 she was a correct young lady looking, in a suitably ladylike way, for suitors among the officers of the British Regiment stationed near Launceston. Her father, Captain Walter Synnot, formerly of the 66th Regiment, had served with some of them at Gibraltar and her stepmother often entertained officers of the regiment, for she did 'not admire the Colonists at all'. The Synnots mixed with the 'most respectable people' and were invited to Government House. However, it is interesting that migration had overturned the values of one member of the family; Walter, Jane Synnot's brother, had an 'infamous companion' to whom Jane could 'hardly suppose him to be married'.

The Synnot family arrived in Van Diemen's Land from Country Armagh, Ireland, on the *Amelia Thompson* in 1836. Two of the numerous children, Marcus and Albert, moved to Port Phillip in June 1837 with many other adventurous and land-hungry young men from families later to be famous as the founders of the pastoral industry in the rich Western District of Victoria.

Jane wrote to her aunt on 6 March 1838, addressing her as 'My dear Mrs Synnot':[20]

'I have long wished for a letter from you but I know that your ill-health prevents you. I hope however that you have been better since we left next month it will be two years since we saw you all the time has passed very quickly with me for we have been in four different dwelling houses in this country the one which we are in will be ours for four years and a half before that perhaps the most of us may be in the *Hades*. We have not had a servant maid for 7 or 8 months and of necessity there is much to be done. I dare say you think the good people do not care for dress here but I can assure they are as fashionable and more so than they are at home the ladies walk every day in black and the lightest colored satins thro' the streets and in Church their dresses are superb neither Mamma or I will be so extravagant as to wear satin for a dress costs about *20 pounds* and the making £4 10 but that is included in the above muslin and calicoe are proportionly dear as for linen you cannot get any fit to be used and that enormously expensive. Mamma, Papa and I were at the Government house the other evening at a nice party, the most respectable people in this side of the Island were there I danced merrily all the evening, all the Officers were there theirs is a very nice regiment and they are our constant and almost only visitors (for Mamma does not admire the Colonists at all) one of their officers Captain O'Hara is nephew to the Governor of Gibralter he was there at the time Papa was and the best Military friend he ever had. Papa was very glad to meet the relation of his old friend General O'Hara another Lieutenant Stapleton is nearly connected with Lord Stanley I am very sorry to say they expect to be moved in a few months. They are shortly going to give a party they asked me to assist in making pastry custards and things of the kind but I am afraid I shall not be able as I am no cook. I shall now tell you every thing about myself as Maria and Anne Jane complained of my remissness on that subject in their last kind letter which I hope you will thank them for my dear Charlotte is still at school I suppose *yet* bye the bye I must not think of her as the little girl I left but a fine grown up woman she must write to me in the next vacations as Maria said she was not allowed to communicate with any but her immediate family. I am as happy as the day is long I love my dear Mamma more *and* she is every thing my heart could *wish* I know you would like her if you were better acquainted tho' we have all the cleaning to do we do a great deal of work both plain and fancy Mamma's chief delight is in having the house nice, we are always thinking of some new ornament for the drawing room which every one says is almost the nicest in the island. Maria and Anne Jane & Susanna are very handy will you ask them when they next write to describe some things of the kind which they have seen lately they are always inventing new things in England. I hope poor Susanna is better the last accounts were not very good which gave me sincere regret but I hope that change of air may do her good as I suppose you have moved before this. I am sure you will be sorry to hear of the scandalous behaviour of Walter we have long since given up the ac- quaintance of him and his *infamous companion* for we can hardly suppose him to be married to one like her but any thing would be mean or fallen enough for him to do when they first came out Papa would not have asked them to our house but Mamma persuaded him to invite them which he did no sooner did they come after having the greatest work at Mr. Gages who declares if he hears what he suspects about Mr Synnot to be true he will come all the way from Hobart Town to fight him. Would you believe it he and Mrs. S. did all in their power and Walter you know had some influence with me I used to be very fond of him to make a disturbance between Mamma and I and to make me dislike even Papa. Mamma bore all this and stopped Papa several times from turning them out besides she treated them with the greatest civility when they did go they tried to take away Mamma's character in the most dreadful manner to all their acquaintances who are all among the lowest of the low. I do not suppose more than one or two gentlemen speak to him and no ladies. However when this came to our ears Papa as his father would not say any thing to him but Mamma wrote to him which letter he said he would send home [if he] did so you may be sure he did not tell the provocation which would make it seem very violent. I would never have told you this if I was not afraid that you might see it and not knowing the circumstances you might think it odd we were here for 7 or 8 months before he came to see us and then only once because he heard Papa was very ill it was before what I have told you happened he never inquires whether we are dead or alive tho' living about two miles from him have not seen him except in church for this year nearly if I did I would not open my lips to him Mrs Synnot I cannot bear to call her by that name but I do not know any other for her has met several gentlemen in this country who knew her well at home every one here and at Hobart know about her much better than we do as you may be sure we never ask as we know quite enough but I have written enough on such a subject . . .

'Papa hopes to be able soon to send home wool as the sheep at Port Phillip are increasing wonderfully and to commission you to get us some articles of clothing. I know you have a good taste in that respect if you send us any more papers I would be very much obliged if you would send those in preference which have the fashions in them. They are greatly altered since we left England.

'Mary Anne Catharine & Nugent are greatly improved, George & Monkton are at home the latter attends a day school in Launceston. Marcus and Albert have been at Port Phillip since June last. Mrs Trappes is quite well but has never come to see us the expense of travelling is too great. I will drop a few seeds in the letter in hopes that they may reach you if you have a green house at the place you go or are gone to.'

The letter provides only a momentary glimpse of the life of Jane Elizabeth Synnot, who was to become one of the matriarchs of the squatting families of the Victorian Western District. Four months later, on 4 July 1838, she married not an officer from a British regiment, but a farmer, Thomas Manifold. Thomas had arrived in Hobart in 1828 on the *Greenock* at the age of 18 and received a grant of 1280 acres at Kelso on the west bank of the River Tamar. When news reached Launceston of the excellent country in the Port Phillip district, Thomas sailed over Bass Strait to investigate and in July 1836 with his brother Peter landed sheep, stores and other supplies and squatted in what was to become the Geelong district. After a spell back in Van Diemen's Land, during which he married Jane, he rejoined his brothers Peter and John on the mainland. In January 1839 they took up Lake Purrumbete, a property of 100 000 acres which included the present site of the town of Camperdown and in 1844 Thomas bought Grasmere station of 24 000 acres, near the present city of Warrnambool. He was briefly a member of the Victorian Legislative Assembly for Warrnambool.

Jane Manifold lived until 1912. Her stepmother, after the death of Captain Walter Synnot, became the second wife of Charles Macarthur, second son of Hannibal Hawkins Macarthur and his wife formerly Anna Maria, daughter of Governor Philip Gidley King.[21]

# 12
# Work in isolation

**Ann Gore**

*Society we have none*

By the latter part of the 1830s, many women were living in very isolated circumstances in bush homes in Australia. As land nearer the major capitals was taken up, land-hungry migrants pushed further and further beyond the limits of settlement for sites for their cattle and sheep runs. Isolation sometimes brought out the best in women and the resourcefulness and independence of women in the bush was to become legendary. But it also had a stultifying effect in cutting them off from the society of other women and in denying them female assistance and advice. Some women found it easier to adapt to the loneliness of isolated farms than others.

Ann Gore's letters add to our cumulative knowledge of the lives of pioneer women. She writes of a time between arriving at a new station and the building of a home. This small collection of three letters which she wrote to her cousins in England was discovered at the Cambridgeshire and Isle of Ely County Record Office. She wrote them while living with her parents at an isolated property named Gilmour, near Lake Bathurst, between Goulburn and Braidwood, which had been granted to her father Captain John Gore RN. Ann's brother Edward helped in running the property, but was often at an outstation. At the time she wrote these letters the family hoped that another son, Lieutenant Graham Gore, would join them.

Although Ann remarked about the young age at which girls married in Australia, she said she did not expect to marry herself. In her isolated position, her opportunities for meeting suitable young men must have been very rare.

Ann Gore wrote on 29 September 1837 to Mary Ann, Henrietta and Ellen Collinson at 47 Guilford Street, Russell Square, London:[1]

To Mary Ann:

'I am very glad you have seen dear Graham we are in hopes he will come out to us now he has gained his promotion—he would be a great comfort to Papa particularly as Edward is obliged to leave us with some part of the stock and it is rather too much for Papa—the management of the Farm with the many annoyances attending it. My dear Mother has been confined to her bed all the Winter as the unfinished state of our house was unfit for her and the weather has been very cold, her general health is good and her spirit not withstanding all her sufferings keeps up wonderfully. I hope as the Summer is now fast approaching she will be enabled to get out amongst us again. We find it rather dull now Edward has left us as he was our constant companion and used to ride out with us. We are now obliged to go a short distance from home and ride whilst the others walk . . . How very much I should like to see you all again—Henrietta—Ellen and George—I suppose I should scarcely know [you]—a few years make such a difference in young people. I must now tell you how we got on with the Farm; we have about 26 acres of wheat in, and our garden produces plenty of vegetables, fruit we have not any yet, but, I hope in the course of a few years we shall have some. My Sisters are both quite well and desire to be kindly remembered to you. Edward has been staying with us for a week, he has many difficulties to contend with in his new establishment, his health is very good.'

To Henrietta:

'Your letters my dear Henrietta give me great pleasure as it shows me that, altho so far distant, you have not forgotten me, the least scrap from England is most acceptable and I hope now you will constantly write to me. I do not know that I have seen a great deal, in our voyage out we stopped at the Cape three days and was kindly entertained by Mr and Mrs Jones, after landing at New South Wales we only remained one day in Sydney and I have only been there one day since. I understand there are a great many houses built, it was when I saw it, an improving town. Parramatta where we resided for a twelvemonth is prettily situated but exceeding warm and musquitoes in abundance—not very pleasant you will say, the part of the Country we are now living in is very different, the climate more resembles that of England, the Winters are very cold and we keep in large fires to keep us warm, wood being very plentiful we can easily do it, the scenery is monotonous and a great many of the trees having white stems gives them the appearance of being white washed, the Native Blacks are I think the ugliest race I ever beheld and there are no means of civilizing them—preferring there [sic] roaming kind of life to a settled habitation; their chief covering is a Blanket, which Government allow them or else a kind of Mantle made of Opossum skin which they wear over the shoulders, they have a chief or king to each tribe, we took one of the little Black Girls thinking to bring her up but, she only remained two days rejoining her tribe on the second day . . . We are now comfortably settled in the Bush, our house is not yet finished—and I think it is probable it will be some time before it is, as to being as comfortable as in old England we cannot expect it, the annoyances you have with bad servants prevents that, and there is no possibility of getting others. Yes my dear you will receive many letters from Ann Gore, for I do not think it is at all probable I shall ever change my name, the Ladies here marry very young I have heard of several being only sixteen . . . '

To Ellen:

'I must write you a few lines in answer to your kind letter although I fear I have not anything very interesting to tell you. Our House is pleasantly situated with an extensive view in Front overlooking our wheat field. I dare say you would fancy the scenery must be very pretty from the trees being all evergreen, but I can assure you it is not to be compared to old England, the white gum which is the principal tree growing in this part of the Country is very ugly, the Mimosas are very pretty as also many of the Flowers but they have very few of them any perfume, there are great many parrots of every variety and Black and White Cockatoos not any of the birds sing with the exception of the Magpie which has a kind of whistle. Society we have none as there are not a great many Families residing so far in the interior and what few there are reside twenty miles off. When we first came up we found great amusement in Music but unfortunately our piano is now out of tune so much that we are unable to play and there is no possibility of getting it repaired.

'Since we have been here we have been left for two months together without servants and obliged to do all the work ourselves not very pleasant I can assure you. Papa is looking very well, what do you think of his taking a walk of twenty miles and without much fatigue. I shall expect to hear from you and very soon, hearing from our Friends is one of our greatest pleasures.'

Neither Ann nor her sister married. When their father died, the property was taken over by their brother, Edward Gore. Another brother,

Lieutenant Graham Gore, was lost with Sir John Franklin's Arctic expedition and another, John, was lost at sea.[2]

## Margaret Menzies

*We made ourselves comfortable in one room*

The journal Margaret Menzies kept during her voyage to Australia and while settling on the land describes very well the problems of adjustment to a new way of life. Although she and her husband came to New South Wales with sufficient capital to give them a good start with no real danger of failure, they experienced some months of very rough living. Margaret became so absorbed in these problems that when a well-known traveller, Lady Franklin, wife of the Governor of Van Diemen's Land diverged from her overland journey from Melbourne to Sydney to visit the district, (see Chapter 9) she noted it only very briefly in her diary. Margaret's more immediate concern was to find women who would make congenial friends and with this in mind she looked shrewdly and critically at her neighbours.

Margaret Menzies and her husband Robert, a doctor, left Perth in Scotland on 1 August 1838 to migrate to New South Wales, which Robert had already visited during a voyage in 1837 as ship's surgeon on the *Hope*. His health was a cause for concern and, apart from the benefits of a milder climate, he was also apparently impressed with the prospects for farming. Before emigrating, he married Margaret Tindall in Perth, Scotland in June 1838. They travelled on the *Earl Durham*, accompanied by Margaret's brother, Charles Tindall, and her maid, Jessie, arriving on 2 January 1839.

Following what was almost a custom, both Margaret and Robert Menzies kept journals during the voyage and Margaret continued hers for some time after their arrival. During the long journey she prepared herself by reading both volumes of *Major Mitchell's Australia* and John Dunmore Lang's account of 'our adopted country'.[3] She thought Lang wrote not 'in the spirit of a Christian. There is much sarcasm & spite throughout the works.' She was very critical of some of the passengers— Mrs McAlpin was 'a disgusting woman & ought to be ashamed of herself' and her daughter disgraced herself in Mrs Menzies's eyes by having a romance with a fellow passenger. On 14 December 1838, after they had been at sea over three months, Margaret Menzies wrote comments that were typical of many who had made the long sea voyage to Australia:[4]

'I sincerely hope the 17 days remaining of this year may take us if not to Sydney at least very near it for never was I so tired of any place as I am of this ship & never was I so tired of people as I am of some folks here, whose mean conduct is too despicable to take notice of and yet sufficiently annoying—'

While looking for land, Margaret and Robert Menzies stayed with Dr and Mrs Patrick Hill at Liverpool, friends of Robert's uncle, Alexander Stewart who had succeeded his nephew as surgeon on the *Hope*. After inspecting land at Mittagong and Windsor, Robert Menzies bought '3 hundred acres from Government and 300 from Dr Thomson adjoining the government land' between Shellharbour and Kiama, south of Wollongong.

Towards the end of February, the Menzies put their possessions on board the *Alexander McLeay* with Charles Tindell in charge and also sent Jessie for the voyage down the coast from Sydney to Wollongong. Margaret and Robert travelled overland from Liverpool through Appin and down the mountain to Wollongong. The following extracts from Margaret's journal describe their arrival and settlement at their property.

*'Saturday 29th February [1839]*
'. . . Passed a very uncomfortable night at Wollongong suffocated with *spirits* & *tobacco* & eaten up by *bugs*. On Sunday called at Dr John Osborne's[5] rather a Gentlemanlike man but not as sterling as Henry & Mrs John the most *unladylike lady* I had seen for a long time—the children Bah! want civilization sadly.

'Proceeded in the afternoon to Marshall Mount 15 miles Mr H. Osbornes[6] & met a very hearty welcome. Mrs Osborne a very gentle nice woman, hope to know her better & Mr O one who I think will be a valuable neighbour to dear Bob—they wished us to remain but I felt anxious to finish my journey and we left next morning calling at O'Mere's on the way where I had my first meal in a log hut & enjoyed it very much—arrived at Kiama about 5 afternoon 3rd March, heartily glad my journey was at an end but surprised the *Alexander Macleay* had not reached this harbour before us, we remained in great anxiety respecting it until the Monday following when she arrived & our cargo living & lifeless in safety but the former quite sick of the sea—that evening & the next day the 12th March got all our goods on shore & took possession of our 3 rooms which we rent from Smith at £2 per week. Robert had been to the Farm the 2d day after our arrival here & saw our huts commenced—he & Charles have been going every second day since but Connor the carpenter being given to drink gets on very slowly & keeps us anxious about being settled there before winter sets in—Robert is very much pleased with his property which we have named Minamurra from the violet which bounds it in part & every one says he has been very fortunate. Were we only there which I trust we will be soon I have no doubt we should with the blessing of God get on very well—Charles went to Sydney a fortnight since & hired a Farm servant who arrived here last Saturday and on Monday he & Charles went to Minamurra & commenced erecting a hut for themselves which they took possession of last night & intend being busy erecting our houses & putting in some garden seeds &c &c. John Cusack is a strong & seems willing man, an Irishman, hope he will turn out better than Garrit Lynch our first servant who was sent to Wollongong to bring back the horse I rode—got drunk— was put in the watch house & did not return till a day after his time— he was dismissed instantly for his conduct most happy I was to get him off having disliked him from the beginning.

'Robert went to Wollongong yesterday. I expect he will return tomor- row evening—feel lonely when he is absent having little variety of work to amuse me—Kiama is a very pretty place to be sold in town allotments & will be most convenient for our sending our crops to Sydney the harbour being such as to admit of small vessels. The coast is very [?indented] to numerous pretty bays & [?diversified] rocks indeed had we only ruinous castles & valiant knights there could not be a more romantic country—you may lose yourself amidst the vines & creepers of an in- terminable forest & in five minutes if you be like minded throw yourself from a precipice into the Pacific Ocean.

'There is no society here & I sometimes feel that we have left a great deal behind us there is some chance of our becoming savages but while dear Rob is happy I ought to be so too & certainly the great improve- ment of his health more than makes up for many comforts enjoyed in Scotland which we cannot expect here—intercourse with well bred people "one" Mrs H. Osborne is the only Lady near me I expect to enjoy—went with Robert one day to Mr [Michael] Hindmarshs Alne Bank. Mrs H a regular dowdy & a *currency*—Kind & well enough but quite a money making couple seemingly now although money is all very well & certainly the great cause of our coming to N S Wales it ought not to be the sole aim of creatures born for nobler purposes & I trust neither R C J or I will ever so far debase ourselves as to make that the chief aim of our existence which should only be sought in so far as it may in- crease our own comforts & the means of doing good to our fellow creatures in need—had a walk this afternoon took Morwen & Tay with me, when shall I be on the Banks of the sweet winding Tay again I do not like to be so long alone it only makes me think of & long after home

& its dear minister & all to no purpose I wish I had a letter from Minnie or some one else how many changes may have taken place since last September.

### 'Friday 19th April

' . . . Some weeks since 3 emigrant families arrived in the harbour to take a clearing lease on Mr Robbs farm—they are from the north of Scotland & only 2 of them can talk English—poor creatures they have been badly off since coming here living in the bush & before they got a hut erected suffering from the rain which commenced about that time as well as from hunger having brought no provisions expecting to receive them from their employer & finding they could exist no longer in that way they have procured places elsewhere—one man goes to Mr Stevenson—the Mackenzies to Mr Osborne & the Smiths as yet undecided whether to go to Mr Osborne Capt [J. G.] Collins or come to us— we took one of their boys James who is just beginning to understand what he has to do & his Father takes him to Marshall Mount which I am sorry for, we are uncertain about taking his Brother who is a smarter boy but of inferior disposition being pert & not given to tell the truth I fear however if he comes I will try to drive that out of him—

### 'Thursday 25th April

'Robert and I set off to Marshall Mount remained at Minamurra 2 hours while the rain lasted & reached Mr Osbornes by 6 oclock, was more pleased with the hut at the Farm than I expected—wish it was finished Charles & John Cusack living in primitive simplicity working hard—Robert left Marshall Mount on Saturday taking a Timor Poney with him which he exchanged with Mr Osborne for old Charlie & very glad R was to get rid of the lazy beast—on Saturday Dr Alick Osborne & Family dined at Mr H O's & on Wednesday Mrs B & I went there to dinner—they seem a nice Family much more agreeable than Dr John Osborne's at Wollongong—Mr H O went on Tuesday to the Kangaroo ground with Mr Brown . . .

'When we arrived in the Colony the country was in a dreadful state for want of water and from that time 2d January till about the beginning of April we had scarcely a drop of rain excepting occasional thunder showers which did not at all benefit the ground—complaints were loud from all quarters of the want of water for man & beast & even in this district which is truly a Paradise when compared to other parts was parched & the grass withered up—every thing rose tremendously in price & dreading there would be no wheat crop next year ships were to be sent to foreign parts for supplies—first flour is now 46/- per cwt & second do 43/- an immense price & actually ruinous to those who like

ourselves are newly arrived and have to lay out money for every thing—
we ought to be thankful for having the needful and trust next year may
be better—the rain came on about the lst April we had several days of
continued & heavy rain which has done an [?] deal of good—it is truly
wonderful the change that has taken place I could imagine I saw the
grass growing & although we have had some very *dry* days since what
before was a field of black earth is now covered with green grass
& although short affords a good picking for the horses—Winter
commences next month & I trust we may have yet abundance of that
most necessary article, rain which would quite change the present aspect of things & make us all look cheerful . . .

'*Monday 6th May*
'The first dray load of things went to the Farm; house nearly finished
on Friday 10th Mr Tait [Rev. John Tait, Presbyterian Minister at
Wollongong] dined with us on his way to Shoalhaven & on Sunday Dr
[G. U.] Alley—Mr Brown & Mr Annesley came about 11 oclock the two
latter gentlemen to see the district—they lunched with us & returned
same afternoon—Monday saw Mr Tait again, Robert went to Minamurra
in the afternoon was called to see a man at Shoalhaven who was said
to be dying—he set [?off] with the messenger had some tea here in
passing & did not reach Shoalhaven till 6 oclock; found the man not so
ill & came home next day very much knocked up—hope he will not
be called away again is a great nuisance & he is not fit for exertion—
before he returned on Tuesday evening a whole cavalcade had arrived
here from Wollongong consisting of Lady Franklin, the Governor's Lady
of Van Diemen's Land & companions . . .

'*May 18th*
'Left Kiama *May 18th* Robert came to Minamurra 2 days before & is
much engaged with a man at the Mills who had his hand dreadfully
lacerated so that when Jessie & I arrived here we found no one to
welcome us & the hut in sad confusion—set about making tidy & by the
time Bob came from his Patient had tea ready—only 2 rooms finished
then one serves as kitchen & Jessie's sleeping place & the other as our
bed room sitting room &c &c—Charles slept in a place off the store
erected by himself & John Cusack—very busy afterwards inspecting
china &c & soon managed to make ourselves comfortable in the one
room where we remained for 4 weeks—had 2 visits of Dr B Brien 1 of
Dr Alley & 2 from Mr Tait during our stay there & could not have
believed some time ago that we could have put up with so little accommodation & at the same time had things tidy about us—found one sofa
most convenient for sleeping on, it was made down every night & up

in the morning & was really useful—Mr Tait remained a night with a Mr Reid from Greenock & fortunately our second bed room was so far finished as to admit of his sleeping in it—funny that a Minister should sleep the first night in it—we are now 24th June fairly settled & confortable in a nice sitting room 22 feet long containing a side board—Piano—Book Case Sofa—large table & 8 chairs & a snug bed room off it where we have many mercies & comfort to be thankful for—getting a Porch made at the door—weather excessively cold—5 assigned men assisted on the 23d much to Bob's joy who will now get on with his opperations . . .

### 'Wednesday 17th [July]

' . . . white cow died Tuesday obliged to buy milk again much good we have derived from Mr Osborne's cows truly—we know what we know—during Bob's absence had Gardener here putting flower borders in order and sowing vegetable seeds in small kitchen garden behind the house vines planted round the walls & 4 fruit trees. Dr Alley fixed on coming to Farm in our neighbourhood—hope they may prove pleasant neighbours—Jessie put her wages in the Saving Bank—Tay had 5 pups, one died . . .

### 'Friday 26th July

'Dr Alix Osborne, Mr Henry Osborne, Holden called here former invited us to a dancing party on the following Monday—got loan of a horse from Mr Osborne & went, very tired & passed a wearisome night disappointed of half the Party—left about 5 this Morning—went to Marshall Mount & slept for a few hours intending to return home in the afternoon but prevented by rain—came home Wednesday Morning & think I shall not leave for some time again—saw no place like home—

### '[11th August]

'On Sunday *11th August* James Ainsworth & Allen were Pleased to take to the Bush—Charles saw Allen in bed at 9 oclock & James was in at Players at half past 8; next morning both were missing—they were caught at Appin on the following Thursday. Robert goes tomorrow to see them tried at Wollongong, been very busy had a bullock killed last week & another this week have now plenty of Beef in the store—

### 'Thursday August 18th

'Robert went as intended, to appear against our runaways on *Friday 19th* they were sentenced to twelvemonths work in an iron gang & to be returned here at the end of that time. R returned on Saturday afternoon.

'Minamurra *4th September*
'Took a walk on Sunday, with B & Charles and saw some beautiful creepers one a scarlet or crimson flower very splendid & another little simple thing as graceful, wish the folks at home could see them!—'

That was the end of Margaret Menzies' journal. In the remaining pages she made notes on diverse subjects—recipes for pasties or meat pies, bread and fruit pudding, common batter pudding, a listing of bivalves, notes on the cleaning of shells, the words for some Scottish songs and a list of expenses 'attending an assigned female servant'. The latter lists the expenses Margaret Menzies incurred when Bridget O'Shanessey arrived at Minamurra on 28 October 1839 and apparently absconded soon after.

| | |
|---|---|
| 'paid for her passage down | £12–6 |
| sent man & horse to meet her | — |
| breakfast for him & feed for horse | 5— |
| value of day's work to him | 2— |
| gown for her | 7–6 |
| cotton for 2 chemises | 4–9 |
| stuff for petticoat &c | 3–6 |
| pair of shoes | 7–6 |
| man going to Wollongong to report her absence | 8— |
| paid Ann for week's work | 5—' |

Margaret Menzies, pregnant at the time she kept her journal, had her first child, Elizabeth, later in the year, followed by several others. Gradually the Menzies gathered relatives around them in their new land. Robert's uncle, Alexander Stewart, returned to New South Wales and bought a town lot at Kiama, Margaret's sister arrived from Scotland in 1843 and her mother in 1859. Robert Menzies died, aged 48, in 1860 and Margaret died the following year aged 44. They were buried beside the graves of two sons who died in 1849 and a daughter. Four daughters survived.[7]

## Sarah Burnell

*I have not been out of the valley for two years*

Sarah Burnell began married life in an established home, but its situation in a valley cut off from the rest of the country tested her self-reliance. Her home was at Araluen, south of Braidwood, in a valley so isolated that supplies had to be put on sledges for the descent down the steep mountain track. As she describes in a letter to her sister-in-law, Mrs Emily Curtis of Old Windsor, England, Sarah made the ascent to the tablelands very infrequently. She was happy to remain in the beautiful valley, later to be the home of poet Charles Harpur and the scene of spectacular gold rushes.

Sarah was native born, a daughter of Charles Henry Gray, who had arrived in Sydney on the *Royal Admiral* in 1800. On 14 February 1836 she was married in Sydney to Henry Burnell by Presbyterian minister Rev. John McGarvie and went to live in a convict-built house on Burnell's 2346 acre station at Araluen.[8] When she wrote on 18 October 1839 to her sister-in-law,[9] Sarah had two daughters, Laura born in 1837 and Margaret born in 1838.

'I only waited the arrival of the box to write to you as you very kindly expressed a wish that I should do so. I am happy to say it came safely, and the things were not in the least injured by salt water. I am extremely obliged to you for your share of its contents. The dress we much admire and the books. The sermons Henry is much pleased with as well as the numerous other presents which we both dearly appreciate, as coming from you and fancying to have been made by yourself . . .

'I have a sister with me so do not feel the loneliness of the bush much, although you may imagine I am a close housekeeper when I tell you that till last week I had not been out of the valley for more than two years, but the fact is there is little inducement to go beyond it, the Mountain is so steep. While I was up I visited all the ladies in the neighbourhood who are not very numerous, they are very agreeable persons. I remained two or three days, and although the distance was only 16 miles, I was so fatigued that I was glad to get home. I rode up and down the mountain and drove in a gig the rest of the way I saw no part of the country anything to equal our own beautiful valley, and persons do not seem to attend to the cultivation of their gardens or else the climate is not so favourable. Ours is very pleasantly situated, the verandah opens into it, which affords the opportunity of amusing ourselves when we feel inclined to garden. Little Laura is already becoming a most useful assistant to her Papa, although I fear she destroys more flowers than she cultivates. Our peach trees, grapes, strawberries and raspberries promise well.

'You wished to know how I amused myself, I can assure you, what with visitors calling as they often do three or four together, people living in this country being obliged to keep sort of open house for travellers, particularly at this distance, where there are no Inns, and my dear little ones and work, I find any time fully occupied. Henry takes us for a ramble occasionally between the Mountain ranges, where at this season of the year most beautiful wild flowers grow, the rock lily is a splendid flower. You would be astonished to see it growing on a solid block of granite without the slightest appearance of earth about.'

In 1842 the Burnells left Araluen to live at a slightly more accessible property, Runnymeade, near the Clyde River, inland from Bateman's Bay. They had twelve children, several of whom settled in the Bateman's Bay district.

## Annabella Innes

*I like my studies very much indeed*

Since its publication in recent years, Annabella Boswell's diary has become immensely popular and has been republished in many editions. Less well known is her own account of her early schooling, at first at a boarding school in Sydney and then by governesses at her parents' property. It is particularly valuable as one of the rare first-hand accounts of early schooling in the 1830s.

Annabella was the elder daughter of George and Lorn Innes of Bathurst. Her mother, formerly Lorn Campbell, was a daughter of Colonel John Campbell who had arrived in the the *Lusitania* in 1821 and settled in the Bathurst district. On 25 November 1825, at St John's Church, Parramatta, Lorn married George Innes, another Bathurst landholder. Lorn Innes was a close friend of Janet Ranken (see Chapter 11).

Annabella Innes was born in September 1826 at The Yarrows, near Bathurst, but when she was an infant the family went to live at an isolated cattle station, Capertee, about 100 kilometres from Bathurst. At various times the family left Capertee to live in Sydney or at Bathurst, sometimes staying with the Rankens. When Annabella was seven her family, then living at Erskine Park near Liverpool, decided to return again to Capertee. It was at this time that she was sent to a boarding school in Bridge Street, Sydney (later located at Albion House, Millers Point) run by Mrs Evans, wife of G. W. Evans, bookseller and stationer, and her partner, Miss Ferris.

Annabella was sometimes unhappy during her year at boarding school and she was overjoyed when her father arrived to take her home to Capertee. A very competent governess, Miss Willis, was engaged to be her teacher. Under Miss Willis, Annabella read many history books, learnt to play the guitar and was drilled in grammar and spelling. As part of her writing lessons, Annabella had to write a letter each week. The following is the letter she wrote on 16 April 1836 to her uncle, Major Innes at Lake Innes, Port Macquarie:[10]

'It gives me very great pleasure to write to you, my dear uncle, and papa tells me I must send you the little drawing I have just finished this afternoon. Had I known it was to be sent to you I would have taken more pains with it.

'We have got a governess now. I like it much better than being at school, because I do not require to leave dear papa and mamma. I am learning to play the guitar; I found it very difficult at first. I made my fingers so sore and my arms ache, but now my fingers have got quite hard at the points, and I am getting on very well with it. I can play the accompaniment to "Ye Banks and Braes" and to "Ah Vousdirais", "Rondo", and a few other little airs. I am reading the history of England, and have got the length of James the First, who began the reign of the family of the Stuart's in England. I like my studies very much indeed; they are a pleasure to me. Miss Willis explains them as I go on, which makes them easy to be understood. I think I like geography better than any of my other lessons. I have gone through the four quarters of the globe with Miss Willis, and I begin again on Monday at the map of Europe and through each country, beginning at England. My sister gets on very well with her lessons. She writes very well indeed, and seems to have a great taste for drawing. She is also learning to play the guitar. I wrote to Grandmamma in December, and since then I have written to aunt Jane. They cannot have got my letters yet, and very much pleased I shall be if my aunt writes to me . . . '

Annabella's next letter, written on 17 May 1836[11] from Glen Alice, Capertee, was to her aunt Isabella in Sydney:

'I am quite glad to have an opportunity of writing to you. I fancy I have got so much to communicate that I scarcely know which subject to commence first. I received your very nice letter when the drays came back from Sydney. I assure you I was very proud of it, and Maggie thought herself quite a big lady because she had got a letter from you. She kissed it over and over again, and went about showing it to every one.

'I am making a basket of cardboard, which I intend to present to Mr Ranken; it is nearly finished. I have painted an Indian tare on the one side, and that pretty blue flower called native flax on the other. On one end I have put a little purple aster and on the other I have sketched the Deil in the Bush, which I intend to paint. I think it will look very pretty. Miss Willis paints all the native flowers we can find for copies for us. If I have time I shall endeavour to take one from nature to send to you. I am getting on very well with the guitar, and can play several long pieces, besides three pretty waltzes and the accompaniments for three songs. I assure you I never look off the book now when I am playing.

Miss Willis took a great deal of trouble with me at first. I am so glad I can do it now.

'I write a long letter every week: it is sometimes three pages and sometimes four. I wish you were here to read them; I think they would amuse you, there is something about you in nearly every one of them. In the one for this week I have you lost in the bush with Margaret,[12] Miss Willis and me, at Hunter's River, where we are supposed to be on a visit to Aunt Ogilvie, after having spent a month in Sydney with Aunt Mcleod. I have written to her after going to Hunter's river: the letter this week is in answer to one I imagined Nancy to have written to me . . .

'Mamma is very busy getting trees planted out. She hopes you do not forget to collect all the seeds you can find for her. Our garden looks very well at present. There has been a great deal of rain. We have plenty of green peas, and all kinds of vegetables. The fowls are not laying, so I am little use as a hen-wife . . . '

After a visit to White Rock, near Bathurst, for the marriage of Annabella's aunt, Annabella Campbell, to Arthur Ranken on 7 March 1837, the Innes family returned to their home where Annabella and her sister Margaret resumed their lessons. Later in the year Miss Willis left, being replaced by Miss Smith, who introduced a stricter style of education. Instead of painting native flowers, Annabella found herself copying drawings of exotic trees and playing the piano, not the guitar.

Her account of her early schooling ends in 1839 when the family left to spend the winter at Lake Innes House, Port Macquarie, as her father had been advised to avoid the cold winters in the Bathurst district.

After her father's death, Annabella, her mother and sister moved permanently to Port Macquarie, where they lived at Lake Innes House just outside the settlement. It is from this period of her life that her journal dates.

In 1856, when she was nearly 30, Annabella married Patrick Charles Douglas-Boswell, accountant and later manager of the Bank of New South Wales at Newcastle. Eight years later they returned to his native Scotland, where he inherited estates at Cumnock. They had four children.

# 13

# *Health care*

**Ellen Viveash**

*In sickness and in health* [1]

The Tanner family were a well established and staunch Anglican family with considerable property holdings in England, which made the migration of Ellen and her brother William rather unusual. Although both originally intended to settle at Swan River—'the first colony to be established exclusively for private capitalists' [2]—their willingness to leave the comfort and security of England seems to require some explanation. That both married into the Unitarian Viveash family and the fact that this might have been an unpopular move with the rest of the Tanners could perhaps account for the move to Australia.

In England, William Tanner chartered the *Margaret* to transport to Australia himself and wife Hester, his sister Ellen and her husband Charles, as well as all their goods and chattels, their servants and seeds. But at the Cape, rumours abounded about the conditions at Swan River, which were said to be so desperate, with starvation threatening, that another vessel, the *Dunmore*, which was prepared to continue on to Van Diemen's Land if necessary, was chartered. This delay meant that the Tanners and the Viveashes did not arrive in Fremantle until February 1831, too late for the most generous land grants. Despite the difficulties and disappointments, however, Hester and William Tanner decided to stay at the Swan River, while Ellen and Charles Viveash continued on to Van Diemen's Land. Both branches of the family called their properties Baskerville.

180

Ellen and Charles became successful farmers, as Ellen was reporting in her letters to her mother in 1834. (Ellen's letters also contained references to her correspondence with the Tanners in the west, and constitute one of the earliest examples of inter-colonial and international communication in the colony.) With all the detail about costs and co-lonial customs (one could be forgiven for assuming that Ellen Viveash was particularly thrifty), these 'itemised accounts' provide a graphic picture of work and social life in Tasmania during this period. They also contain some shocking accounts of the accepted standards of medical knowledge and health care.

Ellen Viveash was often not well, particularly in 1834, the year she was confined with her first and stillborn child: 'I told Martha a few months ago that I was not looking older than my age,' she wrote to Eliza, in England, on 18 September 1834, 'but this is not true *now* as during the last 13 months I am looking at least 5 years older (than before) in consequence of fatigue, anxiety, confinement and broken nights'.[3]

On 26 January 1834, on her return from a trip to Hobart Town, Ellen informs her mother that she has not been at all well. 'The first 3 or 4 days I was very unwell. Mrs Pedder called and I was too ill to see her, and too ill to dine either of the two first days she invited us, but we dined there the next week' she explains.[4] And while it is not quite clear what 'ails' her (she later describes herself as having an intestinal blockage), Ellen goes on to provide—by today's standards—a rather frightening report of the treatment prescribed.

'The last week I was there I was better than I had been for a long time, which I attribute to the fruit. Did not require either medicine or injec-tion. Dr Scott has confirmed my suspicions of my complaint and I used (Charles did at least) the smallest instrument, but could not the next size as it produced too great an irritation and brought on vomitting which compelled me to desist. Tomorrow I begin again with the smallest and I must persevere and Dr Scott says I shall get quite well. He had Salmon's book which he quite approves of. We paid some 4 visits and we had some medicine of him for ourselves and Swan River and his charge was only £5. Strang charges £1 a visit here.'

Ellen Viveash is in a position to discuss the relative merits of the various medical men available (and their fees!); apart from Dr Scott and Mr Strang, there is 'Cotter (district surgeon who is anything but clever) or Mr Cameron an old man and I should think not clever or Mr McNab (very clever but *very* drunken)'.[5] For many women, however, the choices of Tasmanian society would have been unheard of; during the first fifty years of colonisation, the majority of women who were on farms outside the few towns were without medical support and had to be their own 'physicians' in the event of illness. And rarely could they prescribe rest and relaxation as their own remedies!

Pregnancy and childbirth increased women's vulnerability to illness, and it is saddening and salutary to note just how many women there were who died in childbirth, or soon afterwards; or women whose health was drastically impaired by constant pregnancies (which could have been a contributory factor in Eliza Marsden's stroke, although no doubt there were other sources of stress in her life); or women who died prematurely after having given birth to a number of children (such as Christiana Jane Blomfield, mother of eleven children who died age 50— see Chapter 8). Ellen Viveash had acknowledged the toll that her one confinement had taken of her health, and that was without any children to make demands on her time and energy during her recovery. Hester Tanner, her sister-in-law, was not quite so fortunate.

In a letter to her mother (May 4th, 1834) Ellen refers to a 'packet' she has received from her brother William at Swan River (dated 27 February 1834):

'[in] which it appears Hester is again in the family way and has been obliged to wean little Mary Ellen. William says the little girl is very small quite a doll, very good tempered. Hester and the children are quite well. William thinks if they come here (which is not certain for reasons given under) Hester will be confined here. I suppose they must be leaving Swan River in about seven months. What an awful thing it appears to me having children so fast! William says he fears they love their children too much.'[6]

Further correspondence reveals that life for Hester and William was quite a struggle (despite their capital and claims), with Hester's confinements and poor health also a terrible handicap when it came to domestic duties and caring for the children. In sickness and in health, women had to keep working.

By 1835, Ellen Viveash is confiding in Eliza (30 January from Baskerville, Tasmania) that:

'Poor Hester has told us for the first time that 3 doctors have given it as their opinions that she has an enlargement of the breast and she is so unhappy at the idea of leaving her little children without a female relation to take care of them for, as she says, a man, however kind cannot do all which is required and William is so much from home. I am writing to her that should anything happen to her I would go to Swan River and take charge of the younger ones. She had a still born child last time so has only three children, but she is in the family way again and suffers more than in former pregnancies.'[7]

Women had their own work to do, whether healthy or ill, and some-times part of the work was nursing other members of the family who were sick. Many a mother spent sleepless nights with a fevered child (Georgiana Molloy, for example—see Chapter 14), but many a wife also nursed her husband through an illness, even when in poor health herself, and sometimes to the point of her own exhaustion. Ellen Viveash was no exception.

When Charles Viveash 'collapses', Ellen becomes the nurse. Because it gives some idea of the work involved (and of the types of cure that were then canvassed), her letter to her mother, (dated 22 June 1834), describing the period is included here.[8]

'My dear Mother,

I have a great deal of domestic news and chit chat for this letter. I think it will be some weeks before a ship will leave for England and I therefore think I shall more than fill this sheet . . .

'On the 9th of this month Charles complained a good deal of a fixed pain in his stomach which he had felt something of nearly a week before, tho' I could not before the above named day get him to take any medicine, but that morning he took 5 grains of calomel stayed in bed till 2 o'clock when some neighbours came and he got up. They left about 6 and had not been gone more than 20 minutes when Charles complained of sickness . . . and in a moment after Charles complained of his head (I must make another parenthesis to say Charles is nearly well now) and I could not make him place himself on the floor until he half fell there insensible, almost on his face. He was quite immovable in my hands—I rang and Rossiter happened to be out of the house a few minutes and the wet cloth, braces etc. to be undone, windows opened, head to be raised—all done in ten minutes at farthest, but tho' I constantly bathed his face with water I think 20 minutes must have elapsed before he showed any signs of life. I then thought it was more than a fainting fit and sent a man for a neighbour who can bleed. In a few minutes Charles became slightly convulsed and kept up a moaning—then relapsed into insensibility. *Twice* this happened, at last the men took him to bed when he became so much better that we did not bleed him (fortunately).

'I wanted him to take 10 grains of calomel but he said he should be well tomorrow (I knew better). The fit was on Wednesday. That evening I wrote to Mr Strang to come and sent the letter the next morning but he was from home and did not come until the next evening, when Charles was so much worse that Strang did not leave him night or day till the following Monday afternoon. The constipation of the bowels was such that 2 drops of croton oil given twice in six hours with injections of oil and salts given, had no effect except in allaying pain. Mr. Strang then gave him 3 pills of calomel and gums which Charles brought up, likewise 3 drops of croton oil which shared the same fate. The nausea and vomiting was so constant . . . that on Saturday we thought a warm bath was the only hope and we trusted it might make the bowels act. We had sold all our puncheons but one which was carried away with the flood last winter, however, on Saturday before light I sent to a neighbour for one and was unsuccessful but I luckily thought of a case the wool bagging came in from Milroy and had it pitched and the bath was ready between 12 and one which so refreshed him (tho' it did not aid in moving the bowels) that we had time to take other measures.

'That morning, Saturday, Charles had looked deathlike and all feared he would not live. Thomson came and I got him to stay to help in bathing as we feared Charles would faint in the bath but he did not. Mr. Strang had proposed calling in Cotter (district Surgeon who is anything but clever) or Mr. Cameron an old man and I should think not clever or Mr. McNab (very clever but *very* drunken) I asked Thomson's advice, and he decided at once for the latter. We sent in the night and he came almost as soon as light on Sunday, very steady. He stayed till the evening thinking most seriously of the case and putting innumerable questions as to constitution etc. He ordered 6 grains of calomel every 3 hours which Charles took the whole of Sunday and during the night. As that gave *very* partial sleep it was changed to blue pill and cole-sinth [colocynth?] every 2 hours. Pray all bear in mind what McNab dwelt much on, namely if one medicine does not act a change of medicine may, even a less powerful one act even in cases of less importance than this.

'On Sunday afternoon Mr. Sutherland came and his loud talking quite knocked me up having been only just able to wait on Charles. The annoyance of Mr. Sutherland, who is always imprudent, made my spirit give way perhaps a night earlier but this was I believe the saving of my life. I had eaten nothing since Thursday night when I took some bread and tea with Mr. Strang most ravenously and until Monday it remained in my stomach—I felt just as I swallowed it notwithstanding 6 grains of calomel 4 other pills and salts besides 2 injections of salts. I had drunk the cocoa and fowl broth 2 or 3 times day and night which with the necessity of my presence near Charles had exerted me to rush about. At 9 on Sunday, I gave way and from exhaustion could neither stand or sit, my legs seem paralized (from fever I now know and the want of rest to my back). On Saturday morning I had sent for the washer woman who came quickly tho' she had saved me immense fatigue in changing the beds and making the drink for Charles, (he could not endure any one but me or Mr. Strang to stay with or wait on him).

'On Sunday night we went for Thomson to sit up with Charles to give pills every 2 hours, between which he was to have nourishment and *soda water* to *allay the sickness* which had the excellent effect and the bowels began to act slightly. The soda water was continued many days. On Monday I was just able to crawl in to see Charles and then returned to my bed till Tuesday when I was again able to be with him and danger was over unless he made a relapse. Charles said Thomson was the best nurse except me. Mr. McNab slept here on Monday, Charles was so recovered as to be up on Thursday. This was wonderful but I attributed it to the great attention in giving him during the night beef tea, fowl broth, arrowroot etc. every hour and a half, night and day, after the danger was over (a relapse would have destroyed him). McNab said if Charles had been a robust man inflamation would have carried him off but he was of so low a habit that he had fever only one night and *no thirst*. This latter made him very weak, together with the nausea, for he took scarcely 2 drinks in the day till Sunday night.

'When I got ill Mrs. Allison came to nurse one day, Mrs. Thomson one, and Mrs. Allison again. It would be impossible to express to you half the kindness and attention shewn us by our neighbours during this illness, all offering to sit up, help in the day and sending fresh beef, white bread, light cakes, eggs, oatmeal, coffee, jelly (cows feet), milk. I never can forget it and am confident nothing like it would have been met with in England. But they say "in England you would have had your relations and friends to have aided you instead." It is true, but we shall always like this country infinitely better. Charles cares less about leaving it now.

' . . . Charles thought on *the* Saturday he could not live (I did not know at the time that he was so fully sensible of his danger but found he most narrowly observed my countenance) and was most anxious to appoint Mr. Simpson joint executor with me seeing I should be incapable of business for some time. He has now asked Mr. Simpson if he may. Rossiter behaved incomparibly well night and day coming as long as I was well to ask me what the men should do next day. Bill the gardner and factotum likewise very well, 3 other men *very* badly, refusing to even chop wood. One I sent on Monday mid day to Campbell Town for medicine remained out till Tuesday mid day, tho' told by McNab when the medicine was given him to return quickly. He is sent to a chain gang for a year. 2 others Charles wanted me to get punished but it made me so nervous being still weak (on Wednesday when I made the charge against the other) that I begged them off, besides I thought one as an example would do much good and it has. They thought Charles would die and did not perhaps know that I could act, that I had the power of acting. This would now never happen again. Charles has given Rossiter and Bill a pound each and spoken severely to the others and told them he will be severe with them until by good conduct they made him forget this . . .

'Mr. McNab came 4 times to Charles and slept twice and came twice to me and we payed him £10. He said half would amply pay him but we thought it not too much as he doubtless saved Charles life. I had not been very well some time before Charles' illness but I am now very well. McNab, after several consultations and deliberation, says he could swear I never had the complaint I and Dr. Scott believed I had, and if he has not quite convinced me he has made me hope I have not. I have no doubt McNab is the most clever of the two and has had nearly as much experience and certainly is less trusty in his conclusions. He is likewise particularly clever in complaints of females midwifery and was under (in Edinborough) a man who wrote on stricture (White I think). He thinks the inactivity of the bowels has proceeded from the deranged weakened state of the stomach. There is, he says, an enlargement of the colon . . . which produces nearly the effect of a stricture . . . He has ordered me castor oil as often as I like (never pills they increasing my complaint of stomach and bowels) and by way of change rhubarb and magnesium (3d. the former 3s. the latter) and 3 wine glasses daily of camomile tea—the best stimulative, he says, its simplicity alone having sent it out of fashion.

'He says *his* stomach was so debilitated that from weakness of body and mind he was obliged to have some one lead him about, when he luckily saw at an auction a jar of camomile and purchased it which cured him. He will see me again in some weeks to know how I go on and if it should be necessary to use mechanical means (which he does not believe) he will use the intestine of a pig . . . [?] . . . introduced with the bougie [?] and filled by injecting water which may be retained many hours without irritation. If it should be stricture he says it would be easily overcome. He is a very well informed man as well as being so clever in his profession. He is a Highlander. He says my digestive organs are in the most damaged state but by following his plan I shall enjoy better health than for many years past. I think this would do for you dear Mother. If the camomile tea is taken warm it will produce nausea or vomiting. The wonder is I lived through taking pills so many years. He gives reasons for everything. He said Charles should eat often, always having only a small appetite and being debilitated, every 4 hours. He should above every thing keep his feet warm by wearing cork shoes and worsted stockings . . .

'There is a meeting tomorrow at Campbell Town to express gratitude to Mr. Robinson who has succeeded in peaceably capturing the Aborigines. Charles will not attend but will send £5 . . .

'I am going to send this by way of Sydney. Charles began a very long letter to you about 5 weeks ago and he will send it by the first ship which leaves this colony for England. Charles still complains of nausea frequently, this I do not like but probably he is quite as well as he ought to expect, he is still very weak but has been out 3 or 4 days and gets up at 9 and stays up until 10 without complaining of fatigue. I am much better than I have been for many weeks . . .'

Hester and William arrived in Tasmania (en route to England) in May 1835 in the *Harriet*. Hester's fourth child was born at Baskerville a few weeks later. Ellen—who helped with the children during Hester's confinement—became very fond of the 2-year-old, Mary Ellen, who stayed on and later accompanied the Viveashes to London.

Ellen Viveash died in London in 1842 from bowel cancer. Charles remarried, settled in England and went on to have a large family.

# 14
# *Sacrifice and science*

## Georgiana Molloy[1]

*She could not be without flowers*

Georgiana Kennedy gave up a gracious existence in England when she married Captain John Molloy and immediately set sail in 1829 on the *Warrior*; the sacrifice of a comfortable home, congenial society and committed friends was just one of many which Georgiana Molloy (1805–1843) would be required to make during her comparatively short lifetime. Just 24 years old when she married Captain Molloy (who was 48) she became pregnant on the voyage to the Swan River settlement. In May 1830, after a brief period in Fremantle, and having chartered the *Emily Taylor* to transport the small party and their goods south, Georgiana Molloy landed at what was to become Augusta.

Nothing could have prepared this sensitive and educated woman for the birth of her first daughter; on 24 May 1830. In steady rain, with an umbrella held over her in the tent, on a rough bed, Georgiana was 'confined' with her husband in attendance. The baby died three days later.

It was to be three years before she could bring herself to write about this loss to her close friend Helen Story (nee Dunlop), who was now married to a clergyman, and living in Scotland.[2]

'My dearest Helen,

'This I know will be seized by you both and I now see my dear Mr Story almost tearing it out of your pretty white taper fingers. Were you

188

not composed of the charitable and stirling feelings towards your fellow creatures that I know you are you would perhaps think that I had behaved ungratefully in not writing personally ere this . . .

'My dear Helen, I fancy myself newly arrived in the parlour and standing at the fire, then would you have introduced your little flock to me, and I should show you Sabina Dunlop, a darling good little child, now nearly two years old.

'I was indeed grieved, my dear Nelly, to hear of your poor infant's demise, for your sakes not for its own, I could truly sympathise with you for language refuses to utter what I experienced when mine died in my arms in this dreary land no one but Molloy near me. O, I have gone through much and more than I would ever suffer anyone to do again. I fear—I need not say fear—I know I have not made the use of these afflictions that God designed—it was so hard I could not see it was in Love. I thought I might have had one little bright object left to me to solace all the hardships and privations I endured and had still to go through. It was wicked and I am now not thoroughly at peace . . . '

Life at Augusta during those years was harsh and lonely; writing to her sister Eliza (on 7 November 1832), Georgiana tried to explain her circumstances:

' . . . it must always be remembered that we are a hundred & eighty miles from Fremantle, the Port on the Swan, and Vessels only occasionally touch here to supply the wants of a few settlers.'

For Georgiana, to be cut off from family and friends was undeniable deprivation, but so was being cut off from news, current affairs, from intellectual discourse and stimulation. 'Tell me what you think of the present state of affairs in England,' she requests of her sister. 'We know nothing but what we glean from newspapers and those so old that a Revolution might be begun and ended long before we should know.'[3]

Georgiana Molloy was not the only woman at Augusta, although until the arrival of Fanny and Bessie Bussell (see Chapter 15), there was no one who shared her interests or with whom she felt she could converse. While she deplored the lack of cultured conversation, she was also extremely grateful for the presence of Kitty Ludlow, who had preferred service with Mrs Molloy to abuse by her husband. Crippled and on crutches, Kitty was nonetheless an asset when it came to women's work in the bush.

But if life at Augusta was one of privation, it was not without its primitive dramas, as Georgiana recounts to her sister Eliza, with whom relations were slightly strained, but who no doubt responded to this tale of suspense.

'Another incident which I know you will see the propriety of making a subject of thanksgiving occurred on Friday the 15th September 1833 Molloy has lately had a mud wall and fire place built adjoining the House—On the coming of that day. Kitty—her husband, (Ludlow) Tom (a most interesting servant boy) on going out for the Kettle said "The wall is coming down." They said "Oh, no it's the noise of the rain on it." Kitty caught up her crutches. Tom replied, "I tell you it is." Ludlow, who was sitting behind his wife on the hencoop had only time to thrust his wife into an adjoining tent down a step—when down came all the chimney and wall and broke into the side of this tent which comprised of Bulrushes and [?] (you must remember our primitive state) Kitty now seized her crutches and most providentially when Tom spoke the second time and she was first down the step (owing to Ludlow's push and expression, "Like enough it is, Get out of the way, old woman") when the clay fell just at her heels and with its force—although it did not *touch* her—she fell against a box from the concussion. But for this miraculous interposition the poor lame creature must have been crushed to death. Tom exclaimed, "Thank God I have saved your life Kitty" but judge of my situation and inexpressible gratitude to the Almighty when just as we heard the noise of it falling—I was [?] Sabina to go into Kitty at the new fireplace and she said, "No, tay (stay) with 'Mama'." I was on the point of telling Tom to take her out on his going for the Kettle—but was withheld by mercy from the Lord who had compassion recall the threatenings sent out against us She every evening sits on Kitty's knee about that time.

'I cannot express my feelings to you . . . for had the child been on Kitty's knee—and she not able to walk without her crutches, they must inevitably have perished. I forgot to name that Ludlow had leapt into the corner whilst the ponderous mass was falling. It was the work of two days to recover the clay matted together as it was with stones and rushes (for want of straw) and had not the Almighty spared them—judge of the care and time required to extract their bodies. Every time I embrace Sabina I feel how different it might have been—that instead of a dear little child blooming with health, she might have been a mutilated, pallid corpse. Oh dearest Helen and Mr Story—I tremble now and wonder— Do return thanks and praises although inadequate I feel they are . . . '

Of all the examples of the diary-cum-letter in these early years, none could be better than the 'entries' of Georgiana Molloy. Whether writing to her sister Eliza, to her good friends Helen, Margaret and Mary (Dunlop), or later to the scientist Captain Mangles, Georgiana was likely to linger for months over her correspondence. While there were real practical reasons for this 'serial' approach (it would have been frustrating to have 'finished' a letter and to have it waiting for weeks or months until some means of despatching it could be found) it still seems that it was Georgiana's preference to conduct an ongoing 'conversation' with those back home.

In her letter to Eliza, she continues her description of the memorable Friday, 13 September 1833.

'We had not long retired to bed the same night when a person in a very disturbed state of mind burst into the house (for we lock no doors or windows) calling on Captn. Molloy to save him from two men who had attempted to shoot him—He rushed into my room—adjoining the room he entered—Sabina did not cry and I was not much alarmed at anything but the cause of such abomination as I regret to state it arises from great intemperance.

'Molloy had to go for a light from the kitchen about 40 yards, whilst Molloy was about, the person was trembling and begging protection— he had jumped from a window 12 feet high. On Molloy's bringing a candle, the gentleman perceived some blood on his trousers and fell into a dreadful convulsion fit—foaming at the mouth and kicking violently as he lay on the floor. This was too much for Sabina—she and I were up by this time—and she clung alarmed to me—I was obliged to walk out with nothing but my nightdress on—and no shoes—up to Mrs Dawson's rooms about the same distance as the kitchen—I sent down the menservants with some cold water and remained absent on dear Baby's account until the person was taken back to Charles Bussell's house over the garden he again returned and kept us in a sad confused state until 10 in the morning. Nothing would convince him it was an illusion—

'I spoke to him seriously when he recovered, which was the following day—But I fear without hope of amendment as this is the third fit from the same cause He spoke the most ridiculous things and took leave of us for the last time said he was going to enter on a world of spirits when Molloy was reproving him for his habitual excesses.

'These incidents will interest you and give you some idea of the singular events to which we are exposed in this precarious life.'

As a young woman in England, Georgiana had shown a great interest in the emerging area of 'botanical studies'; at a time when there were many people in England displaying a passion for collecting and classifying all the exciting and wondrous new plants that colonisation was uncovering, Georgiana used her opportunities at Augusta to extend her understandings of the flora and fauna. As she reports to Eliza, her vast 'garden' is vitally important to her.

'This is certainly a very beautiful place—but were it not for domestic charms the eye of the emmigrant [*sic*] would soon weary of the unbounded limits of thickly clothed dark green forests where nothing can be [?] to feast the imagination and when you can only say there must be some tribes of Natives in those woods and they are the most degraded of humanity.

'Our clime is heavenly and while you are burning the front breadth of your frock and the *nebs* of your shoes at an excellent fire of Newcastle coals—I am sitting in the Verandah surrounded by my little flower-garden of British, Cape and Australian flowers pouring forth their odour. (for the large white lily is now in bloom) and a variety of beautiful little birds most brilliant in plumage sporting around me. These little creatures seem quite delighted at the acquisition they have made in our emigration and are much tamer than any but the robin and sparrow in England.

'There is a small bird called the Australian robin with shining black back and head, and the breast of a very bright scarlet Also a little bird of a complete blue colour all over resembling *Smalt* or *Cobalt* with short green wings and the Honeyeater are so minutely beautiful. I cannot describe them—they have a long curved beak which they insert into the cup of the different flowers and the symmetry of their form is perfect accords with the elegance of their food you see them perch on the most slender flower stalk and apply the beak to the blossom every moment expecting to see the flower drop off, but their light weight does not in the least effect this.

'The native flowers are all exceedingly small but beautiful in colour although that flies when dried. I only know three kinds and those are two white and one blue of the herbaceous plants possessing an odour, Many of the shrubs are powerfully sweet, some like may, some like bergamote. Another remarkable feature in the Botany of this country S.W. Australia is the numerous kinds of leaves with the identical flowers—some of the leguminous now, I know, one purple pea flower with three kinds of leaves, one of which is a creeper and called the blue vine the other is an erect shrub with no smell and leaves like a holly, the third is also erect with leaves like the Privet—and in shady places the blossom emits a scent about 3 in the afternoon like allspice or clover. Another sort is yellow and straw colour of which there are five sorts of flowers with leaves utterly distinct—but I fear this last page may be somewhat tedious as you are not likely to behold all these aborigines.'

Despite the joys of scenery and garden—and of a delightful growing daughter—Georgiana Molloy and her husband were involved in backbreaking work. There are times when she asks whether it has been worth the sacrifice, as when she unburdens herself to Maggie (Margaret Dunlop).[4]

'My beloved Maggie,

'I received your and dear Mary Ker's letters of September 1831, in October 1832. You do us an injustice to censure us for a moment for not writing and thinking of you. Never a day passes that we do not speak of you and, as I have all along told you so few vessels call at this port, except to barely supply us with provisions, that we have not frequent opportunities of sending. Besides, I always hesitate to send a single letter, knowing the expense thereof.

'We have all been quite well since writing. In November Molloy went to the Swan on business. He remained a month, and was brought back in H.M.S. *Imogene*. Capn Blackwood, perhaps a friend of Roberts', as he is a nephew of Sir H. Blackwood, from whose name this river is called. He is a very nice gentlemanly man and connected with the Grahams of Netherby.

'Molloy went away again last Monday to view his large "grant" on the Vasse—a most pleasing country and answering with truth to the description given of its park-like appearance, with long waving grass, and abounding also in kangaroos.

'In the interim a vessel has come in, which has given me not only my own, but Jack's letters to write, which I am almost unable to do, as at the beginning of the week I was confined to bed from over-exertion. For in truth, Maggie, I have not time to say my prayers as I ought. I must unbosom myself to you, my dear girl, which I have never done—but this life is too much both for dear Molloy and myself; & what I lament is that in his decline of life he will have to lead a much more laborious life than he did in one and twenty years' service. He does not despair but I never knew anyone having his losses to bear but who would.

'May God have mercy on us and poor little Sabina Dunlop who is remarkably well and as I lay in bed on Monday she all at once got up and began to walk. She came to my bedside and said "Mam, Mam". She keeps going backwards and forwards the whole day long with something for me & never cries though I dip her in a tub of water. She has 10 teeth, two of which are double. She began to toddle in Molloy's absence. On Monday she was 14 months old. She is a great blessing. I need not blush to tell you I am, of necessity, my own nursery-maid. If I could afford to keep one, they are so exceptional I durst not trust my child with them . . .

'By this I write to Mary and Mrs Caldicott. I have had seven letters of Molloy's relating to business to answer, besides my own correspondent; to weigh out rations, attend to Baby, & although needlework of every kind both for her, Molloy, myself and servant is required, I have not touched a needle for this week. I am now exhausted, and the day uncommonly hot.

'I told you how it would be! I should have to take in washing and Jack carry home the clean clothes in a swill. The last of this has not happened yet; but between ourselves, dear Maggie, the 'washing' is no uncommon occurrence! But time will show! What goes to my heart is that dear Molloy has so much exertion bodily & mental. But I am repaid with interest when any part I can perform eases his burden. The Lord is good and has shown Himself to us in many wonderful instances, but we are sadly forgetful of His Love and bounty amid the hurried concerns of this life . . .

' . . . Oh! my loved "sister"! I cannot contain myself when I think of the past. I never, never trust myself to think of all we have said to one another . . .

'What is all this about Irving and the supernatural gifts? Please tell me. My head aches & I have all the clothes to put away from the wash; Baby to put to Bed, make tea & drink it without milk as they shot our cow for a "trespass"; read prayers and go to bed besides sending off this tableful of letters. I wish I had you here to help me! What golden dreams we used to have about your coming to stay with me! How would you like to be nearly three years without a woman of your own rank to speak to, or to be with you whatever happened?

'Sabina has just toddled in, hiding her little face with her hand in play. She is sometimes so lively she is "neither to hand nor to find", as James Angus would express it. Pray remember me to them all. I wish Andrew would write & find us out. I shall write to him. My kind love to Robert and accept the same with unabated affection from your sincerely attached sister . . . '

On 20 April 1833, life in Augusta changed qualitatively for Georgiana Molloy; that was when Fanny and Bessie Bussell joined their brothers at the settlement. Georgiana was full of eager anticipation at the prospect of cultivated discussion and company, and insisted that Fanny and Bessie be 'accommodated' by her on their arrival. Although even some of the basics were unavailable, Georgiana went to great lengths to make her guests comfortable at the nearby empty house of Mr Dawson—with flowers, a cheerful fire, photographs and ornaments all provided. (For the Bussell sisters' description of this event, see Chapter 15.)

The Bussell sisters soon moved on to their property, The Adelphi, and there is no disguising the fact that Georgiana was somewhat disappointed with them. They failed to return her hospitality and were 'very closefisted' (among other things!), as she informed Eliza later in the year.

Sadly, what Georgiana did not know when she began her letter to her sister on 13 November, was that the recently married Eliza had died.

'One very good way of packing trees or plants is by putting them in tanner's bark enclosed in an iron pot or pan well closed down. Some fig and vine cuttings for the Bussells arrived here the other day in this manner and the figs had shoots on them 3 or 4 inches.

'You could not send old Georgy a greater treat than some seeds, both floral and culinary—but they must all be seeds of that year's growth. In return I will send you some Australian seeds. I should last time, but Molloy had forgot where he put them.

'I hope ere this you will have received some little memento per *Cygnet*. I send you a bunch of emu feathers given me by Mobin, a native chief— you will perceive that they are covered with a sort of red earth. This they paint themselves with and mixed with fat they extract from their food they besmear the hair which is turned up *a la Grecque* and confined by many strings of the oppossum hair which the women spin.'

Georgiana Molloy's attitude to the Aboriginal people is quite interesting. Clearly she did not see herself as depriving them of their legitimate land rights, but nor did she despise or patronise them. Coexistence was her stance, and she was quick to condemn those whom she saw as treating the Aboriginal people in a hostile or provocative manner. Later, when she began gathering plants and seeds in earnest for Captain Mangles, she learnt from the Aborigines and enlisted their help in her scientific projects.

'The natives are very fond of all the settlers at Augusta, and we live on the most peaceful terms—but at the Swan—from the indiscretion of several persons and particularly their servants, they are hostile. The natives call Molloy King Kandarung and me Kymbin. They are delighted with Sabina and she is not the least alarmed at their black figures and rude voices. She will dance opposite the native children with great glee and an old native woman seized her by the leg the other day and embraced it without producing the slightest emotion of fear.'[5]

Meanwhile, all was not going well for the Bussells; their home was destroyed by fire, along with many irreplaceable belongings. But there were some compensations for Georgiana, as she explains to Eliza:

'You are, I presume, acquainted with the existence of the Bussell family. They have lately been so unfortunate as to have their dwelling house, composed of mud and wickerwork, burnt to the ground and the property much injured by the flames. Fanny, the eldest girl, happened to be staying at the time with me. No lives were lost—but all their shoes, needles and thread destroyed, which in this far distant clime is really irreparable. They have a cottage at Augusta and thither they have all repaired, bringing with them their goods and chattels—amongst which Bessie's piano—placed in my sitting room.

'You may well conceive my gladness at this acquisition as I have not heard the sound of music for four years. Sabina at first was a little afraid but in an hour soon overcame it. She seemed to think it was an animal and insisted on tying a piece of cord round one of its legs hearing us speak of the legs of the Piano—She put her fingers to the opening in the front board where the silk is visible, and exclaimed, "Oh! Mama its coming out—It's coming out!" Hearing the vibrations at night when eating her supper, she said, "If the piano had a mouth Mama I could give it some sop." in time she has become fond of it & her great delight is to sit upon the music stool. She asks me to sit by her. She strikes the keys and attempts to sing—it is most ridiculous to see her—she sings, "Come a Rose, my bave Tossy Boy" (Come arouse thee, My Brave Swiss Boy), "Little BoPeep from Ingle (England) I come", "Buy a broom", and "There grows a bonnie briar bush in our Kail Yard". Yesterday morning on entering the room she asked Mrs Dawson the servant if the piano was awake yet?" I should perhaps suppress all these juvenile Details but my dear Eliza to Molloy and me they are not only amusing but instructive more especially when we rarely hear the sound of any loved voices but our own two . . .

'The Bussells always intended leaving The Adelphi, their residence up the river, but this accident has obliged them to halt at Augusta instead of going go the Vasse, where Molloy and they have taken their large grants. They are genteel nice people and that sort of thing—but terribly *close fisted*, which gives us the idea they belong to the *Take All* family, as we have on several occasions been most liberal to them yet they are not ashamed of receiving *everything* & you will hardly believe they have made no return—nor have Molloy or myself ever broken their bread—This must be secret—I told Mama but charged her not mention it.'

The letter to Eliza is resumed on 21 February when Georgiana reports on the departure—and death—of Kitty, who was 'in a most lamentable state, totally deranged and unapproachable, saving by her husband, from disease which the climate made more offensive'. In the absence of Captain Molloy, Georgiana writes: 'Her funeral duties I was necessitated to conduct. She had to be buried by torchlight. Her poor frame was so highly discomposed, it made two of the bearers ill for some days'. Not so Georgiana, however, who had her own added difficulties to contend with: 'I am overpowered with work and expect an addition to my family in the spring, and have not a cap to put on the child's head'.

The many absences of Molloy also added to Georgiana's burdens and caused her considerable distress; not wanting to complain in her letter to Eliza, she nonetheless includes the information that he has assured her that when he returns from a current trip on government business:

'he will never leave me again unless it is to enrich ourselves and procure more comforts than we have hitherto enjoyed. True, we have drunk many dregs since we embarked on this fatal Swan River expedition, fraught with continued care and deprivations.'

The letter to Eliza was not closed until 18 May—six months after it was commenced—and as the time for sending it approached, Georgiana begins to list some of the 'essentials' that she would like Eliza to forward:

'I wish you would send Jack two pairs of List slippers to put on while dressing, and some Honey in jars. If not expensive also 20 yards of *good black cotton velvet* as much as would make me a *very full dress* and some over for children's frocks—I name the uses I shall apply it to as I am ignorant of the width—perhaps by taking a whole piece you might obtain an abatement and I should not object to that quantity, but let it be a *very* good black, as you will be making up a box dear Eliza I will trouble you to get me some other things—the only impediment the reimbursement which Molloy will pay in time.

'A little watering pot for Sabina and any letter book with pictures or other little bagatelle.

'I am very ill off for net to use for children's caps and that if you can meet with any proper width at a cheap rate and good in kind send some also.

'I wrote to Mama for Hail Oil, Pomatum and very fine tooth combs, If she has not got them enclose three combs three short large size two hair and six nail brushes very hard I had better draw out a list.

'You never can do wrong in sending us out soap for which we sometimes pay 3/6 per lb. Let it be yellow or brown. Candles also and glass would materially serve us as what we do not want I could sell to great advantage.

'*Do make me a present* of a nice new tea pot for Molloy and myself I like either biscuit ware or stone ware such as mustard pots are made of with silver rims. The one I use is a black one sine handle and half a spout. The consequence is loss of time and burnt fingers. Ask the price of a tea set of this kind if such are ever made—Its strength is its great recommendation. I mean brown looking, with raised figures . . .'

A life of very hard work continued at Augusta; by the end of 1834 Georgiana was once more writing to her friend Helen, this time to report on the birth of Mary Dorothea and on the frightening illness of Sabina.[6]

'When I last wrote to you my dear Helen—I believe I complained of multiplicity of business—but on 16 June this year—my third daughter was born and I have not only to nurse and carry her about but all my former occupations to attend to having only Mrs Dawson as female servant. I do not hesitate to say that I am overwhelmed with too much labour and indeed my frame bears testimony to it as I every day expect to see some bone poking through its epidermis. My beloved husband much assists me and more than many would do, except such treasures as yours and mine, dear Nelly. You will be able fully to believe me when I say I must either leave writing alone or some useful requisite needlework undone. The latter I would not attempt for Molloy myself and the children but there is not a person to be had here to do any— I never open a book—and if I can read a chapter on Sundays it is quite a treat to have so much leisure.

'Baby will be six months old on the 16th of this month. She is a very large fat child and remarkably healthy With great thankfulness I avow she has never had even infantile illness . . . Everyone says she is a beautiful child and though it may appear very vain, I coincide with them. She is very fair. I call her *French white* and her flesh is so hard and plump that her arms and legs are like polished marble Her face is more like mine than dear Sabina's is. Her eyes are rather dark blue.

'In November poor darling Sabina was seized with a remittent fever, which came on suddenly At last. At 2 o'clock in the day, I perceived her very drowsy, and she would scarcely leave my side—though at another time I cannot get her to remain with baby & me—we are too quiet— Well before ten she was in a warm bath—her head shaved and blistered. She was quite incoherent and at one time convulsed and before this she had never been half an hour ill from her birth. We were greatly distressed—Molloy and I prayed the Almighty to spare her our dearest hope—she was only 3 on the 7th of this month and on the 30th Death was certainly hovering about her. She sat on my knee to have her head shaved she said "Mama, you will bring Baby in," and kept continually talking about Baby, of whom she is very fond.

'Molloy commanded me to go to bed as Baby, who lays all night in one of my arms was restless. I went but not to close my watchful eyes. Molloy dearest creature, sat up with Diddy who remained in the same state till about three when God be praised & glorified the medicine took effect. The instant this occurred she was better her pulse which beat at 130 and had never been lower than 120 fell, she began babbling in her usual gay manner. She had a relapse a few days after but thank God that was the last and though still very weak and ill looking—I trust will shortly regain her strength, though she is not the same looking child she was. I felt peculiarly grieved for though the medicine man thought that it was a stroke of sun Molloy and I were persuaded that the symptoms were more those of remittent fever and I had for some time been lamenting my total inability to look after her who had always been my sole object of care—I know she ran about too much for her tender years—she was often so tired that, when the poor child sat down to dinner she would almost fall from her chair with fatigue & be quite asleep—her spirits which are very great are too much for her strength, and in the winter she would be running about without cap or bonnet from 6 o'clock to 5. Then having baby both to nurse & attend to, the darling child was neglected—I wish now I had a proper person to take care of her, and when I know there are so many that would be glad of such an asylum as my house would be to them, I bewail my smallness of means that I could not offer to pay their passage money. I of course would prefer an educated person, but would be grateful for one of good Christian principles and if you hear of anyone of sickly health wishing for such a situation I hope you will remember me; I would treat her with every kindness and she would only have to do a little needlework and be a companion to Sabina more to keep her from bad examples if she was not able to teach her. Sabina can say the Morning Hymn which Papa regularly hears at Prayers. He has taught her to say the Lord's Prayer and the Grace of our Lord etc. I never knew her to tell a direct untruth till last Saturday, when she was whipt for the first time, but still insensible to her fault—Tell me how you act when they are given to untruth. I have only one spelling book that your kind Father gave me and it is without pictures—for some object to engage her ever active mind I have already begun her letters but she manifests no predilection for them I wish we were nearer good instruction for I am persuaded many dear and precious minds will be lost for want of it. I am delighted you sent me your two year old letter—if you had not I should have been quite ignorant of the highly instructive circumstances it contained and which I had often much wished to be acquainted with.'

In characteristic style, Georgiana Molloy makes her periodic entries in her letter to Helen; during the course of the undertaking, another box arrives from Helen—almost miraculously. More disasters for the Bussells are recorded; these can be assessed more directly and dramatically from the Bussell letters themselves (see Chapter 15).

'My dear & much loved Helen,

'Last Friday the 5th Dec. the box containing your much valued letters & Mary's kind present were given to me through the medium of

Mrs Bussell, to whose care Mrs Taylor entrusted it. A strange fate awaited it. The vessel on which all Mrs Bussell's goods were placed has never been heard of, and it is presumed is lost, as it was only a small craft and a gale came on three hours after she left Fremantle, the Port of Swan River. However, this parcel has been put up with their [books] the only property they have saved from all they have brought out, amounting to upwards of £1,000.

'None but herself would have ventured property of value in such a vessel, as it was only a boat built on. This is not the worst The poor man Captn. McDermott and three hands so sailors were on board. Captn. McDermott has left a young widow and child of about two years and is daily expecting to be confined without a *penny* to support themselves even now, owing to his inadvertent speculations.'

In terms of home and farm, Augusta was proving to be an unremittingly hard existence, and Georgiana's regrets and remorse made their presence felt in her letters to Helen, her dear friend.

'We are so unfortunately remote a distance—you remember my reluctance to come out to Australia and I wish I never had. We enjoy health and our children will perhaps have more than a competency, but Molloy and I have to work as hard, and harder than servants will. In March our servants' indentures are up, and we are literally expecting to be without, and we shall be, unless some vessel most unexpectedly brings people here. I know I cannot do without a woman servant, however bad she may be, especially when there is no one to be got to wash even, and I have to carry baby. So fat she is, she makes my back quite ache. As to Molloy, he is a perfect slave; up at daybreak and doing the most menial work sometimes, so that all the former part of our lives was all lost time, and even reading and writing there is not time for here.'

Georgiana Molloy had given up much, and was asked to give up more. Augusta had not proved to be as successful as the Molloys had hoped and within a few years a decision had to be made whether to persevere with the resistant site, or to abandon the few fruits of their hard labour and move to a more promising and productive location. The Bussells had already decided on better climes, and on 13 April 1834, the Bussell boys transferred to the *Ellen*, the Government schooner, all the equipment that they needed for the move to Geographe Bay and their new property, Cattle Chosen, 60 miles from Augusta on the banks of the Vasse. Despite the sacrifice it entailed in leaving her garden—one of the sources of beauty, joy and replenishment in her life—Georgiana Molloy was asked to make the move inland. And the relocation of her home was not the only transformation she was to undergo. This was the period when her relationship with Captain James Mangles began.

One of the first Fellows of the Royal Geographical Society, a Fellow of the Royal Society, and a dedicated horticulturalist, James Mangles had visited Swan River in 1831 and had become fascinated with the strange flora of the area. When he had returned to England—still with the desire to further observe and study the Australian plants, Lady Stirling (the Governer's wife) had suggested Georgiana Molloy as a suitable collector and contact. With her graciousness and learning, and her own absorbing interest in gardens and plant life, she had seemed a logical choice for Captain Mangles' purpose.

Georgiana's reputation throughout Swan River and its environs as a lover of flowers and gardens, and as a student of the wildlife of Australia, was widespread; Mrs Charlotte Bussell (who was married to John Bussell), on meeting Georgiana, was to observe that 'she could not be without flowers'.[7] For James Mangles she really was 'a find'; for Georgiana Molloy, his interest, and direction of her explorations, proved to be a lifeline.

James Mangles' first letter requesting assistance with his work was received by Georgiana Molloy in December 1836. On 21 March, she replied.[8]

'My Dear Sir,

'Much to my surprise in December last, I received a particularly choice box of seeds, and your polite note requesting a return of the native seeds of Augusta. In truth, my dear Sir, I much fear you have bestowed your liberality on one whose chief pleasure is her Garden, but who does not enter the lists as a Florist, much less a Botanist. If we were nearer, I should much hesitate to accept so magnificent a present of so many long wished for Seeds, and as all my former pursuits have necessarily been thrown aside (by the peremptory demand of my personal attention to my children and domestic drudgery), I feel that it will be long ere I can make any adequate return in Australian productions.

'We have already collected some seeds, as your box just arrived at the proper season. I am not even acquainted with the names of the native plants. I will, however, enclose a leaf and description of the flower in each paper. I had some dried plants by me from the *Vasse*, a *country apparently possessing* some *exquisite floral beauties*, which I feel most happy in being able to send, and when I obtain a sufficiency to make up a small box, I will despatch it and retain the large one until I am *blest* with more leisure than at present. Another impediment to our being able to procure seeds is our approaching removal to the Vasse, where Captain Molloy's larger grant is situated, but if you do not hear from me shortly, I trust that you will not consider me negligent or unmindful of your humble request. I have put some of my old acquaintances (of whom there are but few in this busy Colony) in requisition, and shall feel myself in duty bound to transmit to you their labours. Although my brother George was anxious to employ me as a collector also my time is so much infringed on I have not as yet sent him any specimens.

'It is with much regret that I leave dear Augusta. Our climate is so heavenly and the scenery is so superior to other settlements, the flowers scentless but *minutely beautiful.* I am told we possess *many* unknown in the *other parts of this Colony.*'

In a later letter she reported on the results of her efforts, and on a personal tragedy[9]:

'My dear Sir,

'Having at length complied with your desires to obtain Flowers & Seeds from Augusta, I send you the result of my labours, which at one time I had not the least hope of being able to do in a satisfactory manner.

'Under the afflicting but unscrutable decree of an all-wise Providence, we have recently been overwhelmed with the most bitter loss of our darling infant and *only son* of 19 months old by the aggravated death of *drowning*!! Painful as it is to record, distance of time and place compels me.

'Captain Molloy, myself and his *little sisters* had been playing with him watching his vigorous and frolicsome mood just after breakfast on *11th November 1837*—We separated each to our necessary duties, (that morning I was preparing to bake and churn). I left dear little Johnnie in my only servant girl's charge. She imagined from having seen him with Mary and near his Papa that he was still there. Mary appeared without him, which *instantly struck us*, as they were inseparable. Charlotte had put the dear child in his cradle, and not finding him where she last saw him, she asked Molloy, then me. I had not seen him, but answered he had his bell on (a little bell he wore round his waist, in case of his straying into the bush). I instantly ran out, and on her running up and down and not finding him, I exclaimed: "*Have you been to the well?*" and became quite alarmed. Captain Molloy said, "Do not frighten yourself, he never goes there!" The fatal truth stole over me, and on Charlotte going to the well, she said: "Here's the Boy," and pulled out that darling precious child, lifeless, his flaxen curls and dripping, his little countenance so placid, he looked fast asleep, but not dead; and we do not believe he really was so until some minutes later. But the medical man was at the Vasse, and we knew not what to do. We tried every means of restoration, but to no effect. And that lovely, healthy child, who had never *known pain or sickness* and who had been all mirth and joyousness 5 precious hours the last time we beheld him together, was now a stiff corpse, but beautiful and lovely even in DEATH; the well is in full view of the windows, about a stone's cast off, concealed certainly by the Virgillia and Mimosa trees. He had not been absent ten minutes, but from being a very fat heavy child, and after eating an enormous breakfast I am told, this increased his rapid step from life to Death; but had any Medical Man been near, I am fully persuaded my little Johnny might have been saved.

'Forgive me, my dear Sir, for thus using towards a Stranger the freedom and minute detail that Friendship warrants and desires. Our children and our necessary occupations fraught as they are with uncontemplated interest, engross the sole attention and exertions of myself and my excellent husband;—Acute indeed was the blow, and when you reflect how dead we are to the World, and completely weaned from that sphere of pursuits, actions and modes of life in which we used to move, I trust you will pardon and excuse my entering thus egotistically and minutely on our present affliction.'

After the death of her son, Georgiana Molloy was deeply depressed and one of her few 'distractions' was to wander off into the bush—often on her own—in search of the specimens that Captain Mangles requested. In the evening she could then become engrossed in preparing them for their trip to England. It was an exhausting and exacting task gathering all the specimens, documenting them so that their properties would be understood in England, and ensuring that they were kept safe from damp, disease and digestion by insects while in transition.

It was because she took so much care with the collecting, the labelling and the packaging that Georgiana Molloy made such a valuable contribution to botanical science.[10] She was meticulous in her record-keeping, noting the characteristics of a plant, the conditions of its growth, the period in which it bloomed, the time at which the seeds were collected, etc. She was also painstaking in her preparation of the specimens for their voyage; much of her letter writing of this period is concerned with the best forms of protection for the transportation of the seeds—under difficult circumstances.

On more than one occasion she regrets the fact that the box in which she is packing all the samples and seeds is not lined with tin: '[I have] commissioned Captn. Molloy now absent at the Swan to procure a tin case' for future use, she informs Captain Mangles.[11] Later she feels obliged to explain some of her unorthodox arrangements:

'In reading the other day I saw it recommended to pack seeds in "Raw Sugar". I accordingly ventured to send the *very minute seed* of *no. 199* in this way, and should be glad to know if it is an approved means . . . they ought decidedly to be enclosed in Tin, but that was in this remote place impracticable . . . I looked over every package of seeds just 4 days before the vessel arrived and found notwithstanding all my care a small fly had got at some of them. This accounts for the quantity of Pepper about them which I hope will be a preservative.'[12]

She apologises that this shipment is not up to her usual careful standards:

'The day on which I sent off the box, I was *so unwell as scarcely to be able to pack it*, but as the vessel unexpectedly called and had but a few hours to remain, I put in its contents I fear in a very imperfect manner, rather than lose the quick transport they in all probability will have to England.'[13]

The work was extraordinarily time-consuming, and Georgiana was grateful for any assistance:

'Whilst on the subject of Books, and Paper, I wish if you honor me any more with being instrumental to your interesting pursuits, you would send me *"seed papers" folded* and *ready*, as your first Box was prepared, also *little Paper Bags*, they aid me so very much, My dear Sir, I have everything to do myself, even to the making of the Bags, and searching for the paper, then folding it.'[14]

She points out that she must do everything herself at Augusta, and then at Fair Lawn[15] ('I am my children's sole instructress and sempstress, and that in conjunction with innumerable other peremptory duties.'[16]), and that the materials for the job are so very scarce, are conditions that she brings home to Captain Mangles, when thanking him for the supplies that he has already forwarded:

'The Brown Holland you sent me I really had not the heart to cut it up for Seed Bags, for which I presume you meant it, so I substituted some of inferior quality and availed myself of the very excellent and superior material you enclosed . . . '[17]

But if seed gathering began as a way of dealing with depression and despair, the exercise soon had its own momentum and rationale, and towards the end of her life it became for Georgiana Molloy something of an obsession. Given that a knowledge of the flora and fauna—indigenous and imported—could well prove for the settlers to be a matter of survival, it is understandable that Georgiana gave the work such high priority; but as an educated woman, who was interested in the world beyond her immediate, narrow circle, the intellectual and social satisfaction that the project provided was equally important. As she changed the order of her days to accommodate the departure of ships, the need to travel to distant places and the demands of the different seasons, the circumstances of the entire Molloy family began to revolve around the botanist's calendar. The task was 'too valuable not to demand care and attention', she wrote, 'and such I render it',

'to the cessation of other concerns. Often has Molloy looked at a buttonless shirt, and exclaimed with a *Woebegone Visage*, "When will Captain Mangles's seeds be sown?" And recently he has laid aside all his own operations and accompanied the children and me by *Land* and *Water*, for a day's search in *quest of* seeds and Flowers. We had three or four Gypsy Parties on your account, in which *Sabina* and *Mary* were much delighted; Indeed, my dear Sir, I have been more frequently from my house this year in making up your collection than for the whole of *the nearly eight years* we have lived at Augusta—Even three times before my darling child's Death we went up to the *Granite Rock* and *opposite side* for flowers, and I had not been in the boat before for three years. Since then we have return'd for the seeds, so that I have *spared neither pains* nor *trouble* in *Serving You.*'[18]

Captain Mangles, on receiving the seeds and the details of their collection, was determined that the contribution of the children should be acknowledged; in September 1839, Joseph Paxton, the head gardener for the Duke of Devonshire, the then President of the Horticulturist Society, wrote to Captain Mangles to inform him how well the seeds were growing, including 'the "*Floral Gem*" which the infant Botanist, "Sabina Molloy", took so much pains to watch and collect, and which you are anxious should be named after her . . .'[19]

For a year, from the spring of 1837 until the spring of 1838, Georgiana Molloy had been collecting, but not despatching; no ship had been available. But life had still gone on, as she informed Captain Mangles when she added the following page to her letter, dating it 8 January September 1838.

'I am quite grieved my dear Sir, that you have not long ere this received our collection of Seeds. I lament every day I have them in my posession, as their departure has been so unfortunately long delayed, owing to the absence of the Colonial or indeed any other Vessel.

'I hope that as I was *very* particular in preserving and taking the best seeds you may yet not be disappointed, but it is very annoying both to you and especially to me; who so well knew what they might have been. The large *Hortus Siccus*[20] has been soldered up since April and I earnestly hope the little vermin have not made any further havoc.

'I detected some in each book and for want of oil of Petroleum or any other preservative, I made little bags which contain pepper.

'The flowers and shrubs are again beginning to bloom, and when I behold them I exclaim, "Poor Captain Mangles, how I wish he had received those of last year"

'In June baby was born [Amelia] and she engross'd so much of my time, I have scarcely leisure to teach *Sabina* and *Mary*, of whom I wrote to you some months since, or rather I should say, of whom I spoke at the commencement of this volume, within this last six weeks Mary has begun to read and I am unwilling she should escape one day; so between the three and my usual employments, I know not what to do first . . .

'My flower garden has hitherto been quite neglected, but as the season advances I hope yet to be able to work in it. Many of the Seeds you so kindly bestowed have stood the winter, and last week I was transplanting some of them; I have enclosed a small cheque on Captn. Molloy's agent, and would be particularly obliged by your procuring me a *Garden Rake*, fit for a *Lady's use*, as I am obliged to borrow one of Captain Molloy's with the most formidable teeth, spreading destruction next to and annihilation wherever it is applied, the handle I can have affixed when it arrives. It must not *be too fine* . . .

'If the Box you send me is large enough, a *Watering Pot* and Rose (the patent wire) would be of the greatest use to us, as ours are worn and destroyed after eight years' service.

'I now close your box and letter, of couse I cannot but send it away, with many fears and *much* very much interest of a Manifold Nature. So many of its contents were collected under the extremes of joy and acute Sorrow; it has beguiled many a moment and I hope you will receive much success and satisfaction in looking over and sewing your seeds.'[21]

For the next few years Georgiana Molloy collected, labelled, packed and despatched seeds, and kept up a fascinating correspondence with James Mangles. The distress at having to move from Augusta to Fair Lawn and the despair on the death of her son gradually gave way to a sense of purpose, even contentment, as she immersed herself in her botany project—when she wasn't engaged in domestic duties (including pregnancy and birth). And no one in the vicinity of the Vasse was allowed to forget the responsibility of seed gathering. 'Your name has created a great sensation in this district,' she wrote to Captain Mangles on 31 January 1840.

'The soldiers who used to pass between *this* and *Augusta* unmolested and unencumbered with anything but their knapsacks, are now seen to bring from thence specimens of all sorts of Plants *under* their *Arms*. The Native Herdsmen are also employed bringing in some desired "Plant" or "Fruit", which until now they have never perhaps looked upon, for they

dislike Flowers and will not suffer any one to be placed on their heads
. . . Last Thursday the *America* Captn Cole arrived in the Bay having, (to
use a technical term) "filled up"!!! She proceeds instantly to America, and
I am anxious to send what I have been able of Plants and Seeds to
obtain for you; Since Saturday last I have been engaged in your Service.
The children have had a week's holiday and so have I, altho' I have
necessarily been very assiduous, always working from after Breakfast till
12 and ¹/₂ after 12 at night. This seems incredible, but I had first to fix
the *specimens*, to *arrange*, then *paste* on labels to that forbidding *Old
Log Book*,—which looks anything but *neat & clean* then write attempts
on character, make the Bags and Cases, and now, Friday Night, commence this interminable Epistle . . . '[22]

On 8 May 1840, Georgiana Molloy gave birth to a daughter; she
called her Flora. While she was eager to return to her botany work, for
many months she was was too ill to move from her bed. But she did not
give up her commitment to the collection of seeds; in her letter to
Captain Mangles she tells him how she was plagued by the need to
continue with the work.

'My sister Mary declares that three times out of four when she came to
my Bedside I called out, "Oh poor Captn. Mangles! I cannot go on with
his collection and the seeds of the *Nuytsia Floribunda* will be all shed!"
and moreover I bewailed the seedling *Isopogon* I intended procuring for
you and sending by some American Whaler when it leaves this Bay.'

At the end of June she wrote:

'In all my illness and real suffering I did not forget you. As Spring
approached I lamented at not being able to gather the flowers as they
came out, and little "Mary Dorothea" was desired in her rambles with
Amelia (not two years old) to bring in all the first flowers—*which she
did* . . . once Molloy in Kangaroo Hunting, brought me a bouquet of
beautiful scarlet flowers, also dried, and which "please God" I ever get
about again, I shall *send* and *Mark.* I was surprised during my illness to
receive a Nosegay from a *Native* who was aware of my *floral passion.*
These are under preparation for you, and a pretty little white flower
with small brown staminae—I have often exclaimed this was the time I
thought of riding out in search of New Plants, and scarcely a day passes
I am not thinking of what I can do or how in any way I could promote
your cause, especially when I have so many things of an imperative
nature to wholly absorb my thoughts & time, and no female servant . . . '[23]

After the birth of her daughter Amelia, Georgiana Molloy took a long
time to recover; after the birth of Flora, two years later, she was ill for

many months. After the birth of another daughter, Georgiana, on 7 December 1842, Georgiana Molloy never again left her room. Throughout the early summer months of 1843, Georgiana Molloy sweltered, developed bed sores, and did not even have the recompense of being able to look out on her beloved garden, or to be near the graves of her two children. She died in March 1843.

Her contribution to the collection and collation of Australian specimens is incalculable, but unlike other pioneers in this field—such as Joseph Banks, for example—her scientific achievement is not widely recognised. However, her diligence, dedication and talent place her among the first of Australian scientists, and her work, her letters, her life and her death are symbolic of many of the sacrifices made by women during this period.

# 15
# *Working with words*

## Frances Louisa Bussell, Elizabeth Capel Bussell, Frances Louisa Bussell (senior)

*Family correspondents*

Frances Louisa Yates had married the Reverend William Marchant Bussell and when he died in 1820 there were three daughters and six sons to provide for; the entire family realised it would be extremely difficult to maintain their position in society without the Reverend Bussell and, primarily in the interest of 'setting up the sons', they elected to try their luck as Australian colonists.

The three daughters—Frances Louisa Bussell junior ('Fanny'), Elizabeth Capel Bussell ('Bessie') and Mary—were of course at home, as was proper for young ladies; John, the eldest son, was a graduate of Oxford; William was at medical school; and Lenox was in the navy. The three younger boys were still at school (Charles at the Bluecoat School and Vernon and Alfred at Winchester) when the decision was made to emigrate. John Bussell, who had been destined to take Holy Orders, had by chance met Captain Molloy—at a ball in Southampton—and had been interested in the Captain's plans for emigration to the Swan River. The generous land grants being made available in the colony were very attractive—particularly when there were so many younger male members of the family for whom occupations had to be found. And whereas the possibility of becoming landowners in England was quite out of the question, such status and position were readily attainable in Australia.

Everyone in the Bussell household knew that it would not be easy to make a new life in the new world; it would mean painful separation from country and community and unimaginable hardship and 'hard labour', but the consensus was that it would be worthwhile. A family decision was made; the problems of work, and separation, would be minimised if the Bussells were to go as a *family*.

Four of the boys would go first: John, and the younger ones—Charles, Alfred and Vernon. They would find out how feasible settlement was, would stake a claim and set up a home, and then the rest could follow. In October 1829, with a servant, Edward Pearce, the boys set sail on the *Warrior*.

That the girls were keen to be included says much for their spirit of adventure, their willingness to work and the closeness of the family circle. In 1832, Frances Louisa Bussell (junior), a very spirited young woman, and Elizabeth Capel Bussell, along with the servants Phoebe and Emma and brother Lenox, embarked for Australia. Both of the daughters were excited at the prospect of joining their brothers and of establishing a new life, but they were also aware of what they were leaving behind—good old England, their sister Mary, their brother William (who did not join them), 'the little Mother' and an ordered, 'genteel' life which was not without its advantages. The two brave and independent sisters who set sail were determined that their sister and mother should share as many of their experiences as possible and for this reason both 'Fanny' and 'Bessie' kept journals in which they tried to record all the details of their days; these were then parcelled up at every opportunity and sent home as 'public reading property' whenever a ship was available. They wrote letters as well, which were often more intimate and individualised.

The journals were 'conversations' with family and friends. Often written when some sort of drama was taking place, they convey a powerful sense of immediacy. These are *adventure stories*, in which the authors— particularly Fanny—cast themselves in the role of heroine and ensure that those who are safe and sound in England know just what wonderful, strange and sometimes terrifying experiences they are missing in the distant and exotic land.

But keeping everyone informed, maintaining the relationships and helping to shape themselves and their own worlds are not the only purposes these entertaining journals serve for their authors. As with conversations, where there are frequent interruptions and changes of topic, so in these journals there are sudden shifts in direction as the writer thinks of important items to include. Sometimes it is a specific object that is desperately needed, and the little Mother is called upon to purchase and despatch it; sometimes it is just a thought that crowds in— as when Fanny writes emotionally from Perth in April, 1833: 'Oh! may

we be found worthy of you our own Mother and as useful to the dear
boys as we hope to be. We have two cows, one is a heifer and the other
in calf.'

To have written as frequently and fully as they did would have taken
the Bussell women a long time. But if a family unit is to be maintained—if relationships are to be managed and care, comfort and reassurance provided—then there is a great deal of conversational work to
be done. Circumstances prevented the Bussell family from doing this
directly, but the journals and letters of the female members of the family
are testimony to the fact that this work with words was constantly
undertaken.

Fanny started her journal[1] on 17 December 1832 with the departure
of the *Cygnet*; the first entry here is from the time the ship was drawing
close to the Australian shore.

*'January 19th 1833*
'I have taken up my pen which I laid down in disgust to give you an
idea of the penguins which have been our companions on board since
we left St Paul's. They are I think a connecting link between a kangaroo
and a flying fish and its wings are in reality fins and its legs placed so
far back that it walks upright. They are when young of a bright purple
with primrose coloured crests. They are awkward, stupid things, amusing from their very ugliness . . .

'We are running on delightfully, 7 knots an hour, with a bright sky,
smooth sea, and a delicious air. This they tell me is the Swan River
climate. In four days we shall see land, the land which is to be hence-
forth the abode of all our interests, hopes and affections. Dear happy
England already seems to us like the land of shadows, beautiful and
beloved but abandoned for ever, and yet how many dear ones are left
behind. It does not always do to think of this . . .

'We are collecting our property, books, etc etc. Bessie and I have
been very busy with Phoebe's gown,[2] it looks so nicely, she will really
be a princess in it. We shall put the finishing touches to it this morning.
You would smile at the next employment which we propose to ourselves.

*'Monday 21st. January.*
'Almost a calm. I must describe the anxiety and trepidation which
now accompanies every moment bringing us as it does nearer to our
Augusta home. At times I am excited almost to pain when I anticipate
the approaching meeting. I am writing now because I can settle to no
other employment.

'As we were sitting in the Cuddy this morning the alarm was given—
"Two Swans! Black Swans in sight". I cannot say how it overcame me.

They proved however to be albatrosses and were shot accordingly, two beautiful birds 10 feet in width, Capt Rolles has given me the foot.

'I ought not to scribble so much, but where can I go if not to you my own Mamma when I feel as I do now. But I won't tease you any more with my egotism and so on. God grant that we may find the dear brothers, to whom we are going, well and happy, and that we may be the means of making them more so. I shall not now write more until our arrival. Every face has now the appearance of anxiety and watchfulness. We are 60 miles nearer to Augusta than Swan River, 300 miles from the latter.

'*1833 26th January.*

'Now, indeed, we are in sight of the Swan River. Some days later than I had expected when I closed this. Capt Toby was the first person on board this morning and from him we heard that our dear brothers were all when he saw them last, six weeks since, Vernon had accompanied him down to King George's Sound. The boys have a grant at Port Leschenault and at King George's Sound. He says they are grown such rough creatures. Vernon and Alfred are quite young men. Miss Turner is married to a Mr McDermot so there was no truth in the report of Ally's engagement.

'The coast looks very flat, we can discover some houses, or rather wigwams, tho built of stone, as the habitations, it rather reminds me of Stonehenge. Two boats here, just appeared, containing Mr Luke Leake, that shocking affair Mr Philip Dodd, and others. Poor Mrs Leake[3] what a meeting for her! They say she is sadly altered. We have felt much disappointment at not finding Capt. Stirling at home.

'I broke off this morning because a boat was in sight and I was anxious to see a specimen of the creatures who are hereafter to be our compatriots. Quite a crowd of young men came on board, but I have not time to talk about them, as their images have been obliterated by the variety of characters which have since passed in review before us.

'My first sensation was that of desolation. Capt. Stirling was absent, we knew no one in a strange land, we will not go on shore, we will stay in our own ship which has at least been hallowed by Mamma's presence. In the evening when we were alone, we sat down and tried to occupy ourselves. I attempted to dry the seaweed which you will find in this book, but Mr MacDermott soon put a stop to such domestic pursuits.

'In this colony, "NO" is never an answer, and tho Bessie and I virtuously determined to abide by the ship we soon found he was determined not to go without us, so we set off with him and Mr Toby, and were greeted on the jetty at Fremantle by several gentlemen.

'Mr MacDermott's is a splendid house, a nice drawing room with every English comfort except a looking glass, a tea table with all "appliances and means to boot" seemed like home, but the Hindoo servants in attending partook more of the Oriental style. Mrs MacDermott is a nice little woman but as I have left a letter there to be forwarded by the *Cornwallis* I need not dwell upon this period of my narrative any farther.

'On Monday 27th we had a terrible fright. Bessie had sent for her music and portfolio and in the evening we were expecting it when Lenox came in wet through. He had not he said, thought it safe to bring it in the dinghy with him, but had put [it] in the Captain's long boat which had been capsized on the Bar.

'What regrets followed! All Bessies dear songs, her portfolio with our drawings, journals, Len's passing certificates and Charlie's Power of Attorney. Bessie went out to agonise on the sand and got a great deal in her eyes, which brought on a touch of opthalmia, in fact we went to bed full of miseries and self reproach . . .

'Bessie has described our voyage up the Swan, lovely indeed it was! like Chepstow, Clifton, Henley, every beautiful place I have ever seen, only broader, clearer, fuller, than any river in England, and then such a lovely clear sky, and a gentle breeze . . .

'I quite love Mr Brown he speaks of John just as people used to speak of Papa, dearest Mother on such occasions. I can only pray that we may all be equally worthy of him and you, and that you may, when you arrive, hear your girls spoken of as we do, the boys. We are received by Mrs Brown most kindly. She is a very pretty young woman, with the whitest skin, and the prettiest black hair and eyes I ever saw. The first evening we had music, but I derived more pleasure in merely looking from the window even, than in listening to the songs which I most dearly love.

'The heat is great certainly, and the mosquitoes here are very troublesome; and I may truly say I never was better in my life. The warm climate suits me even better than I expected. This is an extremely pretty place with all the comforts and luxuries of an English country house with a few incongruities which by the charm of novelty prevents perfection from becoming insipid . . . The Kingsfords are staying here also, they know the Browns in England and Miss [?] a very delightful girl, so domestic and active and good, completes as cheerful and agreeable a circle as can often be found.'

Fanny Bussell is keen to inform her English counterparts that life in the colony is not only splendidly exciting, refreshing and rewarding; it is also refined and civilised. No doubt it was because the middle-class women wanted to preserve their self image as ladies that they were determined to maintain some of the 'manners' of the old country; in this context it is not surprising that Fanny should find society more circumspect and careful than it might have been back home. She continues her pacy narrative for her mother's benefit:

'The society has not degenerated in the least and instead of anyone or anything for the Swan I should say selectness and refinement are more prevalent than in England. Yet no one scruples to assist in the duties of the "menage"—

'Here I am well aware and at the McDermott's we have seen emigration divested of all its miseries to use the popular term. But the Browns have gone through more than we will have to undergo in exposure to climate and trials unknown.

'To continue my recital—On Wednesday Mr Dawson called much surprised to find John's sister. I could not but view him immediately in the light of an old friend. He had so much to tell us, and I assure you we were not sparing in asking questions.

'John, he says has made a vow not to shave until you come out, tho his beard rests on his shirt, but it looks well as he keeps it beautifully combed. Their exertions have been wonderful and their perseverance, unanimity and industry are quite proverbial. Mr Dawson will tell you all about them as he has promised to see you . . .

'Mr Dawson and Mr Moore, the Judge Advocate (these titles will amuse you I know) dined here and we strolled about in the beautiful moonlight and talked alternately of Augusta and England.

'Perth is a very promising city but the sand is greatly against it. The country residences are far preferable and I do not at all join in the universal regret that we are so soon to retire so completely from the world and its gaieties.

'The boys are so methodical, the mornings are devoted to work, two hours in the heat of the day to study, and then labour again. We have not spend [sic] any of our money and Mr Brown thinks it better to take it to them unbroken and expend it at their own discretion. Candles are dreadfully expensive and would be good things to send out, so would soap, and starch.

'Shoes are more valuable than gold. Our dresses and things have been very well chosen, and we feel quite comfortable, Mrs Brown proposes giving a dance next week, there is much curiosity felt on our account and a great deal of speculation I daresay if we were not so fortunately out of the way of it all.

'Nothing can exceed the hospitality here. Mr Brown advises us not to go on the *Ellen*⁴ but to abide by our property, but Mr Toby is very urgent to take us and our inclinations are decidedly with him . . .

'Everyone is very busy in preparing their despatches for the *Cornwallis*. This will go by Mr Dawson our first journal unfortunately left at Freman- tle cannot go by this opportunity but we will forward them by the *Cygnet* I fear I shall not have time to write other letters, but this is public property . . .

'Mr Brown the other day told us an anecdote of John, which I must retail. The Governor in reward for his great exertions in the Colony presented him with three miles frontage on the banks of the river. Mr Turner and Capt Molloy thought it rather unjust, and John in a beautiful letter to the Governor requested permission to resign one third judging it more advantageous to the Colony that friendly interest should yield to public good . . .

'Whilst we were at the Botanical Gardens Mr Irwin received a packet from the Colonial office which he opened before me. It was directed to Capt Molloy and proved to be a long letter from Mary to the boys. We have brought out a number of newspapers also, which we probably put into the post office ourselves. I shall leave you now . . .

'Bessie tells me her journal is to be devoted to [?] and she puts down everything as it pops into her head. This she intends as an apology for Scramble Hall tho I consider hers far more methodical than my own. Yesterday Saturday we had a pleasant little evening party beginning with music and ending with quadrilles, much amazement but no dearly beloveds. Mr Lewis and Mr Dawson were my partners, with the latter I had one of my tremendous tête-a-têtes despite Bessie's reproving looks but I could not resist hearing all about our darlings. But she will tell you all about this . . . '

Having travelled so far, the Bussell sisters were of course very eager to get to Augusta and to start their new life—but unfortunately the *Cygnet* would not oblige them.

*'Perth April 5th 1833*
'You will be justly surprised my own Mother that we have not yet attained the "Ultima Thule" of our hopes but the fact is that the *Cygnet* has been detained far beyond our expectations, and is only now under sailing orders for next Tuesday. I write this by the *Merope* quite a venture as the mail closes this evening and I have been prevented in a thousand ways from settling to letter writing⁵ before, tho I have daily threatened to do so for the last month.

'You will readily believe from our description of Mr & Mrs Brown's family which closed my last that our stay here has not been wearisome indeed no kindness no attention has been spared and your two girls have found that the spoiling system commenced in England has been rather carried out than counteracted here.

'When we left Bassendean[6] it was to visit Mr & Mrs Roe with whom we are now staying. Delightful people whose kindness have been equal to the Browns' I cannot say more. Society here is on a delightful footing no formality yet a strict adherence to all that is nice and right.

'Shortly after our arrival the Government schooner *Ellen* was ordered South and greatly tempted we were to embrace such an opportunity of joining our beloved colonists without delay. A party was formed consisting of Captain Irwin, the Lieut. Governor, his Aide de Camp Mr Dale and Mr Moore. It was with beating hearts we took leave of them all, feeling that they would so very soon reach our future home but Lenox was so decided in wishing us not to remove from the ship in which all our property was embarked that we declined going and only commissioned these new friends to inform our brothers of our arrival.

'I must confess however that "Time on airy pinions flew" and a fortnight found us alternately domesticating ourselves with the Browns or the Roes, Len making our old Cygnet home his headquarters still as well as Phoebe etc.

'At last however I decided on a trip to Fremantle and a visit to the ship, and accompanied Lenox one lovely morning on this expedition, how little did I dream of the happiness in store for me. I refused all temptations to stay at the McDermotts' by the way and spent the day in packing books, arranging cabins, scolding Emma,[7] who is my most anxious care, and comforting Phoebe.

'It was on Monday 8th of March. "A ship in sight" "A schooner" is announced by the cabin boy. Oh can it be the *Ellen?* It seemed too much happiness to expect for she is to bring us such late tidings of our darlings. I ran on deck to watch her approach, not as I had often done before from the listless desire for something new but with all the delirious excitement of hope. "It is the *Ellen*" for she comes not in as a stranger but as if she knew the harbour well. And now she comes nearer and nearer, red coats are visible, and Mr Toby's form was recognised by Capt Bolles who watched the movement with his glass, and reported it to me.

'A Whaleboat is lowered and makes for the shore. The Lieut. Governor has left the vessel with his suite, and now another boat is lowered nearer and nearer it comes towards us "There's a Bussell in that boat I am sure" said Capt Bolles and shortly even I could recognise a row of white teeth which seemed to claim relationship with my own.

'In a few minutes more dearest John was on board looking so well, my Mother, rather barbarous but quite poetical, large canvas trousers made by his own hands, a broad leather belt, hair and beard both long somewhat and moustaches enough to give a bandit look. All this was seen in a moment (you know how I do see) and then too there was a mingled likeness to you, my Mother, and to Emily which had never struck me before.

'The moment of meeting was decidedly the happiest and brightest I have ever experienced, forgive me if I have dwelt upon it too long but I need not say this to you. Mr Toby the kind Mr Toby accompanied him and really this our meeting seemed an affair of general interest.

'Lenox who had gone to Perth for me a few hours before returned on the news of the arrival of the *Ellen* and surely so happy a trio has seldom met in a merchantman's cuddy. We only wanted our poor little Bessie who had been left at Mrs Roe's. The next morning we started by the sea breeze and the kindness and hospitality which we had so long enjoyed was extended to this, our dear Johnnie.'

According to Fanny, the following is supposed to be a letter, rather than part of the journal—but it is difficult to make such a distinction from the words themselves.

'A month has elapsed since then, which we have passed either here or at Bassendean. Our next remove will be to Augusta to the dear ones there. It is not without regret that we shall say Goodbye to the new friends who have made our stay here so pleasant . . . The weather now is getting cooler, and it is so exhilarating after the heat which awaited our arrival. Our worst evils are the mosquitos, they have no mercy upon newcomers. Bessie is a great sufferer, I am bitten all over but the inflammation is not so great as at first. The fleas here are numerous and tremendous in size, and bugs are not a few.

'Walking at Perth is very disagreeable on account of the sand. From the first and last of these evils we shall be free at Augusta, and the climate there is much more agreeable than here. You cannot conceive the annoyance that servants are here, few and therefore expensive and full of consumate impudence. Yesterday we were all at church for the last time Easter Sunday. How I thought of you dearest Mother and of Winchester, dear Winchester . . .

'My journal I will make up and send by the *Cygnet*, this is so completely a chance letter that you must count it for nothing and we have been so interrupted by visitors that I scarcely know what I have said.

'I commence another sheet because our meeting with the dear boys will obliterate for the time the events that are passing around us. While we were at Bassendean Mrs Brown was confined. I was with her when a dear little boy was ushered into this world of woe I almost felt like a

217

mother myself, I think. But the sequel to my story is a sad one. Our baby only lived two days and dear Bassendean when we left it was a house of disappointment and mourning.

'To turn to lighter subjects which Bessie had called to my mind by mentioning the "Inflamatory Book" you would smile to hear the reports that have been circulated about us. Bessie especially has been given in turn to everyone here almost, and I have been appropriated I am told to the Lieut. Governor and to Mr Lewis I do not know what the people think of us, you will hear when you come.

'Dear Mary[8] will be so petted and admired she must be a favourite as she always has been with all who know her. I see no one, dearest Mother, like my own brothers and sisters. The Harrises have got a very nice grant on the Swan River. Mrs Leake is with her husband. The Kingfords are in quest of land for their mill, and will decidedly settle here. So much for our *Cygnet* companions.'

Much of Fanny's character is revealed in her attitude towards the Aboriginal people—the 'natives'. While sharing some of the prejudices of the period (it never occurred to her that 'the natives' had any real claim to the land, even though she was sensitive to their displacement), she departs from some of the conventional understandings by accepting the humanity of the Aboriginal people, and by according them a certain dignity. As her encounters indicate, she does not patronise them, nor does she treat them with fear and contempt; these may be small compensations for stealing their land and destroying their culture, but nonetheless her attitude was compassionate and radical for her time.

'The natives are very troublesome, Mr Brown had four sheep speared last week, they are such things to look upon these wild brethren of ours. This morning when I came up to breakfast I saw a black face looking at me. "What your name" said I "Monday" was the answer, I suppose he liked my complexion, something akin to his own for in a few minutes he said "Your name Monday" It is a proof of affection I hear, to change names so I of course gave him mine in return. "Bussell" I said "You Monday, I Bussell" He laughed and pointed at some bread, certainly more attractive to him, than my brightest smile. This Monday is a shocking affair however, having speared his wife and mother only a fortnight ago.[9] His countenance is very bad, decidedly ferocious.

'At Bassendean we had a "Corrobborree" (Native Dance)

'One evening a large fire was kindled and the natives having chalked their bodies very tastefully soon commenced accompanying their movements with an ugly panting noise like a thirsty dog. One of them imitated the kangaroo and went through all the movements of the animals eating grass scratching its side. Another very gracefully advanced with a spear, pretending extreme caution until within reach of its victim; I thought of Cooper's North American Warriors. At last the hunt is supposed to be up, and all join in a general dance. I have nearly got to the end of my paper . . .

'Remember me most kindly to Ben and Foot we have not forgotten their kindness to us and we never shall. How delicious will be our meeting in about 9 months. Oh! may we be found worthy of you our own Mother and as useful to the dear boys as we hope to be. We have two cows, one is a heifer, the other in calf.

'Our garden at Augusta thrives beautifully. I long to begin my arrangements there. Send out guernsey frocks for the boys. Bessie would like you to bring out cambric muslin frocks for her. It will be cold enough at Augusta in the winter, to wear anything, and I still have a great weakness for silks. But just one will do Mother. Let our dresses if you have them made, be marked, as to save confusion. We are grown capital dressmakers however and have had some experience.'

As the 'conversation' draws to a close, Fanny—almost breathlessly— gets in all the orders that the little Mother is required to supply.

'Soap is invaluable (at least it is now 8/- per lb). Shoes are still more so. I would like you to bring me out some boots made beautifully neat. I must now close this. Love to all at Henley, no one must forget their fondly affectionate Bessie and Fanny. Straw bonnets are the nicest wear here, so light cool and durable. The boys have received their seeds, newspapers and quarterly review. I do not think many packages have miscarried.

'Don't send or bring many coloured robes for us, simple good shirting stripes we prefer for morning dresses, or things of one colour. Merinos for winter will not be too warm, but remember we shall not want anything yet, but clothes out here do wear out dreadfully, stockings especially from the black sand you are obliged to change them three or four times daily and washing so often does not add to their strength. Remember me to Brown and Wells. Read what you please to Brown. Kind regards to Mr Mayo. Love to La chere Tips I meant to have written her, she must not however think that I am going to break off my promised correspondence because I have not yet. Bess has addressed her journal to her, but she must surely come with you my little Mother. Our sister, our friend will join our circle again, or will it not be incomplete? Once more Farewell.'

After their time in Fremantle and Perth, Fanny and Bessie finally found themselves about to leave the *Cygnet*, which for so long had been their home; they landed with all their goods on 20 April at Augusta and made their way to Mrs Molloy's, as the following letter relates.[10]

'My dearest Mother,

'I have left out my desk that I may scribble to the last moment; we are still in the *Cygnet* and Bessy and I have been busy since 4 o'clock in the morning, we are shipping our goods, all in good preservation & none of the cargo in the least damaged, indeed they look as fresh as when first put on board.

'We have not yet landed; so this cannot be an all satisfactory letter. Dear Alfred was on board us all yesterday. Oh my dear Mother how would your maternal feelings exist in seeing this noble boy & how did his sisters' hearts triumph in looking & listening. Captn Bolles says Charles is a delightful young man, we have not yet seen him nor Vernon who is up the country. John as you will hear from a long letter of mine which I left at Perth, spent the last month of our sojourn there with us. You cannot think how well and how young he is looking. Lenox looks older by far. This is our last day on board the *Cygnet*, pray thank Captn Bolles for his kindness to us if you have an opportunity, with all his occasional violence, his attention to us has been unremitting. Dear Mother your girls are as little inured to unkindness and "roughing it" as when they left England. Bessy is quite tired with her exertions this morning & will not write, she is not so strong as I am, but in this lovely climate & with so many kind nurses she will soon become so . . .

'*Augusta April 21st.*
'I continue my narrative. Yesterday all our goods were landed. Captn Bolles pressed us to dine on board—the last day that we could not nor [?] did we wish to refuse. The boys & Mr Green resigned the honour of wafting us to shore to the Captn, but we were met on the beach by the soldiers & our own darlings. Mr Green (how Lord Halsingham would laugh) escorted me to Mrs Molloys. It was nearly dark, but I could perceive that the river was broad & beautiful & the country more richly wooded than an English imagination can conceive. Mrs Molloy came out to meet us with her little Sabina in her arms looking so youthful & interesting, her house is very comfortable & she is so active. We are to stay here for a few days, but as she has not accommodations for us she has fitted up one of Mr Dawson's houses so nicely, a French bed & all sorts of land comforts; a vase of sweet mignonette upon the table & your picture my mother were its ornaments, & a large wood fire blazing on the hearth cast a cheerful light around. We spent a very pleasant evening but broke up early, and as we had little inclination to sleep, we proposed taking the boys by surprise & walked down to their almost deserted abode. We proposed a walk on the beach, tho' it was getting very late, Bessy with John, myself with Charley & Alfred (how nice to lean on *two* of them again). Now I feel in my element said Alfred

drawing a long *happy* sigh. And so did we. It is here that one sees the magnificence of emigration; at the Swan, European comforts & luxuries have already robbed this life of somewhat of its romance; but here it is in all its wildness & grandeur, don't smile at me, my feelings are not more excited than when I left home, but I feel the same wish to act right, & the same energy to do so. We slept delightfully, & I have slipt away from all society & employment for the sake of scribbling to you. I am now in my *home* (pro tempore). Bessy, Phoebe & Emma are on the beach looking after the goods. Emma is herself again & I hope will improve now I have got her away from the ship—Pearce is grown a very fine young man & is much improved. Alfred relieves Vernon at the Adelphi to day & we shall see him tomorrow. Len is very well indeed. The climate is scarcely warmer [?] than in England—I must not write more as I think my presence must be wanted at the beach—Let the cases be small—many of ours must be unpacked before sent to the Adelphi . . . '

There is an extraordinary amount of correspondence between the women of the Bussell family as Fanny and Bessie make their home, first at Augusta. (Like the Molloys they subsequently moved to less difficult terrain, as Bessie explains in a later letter.) While not all the comforts of home are to be found in Augusta, as Fanny makes clear, homemaking has progressed sufficiently for the little Mother to be accommodated. 'Haste', however, becomes the order of the day as the colonial sons and daughters eagerly prepare to have Mrs Bussell and Mary join them.

As the time for the arrival of her mother and sister draws nearer, Fanny Bussell's sense of elation is hardly contained in her journal and letters. The realisation that she could soon be reunited with her mother raises the level of excitement to a new pitch. The following is from the first entry in her journal for 1834.[11]

*'Friday January 31 1834*
'I ought to have commenced my journal with the new year you will all of you say in England but it so happens that as I was anxious to write several letters I made a "vow" I would not begin a diary until the second visit of the *Ellen* had relieved me from my most urgent correspondents. My desk is once more clear of the letters which had engrossed me during the absence of our little schooner and I find myself at liberty to return to my favourite method of communication with the beloved friends who will not find one line superfluous . . .

'On Saturday the *Caroline* a small cutter belonging to Mr McDermott arrived with Mr Turner the sole passenger, he brought another letter from Mamma which I read aloud to poor old Phoebe and Bessey I will not say with what sensations. Come by [?] the *Brilliant* is now at

Fremantle and will arrive by the next trip of the *Ellen* how we are longing to investigate its secret treasures! Captain Molloy and Alfred are still at the Swan if my dearest Mother and Mary should accompany Sir James and Lady Stirling he will be there to greet them he has been treated with the greatest hospitality there, but are not kindness and hospitality the characteristics of the place. You will soon be there to judge for yourself so I will return to Augusta the present theatre of all our hopes and wishes. Bessey in the closing pages of her diary detailed to you our reception of our two new inmates Mr Tobey and Mr Hillman of King George's Sound. Our still very dilapidated house is not a gloomy one and the task of entertainment is very easy where everyone is pre-disposed to be pleased that we soon forget to blush at the unwalled erections which served our guests for bedrooms with our cots strong and comfortably made the English appendages of jugs, basins, clean towels, and quantities of water they formed singular "oases" in the un-redeemed bush by which they were surrounded . . . '

There is more detail of daily life: the work, the livestock, the natives. Fanny also reports on the pleasures—of books in general and of novels in particular.

'I received by the *Ellen* a letter from my dear Fanny Bonjafield which I intended to answer tonight but find I have resumed my journal instead. As Captain Molloy and Johnny are absent we have had prayers home these last two Sundays, Phoebe and Emma only attending. A sermon too from Wells invaluable collection which we really find a treasure. Books are here inestimable. Mr Tobey brought us from the Swan as a loan "the last Man"[12] and one or two more of the same description. Bessey and I are delighted to welcome a novel once more . . . as I have just finished a long letter I will only enter the articles the boys commission me to mention.

'Blue shirting like the last you sent us
Pea jackets
South Westers
Bedding
Blankets
Scrubbing brushes
Brooms
Mops
A new set of sails for the boat
Oars
Lead pipe water for sheets
Chain cable for boat

'All these things have been mentioned before but we are fearful of losing a chance . . . '

She closes this section of her journal on 16 February 1834; it was received in England on 10 November.

While Fanny was busy keeping her narrative journal (among other things) and sending her letters, Bessie was also enaged in much the same activities. Not long after Fanny despatched the above, Bessie wrote the following 'letter'—virtually indistinguishable from the 'journal' entries—to her cousin Capel Carter; it reached England on 12 October, a month before Fanny's journal arrived (Fanny's went via Hobart Town). Bessie informs Capel that they are again going to move—this time from Augusta to the banks of the Vasse (where they set up the new property—appropriately named Cattle Chosen because the area was much more suitable for grazing). Bessie takes a sensible view of the move, although it must have been quite a wrench to leave buildings, gardens, the port and familiar surroundings. But with the whole family involved and with such positive expectations of the future in terms of the farm and the arrival of more members of the family, it must not have been such a strain as it had been for Georgiana Molloy when she had to pull up roots and undertake a similar 'transplant'.

In this part of the 'serial', Bessie is not sure whether her mother will get to read the account, or whether she has already left for her new home, and this too adds to the sense of suppressed excitement. Bessie also refers to the fire which destroyed so many of the Bussells' goods and supplies—and which Georgiana Molloy commented on with such sympathy (see Chapter 14).

*'April 12th 1834* [13]
'My dear Capel,
  'The discontinuation of my journal for the last four months will perhaps make you expect a letter and I know you will be glad to hear from me altho' you may say why was not the journal continued for it must have been more minute and therefore I should prefer it, the real reason is that I have not had time. Vernon, John and Lenox are going to commence colonization anew on the banks of the Vasse which from all accounts must be far preferable to our beautiful Augusta it is not nearly so thickly wooded but the trees are very much larger (this I can hardly imagine) and of quite a different species denominated by the natives tuart, [?], yate, munyart and [?]. The intermediate country is a beautiful undulating grassy lawn, the river is small in comparison to the Blackwood very steep and with very high banks & full of fish Kangaroos are seen in herds which accounts for the natives being so numerous I hope they may be as harmless as the "Manyungas & Yungaries" which is the name

the tribes about here give themselves I am afraid however their eyes are getting open to the superiority of our food & they will soon find out means to get bread if they are denied it after their repeated exclamations of "bread bread yulibue yulibue" which means they are very hungry They broke into the store the other day & stole & wasted three hundred-weight of flour the Serjeants wife was the first to descry their black forms whitened with "bumla" retreating into the woods to enjoy a delicious meal One of the soldiers was immediately dispatched from "the Spring" to Augusta to inform Charles & get leave from John as magistrate to fire upon them. They had only managed to detain a little girl which its father threw down to expedite his escape Before the news could arrive at Augusta the party at the Spring had been obliged to let their prisoner go; one tribe of natives who had taken some of the flour returned with it & put it at a short distance making signs to give up the child & he would leave the flour, they were obliged to consent to this agreement from want of numbers. John, Lenox & Charles armed themselves & went in pursuit of the other delinquents & came on a place where one party had been making a damper quite a l'Anglaise on the head of a cask One of the soldiers mistaking some grass trees for them cried out "there they are" they heard I suppose white voice [sic] & took flight before John & the others could come up & catch them in the act leaving their dinner to the mercy of their invaders who destroyed it & returned here knowing it would be quite useless attempting to discover them in their wild haunts I was writing quite in the dark & I find I have degenerated into almost an illegible scrawl but if I do not write as quickly as I can the ship may be in tomorrow & then I shall not even have time to thank you for the other volume of the Landscape Annual it certainly is inferior to the others but still very beautiful you can hardly imagine how these elegancies of life are greeted among us & I think you would smile at the sort of incongruous collection of culinary, literary & drawingroom furniture but I do not find that any of us enjoy the elegancies of life at all the less from turning our hand to anything in the course of the day for when evening comes & all our duties are over I open the piano with I think much more pleasure than I ever did in England & all are ready to join in the chorus & then perhaps turn from the piano to admire & readmire [?] the often looked at picture or poem.

'Charles, Vernon & Alfred were delighted with their waistcoats, they are indeed the only things of the sort they have worn since they have been out here—Len would have been quite shoeless but for your timely present Fanny's basket is quite invaluable but when John found that he was the only person who had not a letter or anything he said "Well Bessie is there nothing sent for *me*!" my answer was "I suppose John they think you are on your way home" I am very glad that that is not likely to happen indeed it is not possible I hope my dear Capel it will not be a great disappointment to you but other letters are gone home giving the reasons for & against this proceeding & I will not give you my opinion on the subject—I need not have been quite in such a hurry for the ship must be detained some time longer on account of the equinoxtial [sic] gales & they are certainly most tremendous united with the most awful thunder lightening & hail an English person can hardly imagine what it is—I daresay you would like to know what our employments have been lately but they are really almost always so much alike that I do not think I shall have much to [?] In the first place we have been very busy in converting your old plaid cloak you gave me into jackets for the boys John & Vernon have each got one all think them very pretty they are quite the admiration of the colony Then all their duck white shirts & canvass trowsers have wanted repair & that piece of shirting mamma sent has made them a shirt apiece & a neat dress for Emma. I wish we had much more of it to make frocks for ourselves I once said I did not wish any more mirrors but I have since learnt to appreciate them we drew lots for one sent the other day & the lot fell upon Fanny a pair of old boots of yours have likewise come in the very nick of time for the fire almost left me quite barefoot & the shoes I have obtained from Swan River are immensely dear & immensely larger.

'I think I may say we have never [?] safe our dispatches without being in the most desperate hurry but really I have said before I have not had a moments time to myself I suppose my dear Capel that if mamma has left England that you will undertake to be Fanny's & my agent *if* you remain all the little things we require the needful can be found out of *some* of the *five hundreds* so with this I hope useless explanation I shall begin to enumerate a few requisites; I have worn out all my thimbles— holes all the way up & too small—& am reduced to a pewter horror, stay binding, shoe string galleen [?] coloured *ferret, red* 4d [?] marking cotton, good [?] reel cotton, darning cotton, straw coloured galleen, whity brown, black & green thread We have no [strong?] laces alas! buttons black & white bone small & large another of pearl plenty of worsted I have met with a most shocking misfortune & broken my glass my number is six & four for my spectacles Phoebe has broken her glasses too, another pair of good scissors not forgetting buttonhole scissors, a usual pair to fit my workbox they got very rusty on board & Vernon broke them for me indeed every day we miss something here that the terrible fire has deprived us of You have not an idea of the [mess] & confusion in which I am writing but you must excuse it . . . '

The Bussell family correspondence could not be complete without letters from Mamma, the little Mother. With daughter Mary, Frances Louisa Bussell (senior) arrived in Western Australia aboard the *James Pattison* on 19th June 1834. While concerned about the losses occasioned in the fire, Mrs Bussell is nonetheless enthusiastic about her new life, as her following letter to her niece, Capel Carter, indicates. Mrs Bussell has at this stage transferred many of her goods to the *Cumberland*, a small vessel which will sail for Augusta the following morning.

*'August 27th 1834*[14]

'Perplexed and worried as I am in landing and collecting my property and the ship on the point of sailing I snatch a moment to say we arrived safe and well. We are now at Fremantle with the McDermots and were to have been conveyed to Perth to day to stay with Lady Stirling till the arrival of the Colonial Schooner which is to embark us for Augusta All were well there two months since Alfred has recently been here under Dr Colley for three months some complaint on the chest but considered recoverable, I am of course full of dismay. They have decided on residing at the Vasse Charles of course must stay at Augusta, part of our things are on board a small vessel which will sail tomorrow and I hope bring back one of my precious ones, they are all respected and beloved beyond all description, the Governor and Lady have been very very kind indeed yesterday he came down for me and offered a supply of money if needful which would indeed have been very essential but for my Capels purse. 10/-, which must be supplied from Vernon, a ton for landing and £2 for taking to Augusta, the scarity [sic] of the place is very considerable, many of our things are not forthcoming but the Captain leaves orders for compensation, the confusion has been very great. My Portress case with Butler etc, etc has not yet appeared but I hope it may yet, a box of candles and one of Mr Alders cases of tools serious is it not when they are so much wanted. I have scarcely seen any one so I have no information to give. Mary won all hearts on board, in short we both quit [?] with great eclat; but what can make amends for what we have left behind? Yes I shall be united to my best treasure. I recounted a tale of the fire at the Adelphi from the Cape very serious the books & piano saved but the greatest lamentation is made for all Bessies shoes & Bonnets finery etc. a Merciful God spared their lives and they are not cast down Heavens protection still attend them you will all say, and your prayers I trust will still be heard . . . Mr Alders papers of specification have been incalculably valuable their precision will ensure me indemnification without dispute pray say so to him. We left Atwood at the King Georges Sound he said he could not consent to be a slave but he has adopted a more severe slavery than he would have found with us, he is adopted into the family of a Mr Sherat a merchant & farmer of course I could not refuse the subscribers the £20 as it had been expended on his account but if his friends think it right they must accept it by instalments from the little fund I left under your direction it will take 4 years to do it in. I said I should wait [?] on his fulfilling his engagement to which he replied [? hole in paper] . . . that I could not that he was not indentured by his lawful guardian. I was sorry to leave him but it was unavoidable, I must furnish other particulars at some more leisure [sic] time. Mr Waylen has just called all well God bless my friends I can no more now. The Captain is off.'

With the arrival of 'the little Mother', life at Augusta became quite different—and the journals and letters to friends and family (Cousin Capel Carter, and brother William and wife Caroline, who were still in England) were more in the nature of 'news bulletins' and reassurances of continued affection rather than plans for the future. As 'the woman near the shops', Capel Carter has more than her share of requests for goods, and more than her share of distressing family responsibilities.

The following is a letter from Fanny Bussell to her English friends and family after the arrival of her mother and the tragic loss of the *Cumberland*.

'Feby 6th 1835[15]

'I am determined that another opportunity shall not pass by unmarked by a letter to the dear circle at Henley. I can scarcely imagine that this is the first time I have seated myself to address relatives so dear and so kindly remembered.

'I have trusted to our dear Capel to impart such intelligence as may appear most interesting to the large circle of friends whom we have left behind us and thus I have neglected *individualizing* as much as I intended to do when I left England. I will suppose that the principal events in the last years will have become so familiar to you that I need not recapitulate them, I have told the same story so often that I am sure my correspondents must almost shrink from the perusal of one of my long letters.

'There is however one theme on which I am sure I cannot dwell too often or too long. I mean the safety, the health, the happiness of all our party. In the midst of all our troubles and we have had "perils by fire and perils by sea" we have had more cause for gratitude than for complaint. My dearest Mother is with us in enjoyment of her usual health, and when not as now harassed with perplexing business, in her usual spirit.

'The loss of the *Cumberland* which has been mentioned in our late letters to England has been a severe stroke upon her and the recent discovery of the wreck has rather revived her regrets than allayed them. As you will not have an opportunity of seeing the Swan River papers I will touch on some of the circumstances which have transpired since our last despatches were closed. The *Cumberland* was lost in August last. Seven men sailors and labourers residing at Fremantle in company with Mr Ledyard a person in a most respectable line of life having been educated as a surgeon here were on a fishing party when they discovered the wreck and numbers of packages bearing our name strewed upon the beach.

'The first impulse of Ledyard was to report what they found and to claim salvage, but unfortunately he was over-ruled and the work of plunder commenced. Nothing was sacred from them and what the wreck had spared was defaced and destroyed by these unhappy men. The work of pillage was carried on for several weeks until suspicion was roused by the appearance of one of the wives of these men Mrs Keats a washer woman in a coral necklace a present from dear Capel to Bessie. In the subsequent search quantities of goods linen with the names cut out, and damask table cloths sheets towels, and other articles were discovered. Jewellery broken and mutilated in every possible way has come to light but as yet no traces of plate has [sic] been found.

'This is all very disturbing is it not? The unfortunate owner of the vessel Capt. McDermott was found and the body of one of the sailors but neither the presence of death nor any feeling of future retribution could influence these infatuated men. They have been sentenced to 7 & 14 years transportation and the next trip of the colonial schooner will convey them to Hobart Town.[16]

'This is but a slight sketch of the sad history.

'Mamma has just said that she will forward the Perth gazette to England of course you will see it and thus learn the particulars through a more easy medium than my unfortunate scribble. Miniatures of John, William, poor Grandpa and letters without end were picked up by the party afterwards sent to the spot by the Government to reconoitre [sic], and the little pearl ring, a parting present from Aunt Bowker to Mamma was dug out of the sand by Capt Toby.

'We expect a great many more articles to turn up and do not yet abandon the idea of having our plate restored. The Government officers have been most active in their investigations and we are still busy in making out lists by which some of our property may be identified. I will not longer detain your attention upon a subject which will fill you all with regret and commiseration. I would rather introduce you to our farm on the Vasse where my dear boys are exerting all their energies to form a comfortable homestead for their Mother and Sisters.'

Fanny Bussell's account of life at Augusta, (while things are being made ready at Cattle Chosen) reflects the enormous changes that had taken place in the fifty years of white settlement in Australia. The work that the women are engaged in is still hard, but it is also rewarding; the restrictions in terms of goods, comforts and company are many, but the freedoms are also plentiful—particularly in the absence of children; it is partly the fact that at Augusta, and later at Cattle Chosen, the Bussells were a community of adults, in reasonably good health, that life could be painted so positively. Childbirth, child death and the terrible toll that both could take upon women—as Georgiana Molloy's experience testifies—would have transformed the Bussell pattern of family existence. Fanny writes in another letter[17]:

'The Vasse is still in great favour far preferable to Augusta from the great facility in clearing and the fine grassy plains with which it abounds promising excellent pasture for sheep. Our two cows have been reclaimed from the bush and are now here another at the Vasse and three horses form our principal live stock. We have just added geese and turkeys and our goats are equally prosperous and useful.

'Our Vasse garden too has been very productive second only to Mr Turners though this is the first year in which it has been brought into cultivation. As the Vasse is only 60 miles from Augusta we have frequent visits from different members of our infant colony. A walk of two days and a night in the bush is compensated by a short spell of home society.

'The military escort which is stationed at the Vasse consisting of 4 soldiers is changed from Augusta once a month and this allows of very tolerable intercourse. The natives are numerous and at first showed some disposition to be hostile; but they are now on very good terms. We have sent Phoebe with the boys to wash and cook for them and they find her invaluable. Honesty is a quality of rare occurrence amongst the lower orders here . . .

'We have lately been visited by the Governor who expressed himself much pleased with our little colony. After 3 months of total seclusion it created quite a sensation amongst us to find ourselves invaded by all the heads of the different departments. Mr Wittenoom the Clergyman, Mr Mackay the Judge Advocate, Mr Lewis the Commissary General, and though last certainly not least Mr Roe the Surveyor General.

'The visitations are to be annual and form very agreeable epochs in our secluded lives. It was delightful to hear the church service performed by a clergyman again I could have fancied myself in England had it not been that instead of a church we were all assembled in Capt Molloy's verandah which commands an extensive view of our truly noble river. After the service several of the children were baptised, the parents being glad to avail themselves of the first visit yet received from our [clergyman]. The major part of the guests dined with us and sailed the same [day] for King George's Sound . . . '

Many of the closest ties with 'old England' were cut with the death of William, the only direct member of the Bussell family who had remained in the old country; news of his death—and the arrival of some of his personal belongings, forwarded by Capel Carter—indicates how 'distanced' the colonists felt in these circumstances, as Fanny reports:

*'Augusta, June 1835*
'Your case arrived yesterday my dearest Capel, with all its melancholy contents in perfect preservation. You will hear from letters which we forwarded you a fortnight since that this was not the first indication of the event for which your considerate and lovely letter to me would have prepared us. A letter to my dear Mamma dated Oct 29 1834 was destined to be the first which fell into our hands; was it not another instance of that kind providence by whom the very hairs of our head are numbered that it should so have happened?

'The first dreadful shock had subsided and we were strengthened to gaze upon the different relics forwarded by you and our sweet Cally with something like—I cannot say composure for every article as it was drawn forth seemed to write with an iron hand upon our hearts.

'Oh Capel how different it was from any package before received from England. The *Fanny* appeared in our Bay on Tuesday afternoon but it did not come to anchor until Wednesday morning. There were no joyful acclamations as is usually the case when a sail first dawns upon our sight, no cheerful anticipations, no preparations for writing to England, it seemed impossible to do so until the expected box had been opened and examined.

'The subject was almost avoided yet we all knew that it was uppermost in every breast. After breakfast Charles, Mr Green, Capt Molloy went on board, we three girls had much to do fortunately and had not time to observe how slowly time was speeding away. My little Mother began to look pale and thoughtful and miserable, *you know the look* Capel I proposed walking to the bottom of our garden to watch the arrival of the boats which by this time had crossed the bar. Mr Turner's sons already unloading and Captain Molloy was near at hand.

'We waited until the different goods were deposited when Charles and Mr G., carried up our case to the house together. Scarcely a word was spoken screw after screw was drawn out. Mary and Bessie joined us they were neither of them well and Mamma and I persuaded them to lie down a little after our morning duties had been fulfilled.

'At length dear Capel the box was opened and all that your considerate kindness had collected and our sweet Cally prepared and dear mamma Alder had packed so beautifully appeared. But why should I dwell upon a scene which your fancy has depicted too faithfully, everything seemed to bear the impress of the icy hand of death, everything but your picture my darling Capel and that smiled upon us like an angel from the midst of death and desolation.

'There were some bitter tears shed, yes even on that sweet countenance. My dear Mother could scarcely part with it from her hand. It was so good of you to send it at such a moment when every other memorial was of so mournful a nature, and your sweet sweet letters . . .

'In the short fortnight that has intervened since we despatched our last letters by the *Anne* a small boat sent from Fremantle with provisions of the most infamous description[,] little has happened in our secluded circle. Vernon left us a few days later and was succeeded by John who came over on horseback for provisions for the soldiers and themselves.

'He was a great solace to Mamma who seems to depend upon him almost as she did on Papa in every affliction or trouble. He was looking well but was harassed and distressed, this recent news from England was a severe blow to him for he loved William dearly . . .

'Bessie is making a collection of all the Vasse letters for you one series has already been transmitted in a parcel to Mr Turner. You will find them I think highly interesting and the different characters of our few remaining treasures are sweetly portrayed in the truly domestic correspondence for nothing is withheld from you . . .

'Tell Caroline that she must not yield to the feeling that letters which are to go a great distance must be fraught with wonders. Ask yourself whether it is not the minutest detail of private life which awakens the greatest interest, will it not conjure up a smile upon your countenance when I say that I have been interrupted several times to attend to my bread which has been baking and that I now lay this aside to prepare the rice for dinner and to make a stew of some mushrooms which have grown here most abundantly this season. It is generally my dear Mamma's office to dress these for us but she is now lying down and I must act as her representative.'

Fanny is quite clear that it is the domestic detail, the description of everyday reality, which is the 'drama' of family communications and relationships. It is what she writes about, and what she urges her sister-in-law, Caroline, to write in return. It is in the process of describing and explaining the routine of her day that Fanny can best convey the changes that the Bussels are undergoing.

For example, to be without a servant, to prepare one's own meals, to perform the menial tasks of making bread, preparing rice and stewing

231

mushrooms, would have been unthinkable for a lady in a middle-class family in England, yet Fanny Bussell takes such work in her stride in her new country, and sincerely wants her cousin to understand this new identity. But Fanny is also acutely aware that such activities still have to be handled delicately when they are being recounted to her cousin Capel, who is bound by English standards of proper conduct and gentility. For this reason, Fanny makes out that domestic duties are something of an adventure—no real loss of caste, and no drop in the ideals of dignity and decorum. But it is a mark of Fanny's authenticity as a diarist that she 'explains' the many aspects of her life to Capel, even those which might be disapproved of, despised or held against the new Australians. Fanny is quite insistent on itemising the *work* that she does, and its importance to the family and the community; from her confident and committed tone, and the demonstrably essential nature of her contribution, it is clear that Fanny does not have to worry unduly about her place in the world, about her role or purpose in life. She has found herself, partly through writing.

There was still tragedy of course: fire, flood, drought and bereavement. But by the time Fanny Bussell is writing letters from Cattle Chosen, the family saga—and the role that writing has played in realising and nurturing it—has just about run its course. Her writing becomes more leisurely, more amusing and stylised; it is more polished and distanced, and less personally revealing; her words have moved more towards being a pleasant pastime than the very necessary—and raw—self and family communication work.

'Cattle Chosen
Feb 20th 1836

'Yesterday afternoon my dearest Capel the *Sally Anne* entered our bay and amidst the variety of pursuits and the new faces which her arrival brought amongst us, I have only succeeded in mastering the contents of your precious letters within the last two hours.

'None of your packages have come down by the *Sally Anne* but the *Fanny* is hourly expected with the whole of your valuable cargo. I scarcely know how to thank you for us all as you deserve my own best Capel for all your exertions for us and the beautiful exactitude with which you execute commissions or rather anticipate them. By the *Fanny* we shall write again and shall then be able to notice everything more satisfactorily.

'And now I must notice but briefly the severe afflictions with which it has pleased Providence to visit our beloved friends at Ballard Lodge. They need not me to point out where consolation alone can be found in such an hour of trial. I always feel it is so cruel to dwell upon the losses which however new to us have been softened by the lapse of time and the blessed effects of religion to those on whom the stroke has fallen. To my dear Mother this has been a sudden and unexpected blow, and by us who knew but little of him and yet so enough to love his name most tenderly his loss is felt as the loss of an affectionate relative. And poor Uncle Geroge too! it is sad indeed to find one's early friends and connections thus dropping round us. It makes one look almost with impatience to the time when we may too "depart in peace".

'Oh Capel it is a fearful thing to glance one's eye down the page of an English letter and to shudder as each dear name meets the eye, hardly knowing by what distressing intelligence it may be succeeded. But why do I dwell upon feeling my dear friends which your own hearts have already understood. When there are still so many spared us for a meeting even in this world. I am wrong in encouraging the melancholy which cannot always be suppressed . . . '

Then Fanny tries to give Capel Carter some idea of a woman's life on the Vasse, almost fifty years after the First Fleet arrived in Australia.

'You will be pleased to hear that we are all quite well and delighted with Cattle Chosen. It is indeed a sweet place and improvements are daily springing up around us but there is so much to do that to an English eye we still should appear sadly unsettled. The house which we now occupy would strike at a distance as a comfortable substantial looking mansion. It is white and the four upper windows in the upper story [sic] give it a cheerful and finished look which perhaps it does not quite deserve.

'As you approach it the garden well fenced in and productive in all English vegetables would almost make you forget that you are in Australia. You would stop to admire Phoebe's cottage which is the first building after the barracks in the precincts of Cattle Chosen. John's house near the garden very comfortably fitted up as a bedroom for himself and Vernon and ornamented with shelves containing his books would almost make you in love with the little hermitage, by following the garden fence you approach the cottage shared between Lenox and Alfred. All these buildings have chimneys and as the winter is now approaching a bright fire not infrequently blazes on their hearths.

'I have now brought you nearly to our own house, which you gain by skirting the stock yard bounded by a fence on two sides and by the river on the others. Our sitting room is a well sized and well proportioned room which we are gradually rendering comfortable and civilized. The walls of wattle and daub have been most beautifully plastered so that not a crack is visible. The floor is of clay and the front door opens upon a pretty cheerful looking pasture land ornamented with some magnificent trees but not heavily timbered like Augusta. Our books are now arranged on shelves extending the whole length of the room, indeed by the front door we have manufactured a species of couch covered with your drugget[18] dear Capel.

'The piano occupies its place under the window, our two sea chests which Vernon has painted white stand in a corner and act as a kind of closet. Our noble chimney occupying nearly one side of the room gives promise of many a brilliant winter blaze. This is as yet our only finished room. The room upstairs forms a dormitory for all the females of the family. My little Mother has her cot and we three girls each her cot her toilet etc.

'The windows command a pleasant view of the river up on one side with the country in its unredeemed state which is so completely of the Park like description that you would scarcely believe that a year and ten months only had elapsed since the improving hand of the European was first extended over its glades. This side of the picture is full of beauty and yet I dwell with more interest and delight on the opposite scene which offers to our view the little hamlet, our garden, our hayrick, and our stockyard. It is more esssentially English and it bears the mark of daily improvements.

'My dear boys having rested from our labours are standing round the cooking fire which according to Colonial customs is kindled out of doors. Our fowls have been duly fed and are at roost. The geese have returned from their evening stroll, the ducks my peculiar charge have quacked their last quack and are settling themselves to sleep. Bessy has penned up her turkeys young and old and the signal for the last meal is expected by everyone. At a short distance the cow bells are faintly heard and almost at the same moment dear Alfred's voice pealing forth some favourite song surely never meant for cowherd's lips. "Wilt thou say farewell love" and "Bushman's Dream" are the rage at present, as the sounds approach the gates of the stock yard are thrown open and the business of milking commences.

'I wish you could see our beautiful sleek cattle amounting to 15 in number. Our pretty goats too have been long awaiting admittance and after a few graceful antics have thrown themselves beneath our windows or close to the door for the night, but often in the summer season suffered to run loose as they are sure to return for water from the pond in our stock yard.

'The little filly (Capel) is really a beauty, and a more animated and interesting spectacle than our farmyard in the cool soft evening hour is surely not often to be seen and I turn from it with an emotion of gratitude and happiness which only requires the participation of those we love in England to be rendered complete.

'Within the fence all our offices are to be collected, the store which is already built the dairy which is to be our next work, and the fowl house which at present occupies our two builders John and Lenox and their valuable assistant our little Mother who has regularly converted herself into the builders lad. I think now I have rendered the demesne of Cattle Chosen fairly familiar to your imaginations I will pass on to the inhabitants . . . '

And so proceeds an account of all the family members, concluding with the servants.

'I have in the course of this letter not mentioned Phoebe she is wonderfully well tho the marks of age becoming more apparent as the years advance. Our arrival has made her quite happy.[19] She undertakes the greatest part of the washing but the assistance of one of us is constantly requisite. She makes and bakes our bread and butter at present with the aid of one of us in churning. Besides this she cooks for herself and Ludlow now our only manservant. Everything else devolves upon ourselves and our duties are divided into three departments. Cook, Housemaid and Chambermaid, which offices we change monthly. Add to this the care of the poultry, making and mending for the boys the household and ourselves, to say nothing of catching fleas which we are gradually exterminating and you will not call us idle.

'The great bell erected just before our windows awakens us from our slumbers at daylight, breakfast is prepared as soon as the sitting room is put to readiness our milk boiled and our vegetable soup which we term combustible all in order. My little Mother is never absent. After breakfast the boys separate to their various duties. John and Lenox to their building or carpentering, Vernon to the garden, Alfred to the cows. Bessie prepares the vegetables for dinner. Mary clears away the breakfast things and arranges the sitting room and Fanny armed with her own little dusting pan (a present from Mr Toby) and brush, goes to the different rooms of the boys to make their little dwellings look as comfortable as possible for which she is to be rewarded by a pat of the shoulder in the evenings and the epithet of a most admirable girl.

'After arranging our own room a more elaborate business I generally find that Mary and Bessy have finished their avocations and feel only too happy if I can sit down with them but Phoebe's relentless voice often claims my attention to wash to hang out for her which now becomes very fatiguing or to fold the clothes and distribute them to the different houses. At 12 Bessie's great bell summons us from our work and dinner succeeds.

'Then comes the feeding of the poultry. The turkeys falling to Bessie's share the ducks to mine and the cocks and hens to Mary's. The dinner is concluded consisting generally of salt pork and every variety of vegetable to which Bessie does ample justice the plates dishes are washed put away and we all retire to take a short siesta or a little rest with a book which often falls from a tired hand whilst the unconscious eye not infrequently closes on complete oblivion.

'At three the boys return to their labours the heat of the day has passed away and we again settle ourselves to work for the afternoon. These are long and very pleasant and we work till the setting sun calls in our animals to be fed and settled for the night. The boys also come in and our last meal I cannot call it tea as that beverage is now confined to Mamma is in progress.

'The cows are all milked and the horses are praised and petted and then we all sit down to our bread and milk supper. We retire early but generally have service in the evening and conversation without end in which England and her connections claims her part. At present my little Mother is living low on account of her eyes allowing herself a cup of your delicious tea my own Tip and some of Mr Turner's biscuit which is the only description of bread she now patronizes. We younger colonists do not complain of leaven bread in fact we generally prefer it. The baking pan dear Tippo and Fan will be most useful. We left our camp oven with Charlie and I at least have grumbled ever since. The cover for the lamp is indeed ingenious I think we shall not wait till the other is broken before we use it.

'And I must conclude this long prosey concern who would read it who did not love me as you do? God bless you my darling it is getting dark and I have written till I am quite stiff. I fear I shall not be able to keep a journal here I have no time for writing excepting Sundays and then I am quite bewildered at the accumulation of events which press upon me . . .

'We are now busy in making up the last gown you sent for Phoebe for her birthday the 5th of next month. We like our merinos of all things. We intend making up our shawl dresses sent by dear Mrs Jones and the Clergy school girls to appear on the arrival of our next batch of visitors, but we have so much to do I don't think we shall ever be vain again . . . '

On 15 May 1851 Fanny Louisa Bussell married Henry Charles Sutherland and went to live at Crawley, now the University of Western Australia. Bessie was not to be of such mature years upon marriage; on 12 March 1839 she married Henry Mortlock Ommanney; they had five children. The little Mother, Frances Louisa Bussell senior, died in June 1845.

# *Notes*

**Abbreviations**

AONSW    Archives Office of New South Wales
AOT        Archives Office of Tasmania
ADB        Australian Dictionary of Biography
HRA        Historical Records of Australia
LL           La Trobe Collection, State Library of Victoria
ML          Mitchell Library, State Library of New South Wales
NLA        National Library of Australia
RAHS     Royal Australian Historical Society
WAA      Western Australian Archives

## Introduction

1   The diary is not included in this volume; the original is in the Battye Library, Western Australia and a typescript is held in the National Library of Australia, MS 2801.

2   See Cicely Hamilton, *Marriage as a Trade*, London: The Women's Press, (1909), 1981

3   For further discussion of these women and their contemporaries, see Dale Spender, *Women of Ideas—and what men have done to them*, London: Pandora Press, 1990

4   For further discussion of Frances Sheridan and her literary achievements, see Dale Spender, *Mothers of the Novel: 100 Good Women Writers Before Jane Austen*, London: Pandora Press, 1986

5   Babette Smith, *A Cargo of Women*, Sydney: New South Wales University Press, 1988. See particularly the chapter 'Female Married' (pp. 68–76) for some amusing accounts of the ruses—and deception—that women used to be able to marry.

6   Mary Wollstonecraft, *Maria, or The Wrongs of Woman*, New York: Norton, 1798, 1975, pp. 104–6.

7   See Florence Nightingale, *Cassandra* (1928), published in Ray Strachey's *The*

*Cause: A short history of the women's movement in Great Britain*, London: Virago, 1978, pp. 395–418.

8   For further discussion of Eliza Haywood and the contributions of women's periodicals, see Dale Spender, *Mothers of the Novel: 100 good women writers before Jane Austen*, London: Pandora Press, 1986.

9   See Antonia Fraser, *The Weaker Vessel; women's lot in seventeenth century England*, London: Weidenfeld & Nicolson, 1984.

10   See Janet Todd (ed.), *A Dictionary of British and American Women Writers*, London: Methuen, 1987 for further discussion of Janet Little and Ann Yearsley.

11   See Carol Dyhouse, *Girls growing up in late Victorian and Edwardian England*, London: Routledge & Kegan Paul, 1981, for a review of the medical injunctions against women's education.

12   Virginia Woolf, *A Room of One's Own*, Harmondsworth: Penguin, (1928), 1974, p. 63

13   For further discussion of this phenomenon and of the women writers, see Dale Spender, *Mothers of the Novel: 100 good women writers before Jane Austen*, London: Pandora Press, 1986.

14   Charlotte Lennox was one of the pioneer writer/editors of women's magazines and among the first to introduce the serial. For further discussion, see Dale Spender, *Mothers of the Novel*.

**Chapter 1   Forced labour**

1   Bethia Penglase '1788: That illiterate "Freight of Misery"?' *RAHS Journal*, vol. 75, pt II, October 1989

2   *Historical Records of New South Wales*, British Museum Papers Newspaper Extracts, vol. II, pp. 746–7. (Paragraphing has been added to this letter and others in this chapter.)

3   ibid., pp. 767–8

4   John Nicol, *The Life and Adventures of John Nicol, Mariner*, London: Cassell, 1937, p. 134

5   ibid. pp. 130, 139

6   ibid. p. 141

7   ibid. p. 140

8   According to surgeon Richard Alley, five women died during the passage.

9   *Historical Records of New South Wales*, vol. II, pp. 779–80

10   ibid. p. 779

11   John Cobley, *Sydney Cove 1791–1792*, Sydney: Angus & Robertson, 1965, p. 105

12   *Historical Records of New South Wales*, vol. II, pp. 806–7

13   ibid., vol. III, pp. 509–10

14   *Sydney Gazette*, 11 March 1804

15   Letter 21 January 1802, NLA MS 1116

16   G. B. Barton, *The True Story of Margaret Catchpole*, Sydney: Cornstalk Publishing Co., 1924, letter 2 May 1803, p. 133

17   ibid. letter 8 October 1806, p. 140

18   NLA MS 1116, letter 28 January 1807

19   ibid. 8 October 1809

20   ibid. 2 September 1811

21   AONSW COD 1487, 4/3502, pp. 37–8

22   HRA Series I, vol. X, pp. 320–21

23   ibid. p. 321

24  ibid. p. 322
25  Portia Robinson, *The Women of Botany Bay*, Sydney: Macquarie Library 1988, pp. 191–2

**Chapter 2  Farm managers**
1   Elizabeth Macarthur to her mother, 8 October 1789, ML Macarthur Papers (MP) vol. 12, A2908 Mfm CY1150
2   The Macarthur family's transferral to the *Scarborough*
3   Elizabeth Macarthur, 'Journal of voyage to NSW', MP vol. 12
4   E. Macarthur to Bridget Kingdon, 7 March 1791, MP vol. 10, ML A2906, Mfm CY940
5   The wife of Rev. Richard Johnson, Anglican chaplain, who arrived on the First Fleet
6   Elizabeth Macarthur, to Mrs Leach, 18 March 1791, MP vol. 12
7   E. Macarthur to her mother, 18 November 1791, MP vol. 12
8   E. Macarthur, 21 December 1793, MP vol. 12
9   E. Macarthur, 22 August 1794, ML vol. 12
10  E. Macarthur to Bridget Kingdon, 1 September 1795 (incorrectly dated; should be 1798), MP vol. 12
11  E. Macarthur to John Piper, 15 April 1804, ML Piper Papers A256 vol. 3, pp. 419–30
12  John Macarthur to E. Macarthur, 3 August 1810, MP vol. 2
13  E. Macarthur to Eliza Kingdon, March 1816, MP vol. 12
14  E. Macarthur to Eliza Kingdon, 11 December 1817, MP vol. 12
15  ML Bonwick Transcripts Box 60A, pp. 295–7
16  ibid. pp. 313–14
17  *Sydney Gazette*, 19 October 1811
18  ibid. 29 December 1821
19  ibid. 29 December 1821; 22 February 1822; 24 May 1822
20  Rachel Roxburgh, *Early Colonial Houses of New South Wales*, Sydney: Ure Smith, 1974, pp. 188–92
21  Drennan had a disastrous career in New South Wales. He was dismissed from his position in May 1821 and sent back to England in April 1822 under arrest because of a deficiency in official accounts.
22  *HRA*, Series I, vol. XII, letter 17 January 1821 to Governor Macquarie, p. 351
23  ibid. Governor Macquarie to Eliza Walsh, 19 January 1821, p. 351
24  ibid. Eliza Walsh to J. T. Bigge, pp. 351–2
25  ibid. Macquarie to Bigge, 23 January 1821, pp. 352–3
26  ibid. Eliza Walsh to Governor Brisbane, p. 354
27  ibid. Eliza Walsh to Earl Bathurst, pp. 349–51
28  W. Allan Wood, *Dawn in the Valley*, Sydney: Wentworth Books, 1972, p. 77
29  Eliza Walsh and John Galt Smith, who arrived on the *Britomart* on 8 March 1822, were married by special licence at St Luke's Church, Liverpool, on 8 October 1823.
30  Extracts from Anne Drysdale's Diary, La Trobe Collection, State Library of Victoria, quoted in P. L. Brown (ed.), *Clyde Company Papers II 1836–40*, London: Oxford University Press, 1952

**Chapter 3  The work of the Lord**
1   Although usually known as Elizabeth, her letters are signed Eliza. Samuel Marsden called his wife Betsy.

2   ML MSS 719 CY175 Marsden Papers. Reproduced in George Mackaness, *Some Private Correspondence of the Rev. Samuel Marsden and Family 1794–1824*, Sydney, 1942. Letter Eliza Marsden, 13 December 1794
3   ibid. 1 May 1796, 6 September 1799
4   ibid.
5   The *Lady Shore*, a convict transport carrying badly needed stores, was seized by mutineers near Rio de Janeiro while on the way to Sydney in 1798.
6   Marsden papers/Mackaness, 22 August 1801
7   ibid. 13 November 1802
8   ibid. 15 January 1805
9   This was the second son with this name.
10  Rev. Edward Parry, *Memoirs of Rear Admiral Sir W. E. Parry*, London: Longmans Brown & Co, 1857, p. 247
11  Anne Parry, *Parry of the Arctic 1790–1855*, London: Chatto & Windus, 1963, p. 148
12  Edward Parry, *Memoirs*, pp. 249–50
13  ibid. pp. 261–2
14  ibid. pp. 262–3
15  NLA G2224, Diary of Sarah Broughton
16  Information from Rev. Robert Willson, Deakin, ACT and Sydney Boydell, North Fitzroy, Vic.

**Chapter 4  Shipboard travail**
1   ML MSS 1973X, King family papers 1791 to 1956: Diary of Mrs King—wife of Capt. Philip Gidley King, third governor of New South Wales on the voyage from England to Australia commencing 19th Nov. 1799
2   Information from Mrs Judith McMillan, Richmond, Vic.
3   LL MS9115–21, Sarah Docker 1828, La Trobe Collection
4   LL H15574, Box 1341/1, Mary Jane Docker Journal, 1838, La Trobe Collection
5   Louise Brown (ed.), *A book of South Australia. Women in the first hundred years*, Adelaide: Rigby, 1936, pp. 28–9

**Chapter 5  Charitable works**
1   Marsden Papers Mackaness. Letter Eliza Marsden, 22 August 1801, p. 25
2   HRA I, III, p. 525
3   ML Ap. 36 Paterson papers. Elizabeth Paterson to her uncle.
4   HRA I, IV, p. 101
5   HRA I, IV, p. 98
6   *Sydney Gazette*, 11 February 1810
7   Elizabeth Windschuttle, 'Discipline, Domestic Training and Social Control. The Female School of Industry, Sydney, 1826–1877' in *Labour History*, No. 39, November 1980
8   Brian Fletcher, 'Elizabeth Darling, Colonial Benefactress and Governor's Lady' in *RAHS Journal*, vol. 67, pt 4, March 1982
9   Archives Office of Tasmania (AOT) NS 953/letter 14. Letter from Eliza Darling to Edward Dumaresq, 18 April 1826
10  ibid. letter 15, 24 May 1826
11  ibid. letter 17, 27 November 1826
12  ML A4300 Macarthur papers. Fanny Macleay to William Sharp Macleay, 21 April 1826
13  ibid. 8 October 1826
14  ML A4301 Macarthur papers 25 March 1827

15  ibid. 28 April 1829
14  ibid. 27 April 1831
17  Elizabeth Windschuttle, *Taste and Science. The Macleay Women*, Sydney: Historic Houses Trust, 1988

**Chapter 6  Vice-regal duties**
1  NLA MS 195 Ellis Bent papers. Ellis Bent to his mother, 4 March 1810; to his brother, 2 May 1810
2  ML CY 178 William Bligh correspondence, pp. 570–73
3  ML CY 554 Elizabeth Macquarie Journal
4  NLA MS 2261 Macquarie letters
5  ML Doc. 2801. Anne Thomson, 'Journal of a Voyage to Australia', August–December 1831
6  Louise Brown (ed.), *A book of South Australia. Women in the first hundred years*, Adelaide: Rigby, 1936

**Chapter 7  Political observer**
1  NLA MS 1559 Christiana Brooks Diary
2  Colonel William Stewart, acting governor from 1 to 17 December 1825
3  Alexander Macleay
4  Captain Richard Brooks was a prominent supporter of the Bank of New South Wales.
5  Editor of the *Sydney Gazette*
6  William Charles Wentworth and Robert Wardell began the *Australian* on 14 October 1824
7  Edward Smith Hall and Arthur Hill began the *Monitor* on 19 May 1826
8  Robert Wardell remained editor of the *Australian* until 27 June 1828
9  *Sydney Gazette*
10  William Charles Wentworth
11  Henry Grattan Douglass dismissed as Commissioner of the Court of Request.
12  ML MSS 3080, Letters of Christiana Brooks

**Chapter 8  Working wives and mothers**
1  *Sydney Gazette*, 9 August 1817
2  ML Doc. 1050, Wild family papers
3  *Sydney Gazette*, 15 July 1820
4  ibid. 21 April 1825, appointed Clerk of the Bench, Camden.
5  *Memoirs of the Blomfield Family*. Armidale: Craigie and Hargrave, 1926. Letter from Christiana Blomfield to Louisa Edwards, 16 April 1824
6  ibid. 2 June 1825
7  *Memoirs of the Blomfield Family*. Letter 5 January 1828 to her niece, Louisa Edwards. Christiana corresponded with her sister-in-law and her niece, both named Louisa Edwards.
8  *Memoirs of the Blomfield Family*. Letter November 1828 to Louisa Edwards
9  ibid. 4 October 1829 to sisters and brothers-in-law
10  ibid. 2 April 1830 to Louisa Edwards
11  ibid. 10 November 1839 to Louisa Edwards
12  One child, Barrington Wingfield Blomfield, died in 1835.
13  Rev. William Branwhite Clarke
14  Sir George Gipps
15  ML CY 526 Dumaresq, Henry letters 1825–38. Sophy Dumaresq to Mrs Winn

**Chapter 9   Pathmakers**
1  NLA MS 535 Letter by Elizabeth Hawkins
2  *Proceedings of the Royal Society of Queensland*, vol. XVIII, p. 104; Goshen was a fertile district of ancient Egypt given by Pharoah to Joseph.
3  ML MSS 678 Letter by Elizabeth Hawkins to her daughter Louisa at school in Sydney, 6 September 1832
4  Extracts from *The journal of Mrs Fenton. A narrative of her life in India, the Isle of France (Mauritius), and Tasmania during the years 1826–1830*, London: Edward Arnold, 1901
5  NLA MS 114 Franklin papers, Box 2, Folder 12
6  George Augustus Robinson, Chief Protector of Aborigines
7  Matthew Forster, acting Colonial Secretary

**Chapter 10   Shopkeepers and needlewomen**
1  ML A 1677–4 CY929 Hassall Correspondence pp. 1607–10
2  *ADB* 6 Martha Rutledge, 'George Thornton (1819–1901)'
3  Letter reproduced from Lesley Hordern, *Children of One Family*, Neutral Bay, NSW: Retford Press, 1985, with the kind permission of Lesley and Marsden Hordern. Information on Ann Hordern's career is taken from this source.
4  *Sydney Gazette* 14 July 1825
5  ibid. 23 March 1827
6  *Sydney Morning Herald*, 1834, quoted in Hordern, *Children*, p. 32
7  NLA MS 3334 Indenture of Eliza Ward Euren
8  Malcolm Sainty, & Keith Johnson (eds), *Census of NSW 1828*, Sydney: Library of Australian History, 1980
9  ibid.
10  *New South Wales Government Gazette* 1834, vol. II, pp. 529–31
11  *Sydney Gazette* 19 December 1833
12  Published in England, quoted in *Sydney Gazette* 21 December 1833
13  *Hobart Town Courier* 30 November 1833; *Sydney Gazette* 19 December 1833
14  R. B. Madgwick, *Immigration into Eastern Australia 1789–1851*, Sydney: Sydney University Press, 1969, p. 96
15  *Sydney Gazette* 19 December 1833
16  AONSW Shipping Records CO Reel 1286, Mfm 229
17  ML Doc. 1416
18  Louise Brown (ed.), *A Book of South Australia. Women in the first hundred years*, Adelaide: Rigby, 1936

**Chapter 11   Homemakers**
1  Mrs W. B. Ranken (comp.), *The Rankens of Bathurst*, Sydney: S. D. Townsend, 1916, p. 7
2  ML Doc. 930, Janet Ranken letter
3  Janet's pet name for her husband George
4  Edward Lord, landowner and prominent merchant, formerly an officer in the Marine Corps
5  Mrs Kent, wife of Lt Kent
6  Dr James Scott, married to Lucy Margaretta Davey in June 1821
7  Thomas Davey
8  Ranken, *The Rankens of Bathurst*, p. 15
9  ibid. p. 17
10  ibid. p. 20

11  London *Morning Herald* 27 September 1827; Hobart *Colonial Advocate* 1 May 1828. For an account of Mary Leman Grimstone, see Patricia Clarke, *Pen Portraits: Women Writers and Journalists in Nineteenth Century Australia*, Sydney: Allen & Unwin, 1988
12  NLA MS 2137, Letter by Octavia Dawson; also ML Doc. 1264
13  Stephen and Lucy Adey
14  W. T. Davenport, *Spirit of Clarence*, Rosny Park, Tas.: City of Clarence, 1989
15  L. M. Mowle, *A genealogical history of pioneer families of Australia*, 5th ed. Adelaide: Rigby, 1978, p. 209
16  In 1866, after she had been in South Australia for 30 years, Mary Thomas made a transcript of her journal. She also wrote letters to her brother in which she expressed herself with less restraint than she did in her revised journal. Both journal and letters were included in a publication prepared by a descendant: *The diary and letters of Mary Thomas (1836–1866) being a record of the early days of South Australia* edited by Evan Kyffin Thomas, Adelaide: W. K. Thomas, 1915.
17  Thomas, *The diary and letters*, pp. 49–50
18  The eldest son, Robert Thomas, arrived in Adelaide as a member of Colonel William Light's staff on the *Cygnet* before the rest of the family.
19  Thomas, *The diary and letters*, pp. 91–101
20  ML Doc. 1418, Letter Jane Synnot
21  Mowle, *A genealogical history*, pp. 235, 254

**Chapter 12  Work in isolation**
1  NLA MS 1677. Ann Gore letters
2  Information from Fr Brian Maher, Bungendore NSW
3  Mitchell, T. L., *Three expeditions into the interior of eastern Australia*, London, T. & W. Boone, 1838; Lang, John Dunmore, *An historical and statistical account of New South Wales*, London, Cochrane & M'Crone, 1834
4  NLA MS 3261. Journal of Mrs Menzies
5  Dr John Osborne, a surgeon superintendent on convict ships, settled at Garden Hill in 1836 with his wife, formerly Mary Clarke of Dromore, Co. Tyrone and six children.
6  A brother, Henry Osborne, married in 1828 to Sarah Elizabeth Marshall, Dernseer, Co. Tyrone, settled on a grant of 2560 acres near Dapto, which they called Marshall Mount.
7  Krimhilde and Terry Henderson, *Early Illawarra People, Houses, Life*, Canberra: ANU Press, 1983
8  Lindsay and Roger Thwaites, *The History of Araluen*, Braidwood, n.d.
9  ML MSS 1315. Letter Sarah Burnell to Emily Curtis, 18 October 1839
10  A. A. C. D. Boswell, *Early Recollections and Clearings, from an old Journal* or *Some recollections of my early days written at different periods*, n.p., 1908, p. 19
11  ibid. pp. 19–20
12  Margaret Innes, younger sister of Annabella

**Chapter 13  Health care**
1  The letters of Ellen Viveash are taken from *The Tanner Letters: A Pioneer Saga of Swan River & Tasmania 1831–1845*, compiled and researched by Pamela Statham, Perth: University of Western Australia Press, 1981, pp. 69–124.
2  Pamela Statham, *The Tanner Letters*, p. xv

3  It could be that Eliza and Martha are sisters, or else close friends; ibid., p. 99.
4  ibid., p. 73
5  ibid., p. 90
6  ibid., p. 78
7  ibid., p. 110–11
8  ibid., pp. 88–97

**Chapter 14   Sacrifice and science**
1  When Alexandra Hasluck wrote *Portrait With Background*, Perth: Fremantle Arts Press (1955/1990), a biography of Georgiana Molloy, most of the letters that she used were contained in the Western Australian Archives (WAA). Both references are given here, the WAA reference and the page reference where the letters have been quoted in Alexandra Hasluck's book.
2  WAA 501/A; Microfilm letter quoted in part in Hasluck *Portrait*, 1990, p. 81
3  WAA 501/A; quoted in Hasluck, *Portrait*, pp. 103–7
4  WAA 501/A; Hasluck *Portrait*, pp. 108–10
5  WAA 501/A; Hasluck *Portrait*, pp. 118–24
6  WAA 501/A; Hasluck *Portrait*, pp. 131–7
7  *Western Australian Historical Society Journal* vol. 1, iv, 68; original letter in the possession of Mrs Piers Brockman, Busselton; quoted in Alexandra Hasluck, *Portrait*, 1990, p. 193
8  WAA 479A I p. 67; Hasluck, *Portrait*, pp. 154–5
9  WAA 479A I; quoted in Hasluck, *Portrait*, pp. 161–75
10  For further discussion about the nature of her contribution to botanical studies and to the enrichment of Kew Gardens, see Hasluck *Portrait*.
11  WAA 479A I, p. 309; Hasluck *Portrait*, p. 166
12  WAA 479A I, pp. 294–6; Hasluck *Portrait*, p. 178
13  WAA 479A I, p. 294; Hasluck *Portrait*, p. 178
14  WAA 479A II, pp. 16–17; Hasluck *Portrait*, p. 199
15  The name given to the Molloy property on the Vasse
16  WAA 479A I, p. 308; Hasluck *Portrait*, p. 165
17  WAA 479A II, p. 19; Hasluck *Portrait*, p. 201
18  WAA 479A I, pp. 315–16; Hasluck *Portrait*, p. 170
19  WAA 479A I, p. 323; Hasluck *Portrait*, p. 186
20  'Dry garden, an arranged collection of dried plants, an herbarium' (OED)
21  WAA 479A I, pp. 322–5; Hasluck *Portrait*, pp. 173–5
22  WAA 479A II, pp. 17–18; Hasluck *Portrait*, p. 200
23  WAA 479A II, p. 82; Hasluck *Portrait*, p. 207

**Chapter 15   Working with words**
1  Battye Library; State Library of Western Australia; MN 586 Acc/Nos 294A 12
2  Phoebe Bower, an old family servant
3  It is difficult to determine the nature of the reference to poor Mrs Leake, though it does sound as though she has been required to meet someone who was with Mr Leake, and that this has been most embarrassing.
4  The *Ellen* was the local Government Schooner, and the advice was that instead of transferring to it to go to Augusta, they should wait for the *Cygnet* to make the voyage—even though it meant further delay before they could see the boys. Brother Lenox was most insistent that they should not be separated from their property.

5  Sometimes it is difficult to make the distinction between journal and letters when Fanny is writing to her mother; this entry is still part of the journal.
6  The name of the Browns' residence
7  Emma was a Bussell female servant.
8  The other Bussell sister
9  This story was contradicted in the Perth *Gazette*.
10  Refs MN 586 Acc/nos 337A/334
11  Refs 337A/389
12  Mary Wollstonecraft Shelley, *The Last Man*, published in 1826
13  Letters from Elizabeth Capel Bussell, 'Bessie', born 1812, the youngest Bussell daughter; Battye Library, State Library of WA, MN 586 337A/266
14  Letters from Frances Louisa Bussell (nee Yates), known as 'the little Mother'; this letter to Capel Carter—whom she raised 'as a daughter' was addressed to Ryde, Isle of Wight, Hampshire, England and forwarded to Kentish Town, London; noted as received 26 January 1835, 337A/310
15  337A/346, 347
16  Swan River was *not* a penal colony, so 'convicts', whether from abroad or local, were 'transported' to Hobart Town.
17  337A/347
18  '*Drugget*—formerly a kind of stuff, all of wool, or half wool, half silk or linen, used for wearing apparel. Now a coarse woollen stuff used for floor-coverings ... ' (OED)
19  Phoebe had been sent to 'rough it' with the boys—to do their washing—while Cattle Chosen was being constructed; obviously she found it an improvement when the Bussell women arrived

# Bibliography

## Manuscripts

Bent, NLA MS 195 Ellis Bent papers
Bligh, ML CY 178 William Bligh correspondence
Bonwick, ML Bonwick transcripts, Box 60A
Brooks, Christiana ML MSS 3080, Letters of Christiana Brooks
Brooks, Christiana NLA MS 1559, Christiana Brooks diary
Broughton, Mary Phoebe ML Mfm CY 1483, Diary of Mary Phoebe Broughton
Broughton, Sarah NLA Mfm G 2224, Diary of Sarah Broughton
Catchpole, NLA MS 1116, Margaret Catchpole's letters
Close, R. ML MSS 678, Papers collected by R. Close
Dawson, NLA MS 2137, Letter by Octavia Dawson
Docker, Mary Jane LL H 15574 Box 1341/1 Mary Jane Docker journal 1838
Docker, Sarah LL MS 9115–21, Sarah Docker journal
Drysdale, Anne LL, Anne Drysdale diary
Dumaresq, AOT NS 953/309, Dumaresq papers
Dumaresq, Henry ML CY 526, Henry Dumaresq letters 1825–38
Franklin, NLA MS 114, Franklin papers
Hassall, ML A 1677, CY 929, Hassall correspondence
Hawkins, NLA MS 535, Letter by Elizabeth Hawkins
Henty, ML MSS 967, Henty family correspondence 1825–92
King, ML MSS 1973X King family papers. Diary of Mrs King, England to Australia voyage, 19 November 1799
Macarthur, ML A 2906, A 2908, Mfm CY 1150, Macarthur papers (MP) vols 10, 12
Macarthur (Macleay correspondence) ML A 4300 (1812–26), A 4301 (1827–31), A 4302 (1832–36), Macarthur papers. Letters by the Macleay family
Marsden, ML MSS 719, CY 175, Marsden papers
Menzies, NLA MS 3261, Journal of Mrs Menzies; 'The story of Dr and Mrs Robert Menzies and their home, Minnamurra House, Jamberoo 1839–1861, typescript copied from a damaged manuscript by Arthur Cousins'

Paterson, ML Ap. 36, Paterson papers
Piper, ML A 256, Piper papers
Ranken, ML Doc. 930, Letter of Janet Ranken
Synnot, ML Doc. 1418, Letter of Jane Synnot
Thomson, ML Doc. 2801, Anne Thomson, 'Journal of a voyage to Australia',
    August–December 1831
Ward, NLA MS 3334, Indenture of Eliza Ward Euren
Wild, ML Doc. 1050, Letter by Mary Wild

## Official records

Sainty, Malcolm R. and Johnson, Keith A. (eds) *Census of New South Wales November
    1828*, Library of Australian History, Sydney, 1980
New South Wales birth, death and marriage records
*New South Wales Government Gazette*

## Select books

Barton, G. B. *The true story of Margaret Catchpole*, Cornstalk Publishing Co., Sydney,
    1924
Bassett, Marnie *The Governor's lady. Mrs King*, Oxford University Press, London,
    1956
Bigge, J. T. *Report of Commissioner of Inquiry on the Colony of New South Wales*
    (facs. edn), Libraries Board of South Australia, Adelaide, 1966
Boswell, A.A.C.D. *Early recollections and gleanings, from an old journal* or *Some
    recollections of my early days written at different periods* n.p., 1908
Brown, Louise (ed.) *A book of South Australia. Women in the first hundred years*,
    Rigby, Adelaide, 1936
Brown, P. L. (ed.) *Clyde Company papers II 1836–40*, Oxford University Press,
    London, 1952
Clarke, Patricia, *Pen Portraits. Women Writers and Journalists in Nineteenth Cen-
    tury Australia*, Allen and Unwin, Sydney, 1988
Cobbold, Richard, *The History of Margaret Catchpole*, Henry Colburn, London, 1845
Cobley, John *The crimes of the First Fleet convicts*, Angus & Robertson, North
    Ryde, 1982
—— *Sydney Cove 1791–1792*, Angus & Robertson, Sydney, 1965
Collison, April J. *The Female Orphan Institution, 1814*, Rydalmere Hospital Par-
    ents and Friends Association, Rydalmere, 1986
Commonwealth Parliament, Library Committee *Historical Records of Australia*
    Melbourne and Canberra, Government Printer
Davenport, W. T. *Spirit of Clarence* City of Clarence, Rosny Park, Tas., 1989
Dyhouse, Carol *Girls Growing Up in Late Victorian and Edwardian England*,
    Routledge & Kegan Paul, London, 1981
Fenton, Mrs *The journal of Mrs Fenton. A narrative of her life in India, the Isle of
    France (Mauritius), and Tasmania during the years 1826–1830*, preface by Sir
    Henry Lawrence, Edward Arnold, London, 1901
Fletcher, Brian H. *Ralph Darling. A governor malinged*, Oxford University Press,
    Melbourne, 1984
Fraser, Antonia *The Weaker Vessel: Women's Lot in Seventeenth Century England*,
    Weidenfeld & Nicolson, London, 1984
Greaves, Bernard (ed.) *The story of Bathurst*, Angus & Robertson, Sydney, 1961

Hasluck, Alexandra *Portrait with Background*, Fremantle Arts Press, Perth, 1955/ 1990

Henderson, Krimholde and Terry *Early Illawarra people, houses, life*, ANU Press, Canberra, 1983

Heney, Helen *Australia's founding mothers*, Nelson, Melbourne, 1978

—— *Dear Fanny*, Rushcutters Bay, Pergamon Press, 1985

Hordern, Lesley *Children of one family*, Retford Press, Neutral Bay, 1985

Hughes, Joy N. *The journal and letters of Elizabeth Macarthur 1789–1798*, Elizabeth Farm occasional series, Historic Houses Trust of New South Wales, Glebe, 1984

King, Hazel *Elizabeth Macarthur and her world*, Sydney University Press, Sydney, 1980

—— *Richard Bourke*, Oxford University Press, Melbourne, 1971

Kingston, Beverley *Elizabeth Macarthur*, Historic Houses Trust of New South Wales, Glebe, 1984

Macarthur Onslow, Sibella (ed.) *Early records of the Macarthurs of Camden*, Angus & Robertson, Sydney, 1914; Rigby, Adelaide, 1973

Mackaness, George *Fourteen journeys over the Blue Mountains of New South Wales Part II, 1819–27*, D. S. Ford, Sydney, 1950

—— *The life of Vice Admiral William Bligh*, Angus & Robertson, Sydney, 1951

—— *Some private correspondence of the Rev. Samuel Marsden and family 1794– 1824*, Author, Sydney, 1942

Madgwick, R. B. *Immigration into eastern Australia 1789–1851*, Sydney University Press, Sydney, 1969

Mowle, L. M. *A genealogical history of pioneer families of Australia*, 5th edn, Rigby, Adelaide, 1978

New South Wales Government *Historical records of New South Wales*, Government Printer, Sydney

Nicol, John *The life and adventures of John Nicol, mariner* facs. edn, Cassell, London, 1937

Nightingale, Florence 'Cassandra' in Ray Strachey *The Cause; a short history of the women's suffrage movement in Great Britain*, Virago, London, 1928, pp. 395– 418

Lady Nijo, *The Confessions of Lady Nijo*, translated by Karen Brazell, Zenith Books, Hamlyn, Middlesex, 1975

Parry, Anne *Parry of the Arctic 1790–1855*, Chatto & Windus, London, 1963

Parry, Rev. Edward *Memoirs of Rear Admiral Sir W. E. Parry*, Longmans Brown & C., London, 1857

Pike, Douglas (ed.) *Australian dictionary of biography* Vols 1 & 2, Melbourne University Press, Carlton, 1966–67

Ranken, Mrs W. B. (comp.) *The Rankens of Bathurst*, S. D. Townsend, Sydney, 1916

Robinson, Portia *The hatch and brood of time. A study of the first generation of native-born white Australians 1788–1828* Oxford University Press, Melbourne, 1985

—— *The women of Botany Bay*, Macquarie Library, Sydney, 1988

Roxburgh, Rachel *Early Colonial Houses of New South Wales* Sydney, Ure Smith in association with National Trust of Australia (NSW) 1974

Smith, Babette *A Cargo of Women*, New South Wales University Press, Sydney, 1988

Spender, Dale *Mothers of the Novel: 100 Good Women Writers before Jane Austen*, Pandora, London, 1986

—— *Women of Ideas—and what men have done to them*, Pandora, London, 1990
—— (ed.) *The Diary of Elizabeth Pepys*, Collins, London, 1991
Statham, Pamela (ed.) *The Tanner Letters: A Pioneer Saga of Swan River & Tasmania 1831–1845*, University of Western Australia Press, Perth, 1981
Stapleton, Eugenie *Elizabeth Marsden. The parson's wife*, St Mary's Historical Society, St Mary's, 1981
Todd, Janet (ed.) *A Dictionary of British and American Women Writers 1660–1800*, Methuen, London, 1987
Thomas, Evan Kyffin (ed.) *The diary and letters of Mary Thomas (1836–1866) being a record of the early days in South Australia* W. K. Thomas, Adelaide, 1915
Windschuttle, Elizabeth *Taste and science. The women of the Macleay family 1790–1850* Historic Houses Trust of New South Wales, Glebe, 1988
Wollstonecraft, Mary *Maria, or the wrongs of women*, Norton, New York, 1798/1975
Wood, W. Allan *Dawn in the valley. The story of settlement in the Hunter River Valley to 1833*, Wentworth Books, Sydney, 1972
Woodward, Frances J. *Portrait of Jane. A life of Lady Franklin*, Hodder & Stoughton, London, 1951
Woolf, Virginia *A Room of One's Own*, Penguin, Middlesex, 1928/1974
Yarwood, A. T. *Samuel Marsden. The great survivor*, A. H. & A. W. Reed, Wellington, 1977
*Memoirs of the Blomfield family, being letters written by the late Captain T. V. Blomfield and his wife to relatives in England*, Craigie & Hargrave, Armidale, 1926
*Records of pioneer women of Victoria 1835–1860*, Women's Centennial Council Historical Committee, Melbourne, 1937

## Articles

Fletcher, Brian 'Elizabeth Darling: Colonial benefactress and governor's lady', *RAHS Journal*, vol. 67, pt 4, March 1982
Hawkins, Elizabeth 'Journey from Sydeny to Bathurst in 1822' (intro.) Henry Selkirk, *RAHS Journal*, vol. IX, pt IV, 1923
Norton, A. 'From Sydney to Bathurst in 1822' *Proceedings of the Royal Society of Queensland*, vol. XVIII, 1904
Penglase, Bethia '1788: That illiterate "Freight of Misery"?' *RAHS Journal*, vol. 75, pt 2, October 1989
Windschuttle, Elizabeth 'Discipline, domestic training and social control. The Female School of Industry, 1826–1847, *Labour History* no. 39, November 1980
'A lady's letter', *Parramatta and District Historical Society Journal*, vol. I, 1918

## Newspapers

*Hobart Colonial Advocate*
*Hobart Town Courier*
*Port Phillip Gazette*
*Port Phillip Patriot*
*Sydney Gazette*
*Sydney Morning Herald*

# Index

Aboriginal people xxx, 3, 23, 44, 59, 80, 85, 87–8, 132–3, 162, 168, 186, 192, 195, 207, 218–19, 223–4, 229; corroboree 132, 218; displacement 218; 'land rights' 3; relationship with Europeans 224; women 23
accommodation *see* housing
*Adams* 54
*Adelaide Chronicle and South Australian Advertiser* 162
Adelaide, Debra viii
Adelaide, SA 60, 78, 79, 148, 156, 160–2
Adelphi, WA 194
Adey, Lucy Leman (nee Rede) 154, 155, 243
advertisements 141, 144
*Africaine* 157
agent for shopping 225, 227
Agricultural Society (NSW) 92
agriculture *see* crops, farming, livestock
Allan, Mrs (David) 33
*Amelia Thompson* 163
Anthony Hordern's Department Store 139, 141
Appin, NSW 170
apprentices/apprenticeship 141–3
Araluen, NSW 175–6, 177, 243
architect 73
army wives 94–6, 97

Astell, Mary xiii
Augusta, WA xvii, 188, 189, 194, 195, 200, 201, 219, 221, 226, 228
Austen, Jane xxiv, 238
*Australian* 84, 91, 241
Australian Agricultural Company 43–5, 109
Australind, WA xii–xiii

Bank of New South Wales 83, 85, 241
banks/banking 81, 83
Barnsley, Mrs 4
Baskerville, Tas. and WA 180
Bateman's Bay, NSW 177
Bathurst NSW 111, 119, 120–1, 153, 154, 177, 179
Batman, John 35
Baudin, Nicholas 63
Baxter, Annie viii, ix
Bayly, Nicholas 17, 18, 19
Behn, Aphra xiii
Bellarine Peninsula, Vic. 38
Benevolent Society, Sydney 65
Bent, Ellis 70–1, 241
Bigge, Commissioner J. T. 32–3
Bird, Sarah 8–10
birds 192
Bligh, Mary *see* Putland
Bligh, Governor William ix, 28, 63, 70, 71, 72, 241

Blomfield, Christiana Jane 81, 93, 97–105, 182, 241
Blue Mountains, NSW xiii, xxvi, 63, 73, 78, 110–18, 153; first family to cross 110
Bontharambo, Vic. 59
books xvii, xxi, xxiii, 101, 134, 199, 222, 224, 226, 233; *see also* reading
Booral, NSW 45
Boronggoop, Vic. 35–8
Boswell, Annabella *see* Innes
botanical interests/studies 22, 68, 175, 191, 195, 201–2, 203–8, 244
Botany Bay, NSW 7, 9, 239
Bourke, Anne ix, 74–8, 241
Bourke, Lady Elizabeth 74
Bower, Phoebe 210, 211, 222, 235, 244, 245
Boydell, Sydney 240
Braidwood, NSW 175, 176
'brickfielder' 47, 77
Brisbane, Governor Thomas 33, 34, 149, 153, 239
Bronte sisters xxiv
Brooks, Christiana ix, 80–93, 97, 100, 241
Broughton, Emily 46
Broughton, Mary Phoebe 46, 48
Broughton, Sarah ix, 46–8, 240
Broughton, Bishop William Grant 43, 46, 47, 48
*Broxbornebury* 137, 143
Brown, Mrs 217–18
Brunskill, Sarah 59–60
Brunton, Mary xxiv
*Buffalo* 53
Burnell, Sarah 175–7, 243
Burney, Fanny xxiv
bushfires 45
bushrangers/bushranging 81, 84, 88, 89–90
businesswomen xviii, xxx, 1, 9–10, 27, 137, 138–41, 148; opportunities for 138–9
Bussell family xxvi, xxviii, 195, 196, 199–200, 209–36, 245, importance of letter writing to xxvi
Bussell, Mrs Charlotte 201
Bussell, Elizabeth Capel (Bessie) xxviii, 189, 194, 196, 209, 210, 212, 213, 218, 223–5, 236

Bussell, Frances Louisa (Fanny) xix, xxiv, xxviii, 189, 194, 195, 209, 210–11, 211–23, 227–36
Bussell, Mrs Frances Louisa (snr) 209, 210, 221–3, 226–7, 235, 236, 243
Bussell, Mary 209, 210, 226
Busselton, WA xix
*Bussorah Merchant* 144

Cabramatta, NSW 17
Camden, NSW 96
Campbell, Mrs Annabella 149, 150, 151
Campbell, Annabella 179
Campbell, Lorn *see* Innes
Campbelltown, NSW 91, 136
Camperdown, Vic. 165
*A Cargo of Women* xv
Carpenter, Mary 148
Catchpole, Margaret ix, xix, xxxi, 10–16, 238; crime 11; farm overseer 11; health 15; literacy 11; longs for home 15, 16; midwife 14; model convict 12; nurse 14, 16; observes floods 13, 14–15; 15; owns livestock 13, 15; small farmer 13, 15, 16; storekeeper 16; taken off stores 12; views on marriage 13, 15, 16; work 12
*Catherine Stewart Forbes* 65, 105
cattle *see* livestock
Chamber of Commerce, Sydney 87
charitable works 61–79; *see also* philanthropic women
childbearing/childbirth xxvi, 4, 14, 23, 28, 39–40, 43, 44, 45, 48, 50, 65, 66, 73–4, 94, 97, 99–100, 101, 102, 103, 104, 105, 109, 111, 120–1, 121, 130, 141, 153, 181, 182, 187, 188, 198, 206, 207, 207–8, 217–18, 229; attitude to 94; death in xvi, 182; health risks 45; on board ship 50, 54, 55; rate of 100; *see also* miscarriage, pregnancy
childrearing/childcare xii, xvi, xviii, 27, 28, 56, 103, 107–8, 111, 112, 113, 117, 124, 126–7, 141, 193, 194, 198–9, 200, 202
children 6, 7–8, 61, 99, 120, 123, 190; abandoned 61; contributions to scientific work 205; death of xxvii,

23, 41–2, 59–60, 73, 92–3, 154, 181, 182, 188, 189, 202–3, 217–18, 229; death, writing about 41, 42, 189; education of 41, 42, 100, 102, 153; illness of 122, 124, 126–7, 198–9; separation from 28, 29, 41, 42, 49, 50; stillborn 54; teaching at home 41, 98–9, 100, 199, 204, 206; wretchedness of 3; *see also* education

church *see* religion

Clarke, Rev. William Branwhite 103, 241

Clifton, Louisa xii–xiii, 237

climate 25, 75, 79, 87, 88, 98, 108, 147, 160–1, 167–8, 192, 213, 217, 220, 236; heat 161, 213, 217

clothing *see* dress

colonial life xvii, 231–2; adventures of xxvi; attractions/advantages 30, 120, 160, 209, 213; ceremonial aspect 75; changes over 50 years 229; character 77; conventions 212, 216; corruption 39; crime 88, 89; depravity, wickedness, godlessness 40, 42–3, 139; different lifestyle xix; economy 80; equality and independence 77; exotic 210; intrigue and conspiracy 71; loss of caste in 232; manners xix, 214, 216; materialism 68, 150; moral wilderness 44; novelty 213; personal growth possible xx; politics 73, 83; privations and shortages xvii; privilege xvii, 106; 'refinements' 213, 224; rights of subjects 90, 104; strangeness xxviii; survival in xx; traumas of xxviii

contraception xiv

convents, effect of abolition xxii

convict women xiii, xv, xv–xvi, xvii, xix, xx, xxx, 1–19, 21, 29, 39, 50, 51, 52, 73, 107, 137–8, 150; 'adopted homeland' xix; cost to keep 175; crimes 9, 11, 17, 137; difficulty of letter writing for 2; drink 107, 125; editing of letters 2; employment 1; exploitation and discrimination xix; literacy of 2, 11, 17; need for travel passes 12, 18; numbers of 1; privations 2, 3, 4,

5–6; prostitution and rape 4, 17–19, 39; role of 1; separation from children 1, 6, 7, 8; shipboard mortality 6; shortage of clothing 3, 4, 5; starvation 5; survival xix; success stories 9; and business opportunities 1, 9, 138; and marriage 237; and newspaper publications 2; and shipboard conditions 2, 4, 7, 21, 50; as prostitutes 1; as servants 1, 18

convicts xii, 25, 44, 62, 66, 76, 92, 94, 96, 104, 111, 112–13, 118, 154, 155, 174, 175; bureaucratic bungles 137; cease arriving 104; convict life 138; correspondence, importance of xvi; Irish 62, 76; 'making a fortune' 96; marriage to 152; mortality rate 4; pardons 138; punishment 6, 12, 89; runaways 174–5; sentencing 138; treatment of 33

cooks/cooking 1, 11, 12, 164, 231, 234, 235

Coryule, Vic. 38

counselling xxviii

Cox, Jane Maria 81, 90, 100–1

Cox's River, NSW 118

crime 88, 139; punishment of 89

crops 24, 30; failure 23; wheat 12

*Cumberland* 226, 227, 228

Curtis, Emily ix, 176, 243

*Cygnet* 159, 211, 215, 217, 218, 219, 220, 243

Dagworth, NSW 81, 97

daily routine 214, 235 *see also* domestic duties, housework

dairy 25–6, 235, 236

Darling, Eliza 44, 64–8, 68–9, 83, 84, 105, 106, 240

Darling, Governor Ralph 34, 43, 65, 81, 82, 83, 84, 86–7, 88–9, 90–1, 105

Darlinghurst, NSW 46

*D'Auvergne* 60

Dawson, Octavia ix, xvi, 154–6, 243

death 233, 238; writing about 41, 42, 189; at sea *see* voyages; in childbirth *see* childhood; of children *see* children; of husbands *see* women

Denham Court, NSW 81, 82, 93, 97, 100, 103
*Denmark Hill* 121
Derwent River, Tas. 151, 156
diaries xi, xix, xxiv–v, xxvii–ix, xxx, xxxi, 35, 46, 48, 50, 54, 75, 80–1, 121–2, 131, 157, 162, 169, 210–11, 243; audience for 121; mother and daughter 48; reasons for keeping 50; style 121; *see also* journals
diaries and letters, ages and classes of writers xxx; distinction between xxvii; ethics of publication xxviii; role in women's lives xi; selection criteria xxiv, xxx; state representation xxx; and privacy xxviii; as adventure stories 210; as conversations 210; as literary form xi; as narratives xxvii; as self-realisation xxviii; for an audience xxviii, 243; for oneself xxviii
diary/letter form 75, 121–2, 190–1, 223, 245
Dickens, Charles xxv, xxvii
Dight, Mrs 11, 13–14
divorce xv
Docker, Mary Jane 54, 55, 59, 240
Docker, Sarah ix, 54–9, 134, 240
doctors, absence of 203, *see also* medical remedies/treatment
domestic duties 206, 207, 212, 231, 232; demands of 206
domestic violence 10, 82
double standard 209; *see also* education, marriage, women
drawing/painting 68, 214
dress xix, 3, 52, 58, 67, 70, 79, 84, 90, 121, 128, 138–40, 146–7, 163, 196, 204, 211, 214, 216–17, 219, 224, 225, 236; bonnets 141, 147, 219, 226; shoes/boots 214, 219, 224, 225, 226; stockings 219
dressmaking/dressmaker 2, 107, 143; *see also* needlework, sewing
drink/drunkenness 82, 107, 114, 125, 155, 170–1, 171
Dromedary, NSW 72
drought 101–2, 104, 153, 172, 232
Drysdale, Anne ix, 35–8, 239
*Dublin Chronicle* 7

Dublin *Public Advertiser* 8
Dumaresq, Christiana *see* Macleay
Dumaresq, Edward 65, 66, 105, 240
Dumaresq, Colonel Henry ix, 43, 65, 68, 105, 106, 107, 108, 109, 241
Dumaresq, Sophy, xvii, 105–9, 241
Dunlop, Margaret 193
*Dunmore* 180

*Earl Durham* 169
Edgeworth, Maria xxiv
education xiii, xx–xxi, xxii, 25, 41, 42, 155, 159, 177–9; concerns about 25; curriculum 177, 178–9; double standard 155, 209; exclusion of women from xx; of children 41, 96, 100, 102, 120, 153, 199, 204; of girls 62, 103, 164; of women 204; *see also* children, governesses, schools
Edwards, Margaret 94–5
Elizabeth Farm, NSW xvii, 24
*Ellen* 200, 215, 216, 217, 221, 222, 244
emigrants/migration xii, 10, 79, 90, 104–5, 137, 139, 143, 144–5, 149, 152–3, 154, 155, 166, 172, 180, 209–10, 211, 214, 221; aspirations of 149; complaints about government assisted scheme 144; desolation 212; difficulties in settling 210; enticement to emigrate 29; family commitment 210; female assisted migrants 144; first impressions 212; living conditions 172; reasons for migration 209; settlers' lives 87
*Emily Taylor* 188
entertainment *see* social life
Esden, Lydia 17–19
Evans, Mrs G. W. 177
*Evelina* xxiv, xxv

*Fairlie* 130, 131
Faithfull, Mrs 11, 14
family life xxvi, 97, 157, 209–10, 212; family ties 230; *see also* children, women, women's work
famine/starvation xvi, 4, 5, 8, 12, 180, 224; *see also* food
farming/farm work xvii, xxvi, xxx, 1,

Lifelines

4, 11, 13, 15, 20–38, 43, 59, 87, 88, 101–2, 103–5, 120, 156, 167, 234–6; economics of 26, 101, 102; farm labour 26, 104–5; farm overseer 11
farming women xxx, 13, 15, 16, 20–39
fathering 106, 108
Fawkner, John 131, 134
Female Factory (NSW) 17, 30, 111
Female Orphan School 33, 63, 65, 143
Female School of Industry 64–9, 65, 66, 67, 68, 81, 84, 106, 240
*The Female Spectator* xxi
Fenton, Elizabeth 121–30, 242
Ferris, Miss 177
Field of Mars, NSW 29
fire 195, 223, 226, 232, 233
First Fleet xi–xii, xiv, xv, 1, 2, 4, 6, 22
Fish River, NSW 119
floods 13–15, 70, 232; Hawkesbury 13–14, 14–15, 70
flora and fauna 22, 191, 204, 223; albatross 212; native flowers 192, 207; strange animals 211; *see also* botanical studies
food 96, 235, 236; shortages/supplies xvi, 3, 4, 5, 8, 13, 14, 25, 40, 41, 88, 180; supplies from England 41; *see also* famine/starvation
forced labour 1–19
Franklin, Lady Jane ix, xxviii, 130–6, 169, 173, 242
Fraser, Antonia xxii, 238
funeral 196
Fremantle, WA 180, 188
French Fleet 51
*Friendship* 143
fruit 24, 30, 31, 120, 176
fundraising 67
furniture 98, 220, 224, 234

*Ganges* 55
gardens/gardening 1, 22, 25, 176, 179, 192, 200, 201, 206, 219, 223, 229, 233; flower garden 206
gaslight, introduction 86
Gawler, Maria 78–9
Geelong, Vic. 35, 37
Geographe Bay, WA 200

Gibson, Isabella ix, 144–7
Gipps, Governor Sir George 105, 241
Glenelg, SA 157–8, 160
goods in demand 31, 41, 79, 109, 139, 152, 154, 197, 206, 214, 219, 222, 225; *see also* letters, requests for supplies
Gore, Ann ix, 166–9, 243
Gore, Mrs (William) 33
governesses 35, 146, 177, 178, 179
Government House, 163, Sydney 75, 96, 136; Launceston 163
grandmothers xii, xiii, 110, 114, 116, 117, 120
Grimstone, Mary Leman 154, 243

Hamilton, Cicely xiii, 237
Hasluck, Alexandra 244
Hawkesbury River/District 11, 12, 13–15, 70
Hawkins, Elizabeth ix, xiii, 110–21, 153, 242
Haywood, Eliza xxi, 238
health xiv, xvi, xxii, 15–16, 65, 77, 227, 229, 238; *see also* illhealth
health care 180–7; *see also* medical remedies/treatments
Hill, Dr and Mrs Patrick 170
Hindmarsh, Mrs 171
HMS *Imogene* 193
Hobart, Tas. 121–4, 130, 136, 139, 150, 151–2, 154–6; Museum 135–6
homemakers/homemaking xii, xvi, xxx, 39, 130, 149–65, 221
homesickness *see* longing for home
*Hope* 169, 170
Hordern, Ann 138–41, 242
Hordern, Lesley and Marsden 242
hospitality *see* social life
hostess 71
hotelkeepers/licensees 1, 9, 19, 137–8, 141
housekeepers/housekeeping 11, 29, 62, 124, 137, 176
housework xii, 21, 64, 124, 145, 146, 164, 193–4, 198, 200, 202, 225, 231–2, 235
housing/accommodation 25, 36, 78, 79, 82, 87, 95, 97–8, 100, 103, 115–16, 120, 122, 129, 137, 148, 157–8, 160, 161, 163, 166, 167,

168, 170, 171, 173–4, 175, 176, 190, 192, 195, 212, 213, 220, 222, 228, 233–4; bedding 158, 234; inns 132, 134; tents 78, 79, 157–8, 188
Howe, Robert 83, 241
Howe's Weekly *Gazette* 84
Hunter River/Valley, NSW 34–5, 48, 73, 81, 87, 97, 99–102, 136

Illawarra, NSW 136, 243
illegitimate children 50
illhealth/illness 51, 65, 71, 88, 130, 145–6, 167, 181, 182, 183–6, 204, 207–8, 226; scurvy 45; sunstroke 150–1; *see also* children, health
illiteracy *see* literacy
innkeepers *see* hotelkeepers
Innes, Annabella 177–9, 243
Innes, Lorn (nee Campbell) 120, 149, 177
insects, bedbugs, bugs, flies, mosquitoes etc. 60, 114, 139, 161, 170, 213, 217, 235
isolation xxi, 166–9, 175–9, 189, 194; *see also* loneliness

*James Pattison* 226
Jamison, Sir John 68, 92, 111
*Janus* 17, 19
Jervis Bay, NSW 57
Johnson, Mary 2
Johnson, Mrs (Richard) 22, 39, 41, 239
Johnston, Lt Col George 72
Jones, Hannah 143
journals xxvii, 210–11; audience for 215, 243; compared with serial letters xxviii; reasons for keeping 210; style 215; as companion, confidant, comforter xxviii; as 'public reading property' 210, 215; as therapy xxviii; *see also* diaries, diaries and letters and diary/letter form
journal/letter writing 222; lack of light 224; similarities/overlaps 217, 223, 245; maintains relationships 211; reasons for 212; 'scribbling' 221, 228; shifts in style 210–11, 243; time taken 211
journeys, overland 110–19, 125–30,

crossing Blue Mountains 110–19; difficulties and dangers 112, 125; means of transport 112; inventory 112; sea journeys *see* voyage
*Justinian* 5

Karuah River, NSW 45
Kelloshiel, NSW 153
Kent, Mrs 152, 242
Kiama NSW 170, 171, 175
King, Anna Josepha ix, 24, 49–54, 61, 74, 240
King, Octavia Charlotte (nee Dawson) 156
King, Philip Gidley 24, 27, 50, 51, 52, 61, 62, 63, 165, 240
Kingdon, Bridget xvii, 20, 21, 25, 239
Kingdon, Eliza 28, 239
Kingsmill, Mrs 64
kitchens 98

Lake George, NSW 85
*Lady Juliana* 4, 5, 29
*Lady Penrhyn* 2
*Lady Shore* 41, 240
Lake Bathurst, NSW 166, 167–8
land clearing 101
landholders xix, 15, 32–4
land grants 32, 86, 87, 153, 180, 190, 193, 209, 212, 215, 218; to women 33, 34
landscape 12, 58, 79, 114, 139–40, 148, 155, 161, 168, 171, 192, 202, 212, 213, 220, 223–4, 229, 234
Lang, John Dunmore 169, 243
Lapstone Hill, NSW 112
*The Last Man* xxiv, 245
Launceston, Tas. 133, 163, 165
*Layton* 144, 145; women passengers 145
Leach, Mrs 20, 23, 239
Lees, Kirsten ix
Lennox, Charlotte xxv, 238
letters xi, xvi, xvii, xviii, xix, xx, xxiv–xxvii, xxix, xxx, xxxi, 2, 32, 71, 97, 145, 146, 155, 167, 172, 178–9, 210–11, 217, 231, 243; collection of 231; domestic 231; importance for family contact 145; lack of 145, 146; literary style 232; official 32; requests for supplies in

xvii, xxv, 31, 109, 196, 219, 222, 225; resemblance to serials xxv; suspense and drama in xxv; writer as heroine xxvii; as narratives xxvii; *see also* diaries and letters, journal/letter writing
letter reading 233
letter writing xxiii, xxiv, 221; art of 231; attractions of xxv; availability of paper xxix; conditions 236; confessional style 203; difficulties xxix, 225; distractions from 215; importance of xxvi; making time for xxv, xxix; postage cost xxix; pressures of 215; serial correspondence 190–1; shipping unreliability xxix; women and xxiii; writer as heroine 210; and the novel xxiii; and colonial women xxiv; and entry to literary professions xxiii, xxiv; as art xxvii; as family communication xxiii; as means of forging family unity xxvi; as means of reassurance xxvi; as necessity xxv; as work xxv; by instalment xxv; to preserve contacts xxv, xxiv
literacy xx, xxii, 2, 17, 45, 199; disqualification for marriage xxii; and class xx; of convict women 2, 11
Liverpool, NSW 81, 170, 177, 239
livestock 13, 15, 24, 25, 30, 34, 36, 79, 174, 219, 222, 229, 234
London *True Briton* 9
Long, Mary 17, 18, 19
longing for home xix, 5, 15, 16, 40, 108, 137–8, 145, 146, 147, 159, 162, 171–2, 189; links with home 230; *see also* isolation, loneliness
loneliness xxvii, 22, 23, 29, 62–3, 120, 166, 176
Lonsdale, Mrs 132
Lord, Mrs Edward 150, 152, 242
*Lord Goderich* 148
Ludlow, Kitty 189, 190, 196
*Lusitania* 149, 177
lying-in *see* childbirth, midwives

Macarthur, Mrs Charles (formerly Synnot) 163–5

Macarthur, Elizabeth ix, xvii, 3, xxvi, 20–9, 39, 40, 239, 241; businesswoman 27; childbirth 23; death of child 23; educational concerns 25; failure of male support 28; farmer 20, 22, 24, 25, 28; importance of letter writing xxvi; interest in astronomy 22; botany 22, in flora and fauna 22, in music 22; loneliness 23; separation from children 28; setting social standards 21; social life 24; voyage 21
Macarthur, John 20, 21, 22, 23, 27, 28, 29, 43, 71, 73
McDonald, Mary ix, 29–32
Macleay, Alexander 43, 64, 68, 77, 78, 241
Macleay, Christiana 64, 106
Macleay, Eliza 68
Macleay, Fanny 64, 67–8, 240, 241
Macleay, Kennethina 64
Macleay, Rosa Roberta 64
Macquarie Plains, NSW 119
Macquarie River, NSW 119
Macquarie, Elizabeth ix, 63, 152
Macquarie, Governor Lachlan 18–19, 32–3, 72, 73, 74, 152, 239; bias against women 33
Maher, Fr B. 243
mails 2, 31, 215; time taken 223
Maitland, NSW 97
Manero, NSW 104
Mangles, Captain James 200–1, 202, 203, 204, 205, 206, 207
Manifold, Jane *see* Synnot
*Margaret* 180
*Maria, The Wrongs of Woman* xiv–xv, 237
marriage xiv–xv, 1, 3, 13, 16, 80, 91, 94–5, 102, 145, 147, 155, 166–7, 168, 236, 237; arranged 145, 147; conjugal rights xiv; disobedient wife xv; double standard xv; dowry 95; happy 102; husbands xiv; opportunities 145, 167; patterns 16; rights to children xv; stakes 68, 81, 95, 218; views on 13, 15; and property xiii; as legal prostitution xiv–xv; as a mistake xiv; as a trade xiii, xiv; and property xiii; to convicts 39, 152

Marsden, Ann 39–40
Marsden, Eliza ix, 27, 39–43, 182, 239, 240
Marsden, Samuel 27, 39, 40, 41, 42, 62, 111, 118, 240
Marshall Mount, NSW 170, 172, 174, 243
Martin, Sue ix
*Mary Ann* 6–7, 29
*Mauritius* 122
*Matilda* (arrival of 48th [Northamptonshire] Regiment of Foot) 94, 97
Muswellbrook, NSW 109
medical, absence of medical support 182; charges 181; knowledge 181; profession discourages women from learning xxii; remedies/treatment 52, 77, 127, 181, 182, 183–6, 198–9
*Medway* 136
Melbourne, Vic. 35, 130, 131–4
*The Memoirs of Miss Sidney Bidulph* xiii–xiv
menstruation, taboo associated with, no references
Menzies, Margaret ix, 169–75, 243
midwives/midwifery 4, 10, 13, 14
migration *see* emigrants/migration
military 85, 89, 94–6, 97, 229
milliners 2, 107, 141, 146, 147
Minnamurra, NSW 171
miscarriage 65, 105, 150
*Mistral* 110
Mittagong, NSW 170
Molloy, Georgiana xiv, xvii, xxvii, xxix, xxx, 183, 188–208, 220, 223, 229, 244; botanical achievements 208; childbirth 206, 207, 207–8; collects native seeds 201; contribution to medical science 203; death 208; demands of scientific work 207; depressed after death of child 203; domestic duties 206; illness 204, 208; learning 201; sacrifices 208; scientific interest/ contribution 201, 208; scientific work, demands of 203, 205, 207; meticulous nature of 205; seed collection 201, 203, 206; time-consuming work 204

Molloy, Captain John 190, 205, 209, 215, 222, 230
Molloy, Sabina Dunlop 189, 190, 193, 194, 195, 196, 198, 198–9, 205, 206
*Monitor* 84, 85, 87, 91, 241
Moore, Ann 18
*Morning Chronicle* 4
motherhood 39, 94–5, 96, 106–9, 141
Mount Lofty Range, SA 79
Mount Wellington, Tas. 130
Mowat, Capt Thomas J. 18
Murray River, Vic. NSW 59, 134–5; fording of 134
music 196, 213, 215, 224; concerts 86, 168, 178–9; guitar 178–9; harp 77; piano 22, 75, 77, 179, 196, 224, 226, 234; singing 77

native-born 176
needlework/needlewomen 62, 63, 64, 137, 145, 146, 147, 193–4; *see also* sewing
neighbours 152, 185
Nepean River, NSW 111
*Neptune* 21
New Norfolk, Tas. 125, 128
New South Wales xii, xvii, xxx, 90, 108–9, 139, 153; climate 10; dislike of 106, 107
New South Wales Legislative Assembly 90
Newcastle, NSW 12 (Coal River), 96, 101, 136, 179
Newcomb, Caroline 35–8
*Newspaper Regulating Act* 91
newspapers xxi, 16, 83, 84, 90, 91, 131, 134, 215, 219, 241; censorship 91; freedom of press 91, 162
Nightingale, Florence xxi, 237
*Nile* 11
Norfolk Island 5, 10, 12, 27, 50, 53, 61, 62, 71
novel writing xxiv
novels xxii, 222; feminist 154; Gothic xxiv; as source of knowledge xxiii
nurses/nursing xvi, 1, 11, 14, 16, 122, 183–6, 199; suckling xviii, 44

O'Connell, Mary *see* Putland
O'Connor, Carmel ix

Orphan Institution, Sydney 53, 61–3, 84

Orphan School, Sydney 61

orphans 51, 52, 61–3; family responsibilities for 103

Osborne, Mary (nee Clarke) and Dr John 170, 243

Osborne, Sarah (nee Marshall) and Henry 170, 171, 172, 243

O'Shanessey, Bridget 175

painting 178

Palmer, Mrs 11

Parramatta, NSW 2, 8, 12, 13, 17, 24, 30, 40, 63, 68, 111, 138, 167

Parry, Sir Edward 43, 109, 240

Parry, Isabella 43–5, 240

Paterson, Elizabeth ix, 53, 61–3, 240

Paterson, Colonel William 27, 61, 62

*Patriot* 131

paupers 144, 145

Perth, WA 214, 217; Botanical Gardens 215

*Pestonjee Bomanjee* 78

Petty, Martha 106, 107

philanthropic women xxx, 61–79

Phillip, Governor Arthur 3, 53

*Phoenix* 139

Piper, Captain John and Mrs ix, 27, 128, 153, 239

poets 154, 157

political activist 131, 135–6

political commentary/politics 80, 82, 90, 136; *see also* colonial life

political observer 80–93

Port Jackson *see* Sydney

Port Macquarie, NSW 179

Port Phillip district xxx, 59, 135, 163, 165

Port Phillip Bay, Vic. 38

Port Stephens, NSW 43–5, 109, 136

postage xxix

Post Office 215; establishment 82

poultry keeping 235

pregnancy xiv, xvi, xvii, xxvi, 3, 6, 18, 66, 77, 99, 122, 125, 130, 150, 175, 182, 188, 196; unwanted xiv

prices of goods 9–10, 12, 76, 79, 87, 90, 95, 96, 101, 140, 151–2, 156, 162, 163, 172–3, 214, 219

*Princess Royal* 144

prostitution and rape xv–xvi, 1, 4, 17, 19, 144, 145, 155; Government inquiry into 18–19; *see also* sexual exploitation

pseudonyms, men's use of women's names xxiv

public works 92

Queensland viii, xi; absence of letters/diaries xxx

Radcliffe, Ann xxiv

Ranken, Janet ix, 120, 149–54, 171, 177, 242

reading xxi–xxii, 198, 222; 'cause' of uterine disease xxii; 'dangers' to women xxii; importance to women xxi; women discouraged from xxii; women teach themselves xxii

*Red Rover* 144

rape *see* prostitution and rape

religion xxii, 39–48, 58, 62, 65, 98–9, 180, 194, 199, 217, 222, 229–30; Scotch Church 86; *see also* Sunday schools

religious women xxx, 39–48

relocation 223

Richardson, William 2

Richmond Hill, NSW 13, 15, 16, 32

Riley, Honoria Rose 81, 103

robbery 89

Robinson, George Augustas 133, 186, 242

*A Room of One's Own* xxiii

Rooty Hill, NSW 111

Rose Farm, Ermington NSW 32

Rose Inn, NSW 58

Rosedale, Vic. 156

Rosson, Isabella 2

Rouse, Mrs Elizabeth 11, 13

*Scarborough* 21, 239

scenery *see* landscape

schools/schooling 2, 44, 45, 61–3, 64–5, 67–8, 74, 79, 84, 91–2, 95, 96, 101, 102, 103, 120, 165, 177, 178, 242; fees 95, 102, 103; girls' boarding school 177; infant 86; orphan 143, schooling in England 27; *see also* education

schools of industry (England) 65;
*see also* Female School of Industry
Scott, Mrs Lucy Margarette nee Davey
152, 242
Second Fleet 4–5, 6, 21
seeds, collection of 206, 207;
despatching 207; labelling, packing
206; making seed bags 204; paper
bags for transport of 204; protection
and preservation of 204, 205;
transport of 203; use of sugar in
transport of 203; use of tin in
transport of 203
servants xvii, xviii, 1, 4, 5, 41, 55, 64,
84, 85, 107, 123–4, 125, 144, 147,
159–60, 163, 168, 171, 175, 189,
196, 202, 207, 210, 211, 213, 216,
217, 221, 222, 225, 229, 233, 235
sewing/seamstresses xxix, 4, 5, 62,
145–7, 204, 211, 217, 225, 236;
*see also* needlework
sex discrimination 32, 33
sexual availability xvi; exploitation
xv–xvi, 17–19, *see also* prostitution;
and blaming the victim xvi; and
lack of choice xvi
sheep/shearing 4, 27, 37, 104, 165
Shelley, Mary Wollstonecraft xxiv,
245
Shellharbour, NSW 170
Sheridan, Frances xiii, xiv, 237
*Speedy* 50
shipboard journals 49–59, 50, 51–3,
54–7, 72–3, 169–70
shipboard life *see* voyages
Shoalhaven, NSW 173
shopkeepers/storekeepers 1, 10, 16,
137, 138–40, 140–1, 146, 148;
shop work 146
shops xvii, 26, 90, 105, 137, 140,
141; lack of xvii
Smith, Babette xv
Smith, Miss 179
social classes 39, 150, 154, 154–5,
155
social commentary 81
social life 24, 66, 67, 68, 75, 76, 152,
155, 163–4, 171, 176, 194, 213,
214, 215, 220, 222, 229;
entertainment/hospitality 68, 77, 82,
83, 85, 95, 194–5, 214, 216, 217,

220, 222, 226, 229, 236; *see also*
colonial life
social standards 214, 232; appropriate
behaviour 209; comparison between
English lady and colonial 232;
'keeping up appearances' xviii, xix;
lady-like behaviour 214; loss of
caste xviii; refinement xviii; setting
of xix, 21
society xviii–xix, 39, 95, 154–5, 168,
171, 214, 216, 229
soil quality 22, 87
sources of material viii, xi, 237–45
South Australia xxx, 78–9, 157–8,
159, 160, 240, 241, 242, 243
*South Australian Gazette and Colonial
Register* 157, 162
*Speedy* 50
Spender, Lynne x
spinning, weaving 62, 64
*Spring* 81
Springwood, NSW 113–14
squatting licence 104
station life 103–4, 166–8
staymaker 140
stealing 6, 8
Stirling, Lady 201
Storey, Helen nee Dunlop 188
Stroud, NSW 45
Sudds, Joseph 88–9
Sunday schools 65, 79
Swan River settlement xii–iii, xiv,
xix, xxx, 180, 188–208, 209,
212–36, 245
swimming 106
Sydney, NSW 3, 12, 20, 24, 43, 53,
57, 58, 64, 65, 74, 83, 84, 86, 90,
92, 94, 95, 96, 105, 108, 109, 110,
130, 136, 138, 139–40, 145, 151,
153, 167, 170; architecture 92;
development 95; shops 105
Sydney Dispensary 65
*Sydney Gazette* 83, 90, 140, 144, 239,
241
Sydney Grammar School 96
Synnot, Jane ix, 162–5

Tahlee, NSW 44
Talbot, Mary 1, 6–8
*Tamar* 130, 133
Tamar River, Tas. 165

Tanner, Hester and William 180, 182, 187
Tanner family 180
Tasmania *see* Van Diemen's Land
taxation 104; without representation 90
tea 3, 5, 41, 236; teapot 197
Therry, Fr John J. 19
Thomas, Mary 156–62, 243
Thompson, Patrick 88–9
Thomson, Anne Deas *see* Bourke
Thomson, Edward Deas 78
Thornton, Sarah 137–8, 242
Toongabbie, NSW 12
Torrens River, SA 79
traders 9–10; *see also* shopkeepers/ storekeepers
transport, method of 131; of seeds 203
transportation, public inquiry 32–3; *see also* convicts
travel *see* journeys, voyages
traveller and adventurer 130
trial by jury 90

University of Sydney 78

Van Diemen's Land xxx, 63, 65, 73, 79, 82, 95, 121, 130, 135, 139, 149, 151, 154–5, 180, 181
Vasse River, WA 190, 193, 201, 228, 229, 233
*Venus* 153
vice-regal women xxx, 63, 70–9
Victoria *see* Port Phillip
Viveash, Charles 180, 183–7
Viveash, Ellen 180–7, 243
voyages, sea xii, xxx, 2, 3, 7, 21, 49–60, 72–3, 74, 139, 150–1, 159, 167, 169–70, 211–12, 241; accidents 55; boredom 54; childbearing on board ship 50, 55; death at sea 5, 10, 51, 151, 228, 238; death of children 10, 60; floating brothels 17; food on 51, 57; hardships and dangers 49, 50, 51, 53, 74, 76, 122, 157; illness 51, 59; lack of communication 122; losses 227; pillage 228; sea sickness 54; shipboard hazards and losses 213; shipboard life 139, 150, 151, 169–70, 211, 226; shipboard life and women's responsibilities 21, 49;

shipwreck 228; social life on 52; treatment of convicts on 21

wages 95, 105, 143, 146
Walsh, Eliza 32–5, 239
Wangaratta, Vic. 59
Ward, Eliza 141–3, 242
Ward, Susannah Matilda 33
*Warrior* 188, 210
Warrnambool, Vic. 165
washing/washerwomen 1, 148, 219, 235
water closets 108
Wentworth, William Charles 84, 90, 241
Western District, Vic. 163, 165
Western Australia *see* Swan River settlement
whales 56, 150
wheat *see* crops
Wild, Mary ix, 94–6, 241
*William* 40
Willis, Miss 177, 178, 179
Willson, Rev. Robert 240
Wilson, Mary Honoria 81
Windsor, NSW 58–9, 170
Wollongong, NSW 170, 171, 237
Wollstonecraft, Mary xiv–xv, xv–xvi, xvi, xviii, xxii, xxiv
*Woman's Love* 154
women, absence of liberty xv; companions and partners 35; daily routine 35, 98–9, 106, 107; death of husband 72, 121; demands on time xxix; double standard xx, 32; duty xii, xiv; education xiii, xxiv; family responsibilities 113; financial status xii, xiii; free choice xiii; historical bias xx; hostility to 'learned' 71; identity crisis xxvii; ignorance xxi; importance of writing xxi; intellectual starvation xxi; leisure unknown xxix; living conditions 153, *see also* housing; managerial responsibilities xvii; mobility of 25; occupation xiii; position of xii, xviii; readers xxii; relationship to men xii; relationship to mothers xiv, *see also* grandmothers; restrictions on lives xxi; single 145; views on husbands 14; violence against 10,

16; and 'free choice' xii, xiii, 49;
and independence xii; as mothers
xxx; as wives xxx
women's magazines xxi, 238
women's work xi, xiii, xvi, xvii, xxx,
145, 192–3, 200, 229; aboard ship
xxx; administrative 66; contribution
to colony xx; domestic duties
206, 225; earning a living xviii;
exhausting xi, 193; ignored xx;
letter/journal writing 'conversational
work' 211; organisational rationale
xxx; priorities, scientific work
versus domestic duties 205;
satisfying xviii; tiring 220; value
of 232; while travelling xxx; work
hours 137; and definitions of a lady
xviii; *see also* education, voyage,
occupations
women writers, 154; issues raised by
xxiv
wool *see* sheep
Woolf, Virginia xxiii
writing materials xxix, 2

Yass, NSW 135

Zouch, Maria 81